WITHDRAWN
UTSA Libraries

Mexican Exodus

Mexican Exodus

*Emigrants, Exiles, and
Refugees of the Cristero War*

JULIA G. YOUNG

OXFORD
UNIVERSITY PRESS

OXFORD
UNIVERSITY PRESS

Oxford University Press is a department of the University of
Oxford. It furthers the University's objective of excellence in research,
scholarship, and education by publishing worldwide.

Oxford   New York
Auckland   Cape Town   Dar es Salaam   Hong Kong   Karachi
Kuala Lumpur   Madrid   Melbourne   Mexico City   Nairobi
New Delhi   Shanghai   Taipei   Toronto

With offices in
Argentina   Austria   Brazil   Chile   Czech Republic   France   Greece
Guatemala   Hungary   Italy   Japan   Poland   Portugal   Singapore
South Korea   Switzerland   Thailand   Turkey   Ukraine   Vietnam

Oxford is a registered trademark of Oxford University Press
in the UK and certain other countries.

Published in the United States of America by
Oxford University Press
198 Madison Avenue, New York, NY 10016

© Julia G. Young 2015

All rights reserved. No part of this publication may be reproduced, stored in
a retrieval system, or transmitted, in any form or by any means, without the prior
permission in writing of Oxford University Press, or as expressly permitted by law,
by license, or under terms agreed with the appropriate reproduction rights organization.
Inquiries concerning reproduction outside the scope of the above should be sent to the
Rights Department, Oxford University Press, at the address above.

You must not circulate this work in any other form
and you must impose this same condition on any acquirer.

Cataloging-in-Publication data is on file at the Library of Congress
ISBN 978–0–19–020500–3

1 3 5 7 9 8 6 4 2
Printed in the United States of America
on acid-free paper

To Spiro, and to our children

Contents

Acknowledgments   ix

Introduction: *A Desert Uprising*   1

1. A History of Faith and Conflict   18

2. Religious Refugees, Political Exiles, and the US Catholic Church 39

3. "In Defense of Their Brothers Beyond the Rio Grande"   61

4. Bishops, Knights, Border Guards, and Spies   101

5. After the *Arreglos*   125

6. Memories, Myths, and Martyrs   155

Epilogue: *Cristeros Resurgent*   176

Notes   181

Bibliography   237

Index   253

Acknowledgments

THIS PROJECT BEGAN more than ten years ago, and it has followed me through two countries, four academic institutions, and dozens of archives and libraries—not to mention the countless offices, quiet rooms, and coffee shops where I read, wrote, and thought. Despite the inherently solitary nature of academic research and writing, I was never alone on this journey. Family, friends, and colleagues have accompanied me all along the way.

At the University of Chicago, where I began the research for this project, I received the wise counsel and continuous support of my advisor and dissertation chair, Emilio Kourí, as well as the thoughtful advice of committee members Dain Borges and Mae Ngai. I will always be grateful to them for their dedication, their interest, and their time. I also had the opportunity to share my work with Mauricio Tenorio, Claudio Lomnitz, and the late Friedrich Katz, all of whom asked key questions and offered sound and incisive suggestions. Participants at Chicago's Latin American History Workshop—my fellow students then and my esteemed colleagues now—were among the first audience upon which I tested my ideas. These included Pablo Ben, Lara Braff, Carlos Bravo Regidor, Nancy Buenger, Jessica Graham, Amanda Hughes, Patrick Iber, José Ángel Hernández, Nicole Mottier, Sarah Osten, Jaime Pensado, Ann Schneider, and Mikael Wolfe. All of them have read parts and pieces of my writing over the years, and I am so grateful to them for their insight and advice.

I began my archival research for this book in Mexico, continued it in the United States, and then crossed back and forth again several times. This itinerant process taught me that archivists and librarians are some of the world's most interesting, learned, and patient people. In Mexico, I was especially grateful to the kind staff at the Archivo General de la Nación, particularly those in charge of the DGIPS and D-Gob collections, and the Archivo General de la UNAM, as well as to

Marco Pérez Iturbe and Berenice Bravo Rubio at the Archivo Historico del Arzobispado de Mexico. In the United States, I was lucky to receive the counsel of the late John Taylor, archivist at the National Archives at College Park, who knew the collections like a map of his hometown. He pointed me toward sources I never would have found otherwise. Maria Mazzenga at the Catholic University Archives, Malachy McCarthy at the Claretian Missionaries Archives, and Claudia Rivers at the C. L. Sonnichsen Special Collections Department at the University of Texas at El Paso Library were also particularly helpful. Many other archivists and librarians on both sides of the border provided me with tips and counsel that made the research process not only less onerous, but vastly more enjoyable and productive.

When I moved back to Washington, DC, Georgetown University's John Tutino welcomed me into the vibrant community of capital-area Latin Americanists. It was at Georgetown, as well, that I met Carole Sargent, without whose sage advice and gentle encouragement this book might still only exist as a digital draft in my "to do" folder. As I began my academic career at George Mason University, I was grateful to receive a particularly warm welcome from Latin American historians Joan Bristol and Matt Karush. Since I arrived at The Catholic University of America, the kindness, intelligence, and warmth of my colleagues has been the best part of the job. I am especially grateful to Juanita Aristizábal, Claudia Bornholdt, Thomas Cohen, Jennifer Davis, Kate Jansen, Laura Mayhall, Maria Mazzenga, Timothy Meagher, Nelson Minnich, Jerry Muller, Jenny Paxton, Larry Poos, Ramon Sola, Jason Sharples, Stephen Schneck, Caroline Sherman, Leslie Tentler, Arpad von Klimo, Lev Weitz, and Stephen West. Although they no longer teach at CUA, James Riley and Robert Schneider have served as mentors and colleagues from afar. My experience at CUA has also been greatly enhanced by the History Department's wonderful community of graduate students, especially Vanessa Corcoran and Stephen Borthwick, who helped me greatly in the final preparation of this manuscript. Although they are too numerous to name, my undergraduate students at all three universities have asked thoughtful questions that continue to shape my work.

I am also incredibly lucky to have gotten to know a number of supportive and enthusiastic colleagues at DC-area universities and research institutions, including Adriana Brodsky, Benjamin Cowan, Bea Gurwitz, and David Sartorius. I am likewise very grateful to my non-academic friends for their patience, time, wisdom, and companionship. (Timothy R. Homan, in particular, kindly consulted the University of Arizona Library Special Collections on my behalf.) Finally, as a DC-area historian, I have had the great privilege of reading and writing in the Hispanic Reading Room at the Library of Congress, where I sat under the watchful portrait of Benito Juárez, and the marvelous Barbara Tenenbaum kept a kind (and no less watchful) eye on me. In addition, I completed the final preparations of this book during my tenure as a Kluge Fellow at the Library of Congress, where I was very fortunate to work with Mary Lou Reker and the rest of the wonderful staff of the John W. Kluge Center.

The field of Mexican history is vast, as is that of Mexican migration history. Nevertheless, over the past several years—and in a number of cities on both sides of the border—I have been truly lucky to get to know a number of historians whose interests overlap with my own, and whose thoughtful questions at conference panels and seminars have prompted me to hone my arguments and clarify my thoughts. These include Fernando Saúl Alanís Enciso, Stephen Andes, Ted Beatty, Christopher Boyer, Matthew Butler, Manuel Ceballos Ramírez, Margaret Chowning, Robert Curley, Jorge Durand, Jean Meyer, Timothy Matovina, Aaron Navarro, Servando Ortoll, Julia Preciado, Yves Solis, and many others. I am also very grateful to the anonymous reviewers at Oxford University Press, whose clear, detailed, and incisive comments helped me greatly as I revised this manuscript for publication. My editor at Oxford, Cynthia Read, has been an enthusiastic advocate for this project from the first time she read it, and I am profoundly thankful for her support.

Very importantly, I could never have pursued my itinerant research process (and later, my less itinerant writing time) without funding. I have been the grateful recipient of fellowships from the John W. Kluge Center at the Library of Congress, the Andrew W. Mellon Foundation in Latin American History, the Fulbright-Hays Doctoral Dissertation Research Abroad Program, the Center for the Study of Race, Politics, and Culture at the University of Chicago, the Tinker Foundation, and the American Catholic History Research Center at The Catholic University of America.

My family has provided me with love, support, and strength—not only as I worked on this project, but also in everything else I have ever done. My parents, Robin and Malcolm, brought me up in a household full of books, and never let me doubt that I was capable of writing my own. My siblings, Catherine, Peter, Maria, and Gabriel, have been my best friends for as long as I can remember. As they have married and expanded their families, each new family member—Tom, Noelle, Albert, and Adrienne—has created more joy and fun for us all. In addition, Graciela and Henry Steiner, whom I have known since childhood, planted the first seeds of interest in Mexico in my mind and imagination.

This book is dedicated to four people. The first is my husband, Spiro Roiniotis, who has been a source of calm, love, and focus for nearly all of my adult life. The second is my son Theo, who was born when I was a graduate student. The third is my daughter Helen, who arrived when I was a brand new faculty member. These amazing children—and their bright enthusiasm and fierce energy—light up my life. The fourth is my newest daughter, who will arrive as this book goes to press, and who kept me company while I wrote and edited the final drafts.

Writing this book has taken me away from my children for much more time than I would have liked. Thankfully, they were surrounded by a loving community—including my own parents and siblings, as well as my husband's family, George, Irene, Christine, and Katherine Roiniotis—along with a wonderful succession of nannies and babysitters, among them Anne Lojek, Claudia Esquivel Ho, and the indefatigable Candy Gutiérrez. To them, to all of the people I have listed above, and to the people I have forgotten to name but to whom I owe no less—thank you. I am so lucky.

Mexican Exodus

Introduction

A DESERT UPRISING

SIMÓN TENORIO WAS in serious trouble. It was August 13, 1927, and the thirty-six-year-old resident of Del Rio, Texas, had been sweltering for the past week in a jail cell in the hot and dusty *pueblo* of Villa Acuña, just south of the US-Mexico border. When the agents finally came to interview him—first, a group of Mexican government officials; and later, men from the US Department of Justice—he tried weakly to deny his involvement in any crime. He never actually intended to lead a religious revolt against the Mexican government, Tenorio insisted. Hadn't he turned himself in, back on August 7, in Coahuila? No, it was the other men, not him, who had started everything. It was their fault. They were, he said, simply "ignorant and fanatical men that go about praying all day long."[1]

Before long, however, the prisoner began to confess his own role in the failed uprising. It probably wasn't hard for his questioners to get the story out of him: two of Tenorio's companions had already been shot dead in the desert, and he was scared. Over the next few days, he told the agents everything they wanted to know.

The narrative that Tenorio recounted in Villa Acuña revealed not only that he and his co-conspirators had tried to participate in a border revolt, but also that the men had intended to help support the Cristero War, a brutal conflict between Catholic partisans and the Mexican government that was currently raging some eight hundred miles to the southwest in the west-central Mexican heartland, a region that included the states of Jalisco, Guanajuato, and Michoacán.

The entire episode had started, Tenorio confessed, with his next-door neighbor. Since 1923, when he left the small, mountain-ringed village of

Monclova in the Mexican state of Coahuila, Tenorio had lived with his mother and several siblings in a scrappy *barrio* called Chihuahua, directly south of the railroad station on the outskirts of Del Rio, Texas.[2] The dwellings there were tiny—little more than shacks—and so it would have been easy for Tenorio to meet Pascual Robles, the firebrand Catholic priest in the next house over.

Father Robles, an exile from Mexico, had probably resettled in Del Rio around 1926. Within a year, he was well known throughout south Texas. He was a vocal opponent of the current Mexican president, Plutarco Elías Calles, and published a newspaper, *La Razon*, whose pages pulsed with invective against the "tyrannical" Calles government. Its uncompromising motto was "Victory or Death."[3] His other activities were more clandestine: he served as a recruiting agent for the US-based branch of the National League for the Defense of Religious Liberty (Liga Nacional Defensora de la Libertad Religiosa; known simply as the Liga), a Mexican Catholic organization that supported armed rebellion against the Calles regime. In Simón Tenorio, Robles saw a potential soldier for his holy cause. And Tenorio must have felt the same, for when Robles invited him to help plan an armed uprising in northern Mexico, he accepted.

During the midsummer months of 1927, as Tenorio recounted, the two men had driven to San Antonio to meet with a group of powerful political exiles from Mexico, including Luis Bustos, head of the Liga at the time; Juan Lainé, the organization's purchasing agent; and Bishop José de Jesus Manríquez y Zárate, an exiled Mexican bishop and key ally of Catholic militants.[4] The group convened in the Robert E. Lee Hotel, a recently built ten-story "skyscraper" in the heart of the city. There, they gave Tenorio his assignment: he was to recruit a gang of men, bring them into Coahuila, and then meet with a larger expedition in the foothills of the Sierra del Burro, at the northern edge of Mexico's vast eastern mountain range, the Sierra Madre Occidental. Together, they would proceed deeper into Mexican territory. Then, they would join up with several larger bands of armed men from Laredo and El Paso, and launch a Catholic military uprising that would, they hoped, bring down the Calles government and restore the rightful place of the Catholic Church in Mexican society.[5]

The plan was grandiose and utterly impractical, but Tenorio was apparently convinced it would work. After the meeting in San Antonio, he returned with Father Robles to Del Rio and began collecting war materials: rifles, cartridges, pipe bombs, saddles, and bridles. They also recruited a group of seven men: Genaro Valadez, Merced Godinez, José Guerra,

Jesús Elizondo, Agustín L. Guerra, Plácido Sánchez, and Graciano Vélez. By August 6, the preparations were complete.

That evening, the priest escorted Tenorio and Valadez to a remote spot about six miles west of Del Rio. They met the rest of the men on the riverbank of the Rio Grande (called the Río Bravo in Mexico).[6] Then, notwithstanding all of his fiery rhetoric, Father Robles turned back; unlike numerous priests in the Cristero armies to the south, he didn't join the soldiers as they mounted their horses and crossed the shallow river into Mexico. Instead, the men proceeded without him, eventually making camp in the desert.

In the quiet night, the men perhaps reflected upon their reasons for going to war. We cannot know exactly what they thought, but they carried some evidence of their ideology with them: numerous pieces of religious and political paraphernalia. Tenorio had a manifesto signed by all seven men, as well as Father Robles, stating their intention "to overthrow the Bolshevik tyranny in its most recent incarnation, Callismo" and recognizing the exclusive authority of "the Roman, Catholic Apostolic Religion." He also carried several other religious texts: a long sermon written by the militant bishop Manríquez y Zárate, and a clipping from Father Robles's newspaper, *La Razon*, about the exploits of Catholic soldiers in the northern state of Coahuila. One of these stories—surely meant to be inspirational to readers—ended with two young men in front of a firing squad, crying out "We are soldiers of Christ the King ... Long live Christ the King! Long live the Virgin of Guadalupe!"[7]

Tenorio was not the only one who had brought along religious items. Genaro Valadez carried with him a suitcase containing scapulars, rosaries, mass books, and portraits of the Virgin of Guadalupe. (Figure I.1 depicts one of the scapulars.)[8] The suitcase also held three letters. The first was from the men's patron, Father Robles, who underscored the divine motivations for their uprising and declared that "God wishes that all your preparations bear the fruit that He ... has prepared for you." He also alluded to a broader community of supporters, stating "We pray daily for you all" and asking Valadez "to commend us to God, since you are so close to Him because of your good work."[9]

The other two letters were from acquaintances of Genaro Valadez. The first wrote from San Angelo, Texas, and the second from Detroit, Michigan; both writers offered prayers for the men.[10] But the latter, written by a man named Simón Muñoz, also sounded a strong word of caution. Muñoz urged Valadez to wait until he could acquire more guns and

FIGURE I.I Scapular found at the scene of the Tenorio revolt, August 1927
Source: AGN, IPS, Volume 231, Expediente 30.

bullets. Otherwise, he wrote, "you are going to sacrifice your lives without advancing the cause, without hope of triumph, without glory."[11]

Only a day after Tenorio's band set out, this dire warning would prove wholly true. After breaking camp in the early hours of August 7, the men proceeded south toward the Sierra del Burro, as they had been instructed to do. It was at this point that things began to go wrong. First of all, their horses were too slow. The men from the Liga had promised them good war mounts; these horses, the band of insurgents soon realized, were weak, worn-out nags (they may not have known that, in fact, the organization was chronically short of funds). Even worse, Tenorio and his gang couldn't find the other band of men, who were supposed to be waiting for them near the hamlet of San Vicente. After searching for a while, Tenorio assumed that the Liga had simply failed to send reinforcements.

Feeling thwarted, Tenorio decided to abandon the mission. He deserted the rest of his group and headed alone to the village of San Miguel, right outside of Monclova, his hometown. There, he used the town's telephone to turn himself in to the police. In an act of great betrayal—or perhaps simple desperation—he also told them where the other men could be found. On the following day, Mexican federal troops caught up with the gang and opened fire, killing Placido Sánchez and Genaro Valadez. The surviving recruits fled in disarray for the hills, abandoning the rest of their arms, munitions, horses, and saddles at the scene.[12]

After giving his prison confession, which was written up and filed away in investigative bureaus on both sides of the border, Tenorio was taken further south, to the small city of Torreón in Coahuila. What happened to him afterward is unknown. Someone in the United States inquired to the Mexican military about his whereabouts in December 1927, but there is no record that he was found, and the authorities in the United States presumed that he was dead.[13] In any event, his activities were no longer a concern to Mexican federal agents. Tenorio's religious rebellion had ended, and any potential threat was neutralized. Indeed, shortly after Tenorio's arrest, the garrison chief in charge of the Tenorio case received a letter of commendation congratulating him for closing the case so rapidly, and thus preventing any "alarm or scandal that could besmirch the good name of the Supreme Government."[14]

Tenorio and the Cristero War

Despite these plaudits from his superiors, the garrison chief probably knew better than to rest on his laurels. By capturing Tenorio and his men, the Mexican army had stopped only one uprising in a series of small but significant border rebellions that continued throughout the late 1920s. Tenorio, Valadez, and the other would-be insurgents, along with the peripheral characters in the drama—the exiled priest and his prayerful flock in Del Rio, the emigrant friends of Genaro Valdez in Detroit, and the group of men in the Robert E. Lee Hotel—were among thousands of Mexican emigrants, exiles, and refugees who were taking part in Mexico's Cristero War from numerous cities and towns across the United States.

The Cristero War, a widespread effort by Mexican Catholic militants to overthrow the Mexican government that began in 1926 and formally ended in 1929, is known in Mexico as *la Cristiada* or *la Guerra Cristera*. The war had begun when Catholic loyalists—called *cristeros* for their battle cry of *¡Viva Cristo Rey!* or "Long live Christ the King!"—took up arms in order to resist a set of anticlerical reforms promulgated by the government of Plutarco Elías Calles and his handpicked successors. (In fact, the conflict had much deeper roots in several centuries' worth of Church-state tension in Mexico; Chapter 1 will provide an overview of this history.)

With the backing of militant parish priests, some members of the Catholic hierarchy, and Catholic lay organizations such as the Liga, the Mexican Catholic Youth Association (Asociación Católica de la Juventud Mexicana, or ACJM), the Union of Mexican Catholic Ladies (Unión de Damas Católicas Mexicanas), and the Mexican Knights of Columbus (Caballeros de Colón), Cristero soldiers fought guerrilla-style battles against Mexican federal troops and their rural supporters, the *agraristas*. Although there were outbreaks of violence throughout Mexico, the fighting was most intense in the densely populated, agriculturally productive west-central region, which included the states of Jalisco, Guanajuato, Michoacán, and others. As a result, the conflict ravaged the Mexican heartland, destroying villages, disrupting agriculture, and claiming the lives of an estimated hundred thousand people.[15] Although the war would formally end in 1929, when Church and state leaders forged a series of compromises known as the *arreglos*, Cristero militants would continue to launch sporadic uprisings throughout the 1930s. (These are known collectively as the Second Cristiada, or *la Segunda*.)

Historians generally regard the Cristero War as an event that occurred within Mexican territory. Yet in fact, as the planned uprising of Simón Tenorio demonstrates, the war also involved participants from beyond the Mexican border. The reason for this was simple: by the mid-1920s, there were hundreds of thousands of Mexican emigrants living in the United States, many of whom had been directly or indirectly affected by the Cristero conflict.

Mexican migration had first become a significant phenomenon at the turn of the twentieth century, as Mexican laborers, drawn by new transportation networks and comparatively higher wages north of the border, had started to migrate in ever-larger numbers to the US Southwest.[16] With the outbreak of the Mexican Revolution in 1910, thousands of refugees joined these labor emigrants. By the next decade, the number of emigrants had risen to unprecedented heights. This period (1920–29) saw Mexico's first "Great Migration," larger in scale than any movement that had come before it, and not to be surpassed until the bracero program migrations of 1942–64.

Migration during the 1920s was different not only numerically, but also geographically. For the first time, most of the emigrants came from the densely populated west-central region. And by 1926, the Cristero War would contribute new waves of emigrants, exiles, and refugees to this flow. As the war continued, entire towns in Jalisco, Michoacán, Guanajuato, and other west-central states emptied of working-age inhabitants, while Mexican *barrios* in cities and towns across the United States filled with thousands of new arrivals from the Cristero region. By 1930, there were approximately 1.5 million Mexicans (both people born in Mexico as well as people with Mexican parents or ancestry) in the United States.[17]

The temporal and geographic overlap between the Great Migration and the Cristero War meant that many emigrants had experienced the religious conflict. And in fact, by the late 1920s, there were tens of thousands of Mexican emigrants across the United States who, like Tenorio and his co-conspirators, supported the Catholic uprising from the United States. Ultimately, their actions would not change the course of the war: neither they nor their co-religionaries in Mexico would succeed in their goal of overturning the anticlerical government or even reforming the Mexican constitution. Nevertheless, their activities would have a profound and enduring resonance, both for the development of the Cristero conflict in Mexico and within Mexican communities in the United States.

This book examines the history and the legacy of these emigrant Cristero supporters. This group, which I refer to collectively as the Cristero diaspora, included tens of thousands of labor emigrants, more than two thousand exiled priests and nuns, numerous members of the Mexican hierarchy, and dozens of middle-class lay political activists. These emigrants participated in the conflict in a variety of ways, many of which were nonviolent: they took part in religious ceremonies and spectacles, organized political demonstrations and marches, formed associations and organizations, and planned strategic collaborations with religious and political leaders in order to generate public sympathy for their cause. A few of them, like Tenorio and his co-conspirators, even participated in militant efforts that included arms smuggling, recruitment, espionage, and military revolts. Despite the fact that these emigrants supported the same cause, they did not always act in perfect accord; throughout the war years, they sometimes competed with each other—occasionally quite intensely— as they attempted to determine the best way to further their cause from abroad. Yet by and large, they shared a broad political vision for the Mexican nation: one that advocated a restored role for the Catholic Church in the Mexican public sphere, and therefore diverged sharply from the nationalist project of the Mexican government.

Defining Diaspora

Mexican internal conflicts have a long history of spreading beyond the Mexican interior and spilling into the United States. Since the nineteenth century, hundreds of political dissidents from Mexico have sought a safe haven across national lines, and then continued to campaign from US territory. Such men included national politicians such as Benito Juárez in the early 1850s and Porfirio Díaz in 1876; dissidents such as Catarino Garza in the 1890s; the anarchist Flores Magón brothers in the 1900s; Francisco Madero in 1911; and countless other Mexican revolutionaries and counter-revolutionaries from 1911 to 1920, including Victoriano Huerta and Pancho Villa. For them, crossing the border meant not only that they could escape from their enemies in Mexico, but also that they could regroup, refresh their depleted stocks of war materiel, and plot new military campaigns from the relative safety of the United States.[18]

The Cristero religious movement in the United States shared some similarities to previous efforts by Mexican political exiles. Yet here, religion played a unique role. While earlier dissident activities were organized primarily by political exiles, the Cristero diaspora included hundreds of religious leaders—exiled priests, high clergy, and nuns—who worked to organize their communities in support of the Cristero cause. Additionally, the Cristero diaspora was more geographically widespread than many of these previous movements, which had been largely limited to the border states (particularly Texas). In fact, Cristero activity in the United States was fueled by thousands of religious emigrants, exiles, and refugees in multiple locations around the Southwest and Midwest. And many people within these communities connected with each other across great distances in order to advance a common set of political and religious goals in their home country. As a result, these emigrants formed a religious diaspora within the larger Mexican population in the United States.

In using the term "diaspora" to describe Mexican Cristero supporters, I am building upon recent scholarship that has applied this descriptor to the broader Mexican emigrant community. Although there has been extensive debate about the meaning of diaspora—and about whether

Mexicans can be classified as a "true" diaspora, like the classic historical cases of the Jews or Armenians—I agree with scholars such as Alexandra Délano, who argues that the term is useful because it more accurately conveys "the complex transnational identities and relationships that [Mexican] emigrants and their organizations have developed with their home country."[19] Indeed, the members of the Cristero diaspora held specific conceptions and notions of themselves that were inherently transnational, since they were intricately related to the politics, government, and history of Mexico. Sociologist Stéphane Dufoix describes such diasporic groups as "antagonistic," since they "refuse to recognize the legitimacy of the current regime in their country of origin" and simultaneously form "a political space" for opposition in their destination country. The goal of such opposition is "to liberate their country, nation, people, or land."[20] For the Mexican members of the Cristero diaspora, those political spaces were often church pews and pulpits, and the liberation they were seeking was infused with religious meaning. Even after arriving in the United States, these emigrants continued to see themselves as members of a persecuted religious group; as supporters of a specific political movement; as victims of the anticlerical Mexican government; and even as martyrs for their faith.

The Mexican emigrants who supported the Cristero cause also formed these identities *in contrast to* other groups of Mexican emigrants. Certainly, many Mexican emigrants remained apolitical, or left no record of any political activities. Many others vocally supported the anticlerical policies of the revolutionary Mexican government, and the voices of this group, which several other historians have researched, will appear in the chapters that follow.[21] Yet it is the history of the Cristero diaspora—its formation, activities, and beliefs—that has gone untold, and that this book seeks to recover and reconstruct.

Thus, the Cristero diaspora comprised a smaller group within the wider population of Mexican emigrants—all of whom, following Délano, can collectively be considered a diaspora as well. Here, though, I must present an important caveat: it is impossible to determine the exact size or demographic characteristics of this "diaspora within a diaspora," for there is no concrete way to measure the number of Mexican emigrants who supported the Cristero cause from the United States. Emigrants were not required to state their political affiliations when crossing the border, and in fact, many wished to hide their sympathies for the Cristeros (and their antipathy for the Calles government) in the United States. And of course, most Mexican emigrants who supported the Cristero side of the conflict did not devote their entire lives to the Cristero cause. The majority of Mexican emigrants during the 1920s came from working-class and rural backgrounds, and much of their time was taken up by earning the money they needed to survive and to support their families.[22] Nevertheless, as this book will document, there were tens of thousands of Mexican Catholics in the United States who found the time and energy to publically support the Catholic cause in Mexico: this is most evident from the number of people who attended the numerous pro-Cristero marches, rallies, and demonstrations held in different cities during the war years. Furthermore, these emigrants came from a variety of racial, ethnic, and class groups: the archival materials used for this study provide clear evidence that there were male and female Cristero supporters; Indians, *mestizos*, and people of exclusively European descent; wealthy landowners, middle-class urban workers, and rural laborers.

Archival Discoveries and the Structure of the Book

I first discovered the story of the Cristero diaspora not in the United States, where these emigrants lived and operated, but in the Mexican National Archives in Mexico City. Sitting at a long table in the dim and permanently chilly Gallery 8 (the AGN is the former Lecumberri prison, which was designed as a panopticon, and historical documents are housed within the former prison cells that line each of the long galleries), I came across a voluminous collection of letters addressed to President Calles from people living in the United States. The majority of these letters, written by Americans as well as some Mexicans living abroad, applauded Calles for his stance against the Catholic Church. Yet there was one that was different from the rest.

Handwritten in rough, slanted script and dated April 23, 1926, it was a petition signed by a group of Mexican emigrants living in Perris, California, a small inland town that lies roughly between San Diego and Los Angeles. In the decorous language so common to Mexican letters of the period, the writers addressed the president directly:

> The Mexican Mothers and Fathers that comprise this Colony Elevate ourselves towards You a protest against the unjust persecution that has been made against the Catholic Religion. Today ... we unite [as] brothers in Race to appeal for our rights, for our religious

ideals to be respected and for our Churches as well as its ministers to be respected.

After reminding the president of the historical contributions of the Catholic Church in Mexico, the writers asked the president, "with all respect," to "modify the Articles that attack our religion."[23]

The letter raised a number of questions in my mind. Who were these emigrants in Perris? Were there others like them? Why were they rebuking the Mexican government, when so many were praising its anticlerical reforms? To answer these questions, I soon realized that it would be necessary to conduct archival research on both sides of the border. In a way, I had to follow the trail of the emigrants themselves, who had left Mexico for multiple US destinations, and had then collaborated with allies—and confronted opponents—in both countries.

In Mexico, I visited government, private, and Church archives, mostly in Mexico City. There, I found information about the interactions between Cristero supporters and their allies and enemies at home in Mexico. The archives of the Liga, for example, revealed that the Catholic organization's leadership in Mexico maintained constant contact with exiles in the United States, and eventually even established a US headquarters. And through the records of the Mexican government, particularly officers at the Ministry of Foreign Relations and the Confidential Department of the Ministry of the Interior, it became apparent that numerous state officials—especially consular officers, army officials, and intelligence agents—had collected ample information about Cristero activism abroad.[24]

In the United States, my research was more peripatetic, reflecting the variety of destinations that Mexican emigrants chose during the 1920s. Consulting government, private, and Church collections across the country, I found thousands of newspaper articles, personal letters, petitions, photographs, and other documents that revealed that numerous Mexican emigrants in widespread locations supported the Cristero cause through collective and individual actions.[25]

The story that emerged from this archival research is a transnational narrative of migration, militancy, defeat, and resilience. It begins with an analysis of the two events that formed the Cristero diaspora. Chapter 1, "A History of Faith and Conflict," offers a broad overview of the struggle between Church and state in Mexico, as well as a detailed discussion of the chronological and geographic intersections between the Cristero War and the great migration of the 1920s. Chapter 2, "Religious Refugees, Political

Exiles, and the US Catholic Church," explains how a smaller group of Cristero War–era exiles and refugees arrived in the United States (the latter with the help of US Catholic officials). In the United States, they would play a crucial role in directing the formation and activities of the Cristero diaspora. During the period between 1926 and 1929, Mexican Cristero supporters in the United States began participating in a variety of actions in order to support the religious uprising in Mexico. Chapter 3, "In Defense of Their Brothers Beyond the Rio Grande," discusses and analyzes these forms of transnational Cristero activism. Chapter 4, "Bishops, Knights, Border Guards, and Spies," demonstrates how the efforts of the most militant members of the Cristero diaspora were ultimately thwarted by a number of internal and external impediments that precluded the possibility of a successful armed revolt along the border.

In June 1929, the Mexican hierarchy signed an agreement with the Calles government that ended the armed uprising in Mexico. Chapter 5, "After the *Arreglos*," describes the activities of the Cristero diaspora from the 1930s to the early 1940s, as Mexican Cristero supporters in the United States continued to organize—albeit in a less militant way—in opposition to the Mexican government. The sixth and final chapter, "Memories, Myths, and Martyrs," jumps ahead in time to the present day, examining how Cristero supporters and their descendants retained family memories of the martyrdom, persecution, and exile that they had perceived and endured during the conflict. In the Epilogue to this book, I present a closing case for the importance of the Cristero diaspora for an understanding of contemporary Mexican religious and political identities on both sides of the border.

Contributions to the Historical Literature

The main purpose of this book is to reconstruct an important historical narrative that has gone largely untold. This story also aims to extend and build upon the rich and fascinating historical scholarship in three areas: the Cristero War, Mexican emigration during the 1920s, and Mexican American religion.

My primary argument about the Cristero War is that, because of emigration, it had a much wider geographical impact than most scholars have assumed. Essentially, Mexican emigrants who supported the Cristero cause reenacted and reproduced Mexico's Church-state conflict within their communities, while encountering and opposing the representatives and adherents of the anticlerical Mexican government in the United States. In doing so, they transnationalized the Cristero conflict, bringing it out of the Mexican heartland and into the Mexican barrios of El Paso, San Antonio, Los Angeles, Chicago, and other locations. Furthermore, the activities of the Cristero diaspora also impacted the development of the war itself. In particular, emigrants who sent money and weapons to the Cristero battlefields strengthened the position of the Cristero resistance by providing critical material assistance to the Cristero movement's political and military operations; political exiles contributed to the logistical operations of the war; religious refugees promoted support and loyalty for the Cristero cause in Mexico; and militants such as Simón Tenorio participated in several uprisings along the border that, although they were unsuccessful, drew the concern (as well as time and resources) of Mexican and US government officials.

To be sure, I do not claim that the activities within the Cristero diaspora were directly equivalent to the violence and bloodshed in Jalisco, Michoacán, or other war-torn areas. I do argue, however, that the transnational forms of popular activism and resistance that occurred within the Mexican emigrant diaspora must be considered within the historical context of the Cristero War, and that the Cristero War must likewise be understood as a transnational conflict as well as a regional, national, or international one. In that sense, the Cristero War shares similarities with the Mexican Revolution, or even with the current drug war in Mexico: all three of these conflicts began in Mexico, and became transnationalized by emigrants, refugees, and exiles in the United States.

By arguing that historians' conception of the geographic area of the Cristero War should be expanded to include the territory of the Cristero diaspora in the United States, I am following historian Adrian Bantjes, who called on scholars of the religious conflict to conduct new historical investigations of the Cristero War in order to include less-studied regions and actors, as well as wider variations of popular resistance. And indeed, as the scholarship on the popular dimensions of the conflict has proliferated in recent years, it has also expanded beyond the traditional investigations of the west-central states of Michoacán, Jalisco, and Guanajuato, and into regions of Mexico formerly regarded as peripheral to the conflict.[26] In addition, there is also a large body of historical literature that narrates the international development of the war, particularly as it involved diplomats, representatives of the Vatican, international Catholic organizations, and members of the Catholic hierarchy in the United States, Europe, and Latin America.[27] Nevertheless, none of these narratives include a thorough investigation of emigrant Cristero activism and its impact on the Cristero War.[28]

The story of the Cristero diaspora has the potential to shed new light not only on historical understandings of the Cristero War, but also on the nature of Mexican migration, particularly the massive migration of the 1920s. Most importantly, it shows that, as a result of the Cristero War, Mexican emigrant communities were deeply affected by the religious conflict that was ongoing within their homeland. The members of the Cristero diaspora collaborated with each other across cities and regions in the United States in order to advance their particular political vision: the restoration of religious rights in Mexico and the defeat of Calles and his successors. In the process of promoting their political goals, they confronted other Mexican emigrants who supported the revolutionary government; they also quarreled among themselves about the direction their movement should take. Thus, this book, while primarily focused on uncovering the actions and ideologies of the Cristero diaspora, also explores the political divisions and factionalism that affected emigrant community formation during the 1920s and 1930s.

As a result, this study presents a different picture of the Mexican emigrant community than much of the existing historical scholarship on Mexican migration during this period, which, although it has uncovered fascinating stories about questions of race and ethnicity, gender, labor, and community-level organizing, has not yet fully assessed the impact or legacy of the Cristero conflict.[29] This is not to say that historians of Mexican emigration have ignored the Cristero War; numerous regional studies have noted the impact of the religious conflict on emigrant communities within a particular city or region.[30] Yet that same regional focus of the most recent literature may have steered scholars away from investigating diasporic politics during the Cristero War years. In particular, the regional studies do not demonstrate how some emigrants connected across distances to advance their particular political causes; likewise, they generally do not compare the experiences of emigrants across different regions.

This book aims to provide that multiregional scope, focusing on Mexican religious and political activism across multiple urban emigrant communities, particularly (although not exclusively) in the cities of El Paso, San Antonio, Los Angeles, and Chicago. Additionally, it examines the ways that this diaspora maintained transnational ties to the homeland. Following the methodology of a growing number of historians who have begun using transnational archives, it examines how Mexicans in these locations interacted with the Mexican state and its representatives, and with friends and family members at home in Mexico.[31] This study, then, uses transnational and multiregional sources to demonstrate that, thanks to the Cristero War, Mexican emigrants during the 1920s and 1930s were more religious, more involved in diasporic politics, and more politically divided than the scholarship on Mexican migration has assumed.

By focusing on Mexican emigrant responses to a religious conflict in the homeland, this book also views Mexicans as similar to many other diasporic emigrant groups in the period between 1880 and 1940—including Irish American Catholics, Jewish Zionists, and Armenian Orthodox emigrants—who engaged transnationally with religious and political conflicts in their homelands. Like Mexican Cristero supporters, these other groups participated in activities such as sending remittances to revolutionary causes, arms smuggling, producing a politicized print culture, and lobbying the US government. These emigrants also maintained strong political, religious, and cultural ties to their home countries, and many of them astutely negotiated the political framework of the United States in order to pursue their political goals.[32] By examining how the Cristero diaspora worked across cities, regions, and national boundaries to pursue its agenda, this book presents a different portrait of Mexican migration from that dominant in the literature, which has tended to view the majority of Mexicans as economic emigrants rather than as people who left the country for political reasons.[33]

Finally, this book contributes a new perspective to the growing field of scholarship on Mexican American religion.[34] Reconceiving the Cristero War as a transnational conflict whose boundaries extended outside of Mexico's territory and into Mexican emigrant communities indicates not only that the war had a larger geographical impact, but also that it had a more profound resonance and meaning for many Mexicans: so much so, that they carried the conflict with them, and then reenacted it after they left the country. To that end, I extend to the emigrant community the argument of Lourdes Celina Vázquez, who asserts that Cristero thought, as well as memories of the Cristero War, persist in the contemporary Mexican collective memory, particularly in west-central Mexico.[35] This book, then, does not end with the arreglos in 1929 or even with the end of militancy in the late 1930s, but explores how the war has remained relevant to the identities of Cristero-era emigrants and their descendants. Memories of the conflict, especially of martyrdom and militancy, continue to play a central role in family narratives, religious practices, and even political identity. The intensity of these family memories, despite the passage of time and geographic distance, helps to explain why the Cristero War continues to have symbolic resonance within Mexican American Catholicism.

While a growing number of historians, religious studies scholars, and theologians are paying attention to religious practice within the Mexican diaspora, most do not examine transnational sources, or consider the long-term impact of the conflict between Church and state in Mexico on the religious identities of Mexican emigrants.[36] Instead, scholars have focused on better-known popular religious symbols such as the Virgin of Guadalupe, home altars, *curanderismo*, and other "folk" practices.[37] While all of these are illuminating and worthwhile topics of study, an accounting of the story of the Cristero diaspora in narratives about Mexican American religious life offers a more complete picture of the historical factors that have shaped this particular ethnic identity, and can even help to explain the recent rise of new transnational religious devotions to Cristero saints and martyrs.

A Note on Terminology

Throughout the following chapters, I use the term "emigrants" to collectively describe the great wave of people who left Mexico during the 1920s. I have chosen this label rather than the term "immigrants" because I wish to emphasize that Mexicans during the 1920s, like the vast majority of emigrant groups during this period, retained familial, political, and economic ties to their homeland, even years after settling in the United States. (The term "immigrant," by contrast, places greater emphasis on the relationship between emigrants and their country of settlement.)[38]

Within this group, I discuss two subcategories: exiles and refugees. The term "exiles" is applied here to describe the much smaller group of people who left Mexico involuntarily during the Cristero War. These were the Catholic activists, both laypeople and members of the clergy, who were deported by the Mexican government. Many were subsequently blacklisted, so that Mexican border guards could keep them from returning to their home country. The other group I have designated "refugees," because they were forced to flee the country under threat of violence, imprisonment, or death. The largest group of refugees was the Mexican lower clergy—priests, nuns, and monks—who were barred from wearing their religious vestments or practicing the Catholic sacraments during the war years. They often fled to the border on their own or in groups, and then appealed to US immigration officials to allow them to enter the country. Of course, there was significant overlap between the three groups. Most exiles and refugees were forced to work for a living, bringing them into contact with labor emigrants, who, in turn, often became politicized by the ongoing religious conflict. Whenever possible, however, I have tried to clarify and contextualize these labels within the text.

A second thorny problem related to terminology is the use of the label "Catholic." This is an issue relevant for all of those who write about Church-state conflicts in Mexico, a country where the vast majority of the population was nominally Catholic (some 98 percent in the 1920s and 1930s). Yet "anti-clerical" and "Catholic" are often treated as mutually exclusive categories. In fact, many Catholics were anticlerical, while others supported the Church and the Cristero cause. To address this conundrum, I have generally used terms such as "Cristero supporters" and "Cristero partisans" rather than "Catholics" to describe those who were opposed to the anticlerical state.

I

A History of Faith and Conflict

MEXICAN EMIGRANTS DURING the 1920s came from a culture that was thoroughly steeped in Catholic devotion, ritual, and practice. Across Mexico, from large cities to remote villages, the rhythms of the faith permeated public and private life. Church bells rang to mark the passing of the hours and to announce festivals and feast days; convents and monasteries dotted the landscape in cities and towns across the region; and Mexicans everywhere observed religious festivals such as *Semana Santa* (Holy Week) and the feast day of the Virgin of Guadalupe, the manifestation of Mary who had appeared in 1531 to Juan Diego on the hill at Tepeyac, and had become Mexico's national emblem.

Catholic practices were also central to local identities. Each town, village, neighborhood, and parish church had its particular saint, whose holy day would be celebrated with a *fiesta* of fireworks, music, or a parade. And everywhere—in the stalls of a marketplace, on the colored tiles outside a building, or on little altars inside private homes—were painted, carved, or printed images of Catholic saints, Jesus, or the Virgin. Almost exactly four centuries after the first Spanish Catholic missionaries had arrived to convert the indigenous peoples of New Spain, close to 98 percent of Mexicans identified as Roman Catholic, and popular symbols of the faith and the church held meaning—whether positive or negative—for nearly everyone.[1]

At the regional level, however, there were great variations in religious identities, levels of religious commitment, and types of religious culture. The west-central region where the Cristero War was fought was also the area with the highest overall levels of religious participation, and the largest numbers of Catholic churches and clergy. Yet, as Matthew Butler points out in his study of religious identity in Michoacán, not everyone there was

"Catholic" in the same way as everyone else (and not quite everyone was even Catholic: Protestant faiths were already beginning to make inroads into the region[2]). Additionally, divergent local histories meant that there were great differences in religious practice and affiliation within states, and even from town to town.[3]

Aside from these regional variations, there are also differences between institutional and popular Catholicism. In many places, Mexican popular Catholicism was (and still is) quite different from the more orthodox faith espoused by centralized Catholic institutions and their representatives. This was partly because people's contact with the institutional Church varied widely from place to place. Many Mexicans did not actively participate in Catholic sacraments such as church marriage, baptism, communion, or confession. Those in the most remote villages often went weeks or months without seeing a priest.[4] Furthermore, since the colonial period, Mexicans had often combined indigenous and African religious traditions with Spanish ones, in a process known as religious syncretism. These syncretic rituals and traditions, which were often unrecognized (and occasionally condemned) by the official Church, nevertheless served as vitally important elements of religious culture throughout Mexico. So, too, did the popular devotions, miracles, magical practices, and manifestations—both angelic and diabolical—so common in Mexican religious life. For the townspeople of San José de Gracia, Michoacán, for example, it was an accepted truth that Satan had once appeared to fly off with an unfortunate sinner, only to drop him into a wild olive tree after he drew out his rosary.[5]

Despite religious syncretism, regional variations in religious commitment, and the disjunctures between popular religious practice and institutional Catholicism in Mexico, the Church and its representatives often played an integral role in the development and practice of popular religion.[6] Scholars such as Benjamin Smith have argued that we should view popular and institutional religion as a "constant dialogue" rather than as a purely oppositional relationship.[7] Furthermore, many Mexicans had deeply personal relationships with their clergy. Elite and middle-class Mexicans often had aunts, uncles, brothers, or sisters who were priests, nuns, or bishops, and parish priests were frequently present in the lives and activities of many townspeople, whether administering sacraments, teaching in the local Catholic school, or participating in local devotions.[8] (To be sure, that role could also be authoritarian, paternalistic, and even merciless: take, for example, a priest from the town of

Cacalotenango, Guerrero, in hiding during the Cristero War, who wrote to a parishioner in 1928 to warn him not to betray his location to the authorities, "for if you say something and they discover me, you will go to the eternal fire."[9])

This religious culture—as regionally varied and as complex as it was—shaped the experiences and memories of Mexican emigrants during the 1920s. Some of them were surely glad to leave it all behind: Pablo Mares, an emigrant from Jalisco interviewed by the anthropologist Manuel Gamio during the late 1920s, stated that, since leaving Mexico, "I haven't gone to a single church, nor do I pray except when I think of it."[10] Yet Catholicism—and particularly, the rupture between Church and state during the 1920s and 1930s—would profoundly affect many others. In the same set of interviews, Gamio spoke with an emigrant from Mexico City named Juan Casanova, who worked as a photographer in El Paso. He stated:

> I am a Catholic by conviction. My parents brought me up in that faith, they baptized me and confirmed me and I am faithful to it. That is why I am not thinking of going back to Mexico while there is religious persecution. It should be understood that a nation without religion cannot and should not exist, since religion is the foundation of morality.[11]

In explaining his reasons for staying away from Mexico, Casanova was echoing a perspective shared not only by Cristeros and their supporters, but also by many previous generations of Mexicans who had witnessed earlier conflicts between Church and state. Indeed, the Cristero War itself had deep historical roots in the enduring tensions between civil and religious authorities in Mexico. To understand why the war happened and how it would impact emigrants to the United States, we must first investigate this history of faith and conflict.

Church and State in Mexico

For much of the colonial period, the Catholic Church in New Spain had essentially shared political power with the Spanish Crown, and thus held tremendous power and influence in colonial society. Through the judicial body known as the Inquisition (1571–1820), the Church asserted its authority—sometimes quite violently—over the behavior of colonial sub-jects. Yet even during the first three centuries of colonial rule, civil authori-ties clashed with religious ones over issues of jurisdiction and power such as *fueros*, the special privileges granted the clergy, or the wealth and influ-ence of religious orders like the Jesuits. In the last century of colonial rule, the Spanish Crown—now under the Bourbon dynasty—enacted reforms meant to limit the wealth and power of the Church. One of these was the expulsion of the Jesuits in 1767, an event that sparked a popular backlash in Mexican towns and villages, for the order had educated many colonial subjects.

After Independence (1821), it seemed that the Church-state relationship might improve: Mexico's first national leader, Agustín Iturbide, guaran-teed the rights and privileges of the Church in his founding document, the *Plan de Iguala*. In return, he drew wide support from the Mexican clergy. But Iturbide's regime collapsed in 1823, and the first half of the nineteenth century saw intense political instability, with continuous power struggles between liberal and conservative politicians. Liberals, influenced by the same Enlightenment ideas that had captivated the Spanish Bourbons, aimed to construct a modern, sovereign, and secular nation that would be autonomous from the Catholic hierarchy. While some were atheists, Protestants, or Masons, others were devoutly Catholic, yet felt that the Church should have no role in politics.[12] At times, liberals successfully enlisted the support of peasant groups.[13] Conservatives, on the other hand, aimed to preserve the centrality of the Church in both social and political life. They, too, frequently rallied the masses behind their cause.[14]

As liberals and conservatives vied for control of the state during the nineteenth century, the Mexican Catholic episcopate vacillated. The hier-archy was naturally inclined to align with conservative politicians, but this was only a successful strategy when they actually held power. When liber-als took the presidency, the Mexican Church was faced with the unappeal-ing choice between accommodation to state demands and overt resistance to liberal authorities. During the period known as *La Reforma* (1854–1876), the liberal Mexican government under President Benito Juárez introduced broadly anticlerical restrictions, subsequently enshrined in the Constitution of 1857, which divested the Church of property and politi-cal power. The Catholic clergy responded first by supporting conservative forces in the War of the Reform (1858–1861), and then by overtly welcom-ing foreign intervention and the temporary overthrow of Juárez by the French, who subsequently installed Archduke Ferdinand Maximilian of

Austria as emperor of Mexico. After Juárez's *liberales* regained power in 1872, conservatives were largely defeated, although Catholic peasants in west-central Mexico would briefly rise up against the Juárez and Lerdo de Tejada governments in the *Religionero* Revolts of 1873–1877.[15]

By contrast, the first half of the long regime of the liberal dictator Porfirio Díaz (1876–1911) marked a more conciliatory phase in the Church-state relationship, whereby most Catholic bishops stayed out of politics, and in return, the government did not enforce the restrictions that were still encoded in the constitution. During this period, the Díaz government even admitted papal delegates into Mexico, improving the country's relationship with the Vatican, which had been unstable since Pope Pius IX condemned the Reform Laws and the Constitution of 1857. During the 1880s and 1890s, the Mexican Church saw significant increases in the numbers of clergy (including bishops, priests, monks, and nuns); a growth in pious associations and missions; and an increase in popular participation in the sacraments.[16] Some members of the hierarchy also began supporting new Catholic social initiatives, such as the Catholic press, Catholic education, and Catholic involvement in state-run institutions such as hospitals and prisons.[17] (The picture was not as rosy for popular religious movements that opposed the porfirian state, such as the followers of the visionary folk healer Teresa de Urrea in Tomochic, Chihuahua.[18])

In the first decade of the twentieth century, these social initiatives grew more prominent and well organized, as the Catholic hierarchy and laity began to play an even more active role in public life. This social action was inspired by two developments: first, increasingly visible social inequality during the economic "boom years" of the Díaz presidency; and second, the publication of the 1891 papal encyclical *Rerum novarum*, which called for Catholics worldwide to take a greater role in social and civic affairs and advocated more equitable relations between the classes (without, however, rejecting the capitalist system). By the late 1890s and early 1900s, Mexican Catholics had begun organizing Catholic labor organizations, Catholic social congresses, and other types of lay cooperative associations. In addition, the Catholic hierarchy welcomed a new generation of bishops who had been steeped in social activism at the Colegio Pío Latino Americano in Rome.[19]

By 1911, however, the Díaz regime had collapsed. Growing rural and urban discontent, political competition, and social inequality sparked the Mexican Revolution (1910–1920), which would consume Mexico for the next decade, and fundamentally alter the country's political land-scape for the rest of the twentieth century. During the first few years of the Revolution, Catholic organizations and publications flourished. President Francisco I. Madero (1911–1914) officially recognized the Partido Católico Nacional (PCN), and Catholics founded the Asociación de Damas Católicas and the Asociación de la Juventud Mexicana (ACJM) during his presidency. Nevertheless, many Catholics became increasingly criti-cal of Madero, and some within the hierarchy supported his overthrow by Victoriano Huerta in 1914.[20] When Huerta himself was subsequently defeated and the country descended into open civil war between the Constitutionalists (led by Venustiano Carranza) and the massive peasant armies of Emiliano Zapata and Pancho Villa, the brief previous period of relatively unrestricted Catholic political, social, and civic activism would come under serious threat.

After the fall of Huerta, anticlericalism surged within many revolution-ary groups, particularly the Constitutionalists. The anticlerical revolution-aries viewed the Catholic Church as a counterrevolutionary, conservative force that—because of its historical support for conservative politicians, its opposition to secularization, and its allegiance to Rome—undermined the modernizing projects of the revolutionary state. Furthermore, many revolutionaries believed that Catholic teaching led to superstition, fanati-cism, and other supposedly backward social practices among the popu-lace—all of which inhibited the modernization of the country.[21] At the same time, the social projects of the post–Rerum novarum church, such as workers' organizations and social welfare initiatives, competed with simi-lar revolutionary social projects.[22] As a result, the period between 1914 and 1919 saw widespread anticlerical activity, including violence directed at clergy and the closure or desecration of Catholic churches, schools, con-vents, and monasteries. Additionally, some five hundred priests, nuns, and members of the Catholic hierarchy were expelled from Mexico; most fled to the United States, although a few also went to Havana or Rome.[23]

The anticlerical faction also won out at the Constitutional Convention of 1917, where attendees crafted legislation that severely restricted church power, as well as religious expression. These laws were subsequently incorporated in several articles of the Mexican Constitution of 1917. The most comprehensive, Article 130, aimed to excise the Church completely from the political sphere in Mexico. It denied the Church legal personal-ity, granted the government the ability to intervene in religious affairs, and allowed governors to limit the number of priests in their states. It also

banned foreign clergy from living and working in Mexico, and prohibited all clergy from commenting on politics. Article 24 outlawed religious
worship in public spaces. Article 27, which dealt with land ownership
in Mexico, nationalized all Church property. Article 5 banned religious
orders. Finally, Article 3 outlawed religious education at the primary level.
Taken together, these constitutional restrictions reiterated and expanded
the 1857 Reform Laws of President Benito Juárez.

Despite the comprehensiveness of the 1917 anticlerical laws, Mexican
politicians during the administration of Venustiano Carranza (1917–1919)
applied them only sporadically, and even then only at the state level. By
1919, the government began allowing the exiled Catholic clergy to return
to Mexico. Increasingly, Catholic activists in Mexico were able to renew
their activities in opposition to the Revolutionary government.[24] In fact,
the early 1920s saw growing activity and membership in lay Catholic associations such as the ACJM (which had established ten regional centers
and one hundred local centers across Mexico by 1919) and the Knights
of Columbus (an American organization that, since arriving in Mexico
in 1905, had grown to forty-five councils by 1923).[25] The Mexican Social
Secretariat, meant to serve as an umbrella organization that would unite
the various Catholic associations and organizations in a coherent program of social activism, opened in 1922 and attracted the participation of
numerous prominent Catholic activists. This period also saw the formation of a secret organization, the Unión de Católicos Mexicanos (known
as La "U"), which aimed to resist the revolutionary government's anticlerical projects.[26] During the presidency of Alvaro Obregón (1920–1924),
the Mexican hierarchy began to enter more aggressively into the public
sphere, organizing religious spectacles such as the 1923 consecration to
the Monument of Christ the King at Cubilete, in the state of Guanajuato,
and the Eucharistic National Congress of 1924 in Mexico City.[27] In 1925
Pope Pius XI designated the last Sunday in October as the official feast
day of Christ the King. Although this initiative was primarily crafted as a
response to the perceived threats of communism, socialism, and fascism
in Europe, Mexican Catholics seized on the feast day as a way to elevate
Christ as the true leader of the Mexican nation.[28]

The Obregón administration was increasingly unwilling to accept
these acts of resistance and antagonism by the Catholic clergy and laity.
Furthermore, numerous governors, such as Tabasco's Tomás Garrido
Canabal, had begun enforcing the anticlerical constitutional articles within
their states.[29] Yet it was Obregón's successor, President Plutarco Elías

Calles (1924–1928), who would present the most direct and widespread challenge to the Mexican Catholic Church. Calles, a Constitutionalist general during the Revolution, was passionately anticlerical. During the Revolution, he had served as governor of his home state, Sonora, where he had personally taken charge of evicting the clergy. As interior minister during the Obregón administration, he had worked to enforce the anticlerical laws. From the beginning of his presidency, he was determined to apply the constitutional restrictions comprehensively at the national level. By 1925 it was obvious that the Church and the Calles government were headed toward direct confrontation.

Although many members of the Catholic hierarchy wanted to negotiate with the government and avoid further conflict, numerous Catholic organizations—and some of the more militant bishops—began to mobilize even more intensely. In March 1925, Catholic activists—including Miguel Palomar y Vizcarra (a founding member of the Partido Nacional Católico), Luis Bustos (head of the Mexican Knights of Columbus), and René Capistrán Garza (head of the ACJM)—formed the Liga Nacional Defensora de la Libertad Religiosa, known as the Liga, an organization that demanded that the anticlerical provisions be struck from the 1917 Constitution, and aimed to direct popular resistance to the anticlerical state. After the founding of the Liga, the Central Committee of the ACJM ordered its local chapters throughout Mexico to organize Liga committees, and by June 26, 1925, the Liga's Executive Committee reported a membership of thirty-six thousand individuals, with dozens of chapters throughout the country, especially in the west-central states of Jalisco, Guanajuato, and Michoacán.[30]

In subsequent months, the situation deteriorated further. In January 1926 the Mexico City daily *El Universal* printed an inflammatory statement, originally published in 1917, by Archbishop and Primate Mora y del Río that declared that Mexican Catholics "do not recognize and will combat Articles 3, 5, 27, and 130 of the present constitution."[31] Soon afterward, the Calles government began cracking down on Catholic bishops and priests, giving notice that the constitutional articles would be strictly applied, expelling foreign-born clergy from the country, and closing some Catholic schools. On February 23 the first violence occurred when government agents clashed with a crowd of women at the Sagrada Familia church in Mexico City and two of the protesters were killed. The situation would only deteriorate further over the next several months, as state legislators passed numerous restrictive laws and Catholic organizations responded with protests and armed resistance. On May 15, the government ordered the expulsion of the latest papal delegate, George J. Caruana, who had entered Mexico by illegally crossing the northern border.

The following month, Calles announced a set of penal code reforms called the *Ley Reglamentaria* and popularly known as the *Ley Calles*, or the Calles Law. The reforms attached explicit monetary and prison penalties to the religious restrictions in the 1917 Constitution. It prohibited religious education in primary schools, outlawed religious orders, and forbade people from taking religious vows. It also provided penalties for clergy who took part in political activities, outlawed religious political parties, and forbade any religious acts from taking place outside of churches.[32] In response to the new law, the Liga condemned the Calles government and circulated a protest petition, eventually collecting some five hundred thousand signatures. The organization also sponsored a national boycott in which Catholics refused to buy everything but bare necessities. Catholics throughout Mexico participated in this and various other forms of popular protest, including public marches and propaganda campaigns. For its part, the Catholic hierarchy published a pastoral letter repudiating the law and threatening its proponents with excommunication, although it stopped short of endorsing the Liga-led rebellion. It also ordered that, after July 31, all religious services in Mexico would be suspended. Despite all of these protests, the Calles Law nevertheless went into effect on August 1, 1926.

The Cristero War, 1926–1929

In the late summer and fall of 1926, Catholics across Mexico began to militarize. At first, there was no single military leader. Rather, small bands of rebels, acting without collaboration or coordination, launched numerous spontaneous revolts, riots, and uprisings, many of which were directed at federal troops. They also launched guerrilla raids on villages or army depots, for the insurgents were in chronically short supply of arms, ammunition, food, and other necessities. Their enemies would dub the religious militants "Cristeros" for their battle cry of *Viva Cristo Rey!*; soon, they themselves adopted the term.

The disorganized fighting of the initial period (the summer and fall of 1926) meant that the Cristeros could not seize significant territory; rather, they launched their attacks and then fled back to mountain hideouts.

During this period—and indeed, throughout the war years—the movement was particularly concentrated in the west-central heartland, including numerous areas within Jalisco, Guanajuato, and Michoacán (especially the highland regions of Los Altos de Jalisco and the Bajío). Here, the Church had, historically, the highest number of priests and the highest rates of sacramental participation. In addition, these areas had the highest concentration of local and regional Liga chapters.[33] The states of Aguascalientes, Zacatecas, Colima, and Querétaro also saw sustained fighting, while periodic uprisings would erupt throughout much of the rest of the country, from the northern border to the southern states of Tabasco and Chiapas.

By the fall of 1926, the Liga had begun making serious efforts to direct the armed response, creating a War Committee, appointing its military leaders, and consulting with them about tactical decisions. The head of the Liga's military wing, René Capistrán Garza, announced that a general uprising would take place in January 1927.[34] As a result of Capistrán Garza's call to arms, according to Alicia Olivera Sedano, there were sixty-seven different uprisings across Mexico; regional Liga chiefs led many of these.[35] Throughout early 1927, localized revolts erupted all over west-central Mexico, as well as in peripheral states like San Luis Potosi, Coahuila, and Tamaulipas. From June 1927 onward, there would be continuous and widespread fighting between Cristeros and federal troops and their paramilitary forces, known as *agraristas* because of their support for the redistributive agrarian policies of the federal government.

While religion may not have been the only reason people chose to join the Cristero army (after all, the war attracted its share of bandits and adventurers), it is certainly true that Cristero troops and their supporters articulated vivid expressions of religiosity. Cristero soldiers were known for wearing crosses, medallions, and scapulars and carrying the banners of Christ the King and the Virgin of Guadalupe, and it was common for priests to bless the armed bands and provide them with the Holy Eucharist before they headed into battle, as shown in Figure 1.1.[36] Additionally, Cristero hymns, *corridos* (popular narrative ballads), prayers, and poems framed the conflict in explicitly religious terms, lamenting Christ's "absence" from Mexico, equating Calles and the anticlerical government to Satan, and promising to sacrifice themselves, as Christ did, for God. A particularly vivid hymn, entitled "Death to Calles!!! Death!!!"

FIGURE 1.1 Cristero troops presenting arms at Mass
Source: UNAM-MPV, Sección Gráfica, Serie IV, Expediente 20, Document 268.

and mirroring the tune and lyrics of Mexico's national anthem, incorporated themes of martyrdom, religion, and nationalism in its lyrics:

> *Oh Fatherland! How beautiful to die*
> *To save your flag and your faith*
> . . .
> *May the Cross be embraced by your flag.*[37]

This vision of sacrifice and victimhood at the hands of the government could sometimes mask the Cristeros' own role as aggressors in the conflict. As Fernando M. González points out, many Cristeros and their supporters had a particularly passive vision of themselves as a persecuted people who were simply defenders of their faith, and ultimately—if they died in battle—martyrs.[38] Despite this self-conception, however, there is plenty of evidence that Cristero troops could be as ruthless in the field as their enemies. Cristero troops were known to take hostages, raid and loot villages, and participate in torture. Most notoriously a group of Cristeros attacked a Mexico City—Guadalajara, passenger train in April 1927. After wounding and killing many passengers, they then stole cash and jewelry from its surviving occupants, collecting more than $200,000 and setting the train on fire.[39] Additional instances of similar banditry and violence against civilians were numerous. These episodes sometimes had the effect of driving people to join the agraristas or the federal forces.[40]

Thus, by the summer of 1927 and throughout 1928, Cristeros, agraristas, and federal forces were heavily engaged in violent battles across much of west-central Mexico, resulting in ever-increasing civilian and militant fatalities.[41] In July of that year, the Liga made further efforts to consolidate the varied military uprisings into one coordinated campaign, naming Enrique Gorostieta y Velarde as chief of the Cristero forces in Jalisco. A seasoned militant who had fought in the Revolution under Victoriano Huerta, Gorostieta would help the Cristeros capture large parts of Jalisco. In October 1928 the Liga officially appointed Gorostieta as the supreme leader of the Cristero army. Shortly thereafter, he published a manifesto in which he proposed the reestablishment of the Constitution of 1857 (exclusive of Juárez's Reform Laws); suggested a constitutional reform by national plebiscite and referendum; and stated that women would have the right to vote. He also recognized the rights of workers to unionize.[42]

Despite the Liga's effort to develop a Cristero political platform and ensure a wholesale military victory, the Cristero forces were never able to conclusively defeat their opponents in the field. As the war proceeded into 1928 and early 1929, the Cristeros and the federal army battled on, eventually reaching a kind of bloody equilibrium. "It had become clear that the rebellion could no longer be crushed," surmised Jean Meyer. "Likewise, the government could last indefinitely; therefore, the war would drag on forever." The Cristeros had gained control of a large region that included Los Altos and western Guanajuato, and had even installed a Cristero civil government. Cristeros continued to battle *federales* and agraristas across Michoacán, Jalisco, Guanajuato, and the south of Zacatecas. In April 1929, Meyer continued, there were "25,000 men [in the west-central region] armed and organized in regiments, usually operating as guerrillas for lack of ammunition." In the rest of the country, according to Meyer, there were another twenty-five thousand Cristero fighters.[43]

Although the Cristero troops were primed to fight until either they or the government was defeated, the war ended formally on June 21, 1929, when Mexico's apostolic delegate, Leopoldo Ruíz y Flores, reached a settlement with the Mexican government. The agreement, also known as the arreglos, was also brokered by US Ambassador Dwight Morrow, as well as prominent American Catholics such as Father John Joseph Burke, director of the National Catholic Welfare Conference, and Father Edmund Walsh, the vice president of Georgetown University.[44] After the arreglos, the Mexican Catholic clergy resumed religious services, and the Cristero army laid down its arms, at least temporarily. Yet many Mexican Catholics, including some of the clergy and the hierarchy, felt that the agreements did not do enough to protect Cristeros and Catholic clergy from religious repression. They would continue to launch sporadic rebellions until the late 1930s, although these were much less coordinated than those of the 1926–29 war. These uprisings, known as *La Segunda Cristiada*, will be discussed further in Chapter 5.[45]

Mexican Migration during the 1920s

As we have seen, Mexico's west-central region—Jalisco, Michoacán, Guanajuato, and the surrounding states—was a place where popular religion and religious conflict had deep historical roots. It was for this reason that the Cristero War of 1926–29 was fought most intensely there. And it was this area that, by the early 1920s, had also become the primary producer of emigrants to the United States.

The reasons for this out-migration were complex, and predated the Cristero conflict. The west-central region had long been the most densely populated part of Mexico. With a topography ranging from fertile plateaus dotted with lakes to arid, rugged mountain ranges, the area was filled with rural hamlets, small *pueblos*, and several cities, the most prominent of which was Guadalajara, Mexico's second-largest urban center. Three overlapping areas within these states were particularly heavily populated and economically productive: the highlands of Jalisco (known as Los Altos), the Lerma River Basin in Michoacán and Jalisco, and the Bajío, which spans Michoacán, Querétaro, and Guanajuato. Yet the population of the region was also vulnerable to disruptions in the agricultural cycle, to the effects of successive agrarian reforms that had pushed workers from the land, and to the violence of the Revolution and the Cristero War.

Migration from Mexico to the United States had, of course, begun much earlier than the 1920s. In the period between 1850 and 1910, most Mexican emigrants had come from northern border states such as Sonora, Coahuila, Chihuahua, and Tamaulipas, and most of them went to destinations in the US Southwest—areas that had been part of Mexican territory before the Mexican American War (1846–48).[46] By 1920, however, several developments had permanently changed these earlier patterns of migration, resulting in an unprecedented "Great Migration" of Mexicans from west-central Mexico to a variety of new destinations in the United States.

The first of these developments was population pressure. Thanks in part to economic gains and relative political stability of the Porfiriato, the Mexican population had doubled in the years between 1875 and 1910. This created food shortages and increased competition for jobs, which in turn led to higher food prices and lower wages. These problems were particularly intense in the populous west-central region, helping to prompt the first waves of emigration from that area.[47] At the same time, new land laws and colonization schemes between 1883 and 1910 privatized communally held lands, dispossessing millions of agricultural workers.[48] By 1911, according to Paul Friedrich, close to 97 percent of all rural families were landless and "trapped in a system of hired labor" from which they were only too happy to escape by emigrating to the United States.[49]

Because of changes in Mexico's transportation networks, they could now do so more quickly and cheaply than ever before. Under Porfirio Díaz—and with the help of significant foreign investment—Mexico had constructed its national railway system. By the end of the nineteenth century, the railroads had begun to penetrate the previously isolated west-central region, linking the people in the west-central region to larger towns and cities in Mexico, as well as to the United States. By 1888, two trunk lines—the Ferrocarril Central Mexicano and the Ferrocarril Nacional Mexicano—connected the Mexican heartland to El Paso and Laredo, Texas, providing a faster and cheaper way north for potential emigrants from the area.[50]

Wars have always created waves of refugees and emigrants, and the Mexican Revolution was no different. For almost a decade between 1910 and 1920, violence plagued the countryside, agricultural production deteriorated, prices rose while wages remained low, and people began to starve.[51] Early in the decade, migratory flows were mostly comprised of refugees from the northern states, who made the comparatively short journey across the border and often returned to their villages as soon as active fighting had ceased. However, as the battles moved from the country's periphery and engulfed the populous west-central states, emigration from that area continued to increase steadily throughout the 1910s.[52]

By 1920, despite the end of the active phase of the Revolution, emigrants had begun leaving the west-central region in even greater numbers.[53] Thanks to continued population pressure, the new transportation networks, and the legacy of the Revolution, the Mexican peasants of the west-central region had been transformed into a mobile workforce, and slight improvements in Mexico's economic and political situation after the Revolution were not enough to alter these labor patterns. In addition, wages in Mexico remained markedly lower than those in the United States—a long day of hard labor in rural Mexico would bring in only half of what could be earned in ten hours of comparatively less taxing work north of the border.[54]

Between 1880 and 1920, parallel developments in the United States acted to attract increasing numbers of Mexican emigrants. In the United States, just as in Mexico, the expanding railroad system created new demands for labor while simultaneously drawing workers further into the country. The development of irrigation, in tandem with the increased capacity to transport agricultural goods, helped labor-intensive agricultural products such as sugar beets, lettuce, citrus, and cotton to be cultivated on a much larger scale in the American Southwest. Likewise, older industries such as copper and coal mining expanded and created new employment opportunities for Mexican emigrants. During this period, an extensive system of labor recruitment developed, whereby contractors or *enganchadores* traveled into Mexico to find and hire Mexican workers.[55] American companies also solicited Mexican labor via newspaper announcements and word of mouth.[56]

After 1914, the demand in the United States for Mexican labor increased yet again. With the start of the First World War, native-born workers were conscripted into the armed forces, and created a labor demand that Mexicans were able to fill. Although cyclical economic downturns after the war led to the loss of employment and repatriation of thousands of Mexicans, by 1923 the recession had passed. From then until 1928, the United States entered the period of unprecedented prosperity and expansion known popularly as the Roaring Twenties. This economic growth coincided with new laws that made possible increased levels of Mexican migration: the Immigration Acts of 1921 and 1924 established restrictions on the number of migrants from Europe and Asia, but did not apply them to those from the Western hemisphere. Additionally, by the early 1920s some Mexican emigrants had begun looking beyond California, Texas, and the Southwest for jobs. While the majority still went to these states, competition from the continuous influx of Mexican emigrants had lowered wages in the Southwest, providing increasing incentives to travel further north in search of work.[57] Thus, the early 1920s saw the growth of Mexican communities in Chicago, Detroit, Milwaukee, and other Midwestern cities.

By the early 1920s, Mexican migration had been transformed on both sides of the border. In the United States, it had become more urban and industrial, and had expanded beyond the historical Southwest region. And in Mexico, it had become a solidly west-central phenomenon: by 1923 close to 60 percent of emigrants passing through the border town of Laredo claimed origins in Michoacán, Guanajuato, and Jalisco, with the remaining 40 percent coming from the northern region.[58] This migration drew from a wide swath of social groups that included rural and urban emigrants, and from all sectors but the very rich and the very poor. In one municipality in Jalisco, the sociologist Paul Taylor noted that

> almost all occupations and classes in the community have been represented among those who have gone ... Small street vendors, small rancheros, both proprietors and metayers, day laborers with or without property, handicraftsmen such as shoemakers, carpenters, stone masons, *sombrereros*, and many young sons of persons of practically all classes, have been among those to go.[59]

Over the course of the 1920s, new political disruptions would continue to affect many emigrant-sending areas, particularly the west-central states.[60] In late 1923 the de la Huerta rebellion caused new violence in central and southern Mexico and led to further decreases in agricultural production.[61] When the Cristero War broke out in 1926, it produced new waves of emigrants, exiles, and refugees who were forced to flee the countryside to escape the constant clashes between federal and Cristero troops. Adding to this violence, the army launched reconcentration campaigns across the west-central region, in which townspeople were forced to evacuate their villages. Soldiers would then destroy their houses and possessions, and would sometimes use fighter planes to bombard the evacuated area. Anyone who refused to leave was killed.[62] Luis González y González describes the town of San José de Gracia, Michoacán, after one such campaign as "a place of roofless walls and rubble, ashes, and charcoal, with green grass sprouting in the street and on garden walls, and soot everywhere. The only sound was the howling of starving cats."[63] Although some villages recovered their populations after the campaigns, others were "simply wiped off the map" as exiles fled to towns or urban areas, or across the border.[64] For their part, Cristero troops provoked similar waves of migration. Heliodoro Barragan, a farmer from Jalisco who migrated to the United States, recalled that Cristeros

> were chasing me. They wanted money; it was very dangerous. They had already killed José Luis Chávez and raped two young women down by the bridge. When I heard they were looking for me I went into hiding . . . I left with five hundred pesos in gold. It was Easter Monday, April 11, 1927.[65]

The tumultuous conditions throughout the region continuously generated new waves of emigration, compounding the trends established earlier in the decade. Villagers and city residents were well aware that masses of people were leaving during the Cristero War period. One woman reported that "everyone who can is preparing to leave for the United States" since "there are families who do not have the necessities of life and who pass entire days without eating."[66] Newspaper and consular reports also described the widespread misery caused by hunger, disease, and overcrowding in the west-central area, particularly in Los Altos de Jalisco and Guadalajara.[67] "The people have been streaming out of this district," lamented one Guadalajara-based US consular official in May of 1927, "and their plight is said to be most pitiful."[68]

During 1927 and 1928, US consular agents in charge of issuing visas to would-be emigrants noted that emigration to the United States was "heavier than usual," and linked this increase to the political and economic unrest of the war.[69] One prognosticated that "it is probable that heavy immigration to the United States will continue if business conditions remain as bad as they are and the political situation does not improve."[70] Consular officials were not the only ones to note the link between growing emigration and the west-central region: even the national newspaper *El Universal* lamented that

> each day the number of Mexican emigrants [*braceros*] that cross the border and head to the United States in search of work is greater. Every day a huge quantity of people arrive in Ciudad Juárez from the Bajío, Michoacán, Jalisco, Zacatecas, and other regions of the Republic, in order to find employment in California and Texas.[71]

These Cristero-era emigrants followed the northward paths established over the past several decades by earlier Mexican emigrants from the north and west-central regions. Many simply joined relatives or fellow townspeople who had emigrated prior to the war. As numerous scholars have noted, emigrants from Los Altos de Jalisco, Michoacán, and Guanajuato went to US destinations where other *alteños, michoacanos,* or *guanajuatenses* had settled. According to José Orozco, by the early 1920s emigrants from Los Altos de Jalisco were already "an established presence in Mexican immigrant communities in the United States' industrial and agricultural centers . . . and it is to these areas that many Alteños fled during the Cristiada."[72] Francisco Rosales wrote that in March 1927, many of those refugees arrived in Chicago "from such towns as Chavinda, Michoacán, or San Francisco del Rincón, Guanajuato, where Cristero activity was prominent, and joined relatives already there."[73] Zaragosa Vargas, too, noted that hundreds of new emigrants from the west-central region arrived in Detroit in 1926 as a direct result of the war, increasing the size of the city's nascent Mexican community.[74] Dolan and Hinojosa conclude that new communities of refugees, particularly from Jalisco, also formed in within Los Angeles, San Antonio, and other Southwestern cities where the Mexican population had roots going back to the sixteenth century.[75] Finally, in his study of the Cristero War, Jean Meyer asserted that emigration during this period "established on a definitive basis the big Mexican colonies in Detroit, Chicago, and Los Angeles."[76]

By the end of the 1920s, emigrants from the west-central region were becoming an increasingly large presence in communities of Mexicans all over the United States. In Texas, with its long history of emigration and settlement by northern Mexicans, west-central Mexican populations were a growing minority. In Corpus Christi in 1929, for example, close to 20 percent of the Mexicans registering at the consulate were from Guanajuato, Jalisco, Michoacán, and Zacatecas.[77] The available data from California also lends a sense of this population shift. In his study of Mexican communities in the Imperial Valley, sociologist Paul Taylor found that Guanajuato and Jalisco were among the top five states of origin among Mexicans.[78] Camille Guerin-Gonzáles determined that Mexicans from Guanajuato, Michoacán, and Jalisco made up the largest group of emigrants in California's San Bernardino and Riverside counties, comprising close to 50 percent of the 3,038 repatriates who left the region in 1930 and 1931.[79] And Sánchez's study of Mexican immigrants in Los Angeles during the 1920s demonstrated that almost 37 percent of adult male Mexican emigrants recorded in the US Naturalization Service records came from the west-central states, with 21 percent from Jalisco,

Michoacán, or Guanajuato. Manuel Gamio's tally of money orders from the same area found that about 30 percent came from these three states, with the majority arriving from Jalisco.[80]

Mexican emigrants from the west-central region were even more predominant in the Midwest and Great Lakes regions. Taylor's survey of 3,132 Mexicans in the Chicago and Calumet region showed that about 74 percent came from the west-central region.[81] In Detroit, too, the majority of Mexican emigrants came from Jalisco, Michoacán, and Guanajuato.[82]

These precise intersections between the demographics of migration and the geography of the Cristero War happened just as Mexican settlement patterns across the United States grew more permanent. Prior to the 1920s, Mexicans had worked primarily as agricultural laborers, and their migration patterns were therefore seasonal and circular: workers went from the farms of Texas in winter, to the sugar beet fields of Illinois and Michigan in the spring, to the southern cotton fields during the high summer, and home to Mexico in the off-seasons.[83] During World War I, however, the US economy became increasingly industrialized as a result of emerging technologies and increased demands for factory-produced goods. As a result, Mexican laborers could now find comparatively stable jobs with railway companies, canneries, automobile factories, meatpacking plants, steel mills, and other urban industries. These jobs offered year-round employment, and allowed workers to stay in one place.[84] More Mexican men began to bring their wives and children with them, and some women migrated alone, as well. By 1926, according to one source, the Mexican-born population in the United States was composed of about two-thirds as many women as men.[85]

The increased emigration of women and families meant that Mexican emigrants in the United States during the 1920s could begin to build more permanent, established, and socially complex communities. Life in urban centers, in particular, allowed Mexican emigrants to form clubs and associations, publish newspapers, and establish markets, restaurants, social halls, and other commercial and social gathering places. These types of spaces would prove crucial to community formation—that process of creating communal connections and a shared sense of Mexican American ethnic identity—in Chicago, Detroit, El Paso, Los Angeles, and any number of other towns and cities where Mexicans settled. As Douglas Monroy put it, this process of "creating a rich institutional life, the patriotic societies and mutualistas—the structural underpinnings of this immigrant culture—encouraged [people] to continue as Mexicans at the same time that it rooted them in el norte."[86]

Community Formation in the Context of Religious Conflict

Mexico's Great Migration of the 1920s, then, had brought unprecedented numbers of emigrants to the United States. A large proportion of these had geographic ties to the deeply religious Cristero heartland, which meant that their lives, or those of their friends or relatives, had been impacted in some way by the religious conflict. (Furthermore, as the subsequent chapters will demonstrate, numerous emigrants from Mexican states outside of the west-central region, such as Sonora and Chihuahua, would support the Cristero cause as well.) Finally, many of these Cristero-era emigrants were settling in urban areas, and joining more stable communities with complex social networks and access to Mexican print media. All of these factors would contribute to a sharp rise in activism by Cristero supporters in the United States during the war years.

Yet the formation of the Cristero diaspora was certainly not inevitable. Even the most ardently Catholic Mexican emigrants would find that migration to the United States offered not only new economic opportunities, but new social, political, and religious options as well. Within many communities, competing social organizations such as mutual benefit associations (*mutualistas*) offered social connections without a religious affiliation. And patriotic clubs (*comisiones honoríficas*), often sponsored by the Mexican consulates, presented a way for emigrants loyal to the revolutionary state to express their allegiance. In addition, the growing labor movement in cities and rural areas across the United States attracted the participation of both agricultural and industrial Mexican workers.[87] Finally, a small but increasing number of Mexican emigrants were responded to Protestant ministry within Mexican communities by joining other faiths. In some ways, it is easy to see why Manuel Gamio, the Mexican anthropologist who conducted interviews with emigrants during the late 1920s, concluded that Mexican emigrants underwent a "change in religion" after they left their homeland. With enough time in the United States, he asserted, "the burden of fanaticism which the immigrant carries with him . . . little by little slips away."[88]

Gamio was not the only scholar of Mexican emigration who believed that emigration to the United States would inevitably lead to secularization and modernization among emigrants. Other contemporary observers during the 1920s, as well as some scholars writing even more recently, have attributed this supposed secularization to a variety of causes, including more rigorous work schedules, Protestant evangelization, exposure to liberal and secular philosophies, and prolonged separation from parish priests.[89] Yet, as the story of the Cristero diaspora shows, these factors certainly did not cause all Mexican emigrants to leave religion—and religious politics—behind them in Mexico. Instead, thousands of them would organize in support of the Cristero War from the United States. Integral to this movement, however, were two smaller, but equally significant, groups of Mexicans who arrived in the United States during the Cristero War years. The first of these was comprised of the religious refugees who began arriving in the United States after 1926, thanks in large part to logistical and financial assistance by members of the US Catholic Church. The second was a much smaller (but highly vocal) group of Mexican political exiles. Together, these religious refugees and political exiles would play a crucial role in rallying their emigrant compatriots around the Cristero cause. In doing so, they would help establish Mexican Catholic practices and politics within growing Mexican emigrant communities in the United States.

2

Religious Refugees, Political Exiles, and the US Catholic Church

IN THE LATE summer of 1926, the Mexican consulate in San Antonio was making arrangements for the community's annual patriotic festival.[1] The event, which would take place on September 16—Mexico's Independence Day—would, like all such celebrations in Mexican communities around the United States, feature dancing, a parade, music, flags, speeches, and various other colorful displays of symbolic nationalism. In general, it was a tremendously popular event. But there was a problem: many of the city's Catholics, including some within the Mexican emigrant community, were very publically refusing to take part. On July 30 the Catholic archbishop of San Antonio, Arthur Drossaerts, had asked all Mexican Catholics in San Antonio to abstain from participating in the festival. On the following day, Aurelia Avila, the president of San Antonio's "Young Catholics Club of San Fernando," withdrew her candidacy for queen of the festival. Even the city's mayor, John Wallace Tobin, announced that he would not attend the event.[2] Over the next several years, such organized public dissent would continue. On the morning of December 4, 1927, some five hundred members of San Antonio's Mexican community assembled downtown in the square facing the Mexican consulate. There, they presented a signed petition blaming the Calles government for provoking the Cristero rebellion, protesting the violence and brutality of government forces, and requesting that Calles "re-establish law and order and [reform] the Constitution and the legal codes to meet the wishes of the people."[3]

Six months later, there was an even larger gathering in the city of El Paso. On the evening of June 18, 1927, about five thousand Catholics attended a public reception honoring several bishops from Mexico in exile in the United States. After speeches by the Mexican bishops and El Paso's bishop, Anthony J. Schuler, the audience responded fervently. As one historian recounts, "What was now the familiar Mexican Catholic cry of fidelity, 'Viva Cristo Rey!' ... was frequently heard during the reception and was shouted periodically by the great throng." The next morning, which was the Sunday after the feast of Corpus Christi, some thirty-five thousand people, "many of them [Mexican] refugees," marched through the city's streets in a massive religious demonstration.[4]

A year later, in June 1928, Mexicans in Los Angeles celebrated the feast of Corpus Christi in the same way—with a march. Organized by exiled bishop José de Jesús Manríquez y Zárate, the procession began at Nuestra Señora de Guadalupe Church in Belvedere and attracted more than ten thousand people, most of them Mexicans. According to newspaper reports about the march,

> Almost all of the streets where the procession passed were adorned with flowers intertwined on Mexican and North American pavilions; and placards reading *"Viva México"*, *"Viva Cristo Rey"*, were placed in large lettering across the same avenues and in great number.[5]

Meanwhile, in the Chicago, Mexicans also came out in large numbers for a religious event. The occasion, depicted in Figure 2.1, was a cornerstone-laying ceremony in the spring of 1928 for the newly constructed Church of Our Lady of Guadalupe in South Chicago. The powerful Mexican bishop Pascual Díaz attended the event, riding in an open car that headed a procession of the city's numerous Catholic societies—including some 500 Mexicans.[6] During the ceremony, Our Lady of Guadalupe's canon priest, a Claretian named Father James Tort, discussed "the terrible conditions in which can be found thousands of Mexican Catholics who are denied in their own fatherland the right to worship God." Later, Bishop Díaz "protested against [these] calumnies, and exhorted the Mexican colony to be always grateful for the religious liberty of this Nation the United States and to always preserve their faith and their religion."[7]

Throughout the Mexican diaspora during the late 1920s, thousands of people participated in public events in which Mexican emigrants and Catholic clergy—both Mexican- and US-born—strongly critiqued the anticlerical policies of the Mexican government. While Mexican emigrants

FIGURE 2.1 Inaugural procession to Chicago's Our Lady of Guadalupe parish, September 30, 1928

Source: Archivo Histórico del Arzobispado de México, Fondo Pascual Díaz y Barreto, Caja 7.

had openly expressed their faith at religious processions and public ceremonies in the decades before the 1920s, these Cristero War-era events were tangibly different. Indeed, by the mid-1920s, Mexican Catholic religious devotion would incorporate a markedly political agenda: resistance to the anticlerical government of Mexico, and support for the Cristero cause at home.

To understand how Mexican emigrant Catholicism became so politicized—and so oriented around the Cristero War—we must examine the role of a core group of advocates, organizers, and leaders who came to form a vocal minority within the Cristero diaspora. This core group would materialize when the Catholic clergy, members of the Mexican Catholic hierarchy, and lay Catholic political activists began fleeing Mexico. A few of them came during the early 1920s, as regional and state leaders began enforcing anticlerical laws. The majority, however, came after 1926, when the Ley Calles went into effect. While some would leave the country on their own after determining that their lives were in danger, the Mexican government deported many others. Once in the United States, the religious refugees received significant help and support from the US Catholic Church, and many were resettled within Mexican Catholic parishes. Lay political exiles, too, chose to reestablish themselves within Mexican

communities in various cities. Together, many of these religious refugees and political exiles would persistently rally the Mexican community
around the Cristero cause.

Religious Refugees

Between 1926 and 1929, some 2,500 Mexican religious refugees—priests,
nuns, monks, seminarians, bishops, and archbishops—either fled or were
deported to the United States, as the Mexican government enforced the
anticlerical laws that limited the allowed numbers of priests and dissolved
religious orders, and subjected the clergy to direct persecution. A smaller
number of religious refugees fled to other nations, including Guatemala,
Cuba, and several different European countries, including Italy.[8]

This period of exile shared some of the characteristics of the
Revolutionary expulsion of approximately five hundred bishops, priests,
seminarians, and nuns that had begun in 1914 and continued through
the presidency of Venustiano Carranza (1917–1920).[9] Yet there were also
key differences. This new wave of religious exiles was at least five times
as large, which meant that the US Catholic Church had to orchestrate a
much more comprehensive response. For the most part, the US Church
placed the Mexican religious refugees within dozens of Mexican Catholic
parishes that were themselves growing in number and population across
the United States. As a result, this wave of refugees would have a lasting
impact on emigrant community formation during the 1920s.

The refugees had begun crossing the border even before the outbreak
of the war, as it became increasingly clear that the Ley Calles would be
enforced. The new law only explicitly required foreign-born nuns and
clergy to leave Mexico. (This was nevertheless a substantial number: as
early as July 1926, the American consulate at San Luis Potosí reported
that it had received 360 visa requests from "alien priests and nuns," most
of whom were in imminent danger of arrest and expulsion.[10]) Native-born
Mexican clergy, by contrast, were initially allowed to stay in the country,
as long as they registered with the Mexican government and complied
with the new laws. Nevertheless, many chose to leave, since it was essentially impossible for them to continue living in religious communities.
As one group of priests stated to Archbishop Drossaerts, "we could not
do anything. We could not say Mass, we could not perform marriages, we
could not christen the children."[11] By the fall of 1926, growing numbers

of seminarians, nuns, and monks had their convents confiscated, and prohibitions were levied against communal living or wearing of religious habits.[12]

By early 1927, however, exile was no longer a matter of personal choice. Priests, the high clergy, and members of religious orders were increasingly arrested and forcibly deported by the Mexican government, which had issued a decree in January of that year stating that any priests who were apprehended "with arms in hand, or who ostensibly dedicate themselves to conspire against the government," would be immediately expelled from the country.[13] Since Catholic priests often were accused of sedition regardless of their actual activities, and since even those who went into hiding often were found and arrested, leaving the country was their only sure way of avoiding imprisonment or death.[14] In many cases, when they did not leave on their own, the federal government's Confidential Department assigned secret agents to track down these priests and deport them. One such priest was Moisés Quintanar, who was captured by secret agents and sent to the Mexican Army's garrison chief in Piedras Negras, Coahuila, "so that he can be deported according to the orders of the Superior Office."[15]

Thus, the outbreak of the Cristero War sent a stream of religious refugees to the United States. Often they arrived precipitously and under dramatic circumstances. For example, several orders of nuns were reportedly escorted across the desert by the famous Father Miguel Pro, a Jesuit priest who was eventually executed by the Mexican government, and was beatified in 1988.[16] In another instance, a Father Navarro, whose first name was not recorded, arrived in El Paso after being "bound and loaded in a baggage car in the interior of Mexico. In Juarez, he was put in a taxi and released at the International Bridge." A companion of Navarro's, possibly another priest, "was blindfolded [and] released at Wyoming and Oregon Streets [in El Paso] where he was discovered by sympathetic Catholics the next morning.[17] According to various newspaper and archival sources, by 1928 increasing numbers of individual priests were being arrested, conducted to the border, and expelled from the country.[18] Some, such as the nuns and priests depicted in Figure 2.2, arrived by ship in port cities such as New York. The majority, however, crossed into the United States from border cities. These often came in large numbers: at one point, a group of eighty-seven Mexican nuns arrived in El Paso, nearly overwhelming the ability of the diocese to feed and house them.[19]

El padre Antonio Santandreu, que durante cuarenta años ha regido la iglesia de Nuestra Señora de Guadalupe, y ha sido expulsado de Méjico

Tres hermanas de una comunidad católica de Méjico, expulsadas del territorio, al llegar a Nueva York a bordo del "Reina María Cristina"

Los PP. Fabián, Florencio y Benedicto, recientemente expulsados de un convento católico de Méjico, a su llegada a Nueva York

FIGURE 2.2 Mexican religious exiles arriving in the United States

Source: UNAM-MPV, Sección Gráfica, Serie IV, Expediente 11, Document 160.

The arrival of numerous members of the Mexican Catholic hierarchy in the United States was particularly dramatic. On April 20, 1927, following a midnight robbery on the Guadalajara-Mexico City express train, Mexican government officials claimed that the crime had been authorized and instigated by the Catholic hierarchy.[20] On April 21 some of the bishops were summoned to a meeting with Interior Secretary Adalberto Tejeda. After a terse discussion about the train incident, Secretary Tejeda told the bishops that President Calles had ordered them to leave Mexico that night. At nine o'clock, they were escorted under armed guard to a night train to Laredo, Texas. Among the group of refugee prelates were several archbishops, including the elderly and infirm José Mora y del Río of Mexico City, the conciliatory Leopoldo Ruiz y Flores of Michoacán, and Pedro Vera y Zuria of Puebla, who would write an autobiographical account of his time in exile. The group also included bishops Ignacio Valdespino y Díaz of Aguascalientes, Francisco Uranga y Sáenz of Cuernavaca, and the fiercely militant José de Jesús Manríquez y Zárate of Huejutla, Hidalgo. Two other members of the hierarchy had preceded them to the United States. Juan Navarrete y Guerrero, the bishop of Sonora, had been exiled in 1926 and was living in Nogales, Texas (he would also spend time in Tucson, Arizona).[21] Finally, the powerful Pascual Díaz y Barreto, bishop of Tabasco and secretary of the Mexican Episcopal Committee, had actually arrived earlier—in February of 1927—after initially staying in Guatemala.[22]

After their arrival in Texas, most of the bishops, as well as Archbishop Mora y del Río, settled at the College of the Incarnate Word in San Antonio, where the Mexican Episcopal Committee would formally convene through the duration of the armed conflict. Several, however, would live more itinerant lives in the United States: Pascual Díaz would travel frequently to New York and Rome; Manríquez y Zarate would leave Texas for Los Angeles, where he would stay until at least 1929; and Navarrete always stayed close to the border, where he remained in communication with his diocese in Sonora. As we shall see in the next two chapters, during their exile many of the refugee bishops would frequently engage with the wider community of Mexican emigrants, as well as with members of the US Catholic hierarchy and other powerful American Catholics.[23] They also corresponded with their contacts at home in Mexico, receiving the latest news of the war and sharing it with their Mexican and American contacts in the United States.[24]

By the end of the decade, the refugee religious in the United States were so numerous and so dispersed that nearly every community of Mexican emigrants in California, Texas, and the Midwest hosted exiled Mexican priests, nuns, or bishops. In Texas, refugee priests and nuns went to cities including El Paso, Laredo, Brownsville, Houston, Slaton, Galveston, San Diego, Hebbronville, Woodsboro, Kingsmith, Laredo, Castroville, San Antonio, and Toluca.[25] California was also a key destination: more than a hundred Mexican priests, dozens of exiled bishops, and an archbishop sought refuge in Los Angeles alone.[26] The Midwest, too, saw the arrival of priests and nuns from Mexico after 1926: the Archdiocese of Chicago was particularly assiduous in facilitating the arrival and resettlement of the religious refugees.[27] Other, more far-flung cities included Mobile, Alabama; Kansas City, Missouri; New York City; and Philadelphia.[28]

Coinciding as it did with the remarkable growth in Mexican emigrant population of the United States during the 1920s, the arrival of the religious refugees would have a profound impact on many burgeoning Mexican emigrant communities. By mid-1927, it was a rare Mexican emigrant community that did not host at least a few religious exiles. Within these populations, these priests, nuns, and other religious would found schools, parishes, or small businesses, thus becoming part of the fabric of Mexican emigrant community life. As a result, they would serve as visible and public reminders of the Church-state conflict that was raging in the homeland.

They could not have reestablished themselves so quickly, however, without the logistical and financial support of the US Catholic Church, particularly the National Catholic Welfare Conference (NCWC), the NCWC's Immigration Bureau, and several key American bishops and archbishops. Indeed, these US Catholic organizations and individuals extended crucial assistance to these refugees, whether through management of the logistics of border crossing and legal status in the United States, financial assistance that allowed their resettlement within existing Mexican communities and establishment of new Mexican parishes, or by publicizing the Cristero cause to American audiences.

The Role of the US Catholic Church

The arrival of the religious refugees from Mexico in the 1920s represented both a new challenge and an opportunity for the US Catholic Church, whose leadership had long struggled to respond to the spiritual and material needs of Mexicans in the United States. Since the mid-nineteenth century, when the US Church assumed ecclesiastical jurisdiction over the territories formerly belonging to Mexico, American Catholic leaders—almost exclusively men of European origin—had often misunderstood and dismissed the devotional folk traditions of the Mexican communities in Texas, California, and the borderlands. Additionally, the Church had responded inadequately to the relative poverty of Mexicans, often devoting far fewer resources to them than to non-Mexican Catholic communities, and treating them as "second-class status Catholics."[29]

After 1900, when the number of Mexican emigrants began to increase significantly, Catholic leaders began to devote more money, time, and personnel to their communities. Missionary groups, such as the Oblate Fathers, the Missionary Sisters of Our Lady of Victory, and the Claretians were dispatched to Mexican emigrant communities.[30] Charitable groups also directed funds to impoverished Mexicans. The most important of these was the Catholic Extension Society, an organization established in 1905 that raised and distributed money for Catholic parishes in needy areas of the United States. Bishop Francis Clement Kelley, its founder, took a particular interest in Mexican Catholics, and channeled funding to support Catholic missions in their communities.[31]

As the Mexican emigrant population continued to grow, many of the missions in Mexican barrios and *colonias* would eventually become Mexican national parishes. The establishment of these parishes contradicted the prevailing policies of the US Catholic Church at the time, which was promoting "integrated" parishes as part of its policy of Americanization.[32] Yet Mexican national parishes also offered a solution to several challenges. One of these was persistent racial prejudice and discrimination by non-Mexican Catholics, who often tried to prohibit, or at least strongly discourage, Mexicans from joining "their" churches.[33] Perhaps as a result, Mexicans themselves often preferred national churches.[34] In addition, the US Church was increasingly concerned about Protestant evangelizing within Mexican communities; devoting resources to Mexican national parishes was one way to keep Mexicans within the Catholic fold.[35]

During the first two decades of the twentieth century, the growth of Mexican missions and national parishes helped to foster a vibrant Catholic culture within the emigrant community. Certainly, there were plenty of Mexican emigrants who were not religious or did not participate in the sacraments or the life of the parish community. Yet despite the challenges of poverty, racism, and the gaps in institutional support from the US Catholic Church, many Mexican Catholics did manage to contribute money and labor toward Catholic churches and schools; to celebrate important holidays and feast days; and to form numerous lay Catholic devotional societies including Las Hijas de María, the Sociedad Guadalupana, El Sagrado Corazón, La Vela Perpétua, and El Santo Nombre. By the early 1920s, these organizations were common in Mexican communities across the United States. The societies would sponsor religious processions, novenas and other communal prayer events, and social gatherings.[36]

By the mid-1920s, then, the US Catholic Church had greatly increased its presence in the Mexican emigrant community—particularly in urban areas—and Mexican Catholics had established their own social and organizational life. Yet Mexican Catholic parishes in the United States were still lacking clergy who spoke Spanish. It is no surprise, then, that when thousands of refugee religious began to arrive in the United States after 1926, the US Church made every effort to place them within Mexican emigrant parishes.[37]

The Church had, in fact, done this once before. When hundreds of religious refugees fled Mexico during the Mexican Revolution, the Catholic Extension Society had supported them. Soliciting funds from affluent Catholics, Bishop Kelly directed thousands of dollars to Mexican parishes along the border and in the US Southwest, providing the religious refugees with shelter, food, and clothing. He also helped relocate a large group of Mexican seminarians, establishing the St. Philip Neri Seminary in Castroville, Texas, in 1915. There, nearly sixty Mexican priests were ordained, many of whom returned to Mexico after the Revolution. During this period and into the 1930s, Kelly also spoke out against the anticlerical Mexican government. Using the platform of his widely circulated magazine, *Extension*, Kelley also undertook a publicity campaign that portrayed the Mexican government as a "Bolshevik" threat to religious freedom. In the magazine as well as in *The Book of Red and Yellow: Being the Story of Blood and a Yellow Streak* (1915), he publicized the plight of the refugees and deplored the violence directed at them in Mexico.[38]

By the late 1920s, however, the National Catholic Welfare Conference had replaced the Extension Society as the primary organization in charge of relocating the Mexican religious refugees. The NCWC, originally called the National Catholic War Council, was founded by the US Catholic hierarchy in 1917 as a way to coordinate the Catholic response to the First World War. By the mid-1920s, the US hierarchy had become increasingly concerned with the plight of the Catholic Church in Mexico. Its general secretary, Father John Burke, spent the Cristero War years coordinating a campaign to lobby the US government to withdraw its support for the anticlerical Mexican regime, and spoke out in numerous public venues in order to publicize the situation in Mexico. (Burke would also play a key role as an intermediary among the US hierarchy, the Mexican hierarchy, the Vatican, and the Mexican government; during the war years he made trips to Mexico and Havana to meet with President Calles and Dwight Morrow, in an effort to advance the negotiations between Church and state in Mexico.[39])

As religious refugees began to arrive at the border, they appealed to the US Catholic Church for help. The hierarchy did so primarily through the NCWC's Immigration Bureau. Founded in 1920 to assist the growing number of Catholic immigrants to the United States, the mission of the Immigration Bureau was "to be a clearing house for all matters relating to Catholic immigrants of all nationalities." The activities of the organization (which had offices in New York, El Paso, and San Francisco, among other cities) included visiting and offering assistance to detained emigrants; furnishing clothing to those in need; helping them to prepare affidavits or other legal papers; and, most importantly, helping them to navigate US immigration law by filing applications for visas with the US Department of Labor. Recognizing both the significance of migration from Mexico and the need to minister to Mexican Catholics in the borderlands, the NCWC had opened the Immigration Bureau's El Paso office in November 1922. After the onset of the Cristero War, that office became the primary American organization responsible for managing the arrival of Mexico's religious refugees.[40]

From 1926 until 1968, the director of the El Paso office was Cleofás Calleros, a Mexican native whose family had come to El Paso from Chihuahua in 1896. A devout Catholic, Calleros became the primary liaison for many of the religious refugees seeking legal residence in the United States. His office completed visa applications and sent them to the NCWC's Washington representatives, who handled direct contact with the US Department of State. While Mexican religious refugees were generally granted the visas for which they applied, the paperwork was nevertheless daunting, since many of them had initially crossed the border without the proper paperwork. For example, the Sacred Heart Sisters were already in Laredo on visitor's visas when they sought Calleros's help; he managed to secure extensions on their visas and process their applications on time.[41] Thanks to his efforts, most of Mexico's religious refugees entered legally, and Calleros's work was so effective that even US consular officials in Mexico were known to refer priests and nuns who sought refuge in the United States to his office.[42]

Beyond helping the religious refugees to obtain legal residency, the Immigration Bureau—with the collaboration of other Catholic organizations, such as the Extension Society and the Knights of Columbus—worked with members of the US Catholic hierarchy to place the religious refugees within specific communities. Since El Paso was a particularly poor diocese, the task was often undertaken ad hoc. As Calleros recalled years later in an interview, he once had twenty-seven nuns living in his home for two weeks, where they slept on the floor.[43]

Although the Immigration Bureau processed and resettled the religious refugees upon their arrival, it could not provide all of the financial assistance that they would need. Since so many of the refugees arrived in the United States penniless, they (and the Immigration Bureau) would turn to sympathetic US bishops for shelter, clothes, medicine, and transportation.

Several US bishops would play an especially important role in resettling the religious refugees from Mexico. In San Antonio, a city whose Mexican population had grown by twenty-one thousand between 1920 and 1930, Mexican Catholics found significant resources and support. Archbishop Arthur Drossaerts, the prelate who had urged his diocesan faithful to boycott the Mexican Independence Day celebrations in 1926, was an outspoken supporter of the Mexican Catholic cause. During the war years, he made significant resources available to the Mexican religious refugees, including forty-two priests and 195 nuns, as well as the members of Mexico's Catholic hierarchy who made San Antonio their home for the duration of the armed conflict.[44]

On the US-Mexico border, another sympathetic bishop would play a key role in supporting religious refugees. By the late 1920s, El Paso—which had barely been more than a few buildings in the desert at the turn of the century—was now a booming city of a hundred thousand people, more than 60 percent of whom were Mexican.[45] As one of the major crossing points along the border, El Paso would receive a flood of religious refugees during the war years. Over a period of five years, bishop Anthony Schuler would host at least nine religious congregations of nuns, a total of 150 secular priests, hundreds of seminarians, and members of the Mexican hierarchy.[46] In addition, Schuler provided up to $120,000 of diocesan funds for the refugees.[47] By the end of the war, Schuler's advocacy on behalf of Mexico's religious refugees had almost bankrupted his diocese—but it had also helped to create a supportive environment for Catholic refugees in El Paso and the borderlands.

Just as in Texas, the Mexican community in the city of Los Angeles grew rapidly during the 1920s: between 1920 and 1930, the Mexican population tripled from 33,644 to 97,116.[48] During the late 1920s, Bishop John J. Cantwell granted refuge to more than a hundred Mexican priests, several exiled bishops, and an archbishop.[49] In addition to hosting religious refugees, Bishop Cantwell helped to secure financing for new churches for the growing Mexican population, and sought to ensure the religious education of Mexican children through outreach efforts. By 1930, there were at least a dozen new Mexican Catholic churches (many of them named for Our Lady of Guadalupe or for the emblem of the Cristero movement, Christ the King), several new Catholic organizations (including the Holy Name Society and the Hijas de María), and four Catholic community centers in Mexican neighborhoods hosting recreational activities, debating and religious clubs, and catechetical training.[50]

Chicago's Mexican population had experienced a similar rate of growth during that decade: with about 1,200 Mexicans in 1920, it had grown to about 21,000 by 1930.[51] Chicago's community of Mexican Catholics, despite its small size and relative poverty, received the backing of a particularly influential figure in the US Catholic hierarchy: Cardinal George Mundelein, who had stated in 1926 that he was willing to help the Mexican community in the Midwest "with all the power and all my faculties" due to the urgent nature of the Cristero conflict. In fact, the arrival of clerical exiles, the needs of the growing Mexican community, and Mundelein's sympathy for the Cristero cause led him to "[break] with his established policy of discouraging national parishes" and to support the construction of Mexican churches in cities around the Midwest, including Detroit, South Chicago, and Milwaukee.[52] During the war years, he would host the Claretians and the Cordi-Marian sisters, as well as at least two exiled priests from Jalisco. There, they played a key role in founding Chicago's two Mexican parish churches, St. Francis (formerly home to German emigrants) and Our Lady of Guadalupe.

San Antonio, El Paso, Los Angeles, and Chicago were not the only places where religious refugees received assistance. In Corpus Christi, Texas, for example, Bishop Emmanuel Ledvina, who had been general secretary of the Extension Society, housed and placed dozens of exiles within his large border diocese.[53] Nevertheless, it was these four cities that would emerge as the most important centers of Cristero support during the late 1920s and 1930s.

Despite the relative generosity of these US bishops, however, the disproportionate concentration of religious exiles in California and Texas placed serious financial and logistical strains on the dioceses there. Bishop John Cantwell of Los Angeles appealed his situation to the Catholic Extension Society, stating that

> I have a large number of Mexicans here at the present time, so if any Spanish or Mexican Priests ask for advise [sic], please do not send them to California . . . it is a tremendous problem to find the money to sustain them . . .[54]

Although the US bishops struggled to pay for the resettlement of the refugees, there were also a few alternative sources of funding. The Extension Society would provide up to $25,000 for Mexico's refugees, sending the money directly to the bishops who asked for it.[55] Wealthy individuals helped as well: in one instance, a Mrs. Rafael Lozano Saldana of El Paso donated a home to four nuns of the Perpetual Adoration of the Blessed Sacrament, explaining that she "felt that God had honored her by sending her across the path of these exiled religious."[56] Various members of the Terrazas family, famous for their immense landholdings in Chihuahua, donated money to the Immigration Bureau as well.[57] And *El Diario de El Paso*, a Catholic newspaper based out of El Paso, sponsored a fundraising campaign for the refugees.[58]

At the same time, the US Knights of Columbus embarked on a separate campaign that would provide some help to Mexico's religious refugees. At their annual convention in 1926, they established the Million Dollar Fund, which solicited donations from Catholics nationwide as well as from all KOC chapters and from anyone desirous of "furthering any undertaking of the Knights of Columbus in behalf of those who are of the household of faith in Mexico."[59] The Fund was used to publish pamphlets and other literature about the conflict and to disseminate it among the American public, but some $220,000 of it was used to assist in the resettlement of Mexico's religious refugees. Local Councils, as well, came to their aid.[60]

Although Mexico's refugee priests, nuns, and bishops were largely dependent on US Catholic organizations and donors for assistance in resettlement, they also sought ways to earn a living—and in the case of some priests and nuns, to continue to live collectively in their religious orders—once they had settled in US cities and towns. The nuns, in particular, had to be very creative, since they were responsible for their own financial support. As a result, "they were cooks, laundresses, seamstresses, gardeners, nurses, housekeepers, and needle artisans."[61] A more dependable source of income and stability, however, was teaching, and this became the occupation of many of the refugee religious—particularly the nuns—in the United States. The unprecedented growth of Mexican communities in Texas, California, and the Southwest, occurring in conjunction with the closing of Catholic schools in Mexico, had generated a new demand for Catholic schools that could serve the Mexican emigrant community. New schools that opened during the Cristero War years included seminaries and boarding schools that relocated wholesale from Mexico;[62] schools for poor Mexican emigrants in communities such as Los Angeles;[63] and schools along the border, meant for students from Mexican towns who could cross over for the day.[64]

The efforts by religious refugees to build Catholic educational programs within the Mexican emigrant community coincided with the goals of the US Catholic Church in the 1920s, which had become increasingly aware of the spiritual and material needs of Mexicans in the United States. Yet by helping to relocate and resettle the religious refugees, the US Catholic Church was also—and perhaps inadvertently—fostering the formation of the Cristero diaspora in the United States. For education was only one that the refugee religious interacted with the Mexican emigrant community. Refugee priests were dispatched to Mexican parishes all over the country, where they reinforced Catholic identities by preaching sermons, organizing community events, establishing and overseeing Catholic lay associations, and writing a variety of publications. For their part, numerous refugee bishops would work within emigrant communities to rally Mexicans around the Catholic cause at home. As they interacted with the broader emigrant community, significant numbers of priests, nuns, and bishops would play a leading role in the efforts by the Cristero diaspora to contribute financially or strategically to the Cristero War effort. These activities will be discussed in great detail in the next two chapters. First, however, we examine another group of emigrants that arrived after the onset of the war, and would similarly invoke the support of the Mexican emigrant community for the Cristero cause in Mexico: lay Catholic political exiles.

Political Exiles

Beginning in the summer of 1926, increasing numbers of lay Catholic political leaders, including numerous members of the Liga, the ACJM, and the Mexican Knights of Columbus began arriving at the El Paso and Laredo border, where they sought to settle in the United States. The majority of these settled in El Paso, San Antonio, and Los Angeles, where they spent the war years organizing among themselves and within Mexican emigrant communities in order to try to overthrow the Mexican government. In the United States, these Catholic dissidents had plenty of allies, for by the mid-1920s many Mexican emigrant communities in the borderlands already hosted a variety of other exiled politicians and militants who had challenged the Mexican government at some point, and subsequently lost.

Prior to the Mexican Revolution, most Mexican political exiles were opponents of Porfirio Díaz, including the anarchist brothers Enrique and Ricardo Flores Magón, and Francisco Madero, who would become president after Díaz left. After 1910, as the Mexican Revolution generated endless political turmoil and toppled successive political regimes, a steady stream of exiles arrived in the United States. After 1914, they also tended to be politically conservative, as many of them had been supporters of the regimes of Porfirio Díaz and Victoriano Huerta (both of whose careers and lives also ended in exile—Díaz's in France, and Huerta's in El Paso, Texas). These included Félix Díaz, a nephew of the former president; José Ortiz Monasterio, a general under Porfirio Díaz; and the Mexican intellectual and former *huertista* Nemesio García Naranjo. Another prominent exile was Ignacio Lozano, a Mexican journalist who, in exile in San Antonio, would establish the widely distributed conservative newspapers *La Prensa* and *La Opinion*.[65] Although many of the exiles, whom historian Nancy Aguirre refers to collectively as the "Porfirista diaspora," settled in San Antonio and El Paso, others went elsewhere.[66] Félix Díaz, for example, spent much of the decade in New Orleans, Louisiana, where he received visits from numerous allies and co-conspirators.

Beginning in the early 1920s, a new generation of exiles started to arrive in the United States. These were politicians and militants who had led opposition movements against Obregón and Calles regimes; once in the United States, many of them would continue to try to launch new rebellions. Most prominent among them was Adolfo de la Huerta, a Sonoran who had served as interim president after the fall of Venustiano

Carranza and minister of finance under Obregón, and who subsequently launched a revolt against Obregón and Calles in 1923. After his uprising was defeated, he and his numerous supporters went into exile. These included Enrique Estrada of Jalisco; general César Lopez de Lara, who had served as governor of Tamaulipas; Alfonzo de la Huerta, Adolfo's brother; Antonio I. Villareal, former governor of Nuevo Leon; and various others.[67] Some of the *delahuertistas* were also supporters of the Catholic cause: the most prominent of these was Jorge Prieto Laurens, who had left Mexico in 1924. In addition to backing the de la Huerta revolt, Prieto Laurens had been a close collaborator with Catholic political activists in Mexico: he had helped to found the ACJM in 1913, and in the early 1920s, he became the founder and president of the National Cooperativist Party, which opposed the Obregón and Calles governments and won seats in Mexico's Congress.[68] In the United States, he and many of the delahuertistas would repeatedly attempt to organize new military movements and rebellions to overthrow Calles and his successors.[69]

In the summer of 1926, once the Calles Laws went into effect and the Catholic militant movement coalesced, lay Catholic exiles began leaving Mexico as well. Many of the exiles claimed that they had been forced to leave the country, although the records do not indicate how many were formally deported and how many left voluntarily after having been threatened with imprisonment or violence.[70] By 1926 numerous key members of Mexico's three major Catholic lay organizations—the Liga, the ACJM, and the Knights of Columbus—had fled to the United States. In fact, so many members arrived from the former two organizations that both created new US-based headquarters: the Liga's was in San Antonio and the ACJM's was in Los Angeles. Although the Knights of Columbus was originally a US-based organization, Mexican political exiles formed several new councils in Texas and California.[71]

Two of the most prominent lay Catholic exiles were René Capistrán Garza, military commander of the Liga, who spent the duration of the war in the United States, and Luis Bustos of the Liga and the Mexican Knights of Columbus, who arrived in 1927 and stayed until the *arreglos* of 1929. Other Liga members who spent time in exile included Manuel de la Peza, an aide to the Liga's Executive Committee; Luis Chavez Hayhoe, who would become the organization's director in Los Angeles; Juan Lainé, its purchasing agent; and Francisco Vizcaíno and Mariano Alcocer, both Liga members in Los Angeles. Quite a few Liga members in exile, including Luis Ruiz y Rueda and his brother Ramón, played prominent roles in the ACJM as well. Some of them would go back to Mexico to fight, such as Carlos Blanco, a member of the Liga and the ACJM who came to the United States in 1926 with Capistrán Garza. He then returned to Mexico, where he became a military general in command of the Catholic insurgents in Jalisco. He later returned briefly to the United States in February 1928.[72]

As the war progressed, increasing numbers of Mexican Knights of Columbus members began arriving in the United States. So many of them came to Los Angeles that they founded a new council—the Tepeyac Council No. 2635—in that city. Its meetings were held in Spanish, and its members included Edelmiro Traslosheros, who had been state deputy of the Mexican KOC; his brother Julio Traslosheros, a lawyer who had served as the Order's secretary; and numerous other men, including *Licenciado* Jose Vallela, Mariano Alcocer (also a member of the Liga), Ricardo Vertiz, and Manuel Briones.[73] Knights of Columbus went to other cities, as well. One notable member was Francisco Traslosheros Gutiérrez, who went to New York City and then returned to Mexico, where he died in the war. According to a report on the Mexican Fund by the US Knights of Columbus, the organization had spent $115,799.21 "for the relief of exiled and refugee members and their families."[74]

While most of the political exiles belonged to the Liga, the ACJM, or the KOC (or multiple Catholic organizations), there were a few exiles who did not seem to be affiliated with any of the major Mexican Catholic groups. One of these was Guillermo Prieto-Yeme, a journalist and poet who would frequently express his support for Mexico's Catholics in *La Prensa*. Only a very few of them were women, such as Elena Lascuraín de Silva, the wife of a Porfirian-era exile who was president of the Union of Catholic Women. Carlota Landero de Algara, president of the Association of Mexican Catholic Women, was also once denied re-entry into Mexico, although her visit to the United States was voluntary and she was eventually allowed to return.[75]

The lay Catholic political exiles, like many emigrants of the Cristero War, generally arrived either at the Laredo or the Ciudad Juárez–El Paso border crossings. During the war years, many of the political exiles changed residences and cities quite frequently, since they constantly traveled across regions and cities to solicit support from other Mexican groups or from American Catholics. Like the emigrant class as a whole, many Mexican exiles had to search for a way to support themselves in the United States, and this was one that many of them lived itinerant lives. Victoria Lerner cites the case of Jorge Prieto Laurens, the delahuertista exile with strong connections to the Catholic exiles. During his years in the United States, he worked as an editor of Spanish-language newspapers in Houston, had a restaurant in El Paso that went out of business, worked for a clothing store as a vendor, became chief of sales at *El Diario de El Paso* and the *Revista Católica*, and then went to Los Angeles, where he worked on the paper *El Eco de México*, and eventually went on to jobs in radio.[76]

René Capistrán Garza (shown in Figure 2.3), who served as military director of the Liga for the first two years of his exile, was also highly mobile, at least during those first two years. After crossing the border in disguise, without a passport, and without paying the required head tax at the border, Capistrán Garza had to return to Mexico to get his passport and documents and then reenter the United States officially, in order to

FIGURE 2.3 René Capistrán Garza, exiled Liga leader
Source: GU-Americas, Box 19, Folder 21. Published with permission of America Press, Inc.

avoid being deported. In a sign of Capistrán Garza's ability to secure support from prominent Americans, he was apparently assisted in this matter by Consul Walsh in Nuevo Laredo, as well as by other sympathetic figures such as American members of the Knights of Columbus.[77] Initially, he traveled frequently throughout the United States, soliciting funds from the American Catholic bishops and from prominent Catholic businessmen. He would also make at least one trip to Rome to speak with Vatican officials. Eventually, he would lose the support of the Liga—a story that will be examined in greater detail in Chapter 4—but for the initial phase of his exile, he would prove to be an influential organizer of the Mexican Catholic movement in the United States.

Although many of the lay political exiles traveled frequently to different cities in the United States, San Antonio served as their base of operations during 1926 and 1927, and the place to which many of them would frequently return after their trips. One reason for this was that many members of the Mexican episcopate had settled there, in the College of the Incarnate Word. In addition to meetings there, the political exiles also regularly convened at the Robert E. Lee Hotel (a gathering spot favored by many Mexican political exiles, and the place where they would meet with the militant Simón Tenorio and his mentor, Pascual Robles, before Tenorio's failed uprising of August 1927), as well as at the city's various Catholic churches.[78] René Capistrán Garza would eventually settle in a house near the city's center, after bringing his wife, mother, and son to San Antonio.[79] Yet San Antonio was not the only place the lay Catholic political exiles operated. El Paso became a center of militancy during 1927; and after 1928, Los Angeles would increasingly host a number of political exiles.[80]

Mexico's Catholic exiles continued to remain politically involved from the United States throughout the Cristero War. As we shall see in the next chapter, they made efforts to collect money, create and distribute propaganda, and found newspapers and magazines to disseminate their views about the Mexican government. Through their US headquarters, the major Mexican Catholic organizations worked to support the military uprising in Mexico, organizing gunrunning expeditions, collecting funds, and recruiting young men as soldiers. They also undertook diplomatic negotiations, in an effort to gain the backing of US government officials. Furthermore, they would play a key role in organizing Catholic militant revolts along the border. Although none of these efforts would be successful in overthrowing the Mexican government, they did have a lasting effect on the communities of Mexican emigrants: through their organizational activities, publicity campaigns, and media work, they helped incite and direct Catholic activism within Mexican communities in the United States. The writer Guillermo Prieto-Yeme, in a letter to the influential Jesuit priest Wilfred Parsons, summed up the goals of such dissidents in regard to the broader emigrant population when he discussed his plan to disseminate publicity about the Cristero War in the United States. He closed by speculating about the potential power of this large community, proposing to circulate a petition that could be "signed by fifty or sixty thousand Mexicans who have had to flee from Mexico and live in a foreign country on account of the situation created by the <u>Revolutionists</u>."[81]

Toward Cristero Activism in the United States

By late 1926 and early 1927, Mexican emigrant communities in Texas, California, the US Southwest, and the Midwest had all experienced an infusion of two types of religious refugees: the lower clergy and nuns who had fled after the imposition of the Ley Calles and the bishops and archbishops who had been expelled from Mexico after the spring of 1927. In four cities where many of the religious refugees arrived—San Antonio, El Paso, Los Angeles, and Chicago—they found financial and logistical support from local US Catholic leaders, who were eager not only to help them, but also to place them within the growing community of Mexican Catholic emigrants who could be well served by Spanish-speaking priests and nuns. In addition, these communities—as well as many others—would also be strongly impacted by the arrival of the lay Catholic political exiles, who quickly began organizing in support of the Cristero cause from the United States. Taken together, these refugees and exiles—with the support they received from the US Catholic Church—would change the character of the emigrant experience during the war years, bringing the Cristero cause to the forefront of community activities, especially public religious events.

As a result, thousands of Mexican emigrants, many of whom had already been directly or indirectly affected by the Cristero War because of their region of origin—found that the conflict had followed them across the border. After 1926, political exiles and religious refugees began to rally Mexican emigrants around the Cristero cause, and even to reconstruct some of the religious communities—convents, monasteries, churches, and schools—that had been shuttered in Mexico. For many Mexican emigrants during the 1920s, then, the events and sentiments of the Cristero War had not been left behind when they crossed the border, but rather had been transported from Mexico, and then transplanted into their communities in the United States. By making it possible for emigrants to remain involved in the ongoing conflict, the religious refugees and political exiles helped to make the Cristero War a transnational event that spanned Mexican communities at home and in the diaspora.

Furthermore, the conflict shaped the ways that Mexican emigrants adapted to their new lives and communities in the United States. Over the next few years, Mexican Cristero supporters in the United States would form a diasporic identity that distinguished them from other Mexicans who supported the revolutionary government, or who were apolitical. This identity did not just set them apart; it also bound them together, since Mexicans who supported the Cristero cause collaborated across regions and cities in the United States in order to further their political agenda. By early 1927, Mexican emigrants from Detroit to San Diego were embroiled in a variety of activities that would advance the religious cause in Mexico, provoke the Mexican state and its representatives in the United States, and force the US Catholic Church to sit up and take notice of the Cristero diaspora. For tens of thousands of Mexican emigrants, religion—and religious activism—would come to be an essential part of community formation during the 1920s, and in subsequent decades.

3

"In Defense of Their Brothers Beyond the Rio Grande"

ALTHOUGH VERY LITTLE is known about Anselmo Padilla's life, it is clear that he suffered an excruciating death. It was June 27, 1927, near the pretty little colonial town of San Julian, in the Cristero heartland of Los Altos de Jalisco. A scouting party of federal troops came upon Padilla, whom they believed to be a Cristero soldier. The federales ordered him to prove his loyalty to the Mexican government by shouting *"¡Viva Calles!"* Padilla refused, and so one of the soldiers picked up an old, rusty saw.

Over the next several hours, the group of khaki-uniformed men subjected Padilla to a round of brutal torture. First, the soldiers began hacking at his face; then, someone sawed off his nose. Next, they peeled the skin in strips from his legs. Then, they cut off the soles of Padilla's feet—a common practice during the Cristero War. According to one account, they castrated him. Finally, they made the broken, bleeding man stand up on the ruins of his feet and begin an agonizing walk toward their camp. When he collapsed along the dusty road, they forced him to drag himself along with his elbows. Soon afterward, mercifully, his battered body gave out. As Padilla took his last breaths, he reportedly asked God's forgiveness for himself and for his torturers and then let out a dying cry of *"¡Viva Cristo Rey!"*

A few weeks later, and almost nine hundred miles to the north, the sensational news of Padilla's awful death reached the Mexican communities of southwest Texas.[1] Devout Catholics who read the story in the daily newspaper *El Diario de El Paso* probably felt a mixture of inspiration and fury. On the one hand, the way Padilla died—martyred at the hands of purportedly godless *callista* troops—meant that he was destined for instantaneous sainthood. Mexican Cristero supporters who read the story could feel awed and reassured that yet another of their own had joined the ranks of God's holy martyrs. On the other hand, the news provided direct proof to this Catholic audience of the depravity of Plutarco Elías Calles and his anticlerical troops, and a reminder of the urgent need to defeat his government.

The story of Anselmo Padilla was only one of many similar accounts circulating in Mexican communities across the United States during the late 1920s: newspaper articles, letters from relatives, parish bulletins, telegrams, conversations, and even songs carried brutal stories of the Cristero War from the interior of Mexico to the barrios of El Paso, Tucson, San Antonio, Los Angeles, Chicago, Detroit, and other Mexican neighborhoods in the United States. Churchgoing Mexican emigrants heard even more frequent tales from the Cristero front: Mexican priests, so often the victims of the Calles government's repressive efforts, railed against the regime in apocalyptic sermons from their pulpits, and rallied their congregants to action.

These acts of collective resistance to the Calles regime within the Cristero diaspora would take a variety of forms. Between 1926 and 1929, Mexican emigrants all over the United States launched petitions, boycotts, and public protests against the Mexican government. In restaurants, hotel lobbies, and private houses, young men met to plot the undoing of their sworn enemy, the anticlerical Calles government. In the borderlands, clandestine gunrunners smuggled loads of contraband rifles across moonlit desert landscapes, while in California port cities, they loaded boxes of rifles and bullets onto ships. At border checkpoints, groups of pious women smiled sweetly at stern guards, willing them not to notice the stacks of seditious pamphlets tucked discreetly in their dresses. Finally, a few of the emigrants participated in more secretive—and more seditious—activities: arms smuggling, conspiracy, and even clandestine military uprisings along the border, such as that of Simón Tenorio and his small band of militants. During the Cristero War, religious revolutionaries were active in almost every Mexican community in the United States. Throughout the vast border region, from the Pacific coast of California to the Gulf coast of Texas—and then northward, all the way to Chicago and Detroit—the Mexican communities of the United States would become a site where emigrants, exiles, and refugees participated in the Cristero War from afar.

During the war years, this diasporic Cristero activism happened so continuously and in so many places that it was a pervasive part of the Mexican emigrant experience during the war years. The story of this activism reveals a new, and more nuanced, portrait of the Mexican emigrant population. The collaborative actions of Cristero supporters in the United States, so long hidden from history, demonstrate not only the depth of some emigrants' commitment to the Cristero cause, but also the intricate network of connections among the thousands of labor emigrants, lay political exiles, and religious refugees in the Cristero diaspora and their families and compatriots at home. For thousands of Mexicans in the United States during the late 1920s, the Cristero War had followed them across the border in the shape of the news they read, the sermons they heard, and the tales told by family members and neighbors who had emigrated from their hometowns. Religion and politics became intertwined in their new communities just as they had been in Mexico.

At the same time, numerous Mexican emigrants opposed the Cristero partisans, and supported the efforts of the anticlerical Mexican government to assert control over the Catholic Church, which they viewed as fanatical, reactionary, and counter revolutionary. With the help of Mexican government representatives (particularly consular employees), these anticlerical emigrants confronted Cristero supporters in the United States, and participated in activities to counteract their efforts. The Cristero War, then, caused significant tension within the broader diaspora of Mexican emigrants. This tension did not result in violence: the archives contain no evidence of any physical clashes between Cristero supporters and anticlerical emigrants in the United States. Nevertheless, the Church-state conflict created emigrant political factions that mirrored the deeper divisions in the Mexican homeland.

The Cristero War in Emigrant Print Media

The decade of the 1920s saw a flourishing of print culture within Mexican emigrant communities. Although plenty of Spanish-language publications had been established well before that decade, the arrival of tens of thousands of new emigrants to urban neighborhoods created a growing readership for both existing publications and new ones. During the 1920s, Mexican emigrants who settled in towns and cities could usually read at least one local Spanish-language newspaper, and sometimes several. Mexican emigrants also published numerous magazines, books, and pamphlets, which could then be circulated within the emigrant diaspora. The audience for these materials was not limited to the literate, who made up only around 40 percent of all Mexicans during the 1930s.[2] In fact, as Raúl Coronado points out in his study of Latino print culture in Texas, the Spanish-language written word was often circulated orally as literate emigrants read aloud to their illiterate family members, co-workers, or friends. As a result, print media was "experienced communally," even for those who lacked literacy.[3]

The development of an emigrant print culture helped to contribute to Mexicans' sense of belonging to *"el México de afuera"*—a "Mexico beyond Mexico," or more accurately, a Mexican identity that persisted outside of the country's borders. Indeed, numerous scholars have examined the ways that emigrant newspapers and print media helped to create a sense of diasporic identity among their audience.[4] Yet during the 1920s, the residual tensions of the Mexican Revolution and the growing tensions over the Cristero war meant that there were competing definitions of what it meant to be "Mexican." For some, the crucible of the Mexican Revolution had produced an appealing new vision of a secular, modern country in which the state responded to the demands of the people for land, liberty, and labor rights. For others—including the political exiles of the Cristero diaspora—the Revolution was a disastrous step toward atheism and the "Bolshevism" of countries like Russia. This latter group, which was more conservative, more Catholic, and highly critical of Calles, had a number of broadly distributed outlets for their views.

The most widely read Mexican emigrant newspaper in the United States was *La Prensa*, a largely conservative, staunchly anti-Calles daily that was based out of San Antonio but distributed widely across the American Southwest and Midwest, as well as northern Mexico. The paper was founded in 1913 by the journalist Ignacio E. Lozano, a supporter of Porfirio Díaz who left Mexico during the early years of the Revolution. Between 1913 and 1920, *La Prensa's* writers and editors continuously critiqued the regime of Venustiano Carranza. As historian Nancy Aguirre points out, *La Prensa* offered its readers more than just a critical view of the revolutionary Mexican government; it also covered national US news, the latest gossip from Hollywood, and local events. In addition, it included a Ladies' page, articles for young readers, and literary excerpts.[5] In doing so, it promoted a particular vision of what it meant to be Mexican in the United

States, encouraging its readers to pursue an education, rise above racism and discrimination, and keep abreast of the latest news from Mexico.

By the 1920s, the newspaper would become an important forum for Mexican Catholics—particularly political exiles—opposed to the Calles government's anticlerical policies during the Cristero War. Additionally, in 1926 Lozano launched the Los Angeles daily *La Opinión* (it remains in publication today). Both papers' editorials, which during the period between 1926 and 1929 were often identical, dealt primarily with issues in Mexico, and were occasionally written by prominent Catholic political exiles such as René Capistrán Garza and Guillermo Prieto-Yeme.[6] Another frequent contributor to the editorial page was Nemesio Garcia Naranjo, a *porfirista* who had run his own anti-Carranza publication, *Revista Mexicana*, in the previous decade. During the Cristero War, Garcia Naranjo became a strong critic of Calles and gave public lectures on Mexico's so-called "Religious Question."[7] *La Prensa* and *La Opinión*, then, consistently channeled criticism of the Calles government and support for the Cristero cause during the war years.

Another nationally distributed publication, the newspaper *Revista Católica*, was much older. The weekly paper, headed by Jesuit priest Cruz M. Garde, had been founded in 1873 in Albuquerque and was relocated to El Paso in 1917 with the mission of "saving the faith of the Spanish-speaking people of the Southwest and those of Latin American countries."[8] At the onset of the Cristero War, the paper took an active position against the Calles government, publishing editorials criticizing the Calles regime and opining that Catholic Mexicans had the duty to rise up in arms against the government. By 1927 (if not earlier), the newspaper had been banned from circulation in Mexico.[9]

La Prensa, La Opinion, and *Revista Católica* were the most prominent national pro-Cristero newspapers, but Cristero supporters in the Southwest and the Midwest had smaller local newspapers as well. *El Diario de El Paso*, the paper that had carried the story of Anselmo Padilla's martyrdom, was published by Mexican political exiles from Guadalajara who were strongly sympathetic to the Cristero cause.[10] In El Paso and elsewhere along the border, Mexicans could read *La Razon*, the rabidly anti-Calles publication edited by Father Pascual Robles, the priest who had encouraged Simón Tenorio to launch his ill-fated Catholic uprising.[11] In Los Angeles, the ACJM (Mexican Catholic Youth Association, a Catholic men's organization based in Mexico) published *La Voz de la Patria*, which reproduced speeches by prominent Catholics, published news about the war, advocated the repeal of anticlerical laws, and appealed to its eight thousand readers for donations.[12] In South Chicago, Mexican Catholics founded *La Avispa* (The Wasp), a paper whose main purpose was to inform its readership—most of whom were from Jalisco, Guanajuato, and Michoacán—about developments in the homeland, as well as to serve as "a tool of support for the Cristero movement."[13]

A closer look at another south Chicago newspaper, *El Amigo del Hogar*, offers a sampling of the kinds of messages conveyed by Mexican Catholic serial publications during the 1920s. The newspaper was first published in 1925 by the members of a Catholic organization called El Circulo de Obreros Católicos "San José" in Indiana Harbor, along the southern shores of Lake Michigan. Published for "the working Catholics of the Mexican colony," *El Amigo* became the most widely circulated Spanish language newspaper in south Chicago, reaching more than 1,500 households in the region until it was discontinued in the early 1930s.[14]

In its earliest years, the newspaper stayed away from politics, focusing instead on the moral and spiritual improvement of the Mexican community, and exhorting its readers to contribute to the local church-building fund, to behave as good Catholics, and to set a positive example as representatives of Mexico in the United States. After the Cristero War began, however, the editors of *El Amigo* began publishing more frequent articles lamenting the turn of events in Mexico. First-person narratives, such as "A Day in My Homeland" of May 8, 1927, in which a resident of Indiana Harbor wrote of his experiences in the previous year in Mexico during the closing of the churches, became much more common.[15] Another piece commemorated the month of the Virgin Mary (May) and appealed to her biblical language, declaiming "Oh, my mother! Thousands of children in my homeland will not have the honor of offering you their flowers, because the temples are deserted, the altars full of dust . . ."[16]

As the summer of 1927 continued, more articles appeared that described the conflict in Mexico in vivid detail. The issue of July 7 saw the first of a series of articles that described the trials and deaths of various martyrs in Mexico—first in Guadalajara, then in Leon, Guanajuato, and finally in Zamora, Michoacán.[17] Another regular feature that began in the same issue was a column entitled "Brief Notes About Mexico," which described battles, troop movements, and deaths in the war-torn west-central region.[18] Such reports would have been of great interest to the local community, since most of them came from the same region; these updates would continue throughout the duration of the war.

Additionally, editorials began to speak more directly about emigrants' connection to the conflict, reminding the community to stay aware of events in Mexico. In April of 1927, *El Amigo* reprinted an article from *La Prensa* that explicitly addressed the role of the emigrant community, stating that "Mexico's redemption has to come from outside . . . [from] those Mexicans that form the great colony in the United States."[19] Another story demonstrated a direct connection between its readership in the Midwest and their friends and relatives in the homeland. The article described how copies of the newspaper had reached the town of Irapuato in the state of Guanajuato, where a reader there had become so inspired by the activities of Mexicans in the United States that he had donated a sum of money for the opening of a library in Indiana Harbor.[20]

Newspapers like *El Amigo del Hogar* provided a vital source of information and public opinion for Mexicans who wished to read about the Cristero War from the United States. In addition, new, cheap duplicating technologies such as the mimeograph and the ditto machine allowed individuals, political groups, and religious organizations to print reams of pamphlets, flyers, and leaflets about the religious question. These publications proliferated in almost every community where Mexicans had settled during the 1920s. In Los Angeles in 1926, for example, an anonymous author printed a flyer with the headline *"¡Alerta Católicos!"* [Catholics, Beware!]. The pamphlet condemned Mexican foreign minister Aaron Sáenz and the "anti-Catholic policies of Calles."[21] In El Paso, young members of the Liga and the ACJM, the two most important Mexican Catholic organizations (both of which had outposts in the United States at the time), printed and distributed political pamphlets around town.[22] In Del Rio, Texas—the home of Simón Tenorio—the priests from the church of San José gave sermons that excoriated the Mexican government, and "recommend[ed] revolution," while also collecting money for the religious uprising by selling books and religious pamphlets.[23] In Brawley, California (about twenty miles north of the border town of Mexicali), a priest named Apolinar Ponce distributed "subversive pamphlets" among the population.[24] Among the most widely distributed pamphlets within the Cristero diaspora were the texts written by the exiled bishop José de Jesús Manríquez y Zárate, especially his series of "Messages to the Civilized World." In the first of these, published in July 1927, he asked the "civilized peoples of the world" to help Mexico, which "is sinking, and perhaps forever, into the black abysses of lack of faith and barbarity."[25]

Typically, the pamphlets and flyers were even more aggressive and openly political than the newspaper articles. Many of them called upon their readers not only to be outraged by the religious conflict, but also to act on these feelings by donating money for the Cristero cause. One such pamphlet, published in 1928, was distributed throughout Texas, New Mexico, Arizona, and southern California.[26] After beginning with an emphatic rallying cry ("TO ARMS! LONG LIVE LIBERTY! DEATH TO TYRANTS!"), the flyer called upon readers to

> Go out into the battlefields . . . Launch yourself into the most just and saintly war with a handful of valiant ones. Join yourself to the soldiers of liberty. If you are able, head a new group where one does not exist and fight for the patrimony and for the noble ideals that are mocked by the iniquitous traffickers of Sonora.

If the pamphlet's readers did not want to join the fight, however, its writers suggested another way they could support the cause:

> If you are unable to rise up in arms, help the Liberators with your money; much, if you are rich; little, if you are poor. Having volition, you are able to serve—every day—and be really useful to the cause.

The goal of such publications, then, was to galvanize Mexican emigrants to back the efforts of the Cristeros and their supporters in the United States, either by volunteering to go to the battlefields, or to donate money to the movement.

The militancy of the pamphlets, and that of the most ardently pro-Catholic newspapers, was not surprising given that most were probably produced either by lay Catholic political exiles or by religious refugees. One case in particular illustrates the connections among lay Catholic political leaders, religious refugees, and the pro-Catholic emigrant press in the United States. In Los Angeles in 1927, two men, Carlos de Silva, a leader of the ACJM in the United States, and José Amador Manríquez, the nephew of Bishop José de Jesus Manríquez y Zárate and an employee of *Revista Católica*, were arrested by a Los Angeles police officer for carrying concealed weapons and for participating "in the distribution of propaganda against the Mexican government." During their visit to Los Angeles, they stayed at the home of J. C. Rojos, editor of the ACJM's official paper, *La Voz de la Patria*. They had also collected about seven hundred dollars in donations "from patriotic Mexicans in Los Angeles."[27] Such media campaigns, then, could have concrete and beneficial results for the Cristero movement at home.

Speeches, Radio, Films, and Photography

Newspaper stories could inform readers about events in Mexico, and political flyers and pamphlets could invite them to donate money or take militant action. Yet these were not the only ways that Catholic activists reached out to broader audiences. Through speeches and lectures, as well as new broadcasting technologies, lay political exiles and religious refugees managed to expand their audiences even further.

In various cities in the United States, Mexican political exiles organized public lectures that criticized the Calles government. Some of these were known supporters of the Catholic cause: Luis Bustos, Jorge Prieto Laurens, and numerous members of the Mexican hierarchy spoke frequently to Mexican audiences about the religious conflict in Mexico. Others were political exiles who were not exclusively Catholic activists, but who strongly critiqued the anticlerical efforts of Calles and his successors. One of these was Nemesio García Naranjo, the conservative politician and intellectual who had served in the cabinet of President Victoriano Huerta, and had been living in exile for most of the period since Huerta's defeat. Garcia Naranjo, as mentioned previously, gave several speeches to Mexican audiences in Texas. One of these, on June 10, called on "those of us in exile" to "prepare the fight against the tyrant Calles." The next day, he delivered another lecture—entitled "The Religious Problem of Mexico," in which he argued that, by restricting the rights of Catholics, the Calles government had undermined "freedom of conscience and . . . all human rights."[28] (The flyer for this speech is shown in Figure 3.1.)

Another political exile who drew the support of Catholics was José Vasconcelos, a charismatic philosopher and politician who had served as the secretary of public education under President Obregón, and later became a strong critic of the Calles government. In 1929, Vasconcelos toured various northern Mexican border towns, as well as Mexican communities in the United States, in order to build support for his presidential campaign. Although Catholic leaders did not openly endorse Vasconcelos's candidacy, he received support from Catholics as long as it appeared that he would pursue a platform of religious liberty.[29] His

FIGURE 3.1 Flyer from a public speech by Nemesio Garcia Naranjo about the religious conflict

Source: AGN, IPS, Volume 266, Expediente 39.

efforts drew monetary donations from numerous "refugees on the American side who would like to see the present Government and policies ended," and there were widespread rumors that the clergy backed his campaign.[30] In early March of 1930, Vasconcelos held a conference at the Centro México in Brawley, California, a town where there were numerous supporters of the Cristero cause. At his talk, he "launched attacks against . . . the Government" and stated that the Mexican people needed to rise up in revolt to "restore our country."[31]

By the 1920s, emigrants did not even have to be physically present to hear such speeches: the radio, which was becoming increasingly common in private homes and public spaces, allowed a wider audience to listen to news about their homeland. Although there were no Mexican-owned stations, Mexican radio producers would rent time slots in order to broadcast programs to emigrant audiences. While many of these programs showcased musical performances, they also included information about local job opportunities, as well as news programs.[32] Occasionally, these programs expanded to include religious sermons and, occasionally, political speeches. In November of 1926, for example, a man named José Scott gave a conference in the Shrine Auditorium in Los Angeles about the religious situation in Mexico; it was later broadcast on Radio KNX, a station established in Hollywood "under the auspices" of the Knights of Columbus.[33]

Another relatively new technology, silent films and newsreels, meant that movie-going audiences in the Mexican emigrant community could now view vivid footage related to the Cristero War. Such films were viewed in Mexico and in the United States, and were seen by both Mexican and US-born audiences. One scholar described a newsreel that showed Mexican citizens crossing into the United States to attend Catholic Mass; another clip showed refugee nuns as they left Mexico during the uprising.[34] And a film entitled *Mexican Martyrs* that graphically depicted the horrors of the Cristero War reportedly circulated among parishioners of Mexican churches in southern California, although there are no extant copies, and there is no available information about who produced the film.[35] At least one newsreel still survives, however: entitled *History of Religious Persecution in Mexico*, it was produced in 1926 and displayed images of the closure of Catholic churches in Mexico, massive public pilgrimages to the shrine of the Virgin of Guadalupe in Mexico City, and anticlerical labor groups marching in front of Mexico's National Palace and saluting President Calles. The film was most likely screened in secret in Mexico, but its bilingual subtitles and other evidence indicate that it was meant for

US audiences as well, and may well have been seen by some within the Mexican emigrant community.[36]

Finally, Cristero supporters also used still photography from the conflict to generate sympathy for their cause. In December of 1928, a group of lay Catholic political exiles, led by activist Cristero bishop José de Jesús Manríquez y Zárate, published a hundred-page book entitled "Galería de Mártires Mexicanos" and produced by Imprenta Universal in San Antonio. Written in Spanish, the book featured several dozen graphic photographs of Cristeros killed in action, including images of Cristero soldiers hanging from telegraph wires and pictures of murdered priests. The book had a list price of thirty-five cents and a print run of about five thousand copies.[37] An advertisement in *La Voz de la Patria* raised the price, however, asking readers for a donation of one dollar in exchange for the book of pictures of "our martyrs" and promising that the donation would be used for "the necessities of Mexico."[38]

The proliferation of these messages—photographs, newsreels, radio addresses, public speeches, printed flyers, and newspaper articles—meant that Mexican emigrants in the United States during the late 1920s could easily access vivid descriptions and images from the Cristero conflict. The ubiquity of this information meant that most Mexican emigrants would have been aware of events almost as they were happening. For some Mexicans, this awareness would predispose them toward activism. They would encounter even more invocations to take action when they attended religious services within their communities.

Sermons and Religious Events

Mexican emigrants who attended Catholic church or participated in parish-sponsored events were constantly reminded of the war. As discussed in Chapter 2, most of the Mexican priests who had fled the country after 1926 had settled in Mexican parishes in the United States. There, the priests—many of whom had been harassed or persecuted by the Mexican government—gave frequent sermons about their experiences and about current events in Mexico. They also spoke at religious events such as church fairs and religious processions. As one Mexican government agent in Texas reported indignantly:

> from Brownsville to El Paso, Texas, the Priests and other Catholics ... are taking advantage of all the [public] ceremonies

and festivities ... in order to launch terrible charges against the Supreme Government, and insult our Country and our nationality ... disgracefully, [their efforts] are having a certain unfavorable echo among a certain class of people.[39]

In their sermons, Mexican priests often railed against the sinfulness of the Mexican government and extolled the righteousness of the soldiers in the field. Many then asked their listeners to offer money for the support of the Catholic cause in Mexico.

Mexican churchgoers in many US cities and towns heard such messages at their Sunday services. In Ysleta, Texas, one Father Blanchard, "after making the panegyric of the life of Christ ... spoke especially of the issues of Mexico, expressing the forthcoming defeat of the oppressors of the church." When he asked for donations, he reminded his audience of the "constant persecution" that was tormenting their "brothers in faith" in Mexico.[40] In Del Rio, Texas (home of the thwarted border revolutionary Simón Tenorio), priests from the church of San José gave homilies that vilified the Mexican government and "recommend[ed] revolution," collecting money for the religious uprising by selling books and religious pamphlets.[41] And in South Chicago's Our Lady of Guadalupe parish, the priest told his congregation that "many prayers are needed for our Catholic brethren of Mexico that are giving their lives for the religion and freedom of Mexico."[42]

One particularly provocative priest was Father Pedro Centurioni, a pastor of a Catholic church in Eagle Pass, Texas. In one of his homilies, according to a Mexican secret agent who attended the Mass where he spoke, Centurioni called the men in the audience "cowards, bad Mexicans, and false Catholics" for not joining the religious revolt, and told his female parishioners that they were "ignorant and bad Christians" if they did not convince their husbands and sons to go back to Mexico and take up arms.[43] According to one informant, the majority of his listeners left his sermons "profoundly indignant" toward the Mexican government (although one wonders if some were also indignant at being called names by their priest).[44]

Sermons were not the only way that exiled priests reminded their congregations about the war in Mexico; priests in numerous places organized public spectacles in order to reach a larger audience. In San Antonio, a priest named Camilo Torrente, a Spanish Claretian (the Claretian order had established missions in the US Southwest, and many Claretians were exiled from Mexico during the 1910–30 period), put on a play in 1927 called "El Mártir de Leon," which "climaxed with a graphic description of [a Mexican Catholic's] execution."[45] And in Brownsville, Texas, Father Antonio Vallvé, another Spanish-born Claretian exile from Mexico, organized a public religious festival in order to repudiate the Mexican government in front his parishioners.[46]

Other parishes sponsored collective prayer events, festivals, and shrines: in Chicago, the church of Our Lady of Guadalupe offered a Solemn Novena, "praying for the Catholics of Mexico so terribly persecuted by the bandit and infamous bolshevik Calles."[47] A few months later, the parish priest who had told his parishioners that "many prayers are needed for our Catholic brethren of Mexico" also recomended that they "come to pray for Mexico during all of the Thursdays at the Holy Hour."[48] And in 1928, Mexicans from various southern California parish societies united to erect a shrine in honor of Our Lady of Guadalupe, celebrating "the freedom of religion they [now] enjoyed, that was lacking in Mexico."[49]

Throughout the late 1920s, Mexican Catholics around the United States participated in public processions during the feast of the Virgin of Guadalupe (December 12); the feast of Corpus Christi (mid-June); and, increasingly during the Cristero War years, the solemn celebration of Cristo Rey (late October; Figure 3.2 depicts a flyer from one such event). Some of these, such as those described at the beginning of Chapter 2, drew tens of thousands of people. Such grand processions offered clear evidence to the wider Mexican emigrant community that there was significant support for the Cristero cause, and mirrored similar events in Mexico. As historian Matthew Butler explains, religious marches and processions during the Cristero War years provided a venue for lay Catholics to demonstrate their political strength: they were a visible way of "flexing Catholic muscle" in the face of the Mexican government.[50] The same was true for Mexican emigrant communities in the United States. Large public events celebrating religious feast days provided a spiritual alternative to the secular patriotic festivals and other nationalistic programs sponsored by the consulates during the Cristero War years, and they made a political statement as well.[51] As one reporter in *El Diario de El Paso* asserted, a 1928 procession in Los Angeles presented "a practical lesson of tolerance and freedom, for the supporters of the oppressive regime in Mexico."[52]

¡VIVA CRISTO REY!

CATOLICOS MEXICANOS:

Con profunda pena la Comisión Organizadora de los festejos de la Fiesta de CRISTO REY, anuncia a los católicos mexicanos, un nuevo cambio de local para la celebración de dichos festejos....

Seguramente que muchos preguntarán ¿A qué es debido esto? Una sola respuesta tiene esta significativa pregunta: Es que no estamos en nuestra casa y tenemos que solicitarlo todo y, a más de no estar en nuestra casa, SOMOS MEXICANOS....

El nuevo lugar en donde parece que definitivamente se verificará este imponente acto, es el

CAMPO DE LA ALTA ESCUELA CATEDRAL

regenteada por los Hermanos de las Escuelas Cristianas, en la North Broadway y Bishop Rd., un poco adelante del templo de San Pedro y San Pablo.

CATOLICOS MEXICANOS:

Nada nos haga restar nuestro entusiasmo para nuestra Gran Festividad.. Acudamos todos. Démosle a este acto, con nuestra presencia y nuestro entusiasmo, un esplendor inusitado y que tenga una trascendencia mundial. Repetimos a los señores Curas nuestra súplica de que organicen sus Instituciones piadosas y de carácter social y que vayan con sus estandartes y banderas. Volvemos a rogar a los Sres. sacerdotes y a todas las religiosas, procuren asistir. Insistimos en que ningún mexicano debe faltar a esta grandiosa Festividad.

Carros que deben tomarse para llegar al lugar: El "2", el "3", la "E" y la "W" que hacen parada precisamente en la Broadway y Bishop, media cuadra precisamente del lugar en donde tendrá verificativo el acto.

Los Angeles, California, Octubre de 1928.

Editorial "La Placita"   524 New High St. — Los Angeles, Calif.

FIGURE 3.2 Flyer from the Fiesta de Cristo Rey, Los Angeles, October 1928
Source: UNAM-Traslosheros, Caja 102, Expediente 730, Document 7345.

Collective Associations, Both Regional and National

In the early twentieth century, it was very common for emigrants of all nationalities in the United States to form political organizations. These groups served multiple purposes: they allowed emigrants to connect with their compatriots, adapt and adjust to life in the United States, and stay aware of—and responsive toward—political and economic problems in their home countries. In addition, social groups often allowed emigrants of opposing political persuasions to take public collective action in response to the political conflicts of the homeland.[53]

During the late 1920s, thousands of Mexican emigrants joined Catholic clubs and associations that acted to support the Cristero cause from the United States. In addition, organizations that were headquartered in Mexico, such as the Liga and the ACJM, established branches in the United States. This was because many of their leaders were exiled to the United States during the war years. As described in Chapter 2, René Capistrán Garza and Luis Bustos, who served in executive positions in both organizations, spent most of the late 1920s in San Antonio, Texas. There, they and numerous other political exiles conducted organizational business, communicated regularly with the Mexican leadership at home, and sometimes collaborated with the Mexican Catholic hierarchy, most of which was also in exile in San Antonio. They also traveled around the United States giving speeches and seeking donations for the cause.

During the mid-1920s, the Mexican Knights of Columbus became a more transnational organization as well. The KOC was founded in the United States, but had spread to Mexico in 1905 and become quite successful there in the two decades leading up to the Church-state conflict.[54] As the confrontations between Catholics and the government heated up in Mexico, lay Catholic political exiles helped to form Spanish-speaking councils around the United States, including El Paso, Texas, in 1925; Del Rio, Texas, in 1928; and Los Angeles, California, in 1927. The Los Angeles branch, called the Tepeyac Council, was founded by lay Catholic exiles "as a wholly Spanish-speaking Council [as a direct result of] conditions existing in Mexico."[55]

As discussed previously, the Liga, the ACJM, and the KOC all became transnational groups during the Cristero War, with offices in several US cities as well as in Mexico. Yet by the mid-1920s, Mexican emigrants who wished to support the Cristero cause could join a plethora of regional organizations as well. San Antonio's Mexican Catholic community, with its long and established presence in the city, had already organized numerous Catholic societies and associations. The most important of these was the Vassallos and Vasallas de Cristo Rey, which was established in 1925 in order to raise money for the San Fernando Cathedral and other local parishes, as well as to help fund the construction of the monument to Christ the King at Cubilete, Guanajuato. The activities of the Vassallos aimed to foster religiosity within the Mexican emigrant community and thereby, as Timothy Matovina points out, to encourage emigrants to "address the violence and political upheaval in . . . Mexico."[56] Further south in El Paso, a similar organization, the Catholic Union of San José, held meetings where "the most prominent Catholic Mexicans in El Paso" would discuss the religious issues of Mexico and the hoped-for defeat of the Mexican government.[57]

The Midwest, where most Mexican emigrants had arrived after 1920, was home to a number of Catholic organizations by mid-decade. In Chicago, Catholic emigrants formed Los Caballeros de Guadalupe for men and Las Hijas de María for women, both of which put on patriotic celebrations and dances in the Mexican community.[58] In Indiana Harbor, El Circulo de Obreros Catolicos "San José"—which had founded *El Amigo del Hogar*—embarked upon fundraising and public advocacy on behalf of the church in Mexico during the Cristero War.[59] Finally, Chicago was also home to the Beneficient Society Pro-Mexico, which raised funds to support the Cristero cause in Mexico and published propaganda within the United States to attract attention to the conflict.[60] By May 1928, the Beneficient Society boasted Illinois-based branches in South Chicago, Aurora, Elgin, Joliet, Melrose Park, and Waukegan, as well as in Gary, Indiana Harbor, Detroit, and Milwaukee. Although the organization was founded by a middle-class Catholic emigrant, Carlos Fernández, many of its members were "poor Mexican laborers" who resided in Chicago, Detroit, and other Midwestern cities.[61]

Local, parish-based Catholic organizations and clubs created spaces for Mexican emigrants to gather together to discuss their concerns about the relationship between the Catholic Church and the Mexican state. They also encouraged the emigrant community to oppose Mexican government representatives. One type of confrontation, which Cristero supporters had famously implemented in Mexico in 1926, was the boycott. In the United States, the boycott took the form of refusal to participate in the patriotic festivals sponsored by Mexican consulates in the United States, which had recently received a directorate from Mexico's Foreign

Ministry (Secretaría de Relaciones Exteriores) "to develop special plans for Mexican Independence Day celebrations and other national holidays." The organization of the *fiestas patrias* was often delegated to the *comisiones honoríficas*, groups of emigrants that worked under the direct supervision of the consulates. The fiestas patrias typically featured displays of the Mexican flag, the national anthem, nostalgic songs, poems, skits, plays, music, and dancing.[62]

In the summer of 1926, Catholic organizations in a number of cities decided to abstain from participating in the patriotic festivals sponsored by the Mexican consulates. In San Antonio, as mentioned previously, Aurelia Avila, the president of San Antonio's Young Catholics Club of San Fernando, resigned in protest from the candidacy of Queen of the September Patriotic Festival, which had been sponsored by the Mexican consulate.[63] Meanwhile, in Tucson, an organization called the Hispanic American Alliance instructed all of its lodges in the region to avoid participating in the consulate's Mexican independence celebrations, and another social group called the Club Latino de Tucson voted to abstain from all patriotic celebrations of Mexican independence because of government persecution of Catholics.[64] In Los Angeles, a group of Mexicans also refused to participate in the patriotic festivities. The boycotts in both Tucson and Los Angeles were reported in the emigrant press as far away as Chicago.[65]

In some communities, priests sponsored these boycotts. In Naco, Arizona, an exiled priest named Vicente Guzmán "recommended that no Catholic give help nor attend [the festivals] because the current government is a tyranny that persecutes religion." At least some of his flock obeyed: attendance at the patriotic festivals was reportedly markedly lower that year.[66] Another priest—himself not Mexican, but the head of a Mexican parish in Big Wells, Texas—forbade his parishioners from joining the Cruz Azul Mexicana, a *mutualista* (cooperative) society with ties to the consulates.[67]

Cristero supporters confronted representatives of the Mexican government through petitions as well. In December of 1927, as mentioned in Chapter 2, some five hundred Mexicans organized a rally in front of the consular offices in San Antonio, presenting the consul with a signed petition that asked the Mexican government to restore their religious freedoms.[68] And outside Los Angeles, another group of Mexican emigrants sent a petition directly to President Calles, asking him to end "the unjust persecution that has been made against the Catholic Religion" and appealing him "for our rights, for our religious ideals to be respected and for our Churches as well as its ministers to be respected."[69] While both of these groups did not reveal an affiliation with a particular club or political association, the collective action they took was similar to those of the Catholic social and political organizations that had formed during the same period.

Collective actions such as these were meant not only to generate community support for the Cristero cause, but also to provoke the Mexican government's representatives in the United States. In this, they succeeded. Whenever consuls found evidence of anti-government activity in the United States, they attempted to control or put a stop to it. During the 1927 rally in San Antonio, the consulate convinced the city's mayor to issue orders that no speeches should be made, and to mandate the police riot squad to guard the event. Later, consular officials "made public a counter-protest, which, they said, had been signed within the consulate by Calles sympathizers."[70] In California, "the consuls . . . hired detectives to follow exiled Mexican bishops to see if they were involved in gun-running to antigovernment forces, but they found no evidence."[71] And in Texas, according to Arturo Rosales, the Mexican ambassador asked US government officials to put a stop to pro-Cristero activity by refugees.[72] As late as 1935, the Mexican consul in Tucson pressured the owner of a local radio station to shut down Father Carmelo Corbella's Sunday program, which, the official claimed, "had falsely attacked the Mexican government's policy on education and religion."[73]

Even if Mexican government representatives sometimes thwarted the activities of pro-Cristero collective associations, there were prominent members within the Mexican emigrant community who believed that they were an effective way of expressing support for the Church in Mexico. Guillermo Prieto-Yeme, a La Prensa columnist and a Catholic political exile, argued that the act of collecting signatures and presenting petitions had the potential to "move the Mexican colony all over the border to do something in defense of their brothers beyond the Rio Grande."[74] In El Diario de El Paso, one journalist reflected that the San Antonio protest in front of the consulate had allowed the public to hear the "voice" of the emigrant—which was "loud and sonorous, so eloquent and firm."[75] Through collective action, then, Mexican Cristero supporters could raise their voices in public, and confront the Mexican government in ways that they might not have been willing or able to do at home in Mexico (where the Calles government frequently punished dissidents with jail, violence, or even execution). They also established themselves in political opposition to supporters of the Calles government, thus reenacting the ideological divisions that were tearing at the social fabric in their homeland.

While local collective organizations were certainly useful for organizing Mexican emigrants who opposed the Mexican government's representatives within their community, some members of the Cristero diaspora dreamed of founding a national organization. The most successful of these would be Carlos Fernández, the founder of the Chicago-area Beneficient Society Pro-Mexico. In the spring of 1928, Fernández—a devout Catholic who served as president of the Mexican branch of the Holy Name Society in Chicago[76]—began reaching out to other lay Catholic activists in the United States. With the backing of exiled bishop José de Jesús Manríquez y Zárate, Fernández made contact with exiled members of the Liga in Texas and California, and proposed the idea to them that they form a single organization to channel funds and generate publicity for the Cristero cause. This collective effort would result in the formation of the Union Nacionalista Mexicana, an umbrella organization whose aim was to unite Mexican emigrants across regions and cities. By December of 1928, an article in *La Opinion* reported that the Unión Nacionalista "has been established now for some months, and already counts a multitude of Mexicans living in the United States as members, and has forty-six centers distributed in various cities along the border."[77] Over the next year, the Unión continued to grow, and by April of 1929, Bishop Manríquez y Zárate claimed that the organization held significant "territory" in the United States.[78] (The UNM would continue to expand and develop during the early 1930s, a story that will be discussed in greater detail in Chapter 5.)

Confrontations with Pro-Government Emigrants

Throughout the Cristero War years, Mexican emigrants who supported the Cristero cause participated in activities that were ever more public and visible. These activities, while primarily aimed at the Mexican government and its representatives in the United States, also served to provoke another group of people: the many Mexican emigrants who approved of the anticlerical efforts of Mexico's revolutionary government. Some of these articulated their opinions in conversations with the renowned

Mexican anthropologist Manuel Gamio, who interviewed seventy-six Mexicans in the United States during 1926 and 1927. Among these was Miguel Chávez, a farmer from Sinaloa who had emigrated to the United States in 1911. Chávez told his interviewer that he supported "the attitude of the government in wanting to destroy fanaticism."[79] Similarly, Santiago Lerdo, a porfirista refugee who founded a newspaper in Nogales, Texas, stated that despite his education in a Jesuit school,

> I am not a fanatic. I have always taken part in the liberal struggles and although I have nothing to do with the actual religious conflict I think that the Government more or less is right in the measures which it takes and the laws which it tries to enforce.[80]

Other interviewees shared their disapproval of the activities of Cristero supporters, whom they labeled as fanatical and violent. Angelino Bartres, a shoemaker from Guadalajara, Jalisco, stated that "it is one thing to be a Catholic like me and another to be a fanatic ... I don't say that Calles has done well or wrong by the priests but what I do say is that Mexico is backward on account of the Catholic fanaticism."[81] Wenceslao Iglesias, a farm laborer from Zacatecas who had come to El Paso as a teenager, likewise disapproved of the Cristeros, stating that "I don't believe that in order to be good here one has to go around shouting 'Viva Cristo Rey!' and killing one's brothers."[82] And Isidro Osorio, a railroad worker from Guanajuato, articulated both sentiments—disapproval of Cristeros and approval of the Mexican government—when he stated: "I am Catholic, but I am not a fanatic; and I think that what Calles is doing is well done."[83]

It is not surprising, then, that some of these anticlerical Mexican emigrants pushed back against pro-Cristero activities among their compatriots in the United States. As evidenced by their letters to various government officials at home in Mexico, many condemned the efforts of the Catholic clergy in the United States to foment rebellion, or at least anti-government feeling, among Mexican emigrants.[84] Immediately after the anticlerical laws took effect, one emigrant in Los Angeles wrote to President Calles to ask for help in "rising up with many people that are in agreement with you," in order to oppose the "many men that at the same time are gathering together here in Los Angeles to attack you and your ideas."[85] In addition to offering material support, others reiterated their own feelings of loyalty and solidarity for the Calles government and its anticlerical policies. In Chicago, "a group of workers of different industries, Mexican men that reside in Chicago," published an open letter to President Calles in the newspaper *Mexico*, declaring, "from the fields, factories, and workshops, we support the firm action of your Government, despite the pressure and threats of clericalism and its sympathizers."[86]

Beyond simply expressing solidarity with the Calles government, anticlerical emigrants also attempted to warn the government about the actions of Cristero supporters in the United States, as well as to counteract these pro-Cristero activities. For example, an emigrant and Protestant minister named C. T. Valdiva from Colton, California, wrote in September 1926 to the Ministry of the the Interior that "there is no doubt that the Jesuits of El Paso, Texas, are reviving the spirit of rebellion among the fanatical people from Mexico; this is known by everybody on this side of the Rio Grande." He then explained his efforts to mitigate the problem, adding that he was "trying to hold conferences ... in order to clear up certain dark spots that the Catholic press has placed in the history of the Revolution and its government." He also stated that he had visited San Diego to meet with the imprisoned followers of the failed uprising by General Enrique Estrada, a former delahuertista who had tried to launch a border revolt to overthrow the Calles regime, where he "spoke with them about their duties to be loyal to their government."[87]

Naturally, Mexican government officials in the United States supported the activities of these anticlerical emigrants. In the spring of 1927 in Gary, Indiana, the Mexican consul hosted an assembly in the city's public library during which speakers gave presentations exposing the activities of the local clergy. According to one source, some three hundred people turned out to hear these talks, which included the condemnation of a local priest who "dared to [publish] in the columns of a local newspaper a series of attacks against Mexico and against the colonia in Gary."[88]

Some loyalists even offered to come back to Mexico to fight on the side of the government. J. M. Chávez, from Saginaw, Michigan, offered on August 19, 1926, to organize a body of volunteers on the coast of Michoacán, where he had lived and worked for five years. In the meantime, Chávez was also working with some compatriots in the United States in order to counteract

the ideas that various Catholic ministers try to awake in our countrymen ... incit[ing] them with total frankness to rebel against Your Government, saying to them that it is now time that they follow the example of the martyrs and be ready to spill their last drop of blood in defense of religion.[89]

Chavez's observations may have seemed hyperbolic in tone, but they were based in truth. During the war years, thousands of Cristero supporters in many parts of the United States would participate in a variety of clandestine, illegal, and occasionally violent efforts to overthrow the anticlerical government of Mexico. Although they would never succeed in achieving this goal, their repeated acts of militancy would provoke surveillance and repression by the Mexican government and its representatives in the United States.

Arms Smuggling and the Turn to Militancy

In 1927, Antonio Rodríguez, an emigrant living in Chicago, wrote a letter to President Calles. In it, he professed his loyalty to the government and then launched into a lengthy complaint about the Mexican emigrant population in the United States. In Chicago, he reported, a Spanish priest at the Church of St. Francis was "controlling the whole Mexican colony." Other states were just as full of "fanatical Catholics." These emigrants, he said, "have already purchased a large quantity of arms," which they were planning to send to Mexico.[90]

Rodríguez, aggrieved as he was, was not exaggerating. Across the United States during the late 1920s, Mexican emigrants collected and donated money to buy guns, ammunition, and other war materiel for the Catholic cause. They then smuggled the weapons across the US-Mexico border and into the Cristero heartland in west-central Mexico. When the supplies finally arrived, they were desperately welcomed, since the Cristero troops were chronically short of ammunition. (Indeed, as a December 1927 bulletin from the Liga bluntly stated, the Cristero troops' most crucial need was "AMMUNITION, AMMUNITION, AMMUNITION."[91]) The armies of the government, by contrast, were larger, better organized, and better paid.[92] Through their smuggling operations, Mexican Cristero supporters were able to provide the soldiers with a significant amount of weaponry, and thus to relieve at least some of the persistent problem of weapons shortages.

In launching clandestine arms smuggling operations, Cristero supporters in the United States were participating in what some scholars have labeled a "time-honored occupation along the border."[93] Since the Mexican Revolution, various insurgents had followed a familiar pattern. First, they would enter into the United States to purchase weapons. Then, they would transport them into Mexico by bribing railroad workers to produce false manifests for loaded train cars; or buy fleets of automobiles, pack the guns inside, and then drive them into Mexico, sometimes bribing American soldiers guarding the border. Arms dealers in the United States, who stood to profit from the flourishing weapons trade, were known to help the Mexican smugglers evade the authorities.[94] While smuggling operations were certainly smaller in volume during the Cristero War than they had been during the Revolution, they would nevertheless prove to be of significant help for Cristero troops.

Arms smuggling was also highly illegal. Since the Mexican Revolution, the US government had made numerous attempts to control the shipment of arms across its southern border, and by 1924, a presidential proclamation explicitly forbade the exportation of arms and munitions of war to Mexico by anyone except those that "are approved by the Government of the United States for shipment to the Government of Mexico."[95] Although the law did not seem to deter smugglers, it meant that they were under constant surveillance by the US and Mexican governments. By early 1928, Mexican government officials noted to the US Department of Justice that "the rebels are getting ammunition in considerable quantities, probably from the United States."[96] That spring, a US military informant reported that "large quantities of arms and ammunition are being smuggled into [Mexico] from the United States . . . to the different revolutionary factors [sic]." As a result, the report continued, Mexican federal troops would be sent to assist customs officials in stopping the illegal smuggling.[97] A report from the US military envoy in Mexico from the same time period concluded that most of the Cristero leaders' supplies were coming from the United States, "where they seem to have plenty of sympathizers who are helping out with money and ammunition."[98]

Some of the Mexican emigrants organizing the purchase and shipment of arms for the Cristero troops were priests. One of these, not surprisingly, was Father Pascual Robles, the priest who had organized the unsuccessful rebellion of Simón Tenorio outside of Del Rio, Texas. Robles was apparently quite effective at convincing Mexican emigrants, refugees, and exiles to open their pockets in support of the Catholic cause; in the summer of 1927, he went on a fundraising mission along the border to collect money "from various persons in sympathy with the movement."

Among the donors were the Sisters of Charity at the Good Shepherd Home in San Antonio, who gave him fifty dollars, indicating that at least a few refugee nuns supported the militant effort. He used the funds that he collected to purchase arms and ammunition for Tenorio's group, as well as to outfit at least one other rebel group that he had organized along the border.[99]

To raise money for these gunrunning operations, other militant priests embarked on similar fundraising campaigns within Mexican parishes. In Brawley, California, a priest named Apolinar Ponce—originally from Guanajuato, Mexico, in the Cristero heartland—distributed "subversive pamphlets" among the population and traveled frequently to nearby border towns in order to meet with "conspirators."[100] He was also known to have led a "group of discontents" to smuggle arms and munitions from Brawley to a border area near Columbus, New Mexico.[101] Another priest, Pedro González, was accused of being the mastermind of a vast smuggling network along the border.[102] Sometimes these priests simply provided the space for arms storage, as when Mexican investigators discovered "a large quantity of .45-caliber pistols and ... materials of war ... hidden in the Church at Rio Grande City."[103]

Both US and Mexican intelligence records indicate that many of the lay Catholic political exiles, as well as the exiled Mexican hierarchy, made arms purchases during the Cristero war years. Even the exiled Mexican bishop Pascual Díaz—a conciliator who was not known to be a supporter of the militant movement—was suspected of getting involved in a scandalous incident of illegal arms smuggling in the fall of 1927.

The affair, known as the Pacific Arms Company case, unfolded over the summer and fall of 1927 and was investigated by US and Mexican law enforcement agents on both sides of the border. It involved an impressive quantity of arms, munitions, and supplies. Upon uncovering the conspiracy, US Department of Justice agents near Santa Barbara, California confiscated several trucks with $50,000 worth of contraband, including no fewer than

> thirty thousand 30-30 cartridges, nine hundred seventy Springfield [rifles], ninety-six Lugger pistols with butts and cartridge belts, five hundred extra thirty caliber barrels for Springfield rifles, three Lewis machine guns, six Rattler machine guns, thirty thousand special cartridges for thirty-caliber machine guns, a small motor for a boat, two Smith & Wesson pistols, four Skrag rifles, two thousand

thirty-eight caliber pistol cartridges, two thousand loaded clips for
forty-five caliber pistols, two hundred magazines for machine guns
with thirty-two cartridge capacity, nine Lewis machine gun magazines, one hundred twelve Rattler machine gun magazines, one
packet with antiseptic preparations, one box with miscellaneous
munitions.[104]

According to the agents' reports, the Pacific Arms case had numerous
connections to Mexican Catholics in the United States. The weapons were
meant to go to exiled general Félix Díaz, a nephew of former president
Porfirio Díaz, who some Mexican Cristero supporters hoped would overthrow the Calles regime and restore religious rights in Mexico. Some of
the money used to purchase the arms—a check for $1,290—had come to
the United States from Catholics in Guadalajara, the geographical epicen-
ter of the Cristero conflict.[105] Other funds had come from exiled priests,
and exiled Liga members were implicated as well: Luis Bustos, a leader
of the Catholic organization in San Antonio, had purportedly met with
general Díaz's secretary, Guillermo Rosas, in connection with the case.[106]
Finally, according to a report from the Mexican consul in San Francisco
that cited informants in Ciudad Juárez, even Bishop Pascual Díaz was
said to have participated from San Francisco, where, "in the company of
Manuel García [Herrera]," he had personally ordered "three boxcars full of
war material" to be sent to Mexico through El Paso.[107]

According to intelligence reports, Manuel García Herrera was a priest
who had "been active in Revolutionary matters since his crossing from
Mexico" in March 1927. In exile, according to intelligence reports, García
Herrera had been "closely associated with" both Bishop Díaz and the
more militant Bishop Manríquez y Zárate.[108] Eventually, US Department
of Justice agents would interview Bishop Díaz in connection with the
case, but when they reached him in New York, he denied all involvement
in arms smuggling, and any connection with García Herrera.[109]

Given the fact that Díaz would later withdraw support for the Liga, and
would eventually play a key role in reaching the settlement that ended the
1926–29 phase of the armed conflict in Mexico, it is quite possible that the
bishop's denials were true, and he had no connection with García Herrera.
Bishop Manríquez y Zárate, however, was definitively involved in the
arms trade. During his exile in Los Angeles, where he lived during 1928
and 1929, the bishop was remarkably successful at collecting funds from
Cristero supporters, occasionally sending thousands of dollars back to

Mexico to support the Cristero troops.[110] Indeed, he reported in December of 1928 that he was about to send the *"muchachos"* (he was probably referring either to Liga leaders or to the Cristero soldiers) a *"regalito,"* or little gift, of $13,000, although it is unclear whether this amount was ever sent.[111]

With some of the money he collected from Mexican Catholics in Los Angeles, Bishop Manríquez y Zárate and his contacts bought arms from US dealers and sent them to the Cristero battlefields in Mexico. From his post in Los Angeles, the bishop kept careful track of where weapons were most needed: in one letter, he alerted the Liga in Mexico about a distressing situation in El Salvador, Jalisco, which had been sacked by federal soldiers. "I take this opportunity to beg you to send them [whatever] war materials that you can," he wrote.[112] (Due to the fact that the Mexican government often monitored the mail between Catholic activists, Manríquez y Zárate often referred to arms with euphemisms, as when he wrote "I continue sending goods and toys to the Mexican children,"[113] or "the package of toys for the children of Jalisco is ready to be sent in the coming days."[114])

Laymen were also known to participate in the arms smuggling trade. A few months before the Pacific Arms Case was uncovered, agents had reported that Manuel Cervantes, a prominent lawyer in San Antonio, had brought around $25,000 to exiled Liga leader René Capistrán Garza to be used to buy arms and weapons, which would then be sent "through unpopulated areas in the jurisdiction of El Paso, along the border with Chihuahua." After that, rebel groups would transport the weapons into the interior of the country.[115] Capistrán Garza himself also went to Laredo, in order to send in ten thousand machine-gun cartridges; he was reportedly assisted in this mission by several *"méxico-texanos."*[116]

Catholic organizations took part in arms smuggling as well. During the war years, numerous members of the Knights of Columbus—both Mexican and American—engaged in smuggling activities. In 1927 Mexican government agents reported that the Knights were engaged in an "active campaign" among recently arrived Mexican emigrants from Jalisco, Michoacán, and other states "in order that, upon their return to the *patria,* they would bring back contraband arms and ammunition."[117] In another case, three members of a KOC chapter in Rio Grande City were said to be hoarding weapons on their ranch along the river valley.[118] Edelmiro Traslosheros, an exiled member of the Mexican Knights of Columbus and the Liga, was reported to be purchasing arms and ammunition specifically "for the Catholic rebels in Jalisco" and sending them into Mexico through places like Tucson.[119]

While most of the contraband munitions were sent over the border, emigrants also smuggled the weapons by sea. In 1927, Mexican officials searched the ship *Zamora*, which was traveling from San Pedro, California, to San Blas, Nayarit, and then to Puerto Vallarta, Jalisco. They soon discovered a hidden cache of weapons "destined for the rebels."[120] And in February of 1928, a variety of war supplies were delivered to Cristero troops on the west coast of Mexico, most likely after having been "shipped from Los Angeles in small boats."[121] Additionally, according to one scholar, Cristero sympathizers consistently made use of maritime connections between San Francisco and Mazatlán, Sinaloa, to import weapons.[122]

These transnational, clandestine arms trading routes extended not only southward from the United States, but also in the opposite direction. During the war years, Cristeros on the battlefields also sent envoys north across the border to buy and bring back arms. One was Cristero General Fernando González, who had "recently led the religious fight in the states of Jalisco and Oaxaca," and whose arrival in San Antonio prompted a flurry of "inquiries at different ammunition houses."[123] Another was the "famous Padre Vega," a priest and Cristero general who was known for his role in the assault on the Guadalajara-Mexico City train in the spring of 1927. Later that summer, he reportedly made an appearance in San Antonio to meet with lay Catholic activists in San Antonio.[124] Later, in November of 1928, US border patrol agents apprehended two Cristero soldiers in Eagle Pass, Texas, on their way back into Piedras Negras, Coahuila. The two men, pictured in Figure 3.3, were Bernardo Orizoga, from Techitlan, Jalisco, and Francisco Castellanos, from Guadalajara, Jalisco. They were driving a Ford truck equipped with a secret compartment full of ammunition, which they had purchased from the Garza Hardware Company in San Antonio.[125] Apparently, the men were quite a catch: a Mexican official called them "the most important agents that the rebels of Jalisco have commissioned for the buying and transportation of arms and munitions from the United States."[126] The two men were sentenced to six months of prison in the United States, at which point they were most likely turned over to Mexican authorities for further punishment.[127]

Arrests of arms smugglers, and confiscations of smuggled weapons, did not seem to deter Cristero supporters from continuing their attempts to get weapons across the border. If arms were confiscated in one place, they could certainly get through in another. In one instance, the secretary

FIGURE 3.3 Captured Cristero arms smugglers, October 1928
Source: AGN, IPS Volume 234, Expediente 15.

of Adolfo de la Huerta, the exiled military general who was known to have allied at times with Cristero supporters in the United States, wrote to both his Catholic and delahuertista followers "not to be demoralized by the arms and munitions that the Department of Justice agents had decommissioned in Tucson ... [because] a boat had easily embarked from San Francisco ... loaded with elements of war for the rebels of Jalisco."[128] Like the Revolutionary traffickers before them (and the many generations of twentieth-century smugglers that would follow), the Cristero arms dealers of the 1920s found that the US–Mexico border was highly permeable.

Military Recruitment, Rebellious Plots, and Armed Revolts

While the transnational effort to smuggle arms certainly provided significant help to Cristero troops in Mexico, and hundreds of Mexican emigrants, exiles, and refugees participated in the smuggling operations, arms smuggling was only one of the militant tactics employed by the most ardent Cristero supporters in the United States. Some emigrants simply left the United States and joined the Cristero army. In the Midwest, several emigrants were known to have enlisted: in 1927, two Gary residents, originally from the *pueblos* of Yuriria and Salvatierra in the Bajío region of Guanajuato, planned to go back to the battlefields near their hometowns. Another young man, named Ramiro Sánchez, left Detroit to fight in Uruápan, Michoacán during the same year.[129]

Priests and bishops, in the process of preaching to the emigrant masses, occasionally played a direct role in inspiring potential soldiers. In Big Wells, Texas, a priest from Coahuila "went around trying to recruit people ... telling those who[sic] he spoke with that a formidable counter-revolution was very soon to be unleashed in Mexico."[130] In Los Angeles, the militant exiled bishop José de Jesús Manríquez y Zarate of Huejutla, Mexico, helped to identify emigrants who were willing to become Cristero soldiers. In 1928, the bishop wrote to Miguel Palomar y Vizcarra, the director of the Liga in Mexico City, to let him know that

> there is here a group of young men ... who want to go to Mexico to fight for freedom; most of them are educated and well brought-up fellows [*muchachos cultos y de buena formación*] ... I beg you to make some suggestions to me about the place where these young men can rise up, the time of their uprising, etc.[131]

There were probably other men who went back to Mexico to join the rebellion, although their stories are not recorded in the archives. Still, most of the Mexican emigrants who were known to have participated in military efforts did so from within the United States. In fact, for most of the late 1920s, many Mexican political exiles actually competed with each other to direct the war effort from Texas.

During the first year of the war, René Capistrán Garza, the head of the Liga and an exile living in San Antonio, issued a manifesto, which was printed in El Paso and distributed on both sides of the border, urging Mexico's Catholics to take up arms. When, during the first weeks of January 1927, "rebellion flared in a dozen Mexican states," it was Capistrán Garza's declaration that was displayed and cited by Cristero troops.[132] Ultimately, Capistrán Garza was unable to effectively secure the support of Mexican and US backers, and political infighting between him and other political exiles prompted him to resign from his position in 1927. For him and for others, it proved impossible to direct the entire war effort from abroad. (And indeed, even within Mexico there were continuous disputes between the Liga and the Cristero leadership in the field, as we shall see in the next chapter.)

Thus, political exiles would employ other strategies in order to advance the Cristero military effort from the United States. As discussed previously, lay political exiles frequently collaborated with the numerous other enemies of President Calles who were living in exile. These men— who included Generals Adolfo de la Huerta, the delahuertista Enrique Estrada, and the porfirista Félix Díaz—were not Cristeros. In fact, they held a wide array of political affiliations, but each of them was committed to overthrowing the Calles government. Catholic political exiles held numerous meetings with these generals and their representatives in the United States. Some of them hoped that they could unite all the generals together with the Catholics and lead a coordinated attack, although there were disagreements about who should be the leader.[133] Despite these power struggles, the Cristero dissidents' attempts to conspire with the exiled generals were not completely fruitless. After 1926, many of these secular militants began to incorporate a call for "freedom of religion" into their manifestos and public pamphlets, as it became apparent to them that, in order to gain the support of Mexican Catholics in the United States and at home in Mexico, they would need to attract the Catholic exile faction.[134]

During the period between 1926 and 1929, Cristero supporters engaged in another strategic effort in the United States: organizing military rebellions along the US-Mexico border. Unfortunately for them, most of these did nothing to advance the Cristero cause in Mexico. Instead, they simply attracted surveillance and attention from the US and Mexican governments, while draining the militants of time and money, and occasionally costing some of them their lives.

The case of Simón Tenorio, described at the beginning of this book, was one such rebellion; it unfolded during August 1927. Earlier during that same summer, another military uprising had occurred that—although it would also end in defeat—involved a much larger number of people, over several places along the border. This was the uprising of José Gándara, a Mexican Catholic militant from El Paso, Texas. Even though his revolt was a failure, the way that it was planned and executed reveals much about the motivations and machinations of Cristero militants in the United States—and also helps explain the eventual failure of emigrant Cristero supporters' efforts to overthrow Mexico's anticlerical government.

The Gándara Rebellion

José Gándara was very different from Simón Tenorio, the hapless militant whose uprising collapsed in the desert of Coahuila. Gándara, pictured in Figure 3.4, was an educated, debonair member of El Paso's growing Mexican middle class. Fluent in English and Spanish, he was born in Chihuahua, Mexico, and came to the United States as a child in 1914. His father was an attorney for American mining companies—including the American Smelting and Refining Company, which had offices in northern Mexico—and left during the upheavals of the Mexican Revolution.[135] With such connections and experience, Gándara was able to build a decent livelihood. Prior to the Cristero War, he and his brother Carlos owned a photography studio, the Desert Picture Shop, on one of the city's main commercial thoroughfares. They specialized in providing passport pictures (a new requirement for Mexicans and Americans crossing the border) and sold artwork and photography as well.[136]

FIGURE 3.4 José Gándara, Cristero militant
Source: GU-Americas, Box 19, Folder 2. Published with permission of America Press, Inc.

Gándara was not only an established member of the nascent Mexican American middle class in El Paso, but he was also a devout Catholic. A member of the Knights of Columbus and the ACJM, he was well known in El Paso for his religiosity. In a letter of introduction to Wilfred Parsons, an influential Jesuit priest and editor of the magazine *America*, a Catholic priest in El Paso described the young man's "high enthusiasm and ardor" and affirmed that Gándara was "a staunch Catholic, and a daily communicant."[137] After the Cristero War began, Gándara became involved with the growing community of political and religious exiles and refugees that had been arriving in El Paso and San Antonio, eventually forging an alliance with René Capistrán Garza and other exiled members of the Liga.[138] Shortly thereafter, he took a hiatus from his photography business in order to dedicate himself completely to the Catholic cause in Mexico.[139]

Perhaps because of his longstanding connections with both US and Mexican Catholics in the region, Liga leaders in Mexico selected Gándara to serve as "an agent in the United States for the Catholic rebellion in Mexico." In September 1926, just two months after the outbreak of the armed conflict, he traveled to Mexico City to confer with Archbishops José Mora y del Río and Leopoldo Ruiz y Flores and with Bishops Pascual Díaz and Miguel de la Mora, among others; after the meeting, he claimed to have received their written authorization to raise money and material support in the United States for the Cristero rebellion in Mexico. Although ecclesiastical authorities in both countries later denied having provided Gándara with assistance, archival evidence suggests that, at the very least, his activities and those of his compatriots were regarded with great interest and granted tacit support by at least some members of the Catholic hierarchy on either side of the border.[140] For a while, he and René Capistrán Garza, the exiled Liga leader, worked together to plan Mexico's Catholic rebellion from the United States, although the two men ultimately had a falling out over logistics and finances, and Gándara decided to launch a revolt on his own.[141]

In doing so, he received strong encouragement from an exiled bishop, Juan Navarrete of Sonora, who had been living in both Nogales and Tucson since 1926. Navarrete was not widely known to have been a militant prelate, but there are indications that he was working behind the scenes to encourage the armed movement, particularly among the Yaqui Indian communities in northern Sonora. It was well known that Navarrete was in constant contact and communication with the Yaqui faithful giving Masses in Yaqui towns with the help of an interpreter. In his homilies, he had been known to tell his audience that they were right to take up arms in the government because their liberties had been suspended; and a 1926 Yaqui manifesto against the Mexican government apparently exhibited "the hand of the clergy" (specifically, that of Navarrete) in some of its language.[142] While religion was not the sole cause of the enduring conflict between Yaquis and the state, it seems to have cropped up more and more after 1926; one newspaper article about a band of Yaquis taking refuge in Nogales from Mexican federal troops in the spring of 1927 cited "loss of church" as one of the primary causes for their conflict with the government.[143]

It is not clear how Gándara and Navarrete met each other, but according to a later report about the Gándara uprising, the Sonoran bishop told Gándara that he was a "man of destiny whose duty it was to enter Mexico and place himself personally at the head of the Catholic rebellion." With the Sonoran bishop's blessing and support, Gándara began purchasing supplies of arms and ammunition and rounding up local supporters—many of whom were from the Yaqui Indian communities in the region—to join in the rebellion.[144]

Although Gándara was from El Paso, he decided to make Tucson his base of operations, possibly because it was a smaller town where he was less known. He began buying military supplies—apparently with up to $10,000 of his own money—from Esteban Borgaro, a novelty dealer with a variety shop there.[145] Meanwhile, his brother Carlos Gándara planned to lead a simultaneous attack from a town outside El Paso, and had enlisted a group of between seventy and eighty men in the El Paso-Ciudad Juárez area.[146] The two brothers reportedly planned to join forces with generals Nicolás Fernández, Juan Galindo, and other rebels currently in hiding in the mountainous Sierra de Chihuahua.[147]

Throughout the planning stages, Gándara kept his plot hidden from all but his closest allies. Despite his precautions, however, Gándara was being watched. US border patrol agents and Department of Justice agents, alerted by Mexican consular and secret service agents in the region about Gándara's suspicious activities (and already aware of him as a public figure who had spoken out against the Mexican government), quickly found out about his arms transactions with Borgaro. By the middle of June, just two weeks before the revolt was to begin, US agents arrested Borgaro and charged him with conspiracy to ship arms into Mexico, a clear violation of the President's Proclamation of 1924. Shortly afterward, the arms dealer confessed that he had delivered eight boxes of rifles to twelve Mexicans with a truck, "at a lonely arroyo a mile and a half northeast of Millville, a town just a few miles north of the US-Mexico border."[148] US officials hastened to the drop-off point, where they captured material including two dozen Winchester and Mauser rifles and carbines, fifty-four canteens, various containers for carrying ammunition, and clothes, hats, knife cases, and assorted other supplies.[149]

The rebels who participated in the Gándara plot were also carrying religious propaganda. Several months after the thwarted uprising, a Mexican secret agent, acting on a tip, found some of Carlos Gándara's weapons "buried in a little grove on the shore of the Río Bravo" on the outskirts of San Elizario, which was on the American side of the border. The stash he found included, in addition to a modest amount of weapons and cartridges, "two tricolor flags, a packet with medals of the Virgin of Guadalupe, [and] a box with propaganda and seditious manifestos."[150] Presumably, Gándara's Catholic militants had brought the religious propaganda in order to disseminate it to potential sympathizers in Mexico, just as Tenorio's band would do two months later.

The "lonely arroyo" where José Gándara's arms were recovered was on the outskirts of a Yaqui village; there, Department of Justice agents arrested twenty-five Yaquis and Mexican citizens, including one woman. Their initial testimony provided enough information to arrest Gándara on June 25.[151] Although a sympathetic sheriff had supposedly tipped him off to his impending detention and even offered him the chance to flee the country, Gándara decided that if he did so, "his house and place of business in El Paso would probably be raided and the files of the Rebellion . . . would be discovered." Determined to protect his contacts within the Catholic Church from the scandal that would result if these documents were made public, he turned himself in to police in Tucson. Nevertheless, Bishop Navarrete was arrested at the same time, on conspiracy charges.[152] In the fall of 1927, he, Navarrete, and the arms dealer Esteban Borgaro went to trial in Tucson.[153]

Gandara's Trial and Its Aftermath

The defendants were tried by federal tribunal in the US District Court in Tucson during the week of November 15, 1927. Gándara, Borgaro, and Navarrete were charged with conspiracy; in addition, Gándara was charged with "an infraction of the country's neutrality law by attempting to incite rebellion in Mexico."[154] The case drew daily coverage from the local press, numerous spectators, and "a formidable group of legal talent" in the defense counsel, which was led by Frank Curley, Navarrete's attorney, and W. H. Fryer, who was Gándara's.[155] It was reported that both Bishop Navarrete and Gándara were in good spirits throughout the proceedings, smiling repeatedly "at amusing incidents that occurred during the questioning of jurors."[156]

Testimony from the Yaqui Indians provided the basis for the prosecution's case: several stated Gándara had made a speech to them on or around June 24. One man, Francisco Félix, testified that he had seen Gándara deliver ammunition at the village, which was then "secreted by the Yaquis near the Santa Cruz riverbank."[157] When Gándara took the stand, he admitted to purchasing the arms, although he claimed that he had been assured by a reliable source that the embargo against importing arms and munitions into Mexico was about to be lifted. He confessed that he had bought ammunition for the Yaquis and given it to them, with orders that they hide it until he authorized the revolt. He also made the startling claim that some three thousand Yaquis were to have taken part in the uprising. Asked about his political leanings, Gándara "readily declared that his sympathies were with the Yaquis," claiming that his grandfather had lost his life defending the Yaquis from the Mexican government seventy years beforehand, and that his family home in Chihuahua had been ransacked by a band of Obregón's soldiers, which had caused the death of his mother.[158]

Interestingly, very little of the US press coverage devoted to the Gándara case mentioned religion as a factor in the foiled uprising, and it appears that the religious question was not raised during the trial. Only one article, in the *Tucson Citizen*, noted that Gándara's arrest had forestalled a revolution "based entirely on religious principles."[159] Given that he was well known on both sides of the border as the "Minister of War of the Catholics,"[160] it seems that either the attorneys prosecuting the case were not interested in raising the religious dimensions of Gándara's arrest, or that Gándara himself purposefully avoided making religious declarations during his trial, most likely in an attempt to protect the other Catholics who had supported his attempted revolt.

In the closing arguments, assistant US attorney Clarence V. Perrin called Gándara "one of the most ardent revolutionists that Mexico has seen for a long time ... a traitor to his own government." In response, Gándara's lawyer, William H. Fryer, gave an address "full of wit and sarcasm," in which he belittled the testimony presented by the government and claimed that the Yaqui evidence was inconsistent. He acknowledged that Gándara, like his family before him, harbored a "deadly hatred" for the current Mexican government of President Calles—whom he derisively called "His Turkish Majesty"—but he claimed that the evidence did not convincingly demonstrate a conspiracy between Gándara and Borgaro.[161]

After the arrest of Bishop Juan Navarrete, the exiled prelate who had assisted José Gándara during his attempted revolt along the border, there was much debate within US Catholic circles over how to get the bishop out of further legal trouble (and prevent a potentially embarrassing scandal from becoming public). Although some prominent Catholics suggested that the Navarrete be smuggled out of the country, Father John Burke of the National Catholic Welfare Conference was opposed to breaking the law, and decided instead to start a campaign to have the charges dropped. To this end, important Catholics such as Archbishop Edward Joseph Hanna of San Francisco, Patrick Cardinal Hayes of New York, Dennis Cardinal Dougherty of Philadelphia, Wilfred Parsons, the influential editor of *America* Magazine, and the Apostolic Delegate Pietro Fumasoni Biondi published press releases and made use of their connections with US government officials to lobby for Navarrete's cause. Burke himself secured a meeting with the assistant to the US attorney general, where he suggested that the indictment of Navarrete might harm the NCWC's ongoing attempts to facilitate a peace accord between Church and state in Mexico. The campaign for Navarrete's release seems to have helped him: the charges against the Sonoran bishop were dropped shortly thereafter and he was allowed to remain in the United States unmolested for the duration of the Cristero War.[162]

Like Bishop Navarrete, the arms dealer Esteban Borgaro would also walk free, at least initially: his case resulted in a hung jury and was scheduled to be retried.[163] Gándara was not so fortunate: he was the only one of the accused who was declared guilty. Sentenced to two years at the government penitentiary at McNeil Island and a fine of $1,000, he was not allowed to go free on bond—only to bathe and secure his belongings before going to the county jail. After his father paid the $5,000 bail, he was released; eventually, he was granted a stay of sentence while he appealed his conviction, and it appears that he never served the time in the federal penitentiary.[164] Nevertheless, for rest of 1927 and 1928—as the Cristero Rebellion reached its apogee in the Mexican countryside—Gándara would be effectively decommissioned as a Cristero revolutionist, as his free time was completely taken up with overturning the legal charges against him.

In the aftermath of the Cristero revolt, Gándara sought help from the Catholic Church in recovering the money that he had spent. Destitute and deeply in debt, Gándara traveled to Washington, DC, and New York in 1930 to solicit financial assistance from prominent American Catholics such as John Burke of the National Catholic Welfare Conference, various US bishops, Knights of Columbus leaders, and Wilfred Parsons of *America* magazine—even threatening to make public some incriminating documents in his possession unless he was given restitution. Nevertheless, the Depression-era Church seemed to be in no position to give him money, and representatives of the Knights of Columbus and the hierarchy continuously refused him repayment.

Although Church officials publicly denied responsibility for Gándara's plight, in confidential papers they were less circumspect. A lengthy missive from Wilfred Parsons to Arthur Drossaerts, the archbishop of San Antonio, in April 1930, seemed to claim some responsibility for Gándara's plight:

> I happen to know that Mr. Gándara is a most deserving subject for help. He was led into the adventure by important people and when he could easily have fled the country, he remained and allowed himself to be arrested in order to secure the release of Bishop Navarrete. If your Grace could see your way to doing this, I am sure it would be a very gracious action.[165]

In response to one of the letters, Father Burke, essentially admitted the involvement of prominent Mexican Catholics, stating that Gándara "sincerely believed that he was serving the Church in laboring for a successful armed resistance" and that he had been "no doubt assured . . . that he would be recompensed" by some of the Bishops of Mexico, who had never really accepted the position of the NCWC, which had refused to support the armed resistance. Burke later admitted that there had been evidence that Bishop Navarrete was in touch with organizers of the revolt at least a month before the uprising, and that the bishop "did not disapprove in any formal way" their plans.[166] Furthermore, Burke acknowledged that some of the money raised in the United States by US Catholics had gone "to the cause of armed resistance in Mexico."[167] Indeed, it seems that although the official position of US Catholic organizations such as the NCWC and the Knights of Columbus was to refrain from supporting the militant efforts of Mexican Catholics, there were occasional moments—including during the Gándara revolt—where funding from US Catholics found its way to Mexican Catholic rebels.

As a result of his appeals, Gándara did obtain some help from influential US Catholics, who successfully lobbied the office of Congressman Nicholas Longworth for a full and unconditional pardon from President Hoover on March 31, 1930.[168] Around the same time, Gándara requested and received permission from the Mexican government to return to Mexico, having been banned from entering the country during the height of the religious conflict.[169] By March of 1930, the ambassador of Mexico wrote a letter stating that the Mexican government "does not have any interest in the further prosecution of the case."[170]

After the 1930s, Gándara appears to have lived out a relatively quiet life. Nevertheless, for years after his revolt, he felt disillusioned. He had nearly sacrificed his freedom for the Catholic cause in Mexico, and yet, he thought, no one appreciated his efforts. Although he had received significant behind-the-scenes support from US Catholics during the aftermath of his trial, those connections seemed to have disintegrated once Gándara's pardon had been granted. "They're all for you, and they think you're the good guy," Gándara told his family in a letter after the war ended, "and yet as soon as you complain, everyone abandons you." For a while, according to his daughter Margaret (Mago) Gándara, he developed a drinking habit.[171] He died in 1961 without organizing any further rebellions against the Mexican government. After his death, he was described by a surviving sister as a brave patriot who had "joined the movement for religious liberty" and would "keep on working from Heaven."[172]

Defeat and Persistence

In the end, the Gándara revolt was no more successful than Tenorio's military uprising in the desert a few months later—although, unlike the Tenorio revolt, it would end somewhat more happily for the main protagonists, who managed to stay within the comparatively safer American justice system. Yet both events, despite the failure of their objectives, demonstrated that some Mexican emigrants in the borderlands were willing to participate in the Cristero rebellion, even at the risk of their lives and livelihoods. In the Gándara case, the involvement of Yaqui Indian participants supports recent scholarly arguments that some northern indigenous populations were sympathetic to the Cristero cause.[173]

When military revolts such as Gándara's are considered along with the other activities discussed in the previous pages—military recruitment, arms smuggling cases, fundraising, mass public events, religious spectacles, and even the dissemination of accounts of war through the media—it is clear that the Cristero War was certainly not a regional event limited to west-central Mexico. Instead, it was a transnational conflict that crossed borders—not only because it involved the global Catholic Church and a host of diplomats and international Catholic actors, but also because of the thousands of emigrants, exiles, and refugees who supported the cause from within the United States.

By monitoring, witnessing, and even participating in Mexico's religious rebellion from afar, these Mexican emigrants became political actors in communities that were increasingly suffused with the tense and conflicted politics of the homeland. During the late 1920s, even the simple decision to attend Sunday church services could make a political statement within Mexican communities. To listen to the denunciations of an exiled priest, and then to donate money when he asked for it, was to endorse the cause of Mexico's Catholic militants and condemn the revolutionary government. The most vociferous Cristero supporters overtly supported armed insurrection, and in doing so, they sometimes even attracted the support of US Catholics and members of the US Catholic Church, while simultaneously provoking the ire of government officials on both sides of the border, as well as of the many emigrants who supported the Mexican government's anticlerical actions.

Ultimately, however, Mexican Cristero partisans in the United States would encounter a number of challenges that thwarted their most militant efforts. Ultimately, the obstacles that had effectively put an end to the Tenorio and Gándara revolts would prove insurmountable by 1929, the final year of the Cristero War. First, though, these emigrants, exiles, and refugees would make one last attempt to overthrow the Mexican government from the United States.

4

Bishops, Knights,
Border Guards, and Spies

ON MARCH 3, 1929, the dissident general José Gonzálo Escobar launched a military revolt against the Mexican government from Mexico's northern border, in the state of Sonora. Over the course of the month, Escobar's uprising would prove a serious threat to the stability of the Portes Gil administration, prompting *jefe máximo* Plutarco Elías Calles (by then serving as the minister of war, but actually de facto head of state) to divert thirty-five thousand federal troops away from the west-central states, where they had been fighting the Cristeros, and toward the northern border.

The *escobarista* revolt was certainly not explicitly pro-Catholic in nature, and the conventional wisdom of the time—and the limited historical scholarship on the event—seems to have been that Mexico's Catholics were not particularly interested in the 1929 revolt.[1] Yet in fact, archival evidence indicates that the revolt was at least partially fueled by support from Cristero partisans. The leaders of the revolt included numerous revolutionaries who had previously repudiated Calles's anticlerical policies, including Gilberto Valenzuela, former candidate for the Mexican presidency; Jorge Prieto Laurens, a delahuertista and sometime Catholic ally; and Enrique Estrada, who had led a Liga-backed border revolt of his own in the summer of 1926.[2] Furthermore, Escobar and his collaborators actively courted assistance from disaffected Cristero supporters on both sides of the border. By providing the seemingly powerful escobarista rebels with money, men, and arms, the Catholic militants in the United States hoped to overthrow the anticlerical government of Mexico once and for all.

In California, and especially in Los Angeles, the escobaristas found a receptive audience as they plotted their insurrection. Soon after the revolution broke out in Sonora, the Los Angeles Bureau office of the Department of Justice began to receive reports that a group of exiled Mexican generals, including Enrique Estrada, "were holding revolutionary meetings over the Mexican Theater Building on Main Street" in order to recruit and organize bands of men to travel to Nogales, Sonora, to join the revolt. After the meetings, they began sending small groups of three, four and five men at a time to the border, some "by automobile and others by the Pickwick Stages."[3]

Some of these men were certainly Cristero partisans. A recruiting flyer for the Escobar uprising, shown in Figure 4.1, circulated in Los Angeles in early March. The information on the flyer indicated that the rebels were soliciting both volunteers and funds from among the Mexican Catholic community in California. The inflammatory language of the document explicitly framed the escobarista revolt as a religious rebellion. Stating that "the long-awaited day has arrived" and that good Catholics must seize the opportunity to give "the HOLY CAUSE all of your money and all of your blood," the flyer revealed an address where readers could go to receive instructions on how to donate money or join the rebels in Sonora, and reminded readers not to forget "the great debt and responsibility that we have in these moments for our Church and our Country" as well as the sacrifices of "our martyr brothers in Mexican territory." It closed with the call: "Down with the heretic government of the REVOLUTION! LONG LIVE CHRIST THE KING!"[4]

Cristero supporters in Texas also backed the revolt. The consul in El Paso passed along intelligence that several rebels who had just crossed the border at Nogales had received financing from "the Catholic clergy," as well as "Knights of Columbus along the border . . . of all nationalities."[5] In San Antonio, the gadfly priest Camilo Torrente, known for his overtly seditious sermons, told parishioners at the Cathedral of San Fernando to pray to God that the escobarista revolt would triumph. He also collected donations from "Mexican Catholics and Texas-Mexicans" to pay the passage for a group of militants that planned to go to Ciudad Juárez to join the uprising. Reportedly, some sixty men left San Antonio in order to "serve in the ranks of the Rebellion."[6]

To generate such widespread support from Mexican Catholics in southern California and Texas, Escobar and other rebels had made numerous promises that their movement would guarantee freedom of religion.

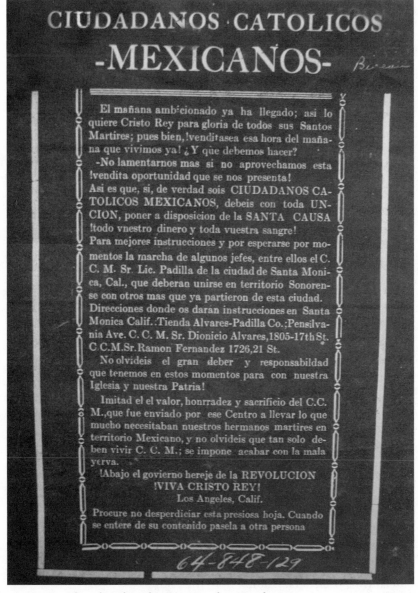

FIGURE 4.1 Flyer distributed in Los Angeles, March 1929
Source: NACP, Justice RG 60, Classified Subject File 71-1-74, Box 12342.

Escobar himself publicly advertised his sympathies in his promotional material. In a manifesto entitled "Libertad Religiosa" and signed by the military leader, he declared that his revolt would make "a national government instead of a sectarian one; a liberal government in place of an intolerant one" and proclaimed "the urgency of ending the fratricidal war provoked by the religious question."[7] Another rebel general and subordinate of General Escobar, Raúl Madera, stated during an interview with US immigration officials that he—as a landowner in Coahuila—had joined the revolutionary movement in part because under the rule of Calles

> the country has been under practically a Bolshevik system of government with agrarian and labor policies in my opinion highly detrimental to the best interests of Mexico ... Furthermore, the religious issue erected by the government against the will of 99% of the inhabitants has brought about a current of unrest.[8]

At least some of the rebel leaders seemed to have followed through with their promises to restore religious freedom in Mexico. In the first weeks of the revolt, the escobaristas briefly took control of Ciudad Juárez, directly south of El Paso, Texas. There, the commanding general, Miguel Valle, announced that churches were to be reopened "any time the priests care to return and conduct masses." When the news spread, crowds of enthusiastic Catholics gathered outside, "eager to hear the tolling of the bell announcing the first mass."[9] Twelve days after the revolt, the conservative Mexican emigrant daily *La Prensa* reported jubilantly (if prematurely) that, within the territory controlled by the rebel forces—which included the states of Sonora, Durango, and Chihuahua—"the rebel forces have solved the religious conflict" and that they had reopened the Catholic churches and allowed priests back into the region.[10]

Unfortunately for the aspirations of the Mexican Cristero supporters in the United States (as well as those in Mexico), the escobarista revolt collapsed in early April of 1929, after a concerted response by Mexican government forces. The rebellion had lasted only one month, and failed to overturn the Mexican government or even to hold on to territory within Mexico. Many of the movement's leaders escaped to Los Angeles, leading quieter lives while recuperating from their stinging defeat.[11]

The failure of the Escobar rebellion marked the final significant effort by emigrant Catholic militants to participate in a border uprising from the United States. Each earlier attempt had ended in abject failure as well. José Gándara was too embittered and impoverished to actively participate in the militant movement after the end of 1927. Simón Tenorio had disappeared into Mexico, and was probably dead. The other exiled revolutionaries who had lent support to the Cristero diaspora at various points over the past several years, such as Enrique Estrada, Adolfo de la Huerta, Jorge Prieto Laurens, and Félix Díaz, did not attempt any further uprisings after the spring of 1929.

This string of military defeats is partially explained by a simple reality: despite all of their efforts, the Catholic militants of the Cristero diaspora never had enough manpower, firepower, or money to overthrow the Mexican government from the US border. Yet there were also a number of other, more complex reasons for the failure of the Cristero border revolts between 1926 and 1929.

First, militant Cristero supporters were unable to elicit financial assistance from the people whose help they most needed: American Catholics. From the beginning of the war, Cristero militants in the United States never received sufficient funding from the US Catholic Church, or from the most vocal Catholic organization at the time, the Knights of Columbus. (As discussed in Chapter 2, however, several Catholic organizations did provide donations to Mexican Catholic refugees, and helped to publicize the conflict within the US media.) Internal conflicts would also undermine the efforts of the Cristero diaspora. Lay political exiles fought with each other over leadership, logistics, and strategy, and these squabbles took up valuable time and resources. Furthermore, the Mexican hierarchy in exile also split into two opposing groups: the conciliatory bishops, who advocated a diplomatic resolution to the Church-state conflict; and the militants, who urged the Mexican Church to support the armed rebellion to the end. Finally, Mexican Cristero supporters in the United States faced another obstacle that was perhaps the most insurmountable at all: government surveillance and suppression. Because they were organizing in one country in order to overturn the regime of another, they provoked the governments of both countries in equal measure. At a time when the US government—especially the Department of Justice—had begun monitoring the border more aggressively, would-be Cristero militants were surveilled and sometimes prosecuted by the United States. At the same time, Mexican secret agents continuously infiltrated dissident communities in the United States in order to curtail their militant activities.

Individually, each of these impediments—lack of US Catholic support; infighting among Cristero sympathizers; and government intervention—might have been surmountable. Taken together, they were simply too difficult for the Cristero supporters to overcome. The Cristero diaspora, despite operating transnationally, was subject to obstacles rooted in factionalism, boundaries, territoriality, and sovereignty.

American Catholics and Cristero Militants

During the late 1920s, Mexican Cristero supporters in the United States hoped to convince the American Catholic hierarchy to support the Cristero cause in Mexico. Initially, they were certain that Catholics in the United States would be so outraged by the atrocities of the Calles government that they would pressure the US government to break diplomatic relations with Mexico. They also thought that wealthy American Catholics would be moved to donate the hundreds of thousands of dollars that they needed to buy weapons and supplies for the armed rebellion. Indeed, many members of the US episcopate were vocal advocates for the Catholic cause in Mexico, particularly Bishop Francis Clement Kelley, the founder of the Catholic Extension Society. Father John Burke, director of the National Catholic Welfare Conference, was a consistent public supporter of the Mexican Catholic cause, and would eventually play an instrumental role in helping to negotiate a settlement between the Church and the Mexican government.[12] In addition, the bishops of heavily Mexican areas such as El Paso, San Antonio, and Los Angeles not only spoke out against the anticlerical campaigns in Mexico, but also provided support and funding to Mexico's religious refugees. Yet by and large, the US Catholic hierarchy was reluctant to provide financial support for the militant effort, refusing to fund either the Cristero uprising in Mexico or Cristero supporters in the United States.[13]

At the outset of the conflict, the Liga's leadership in Mexico persistently sought financial help from the US bishops. In the spring of 1926, the organization—with the blessing of the Mexican Catholic hierarchy—sent two delegates, Carlos Blanco and José Tercero, to the United States to meet with Father John Burke in Washington, DC.[14] At the meeting, the envoys spelled out exactly what they hoped for in terms of support from the US Catholic church: first, a "campaign of ideas in the United States"; second, "facilities offered to students who desire to enter seminaries and universities of North America and funding for . . . a Catholic University in Mexico"; and third, "financing [for] the Defense of fundamental liberties in our country." In other words, they wanted a propaganda campaign, aid for Mexican Catholic education, and money for the military movement.[15]

Convinced that the meeting had been a great success, Blanco and other Liga representatives wrote to Burke two months later, urging him to send them money right away, and informing him that they had already formed a committee to disburse the funds. Burke quickly demurred, declaring that "it is not within the charter of the National Catholic Welfare Conference to raise funds in any large way."[16]

Undaunted, the Liga's Executive Committee continued to seek assistance from individual American bishops. They were surely emboldened by discussions at the Eucharistic Congress in Chicago, held in June 1926, where numerous Mexican Catholic delegations and pilgrims held "secret meetings ... [and] asked for aid in their struggle."[17] Yet apart from sporadic financial assistance from particularly supportive prelates such as Archbishop Drossaerts in San Antonio and Bishop Schuler in El Paso, comprehensive financial support for the Liga would not be forthcoming. This problem first became evident in the fall of 1926, when the Liga's René Capistrán Garza, who had been living in exile in the United States since the summer of 1926, undertook an ambitious effort to solicit funding from the American Catholic hierarchy. Together with three colleagues, José Gaxiola and the brothers Ramón and Luis Ruiz Rueda, Capistrán Garza set out on a cross-country tour of various Catholic dioceses and archdioceses. Everywhere they went, however, their efforts drew a distinctly lackluster response:

> at their first stop, Corpus Christi, the bishop rebuffed them with the comment that people in his diocese didn't like Mexicans. In Galveston the bishop took a ten-dollar bill from his wallet and gave it to René, ending the interview. Houston, Dallas, and Little Rock were much the same—they got twenty, thirty, fifty dollars.[18]

They continued on to St. Louis, Indianapolis, Dayton, Columbus, Pittsburgh, Altoona, Harrisburg, New York City, and Boston—all cities with large Catholic populations. Even so, the trip was an unmitigated failure: they managed to raise only $3,260 (out of a stated goal of $100,000) and they spent most of their earnings on gasoline, food, and other travel expenses.[19]

By the mid-December of 1926, it was clear to the leaders of the Liga that no financial support would be forthcoming from the US Catholic hierarchy.[20] The reticence of the US Catholic leadership was perplexing and frustrating to Mexican Cristero supporters, but it can be understood within the political context of the period. While US Catholic leaders were indeed strongly opposed to the Calles government, and many of them supported the Cristero cause, they were caught in a sticky diplomatic situation. If they provided Mexico's Cristero militants with direct aid—especially weapons—they would be breaking the law, for it was illegal to help a foreign revolutionary movement that aimed to depose an ally of the United States.[21] Given the anti-Catholic sentiment that persisted within American political culture, the US hierarchy felt that it was in too precarious a position in the political firmament of the United States to collectively support the violent overthrow of the Mexican government.

The US Catholic bishops were not the only potential source of assistance, however, and Mexican Catholic exiles had great hopes that another Catholic organization, the Knights of Columbus, would prove more helpful. In February of 1926, Liga leader René Capistrán Garza and José Gaxiola—along with the Jesuit priest Carlos María Heredia, one of the early founders of the Catholic Students' League in Mexico—had attended the Knights of Columbus conference in Philadelphia in February of 1926 in order to lobby for support for the Cristero cause.[22] Later, on their tour of the United States, Capistrán Garza and his companions went to the Knights of Columbus headquarters in New Haven to appeal for donations. There, however, they had no more luck than with the bishops: they were brusquely turned away.[23]

Like the US hierarchy, the Knights were strongly opposed to the anticlerical Mexican government, but the organization's leadership planned to express their opposition exclusively through legal channels. First, they hoped to use their mass membership to put pressure on the Coolidge administration to withdraw diplomatic recognition of Mexico and to lift the arms embargo. Second, they began a campaign to collect donations from KOC chapters nationwide. They then used this pot of money, which they labeled the Million Dollar Fund, to publish pamphlets and other literature about the conflict for distribution in the United States. The KOC leadership in New Haven expressly stipulated that none of this money was to be sent to Mexico, or to be used to finance the Cristero rebellion.[24] As a result, the Liga did not receive any funding from the Supreme Council.

Still, the KOC was a large organization, with numerous chapters nationwide, and individual Knights often strayed from the official position of the Supreme Council by providing financial or material assistance to Mexican emigrants, exiles, and refugees in the United States. During the Gándara trial, for example, it was revealed that members of the Knights were apparently closely affiliated with the arms smuggling company Dunnegan, Momsen & Ryan of Tucson.[25] In addition, José Gándara's defense lawyer, William Fryer, was a Knight as well. As the war went on, rumors developed within the Mexican exile community that the Knights' money, which had been "raised apparently for the purpose of printing pamphlets," was being used instead "for the purchase of arms and ammunition."[26] Such rumors also reached the Mexican consuls in the United States, who were alerted that KOC chapters along the border were "undertaking an active campaign among the [emigrant] workers from Jalisco, Michoacán and other [states] so that when they come back to their Homeland, they will smuggle contrabands of arms and munitions."[27]

Piecemeal support from individual Knights and local councils, however, was not the kind of help that the Mexican representatives of the Liga were hoping for. As one exile wistfully reflected, "a while ago the Knights of Columbus voted a million dollars for the defense of the Catholic faith in Mexico ... If only this money were to pass to the Liga, how much good it could do!"[28]

Although the KOC and the NCWC would not back their efforts, Mexican Catholic political exiles had one final avenue to pursue in their search for money and supplies for the Cristero cause: wealthy Catholic magnates. In December of 1926, Capistrán Garza met with oil baron William F. Buckley (father of *National Review* founder William F. Buckley, Jr.) and Nicholas Brady, both prominent multimillionaires sympathetic to the Mexican Catholic cause. He also held a press conference at the Waldorf-Astoria, where he denounced the Calles government and outlined the main goals of the Catholic activists in Mexico. There, he flattered his American audience. "We millions of Mexicans whose voices are suppressed," he stated, "want you to know that there is a Mexico eager to adhere to and carry out the ideals of liberty that you carry out so gloriously in the United States."[29] Capistrán Garza had reason to hope that this strategy might work. He had received a boost from Wilfred Parsons, the Jesuit priest in New York who used his platform as the editor of the widely read Catholic magazine *America* to generate public sympathy for the Cristero cause.[30]

Yet in the end, this strategy proved just as fruitless as the others: Mexican lay exiles were unable to secure significant financial support from wealthy US Catholics. These men certainly had the same concerns as other Catholics about the legality of providing aid to a revolutionary movement. In addition, the US Catholics had become increasingly opposed to supporting either Capistrán Garza or the Liga-backed militant movement in Mexico; rather, Catholic leaders, along with the US government and the Vatican, had already "started down the road of diplomatic negotiations."[31] Furthermore, American Catholics were also dissuaded from providing financing to Mexican exiles because of the growing infighting between the political exiles and the Mexican hierarchy in the United States. After 1927, the tension between these exiled factions would become so public that any potential donors were most likely scared away.[32]

Political Infighting

By the late spring of 1927, René Capistrán Garza, having failed to secure funding from US Catholics, was dismissed from his post with the Liga. His reaction to the ouster revealed the deep tensions between different factions of Cristero exiles. From Texas, he wrote a bitter letter of resignation bemoaning the conduct "of a large number of Mexican Catholics living in the United States," whom he blamed for "inventing mistakes which I have not committed and calumniating me."[33]

Back in Mexico, the Liga leadership acknowledged that the different groups of Mexican Catholic political exiles in the United States had become remarkably divided. They blamed the split on Capistrán Garza's personality and strategy, and decided to see if a new leader would unite the exiled Catholic factions.[34] They named Luis Bustos, an exile who had been head of the Knights of Columbus in Mexico, as the new representative of the Liga in the United States. With Bustos in charge, they hoped that the Liga could try one more time to convince US Catholics to provide financial support to the Cristero cause.

Bustos began his tenure with optimism. He was certain that he had landed upon a solution to the two problems bedeviling the Mexican exiles: lack of US support and factionalism. This solution was the Partido de Unión Nacional (the National Union Party). Conceived as an exclusively US-run operation, the Unión Nacional would serve as a front for the Liga in the United States. As it was supposedly open to non-Catholics, Bustos and the Liga hoped that it would draw support from prominent Americans who were displeased with the Mexican government but unwilling to back a markedly Catholic cause. The party's platform could potentially appeal to a wider audience as well: while it advocated for freedom of religion and the right of religious denominations to own property, it also aimed to reinstate Mexico's liberal Constitution of 1857, although without its anticlerical directives.[35]

Unfortunately for Bustos and compatriots, the National Union Party not only failed to attract any significant American support, but also further alienated opposing factions of political exiles. René Capistrán Garza, as well as a group of exiled ACJM members including Luis and Ramon Ruiz Rueda, Carlos Blanco, and Salvador and Luis Chavez Hayhoe, issued a public repudiation of the Unión Nacional plan, basing their objections on the grounds that "To restore the Constitution of 1857 . . . was simple madness . . . the notion that such a ploy would gain American aid was a deplorable illusion."[36] Lacking unified support from the Mexican lay exile community or from American Catholics, the Unión Nacional was ready to crumble. The final devastating blow would come when an influential group of exiled Mexican hierarchy withdrew its support for the exiled lay political exiles in the United States.

The Mexican Catholic episcopate like the political exiles, was divided in its response to the Church-state conflict. Certainly, some members of the hierarchy in Mexico had initially supported the Liga and its attempts to organize the Catholic militant effort in Mexico. Other prelates—most famously Bishop José de Jesús Manríquez y Zárate of Huejutla—backed the armed revolt even after their exile to the United States. Another group, however, would ultimately prove more powerful. These were the concilia-tory bishops, who urged a diplomatic resolution to the conflict, and even-tually withdrew their support for the Liga and the armed movement.[37] What doomed the alliance between the hierarchy and the Liga was the rise to power of the man at the helm of the conciliatory wing: Pascual Díaz, the bishop of Tabasco (shown in Figure 4.2).

Díaz, the secretary of Mexico's episcopal committee since mid-1926, had initially supported the Liga's efforts to secure funding in the United States. (As discussed in Chapter 3, it is possible that he even provided help to Catholic arms-smuggling efforts, although he denied having done so.) Yet by the first half of 1927, the relationship between the Liga and Díaz's faction had crumbled. The conciliatory bishops, always uncertain about the legitimacy of the armed revolt, now became opposed to it, as the possibility of negotiating with the Mexican government became more concrete. Furthermore, they openly disagreed with the leadership of the Liga, which was attempting to organize the armed response. Despite the pleas of Liga leaders, the Mexican hierarchy consistently claimed to be without money, and refused to donate to the Cristero political exiles in the United States.

After the collapse of Luis Bustos's Unión Nacional in the spring of 1927, Díaz increasingly limited the Mexican hierarchy's support for the lay Catholic leadership. At the same time, he began to assume a role as the

FIGURE 4.2 Pascual Díaz, Bishop of Tabasco
Source: Archivo Histórico del Arzobispado de México, Fondo Pascual Díazy Barreto, Caja 7.

most powerful representative of the Mexican Catholics in the Cristero-era negotiations among the Vatican, US Catholics, and the Mexican govern-ment. As a conciliatory member of the hierarchy, Díaz aimed to reach agreements between Church and state through diplomacy, regardless of the desires of Mexican lay political groups for continued militancy.[38] Furthermore, after his exile from Mexico, Díaz had begun to develop pow-erful alliances with key Catholic leaders in Rome, New York City, and Washington, who quickly began to regard him as the most competent negotiator in the conflict. Indeed, by the end of 1927 the Vatican—which had never given overt support to the armed movement in Mexico—had appointed him the official Mexican intermediary with the Holy See. When he notified the rest of the bishops of his papal appointment, he directed them to withdraw their support for the Liga's military activities and informed them that they could no longer advocate armed popular action.[39]

To Catholic lay political exiles such as Bustos and Capistrán Garza, it appeared that Bishop Díaz wanted the Mexican lay groups to leave the high-level diplomatic negotiations to him alone. In fact, the bishop overtly asserted his position to Bustos and the lay exile community in January of 1928, when he wrote that

> the Holy Father has seen fit to name me Official Intermediate between the Apostolic Delegate [Pietro Fumasoni Biondi, apostolic delegate to the United States] and the [Mexican] Bishops, ordering me at the same time to let the Liga know (through its chiefs) that they must ... maintain their social and religious activities separately from those of political character, and furthermore, from the armed movement.[40]

Effectively, Díaz now sat in the most privileged position for negotiations among US Catholic leaders, Rome, and the Mexican government, while the Liga had effectively lost much of the bargaining power it once held. By early 1928, Luis Bustos, like Capistrán Garza before him, had given up trying to solicit funding or widespread support from US sources or from the Mexican hierarchy. Bustos retreated to San Antonio, Texas, where he struggled to redefine his relationship with the Liga and to mediate between the Liga and the conciliatory Episcopal Committee. Unable to reenter Mexico or to find employment, he wrote a tortured letter at the end of 1927 to the Liga's Executive Committee to let them know that he, his colleague José Ortiz Monasterio, and several other exiles were operating in a state of disillusionment, uncertainty, and penury:

> I prefer to die in front of a firing squad than to find myself in such anguish. I cannot bear death by starvation, much less that of my family,—YOU HAVE THE LAST WORD.
>
> I want you to give [us] directions ... Without money to move, without documents to show, what can I do? ... You order me to run and then you tie my feet.[41]

After 1928, Bustos, Capistrán Garza, and other lay Catholic exiles seemed to realize that they would not be receiving significant support from American Catholics, nor would they have the backing of the Mexican Catholic hierarchy. Furthermore, the internal divisions among exiled factions and among members of the hierarchy would prevent the exiled Liga leaders from any coordinated, comprehensive militant operation. Instead, other Mexican emigrants—particularly those who worked with Bishop José de Jesús Manríquez y Zárate during his exile in Los Angeles—would continue to try to advance the Catholic cause from the United States through fundraising, arms smuggling, and support of movements such as the escobarista revolt. But these actions were much smaller in scope than what the lay Catholic leaders, in the initial months of their exile, had hoped for. Furthermore, two far more powerful forces would largely thwart even these smaller-scale efforts: the expanding reach of the governments of the United States and Mexico.

State Responses to Transnational Cristero Activism

The experiences of Simon Tenorio and José Gándara, the two Catholic militants whose plans were discovered and thwarted by government authorities on both sides of the border, have already illustrated how a variety of government officials were cracking down on insurgents on both sides of the border. During the 1920s, both the US and Mexican governments were actively trying to gain greater control over the flow of people and goods across the US-Mexico frontier. The rationale was different on either side of the line, primarily because the United States was focused on regulating the entry of people as well as the flow of illegal goods from Mexico, while Mexico hoped to control emigrants' exit.[42] Yet, in their efforts to establish sovereignty and order over their shared frontier, both governments began paying much closer attention to the activities of Mexican citizens as they crossed it.

For the United States, one of the greatest problems was smuggling. Prohibition (1920–1933) had created a market for bootleggers willing to bring alcohol from Mexico to the United States, but the more serious problem, as discussed in Chapter 3, was arms trafficking. Since 1906, US neutrality laws had prohibited military expeditions against any country with which the United States was at peace, and a 1924, presidential proclamation explicitly forbade the exportation of arms and munitions of war to Mexico by anyone except those that "are approved by the Government of the United States for shipment to the Government of Mexico."[43] It was, therefore, the goal of the US government to prevent arms from crossing into the wrong hands in Mexico, and US officials were eager to do so. Yet establishing control over the border during the Cristero War years would present numerous logistical difficulties for US government officials. Multiple agencies were ostensibly in charge of the border the region itself was vast, and the number of personnel in each of these agencies was still relatively small. As a result, and as described previously, Cristero supporters and others who wished to smuggle contraband were frequently able to do so without being caught.

The special agents who conducted most of the surveillance of Mexican emigrants during the 1920s were employees of the Department of Justice's Bureau of Investigation, the predecessor to the FBI. These agents played perhaps the most important role in monitoring the activities of lawbreaking Mexicans in the border region during the Cristero War years. Although no more than ten or twenty different agents followed numerous Mexican suspects, they were responsible for producing in-depth intelligence reports about their subjects, often pursuing suspicious characters until they had enough information to arrest, indict, and convict them—as in the José Gándara case, when department of Justice and Border Patrol agents, as well as the Tucson sheriff, had followed Gándara since at least several weeks before his arrest in late June of 1927, and built an immense surveillance file that they used as evidence in his trial.[44]

Nevertheless, their work resulted in relatively few convictions during the period between 1926 and 1929. One agent, Gus T. Jones, summarized the difficulties in obtaining sufficient evidence to prosecute neutrality cases:

> the professional revolutionists and smugglers ... are very astute, know the border like an open book and are cunning enough to send their arms and ammunition across ahead of them or obtain these munitions from some previous cache in Mexico.

Furthermore, Jones pointed out, one district alone included five hundred miles of the border and had only seven investigators assigned to its office. Since the Department of Justice agents were not responsible for patrolling the border itself (and could not have done so with the number of personnel available), Jones admitted that there were "hundreds of places where [smugglers] can cross with a very slight chance of detection."[45]

Reinforcing the efforts of the Department of Justice was the US Border Patrol, which had been founded only two years before the Cristero War broke out, in 1924. By the late 1920s, the Border Patrol was still a new force, and employed fewer than fifty border guards, charged primarily with preventing the smuggling across the border of alcohol, narcotic drugs, arms and ammunition, and undocumented migrants. Conceived as an elite operation, only men between the ages of twenty-one and thirty-six who stood over 5'7" and passed a grueling physical exam were eligible for the job. Their surveillance of the border was done largely on foot or on horseback.[46]

At the outset, the challenges facing the new agency were just as monumental as those that the Department of Justice confronted, and easily more dangerous. While Department of Justice agents were focused more on investigative work, Border Patrol agents were constantly subjected to greater physical strain and risk. Nevertheless, they managed to seize significant amounts of contraband from smugglers. Articles in two Arizona newspapers described a typical week for the Border Patrol in May 1927, in which the Agency's thirty-four officers "covered 4854 miles of the border country, 3872 by motor, 419 miles on horseback, and 482 miles on foot." During that time, they checked 2,128 individuals for "narcotics, liquor and other contraband" and personally confiscated 24,000 rounds of cartridges, 36 Krag rifles, several machine gun magazines (worth about $1700) as well as two Ford automobiles (worth about $350) and "two burros, one saddle and bridle, one pack-saddle, two dozen cans of sausage, and ten gallons of mescal."[47]

A third agency in charge of controlling border traffic was the US Customs Office. Customs officers were more numerous than those from either Department of Justice of the Border Patrol—there were 150 in 1911—and they were ostensibly "at the forefront of stopping arms smuggling."[48] However, they rarely made arrests, and they confronted the same difficulties as the other two departments in intercepting any contraband, as a report from a Department of Justice agent attests:

> The Collector of Customs in this District advises that it is absolutely impossible with his present force of men to make a search for contraband going to Mexico as it would necessitate several inspector [sic] and a corps of carpenters to open all boxes and cases ... in other words, it is very easy to place a Thomson machine gun in a case of shoes and this no doubt is being done.[49]

Each of the three agencies responsible for monitoring and controlling the US-Mexico border faced immense challenges. As a result, Mexicans who wished to send guns to the Cristeros from the United States were often able to do so successfully. Nevertheless, the combined efforts of the US government agents would certainly put a damper on the arms smuggling attempts. Even more importantly, US agents' investigative work in the border region would prove instrumental in thwarting actual military uprisings, such as those of Simón Tenorio, José Gándara, and other would-be rebels.

In their efforts to crack down on arms smuggling and border militancy, US government agents worked closely with representatives of the Mexican government, which was naturally quite concerned with the activities of Cristero militants in the United States. One instance in which this collaboration was particularly important was the uprising of the exiled militant Enrique Estrada, a delahuertista general in exile in the United States. In the summer of 1926, Estrada tried to lead a revolt against the Calles government from southern California. Although Estrada was not principally a Cristero supporter, he, like other exiled delahuertistas, had some connections to the Catholic movement. (In fact, Liga leaders had hoped that they could ally with him during his 1926 uprising, and he would later collaborate with Cristero supporters in the United States during the Escobar uprising of 1929.)[50]

Estrada's attempted revolt involved numerous Mexican emigrants from southern California. In preparation for the uprising, he and his associates recruited between 150 and 350 men and sent them to the Imperial Valley disguised as laborers and cotton pickers; most of them were from Los Angeles, although a few were from San Diego.[51]

Despite Estrada's efforts to remain clandestine, informants from within the Mexican emigrant community tipped off Bureau of Investigation agents in advance. The agents then followed Estrada's convoy from Los Angeles to the Mexican border. There, they arrested Estrada and 150 of the recruits; most of the detentions were made on August 14th and 15th, 1926. Estrada was sentenced to a year and nine months in the federal penitentiary and a fine of ten thousand dollars. His generals served hefty penalties as well: over a year in prison for most of them, and fines of one to five thousand dollars. The lower-ranked recruits each served around six months of jail time.[52] In recognition of the Bureau's efforts to regulate Mexican uprisings from within US territory, the Mexican government sent engraved pocket watches to the eight agents who had worked on the case (the watches were later returned to the Mexican government by US officials, so as to avoid the appearance of bribery).[53]

Binational cooperation of this sort was not always as smooth during the 1926–29 time period. Indeed, agents on both sides occasionally expressed frustration with each other. In 1927, agent Gus T. Jones expressed his opinion that Mexican Secret Service agents frequently exaggerated their reports about the seditious activities of Mexicans in the United States "in order to stay on the payroll."[54] On the other hand, some Mexican government representatives were convinced that US officials were not doing enough to monitor Mexican communities in the United States and prevent them from undertaking rebellious activities. As Emiliano Tamez, the Consul of Eagle Pass, put it in 1927,

> everyone knows that the enemies that live here go about buying arms, mounts, and other second-hand war materials, but the American authorities don't find sufficient merits to proceed against them and they are closing their eyes so as not to see, and leave them to work in all freedom.[55]

Perhaps spurred by the perception that US authorities were not doing enough to control dissidents, Mexican government authorities in the United States embarked on their own surveillance projects in order to monitor the emigrant community for evidence of militancy, and prevent military uprisings along the border.

The Mexican Government and the Cristero Diaspora

Given Mexico's history of mass migration to the United States, and the tendency of Mexico's political dissidents to use the United States as a haven and a place to regroup for new uprisings from north of the Rio Grande, all of Mexico's presidents since at least the mid-nineteenth century monitored the activities of Mexican emigrants in the United States. The Calles government, however, reformulated and expanded Mexican intelligence in the United States during the Cristero War years, in particular by strengthening the role of the Confidential Department (a department within Mexico's Ministry of the Interior).[56] During the late 1920s, the Confidential Department conducted a range of domestic and international investigations of political rivals, electoral candidates, crimes, and the activities of foreigners in Mexico.[57] These efforts would supplement the longstanding attempts by Mexican consular officials to monitor the activities of dissident Mexican emigrants. Since the Confidential Department's reforms took place at the same time as the Cristero War, numerous Confidential agents were assigned to investigate Cristero dissidents in Mexico and abroad.

By late 1925, the Confidential Department's director, Francisco M. Delgado, had begun efforts to expand the Department's activities into Mexican emigrant communities in the United States. In a memorandum to the Ministry of the Interior, Delgado alerted officials that "enemies of the current administration" were "making a concerted effort" to overturn the Mexican government from the United States, and proposed that some twenty Confidential agents "who would be knowledgeable of the people and the terrain in which they operate," be sent to various border cities and towns. There, he suggested, they could work aboard the trains as they crossed the border into Mexico, as well as in places in the United States where "the dissidents live and work."[58]

By early 1926, the Confidential Department had dispatched at least nine agents to work along the border and inside the United States, and Delgado ordered other agents to the United States in response to specific events.[59] In fact, Delgado was known for carefully selecting the appropriate agent for a given investigation, sending agents with particular talents and characteristics to monitor situations that they were best qualified for and most knowledgeable about.[60] After receiving their assignments, agents traveled to the site of the investigation, and then reported back to the department. Upon reviewing agents' reports, Delgado would then recommend that Calles send federal forces to problem areas.[61]

By necessity, Confidential agents working within Mexican emigrant communities led an itinerant existence. Unlike consular employees, who generally stayed within their assigned city or town, Confidential agents traveled constantly by train and by car—often over great distances–in order to pursue leads, attend rallies and events organized by anti-government groups, and interview their informants. For agents in the United States, the purpose of attending such events was to assess the relative danger that these people or groups presented to Mexican national security. They evaluated whether a particular person had attracted a significant following, and kept track of the communities that were most supportive of the Mexican government.[62]

Confidential agents were very eager to avoid being detected by the emigrants that they surveilled, and they implemented a number of different techniques and disguises. One internal memorandum, for example, suggested that agents carry a press pass and pose as journalists, since "we believe [it is] the best way to introduce oneself into distinct social circles . . . from the modest barrio dance to the Political Clubs."[63] A report by agent Carlos I. Flores began with the question "What Should the Confidential Agent Know?" and shared several practical suggestions, such as to "begin conversations about topics that are different from the true object, [only gradually] directing them toward convenient terrain, to carefully collect the observations, opinions, judgments, and data of the interlocutor."[64]

Many agents were required to send frequent reports—as often as twice a day—detailing both their own activities and those of the dissidents whom they were monitoring. Their work demanded that they exercise diplomacy and tact, and that they cultivate good relationships within the Mexican consulates (where consular employees were also engaged in intelligence-gathering efforts within emigrant communities), among officials in Mexico's Department of Migration, and occasionally with US Department of Justice agents and Border Patrol employees. Agents frequently monitored the mail as well: a wealth of intercepted letters, submitted by agents to their superiors, can be found in the archives, and the Confidential Department kept lists of people, both inside and outside Mexico, who were receiving "correspondence of a seditious nature."[65]

Most of the work of the Confidential agents who were sent to the United States during the late 1920s took place along the US-Mexico border or in nearby cities and towns. San Antonio, where many members of the exiled Catholic hierarchy had resettled during the Cristero War, was reportedly "bristling with spies."[66] Some agents, however, ventured much further afield. In June 1926, for example, San Antonio–based agent Francisco de la Garza (who signed his letters as "Confidential Agent No. 47") traveled to Chicago to surreptitiously attend the Catholic Eucharistic Congress and spy on Mexican participants there.[67] Once in Chicago, the agent attended numerous events hosted by and for Mexicans, compiling lists of the attendees and sending detailed reports about anyone who spoke disparagingly about the Mexican government.[68]

Throughout their travels, Mexican government agents carefully forged alliances with emigrants who were sympathetic to the Calles regime, for such people could serve as valuable unpaid informants. As discussed in the previous chapter, government loyalists in the United States sent dispatches to Mexico throughout the Cristero War years. Sometimes, these reports contained specific information about planned military insurrections. In 1928, one informant wrote to the Ministry of Foreign Relations with alarming news:

> The Catholics, priests and Knights of Columbus, as many Mexicans as Americans, helped by an innumerable amount of dissidents, are surreptitiously preparing a military uprising that will be aimed primarily at Nogales, maybe at Ojinaga, and at Baja California.

The informant also noted that Catholic militants were purchasing arms, horses, and other military supplies "in various parts of the United States" and sending this material across the border in places such as Ciudad Juárez, Nogales, and San Diego.[69] This type of information was extremely valuable to government agents, since it helped them to target their security efforts.

Confidential agents also monitored newspapers and other publications produced by Mexican communities in the United States. During the late 1920s, Confidential and consular agents prohibited Mexican citizens from bringing inflammatory texts into Mexico, and put pressure on Mexican exiles who published anti-government tracts. As early as 1925, Mexican officials along the border attempted to prevent the entry of certain circulars.[70] Although this practice generated complaints of "interference" from US consular officials on the border, it continued through the 1930s, by which time the Mexican government had disseminated a long list of banned publications—most of them produced by Mexican political exiles—that were "treating in an injurious ways the Institutions of the Country, and observing a subversive attitude."[71]

Mexican government agents also created and shared extensive *listas negras* (blacklists) of Mexican citizens who were prohibited from entering Mexican territory.[72] Maintained continuously from at least August 1926 until at least March 1930, the lists included those Mexicans who had been deported by the Confidential Department, as well as Mexicans who had voluntarily left the country and, for any number of reasons, were considered enemies of the Calles regime and therefore barred from reentry. Naturally, many of the names on these lists during the late 1920s were Catholic dissidents.[73]

The intelligence behind the blacklists often came from consular officials, who lived within Mexican communities and could thus keep close track of seditious Mexicans who entered and left their region. The blacklists were shared among the Mexican consulates, Mexico's Migration Service, and the Confidential Department. Agents would then use the lists to verify emigrants' identities, either at checkpoints along the border or on the trains that crossed into Mexico. In February 1927, for example, Confidential agent Fernando de la Garza requested that special attention be paid to "the trains that come to and return from the North" in order to watch for Catholic conspirators who were known to be traveling at that time.[74]

The blacklists also demonstrate that the Calles government frequently targeted Catholics for exclusion during Cristero War years. Not surprisingly, the administration wished to keep out priests and the Catholic hierarchy; several of the lists contained the names of priests along the border and the interior of the United States who were banned from entering Mexico.[75] Immediately after the US Department of Justice thwarted the border uprising of Enrique Estrada in San Diego in August 1926, the Migration Service circulated a general order that agents prohibit the crossing of any "clerical elements against the constitutional Government."[76]

The Calles government also made a practice of blacklisting female religious and any women suspected of collaborating with them, since they were known to disguise their identities and cross back into Mexico with seditious material. In a memorandum to the Department of Migration, Confidential Department head Delgado reminded agents that:

> Catholic elements make use of nuns who enter or leave our country, in order to send correspondence to the Bishops and other prelates as well as to rebel groups, acting as agents in the development of their plans against the Government and public tranquility.[77]

Confidential agents kept lists of such women's names and used the lists to prevent them from crossing the border, as when they successfully blocked the entrance of Sisters Soledad Hernández Vázquez, María Nava, María Villagómez, and Francisca Regalado at Nuevo Laredo in late 1928.[78] As late as 1930, the Department instructed its agents that no nuns could enter Mexico without express written permission.[79] Laywomen who were known to associate with nuns were banned as well: one Confidential agent in the border state of Tamaulipas advised the Ministry of the Interior that a young woman named María García should not be permitted to cross the border, as she was "a hotheaded fanatic" who intended "to enter the country to meet up with some nuns that are incognito."[80]

Between 1926 and 1929, many of the blacklists excluded Catholic lay dissidents, some of whom were longtime residents of the United

States. In August 1926, when the Club Latino de Tucson published an anti-government, pro-Cristero protest in the *Tucson Citizen*, the Consulate of Tucson compiled and distributed a list of all the club's members, so that "in case they cross into our country they can be consigned to the Agent of the Public Federal Ministry."[81] Along with the individuals' names, the list noted their citizenship status and any Catholic affiliations, such as membership in the Knights of Columbus.[82] The use of blacklists continued through at least 1929, when the Confidential Department generated a list hundreds of pages long, with names of Mexicans who had taken part in the escobarista revolt. This list included the religious affiliations of each individual and described several as being *"católico extremado."*[83]

A Problem of Timing

Through their efforts to monitor the organizations, meetings, plots, and publications of dissident Mexican Catholics in the United States—and to keep Cristero supporters from entering Mexico—Mexican government representatives from the Confidential Department, as well as from the Mexican consulates in the United States, helped to undermine the militant movement within the Cristero diaspora. Aided by US government officials, their activities helped to ensure that there would be no successful Catholic militant uprising along the border during the late 1920s. (This binational cooperation in defusing Catholic militancy is particularly noteworthy, given the often-tense diplomatic relationship between the two governments during the late 1920s.) The Catholic militants were further hampered by their own internal divisions, as well as by a lack of financial support from American Catholics.

Taken together, these obstacles would prevent the most militant members of the Cristero diaspora from organizing a sustained revolt along the US-Mexico border. Perhaps even if these obstacles had not existed, Catholic militants in the United States would never have mounted a successful rebellion. After all, the distance between the border and the Cristero heartland was immense, and a successful border uprising would have required an enormous amount of money, weapons, and military recruits. Certainly, most Mexican rebels have historically used the border as a place to regroup, recruit new participants, and gather supplies, preferring to return to the Mexican interior to fight rather than to conduct a rebellion on the border. Yet the Cristero militants along the frontier faced the particular bad luck of timing: the Cristero War occurred in a period when the two national governments that they confronted were asserting greater administrative and military control over the border region. In fact, they may have inadvertently helped provoke the Mexican and US governments to intensify their surveillance efforts, since border agents, Department of Justice agents, and Mexican employees of the Confidential Department were well aware of the problem of Catholic militants, and wished to put an end to their seditious activities.

The Cristero diaspora, in turn, was prompted by these insurmountable obstacles to turn away from militancy after the collapse of the Escobar rebellion in March 1929. Even more importantly, the subsequent cease-fire between Church and state made the possibility of an successful armed revolt even more remote. Although a few of the most militant exiles—especially bishop José de Jesús Manríquez y Zárate—would continue to hold out hope for an eventual rebellion, the rest of the Cristero supporters in the United States gradually began to search for other ways to express solidarity with the Catholic cause in Mexico. During the 1930s, Cristero partisans in the United States would begin to participate in new types of collective action in order to further the Cristero cause. In doing so, they would lay the groundwork for an emerging religious nationalism that was forged by the religious and political conflict in Mexico.

5

After the Arreglos

THE CRISTERO WAR officially came to an end in the summer of 1929, when the Church and state finally reached an agreement that seemed to set the stage for peace. This occurred only after long negotiations among President Calles, his handpicked successor Emilio Portes Gil, conciliatory members of the Mexican Catholic hierarchy (including Pascual Díaz and Leopoldo Ruiz y Flores), American ambassador Dwight Morrow, Vatican representatives, and prominent US Catholic actors such as Father John Burke of the National Catholic Welfare Conference and Father Edmund Walsh, vice president of Georgetown University. The Liga and the Cristero army were largely left out of the negotiations.

On June 21 Archbishop Ruíz y Flores, by then the apostolic delegate to Mexico, and President Emilio Portes Gil each released conciliatory statements to the press.[1] The president declared that it was "neither the spirit of the Constitution, nor the law, nor of the Government of the Republic, to destroy the identity of the Catholic Church or any other church, nor to intervene in any manner in its spiritual function."[2] Ruíz y Flores, for his part, stated that "the Mexican clergy will resume religious services in accordance with existing laws."[3] Soon, the news of the settlement (known as the arreglos, or arrangements) had spread to the battlefields—in some cases, by pilots dropping leaflets from airplanes. Over the next several months, the majority of Cristero soldiers and generals were directed to lay down their arms.[4] Once again, the churches opened their doors, and Mexico's Catholics were ostensibly free to worship and receive the sacraments.

In the United States, Mexican Cristero supporters followed the news of the settlement with intense interest, and mixed feelings. There were certainly many Mexican emigrants who were hopeful that the worst days had passed for the Mexican Catholic Church. Some of the most optimistic were the exiled Mexican clergy, most of whom were finally permitted to reenter Mexico after three years of exile. As soon as they could, hundreds of priests and nuns in the United States packed their bags and boarded trains for the homeland; many members of the Mexican hierarchy, too, prepared to return to their home dioceses and archdioceses. In and around Los Angeles, there were some forty parishes that saw Mexican priests head back to Mexico.[5] (Some of these returnees are pictured in Figure 5.1.) In San Antonio, Mexican Catholics held a "jubilee of thanksgiving" to send off the returning prelates.[6]

Yet such enthusiastic early responses masked the deep trepidation that many Cristero supporters on both sides of the border felt about the settlement. The Cristero soldiers in Mexico, their generals, and the representatives of the Liga had all been excluded from the negotiating table, and their concerns—particularly their desire for constitutional reforms that would overturn the anticlerical clauses—went almost entirely unaddressed in the arreglos. Additionally, the Mexican government refused to allow the return from exile of its most persistent opponents, including Bishop José de Jesús Manríquez y Zárate and Archbishops José María González y Valencia and Francisco Orozco y Jiménez, as well as lay political activists

FIGURE 5.1 Priests returning from Los Angeles to Mexico, July 5, 1929
Source: Author's collection.

such as René Capistrán Garza, Luis Bustos, and Juan Lainé. Indeed, Cristero supporters had little hope that the Mexican government would back down from its anticlerical policies. According to one scholar, many Mexican Catholics—as well as Catholics around the world—would come to see the arreglos as nothing more than "a deception" of the Cristeros by the powerful actors, both clerical and secular, who had negotiated the settlement.[7]

Cristero supporters within the Mexican emigrant community shared this skepticism. Miguel Venegas, the owner of a small Mexican grocery store in Los Angeles and a former Cristero partisan from Jalisco, voiced these doubts when he wrote to his father in Guadalajara in late July of 1929 to ask for news of the arreglos. "We have been following the events step by step through the newspaper," he said, "and I hope that [the settlement], which for now doesn't appear to be enough, will eventually become a reality . . . there may be an agreement, but it is lacking our trust for now."[8]

In fact, the concerns of Venegas and other Cristero supporters regarding further conflict would prove well founded over the next decade. The Mexican government—still under the control of Plutarco Elías Calles, who had established himself as *jefe máximo* during the administrations of Emilio Portes Gil (1928–1930), Pascual Ortíz Rubio (1930–1932), and Abelardo Rodríguez (1932–1934)—continued to support renewed anticlerical campaigns, particularly in states with strongly anticlerical governors, such as Tabasco and Veracruz. Even after Lázaro Cárdenas assumed the presidency in 1934 and the Calles political machine was eventually dismantled, the Mexican government pursued a political and social agenda that many Catholics deeply opposed. In particular, former Cristeros adamantly rejected the Cárdenas administration's socialist education initiative, in which the national government trained teachers in state-run schools to disseminate lessons that promoted Mexican revolutionary nationalism, anticlericalism, and controversial social initiatives such as sexual education.[9]

In response to these developments, Cristeros in Mexico once again took up arms against the state during the 1930s. These repeated uprisings, known collectively as La Segunda or the "Second *Cristiada*," were far less organized—and far more localized—than the Cristero revolt of 1926–1929.[10] Furthermore, by the 1930s, Catholic militants had lost all hope of support from the Catholic hierarchy, now led by the conciliatory Pascual Díaz, who had ascended to the position of archbishop of Mexico City and primate, or highest ranking hierarch, of Mexico. The Vatican rejected Catholic militancy in Mexico as well, even while condemning the Mexican government for its renewed anticlerical actions.[11] Nevertheless, the pattern of Cristero militant resistance and sporadic anticlerical violence would continue until at least 1938.

Mexican Cristero supporters in the United States monitored this resurgence of Church-state antagonism closely throughout the 1930s. For much of the decade, Mexican Catholic emigrants who participated in community-oriented religious activities—attending church, participating in a march or parade, joining an organization—would be hard pressed to escape the continuous flow of news about the ongoing conflicts between Catholic partisans and the revolutionary Mexican government. Yet over the course of the decade, emigrant Cristero activism after the arreglos would diverge from that of the period between 1926 and 1929, when the most ardent members of the Cristero diaspora had participated in fundraising, arms smuggling, and militant revolts along the border. In the years after the failure of these uprisings and the rejection of Catholic militancy by the moderate hierarchy and the Vatican, it became increasingly clear to most emigrant Cristero supporters that an armed response was no longer a viable option. Instead, the Mexican emigrants, refugees, and exiles who supported the Catholic cause and opposed the Mexican government began to participate in more pacific and enduring forms of Catholic social and community organizing in the United States.

Peaceful resistance to the anticlerical government from the United States predated the 1929 agreements, of course. As discussed in Chapters 2 and 3, Mexican Catholic emigrants had participated in boycotts, petitions, rallies, and public religious processions during the 1926–29 period. They had also formed numerous community organizations that would help to rally broad support around the Catholic cause in Mexico. After the failure of the armed movement, then, these non-militant endeavors would continue, and prevail over militancy as the most viable way of protesting the Mexican government from the United States.

In the years after the arreglos, Cristero supporters in the United States would participate in a variety of activities that drew broad public attention to the plight of Catholics in Mexico. The first of these—one that, in fact, began in the years before the arreglos but would continue into the early 1930s—was the formation of the Unión Nacionalista Mexicana, an umbrella organization sponsored by the exiled bishop José de Jesús Manríquez y Zárate. Through at least 1932, the UNM sought to unite Mexican Cristero supporters across the United States, as well as to draw the wider attention of the American public to the religious crisis in Mexico. During the rest of the decade and into the early 1940s, Mexican Cristero supporters would organize impressive public marches, circulate Cristero narratives in emigrant print media, support new religious organizations at home in Mexico, and even build a monumental statue of Christ the King along the US-Mexico border.

Taken together, these efforts helped to foster the development of a stronger form of Mexican Catholic nationalism within the diaspora—one that would survive within Mexican American communities and families for successive generations. This Catholicized national consciousness rejected the Mexican government's revolutionary nationalism; and insisted upon the inseparability of Catholic and patriotic symbols. To understand how this religious nationalism developed and strengthened in the decade after the arreglos, it is necessary first to turn a few years back in the narrative to the 1927 arrival of José de Jesús Manríquez y Zárate, who would become the Cristero diaspora's most important clerical supporter, the sponsor of the Unión Nacionalista Mexicana, and the most forceful proponent of Mexican religious nationalism during the 1930s.

The Bishop of Huejutla and the Unión Nacionalista Mexicana, 1927–1929

Ever since his deportation by the Mexican government in the spring of 1927, Bishop José de Jesús Manríquez y Zárate (pictured in Figure 5.2) played a key role as an organizer and supporter of Cristero partisans in the United States.[12] In the initial phase of his exile from his diocese in Huejutla, Hidalgo, Manríquez y Zárate settled in San Antonio. Almost as soon as he arrived, he began to rally the city's emigrant community around the Cristero cause, collecting funds from sympathetic Catholics and sending them back to his diocese in Mexico.[13]

Then, in July of 1927, only three months after his arrival, he published an essay, *Message to the Civilized World*, which would comprise the first of a series of pastoral letters that he would publish throughout his long exile. In the *Message*, he positioned himself as a spokesperson for the Cristero cause, asking his readership to help Mexico, which "is drowning, and perhaps forever, in the black abysses of lack of faith and barbarity." He also displayed a sympathetic attitude to the "thousands upon thousands" of Mexicans who had "emigrated to the United States ... leaving their

FIGURE 5.2 José de Jesús Manríquez y Zárate, Bishop of Huejutla
Source: UNAM-MPV, Sección Gráfica, Expediente 8, Document 108.

families in Mexico in the most absolute misery."[14] His populism surely endeared him to many Mexican emigrants, as well as to many of the militant political exiles in the United States. In fact, even before he wrote his missive, some members of the emigrant community expressed enthusiasm for his activities. An April 1927 *La Prensa* article announcing his arrival stated that he was "widely known in this country for the valor and virility with which he defended himself from ... multiple persecutions."[15]

At the same time, the bishop's uncompromising stance made him many new enemies. In the *Message,* he excoriated those who were reluctant to assist the Cristero cause: first, priests who did not join the Mexican people in the battlefields; second, the countries of the West, for being complacent; and worst of all, "the rich Mexicans who, to conserve their money, drown the voices of their consciences and submit themselves to the caprices of tyranny."[16] This finger-pointing irritated the conciliatory members of the Mexican hierarchy, led by Pascual Díaz y Barreto.

According to a Liga memorandum, the *Mensaje* "caused displeasure" among the members of the clergy who resided in San Antonio.[17]

As his exile wore on, it must have become increasingly clear to Manríquez y Zárate that he needed to distance himself from the more moderate members of the Mexican Catholic hierarchy. Furthermore, the bishop had begun to attract the attention of US Department of Justice agents, who correctly suspected him of purchasing arms and arranging for them to be smuggled into Mexico.[18] Consequently, in April of 1928, Manríquez y Zárate relocated to Los Angeles. There, he quickly identified a large community of Mexican emigrants who sympathized with the Cristero cause, and began organizing them in support of the Catholic rebellion in Mexico. Many of these clandestine activities, discussed in detail in Chapter 3, involved collecting money for the armed movement, recruiting young men who could return to Mexico as soldiers, and arranging the purchase and distribution of arms and weapons for the Cristero militants in Mexico. Yet the bishop was not interested only in militancy. Shortly after he arrived in Los Angeles, he also began organizing peaceful public gatherings for Mexican Catholic emigrants.

These events were suffused with reminders of the Church-state conflict in Mexico. In June of 1928, for example, the bishop collaborated with community leaders to organize a procession for the feast of Corpus Christi. At the parade, which attracted tens of thousands of participants and spectators, attendees carried signs printed with the Cristero battle cry, "*¡Viva Cristo Rey!*" The bishop gave a sermon in which he "spoke of the vicissitudes that the Church is currently suffering in Mexico, and [advocated] for the soonest possible end to the conflict."[19]

A few months later, in late October, the bishop organized another celebration of Christ the King; some five thousand Los Angeles–area Mexicans attended. Officiated by four bishops and numerous priests, the day's events included a Mass that involved a solemn oath of vassalage to Christ the King, a prayer for the pope, and a blessing. After the Mass, the organizers held a "Literary Soirée [*Velada*]" in which volunteers read aloud from written compositions that, the bishop recounted, "animate[d] the Mexicans to unite with their compatriots in the glorification of Christ the King, above all defending this cause in the battlefields."[20]

It is clear from his writing that Manríquez y Zárate saw these public events as an evangelizing opportunity, and also as a message from the emigrant community to the Mexican government. Furthermore, he was promoting a specific form of Catholic nationalism among Mexican emigrants: one that openly characterized the Catholic Church as an essential part of Mexican history, culture, and identity. This was a direct counterpoint to the revolutionary nationalism promoted by the Mexican government, which emphasized the solidarity of the working classes, a secular national pantheon, and the historical tyranny of colonial institutions such as the Catholic Church.[21] The bishop's religious nationalism seemed to have resonance for the emigrants who attended the public events he organized. After the Christ the King celebration in 1928, Manríquez y Zárate proudly reported to the head of the Liga in Mexico that many of the attendees "that beforehand were embarrassed to call themselves Mexicans, are now honored to announce their nationality."[22]

The bishop's public activities in Los Angeles, and his success at militant organizing in the United States, helped to cement his position as an unofficial leader of the Cristero diaspora by 1928. Increasingly, Mexican Cristero supporters around the United States reached out to Manríquez y Zárate for advice, support, and collaboration, and echoed his messages in their writings and speeches. This was the case when Carlos Fernández, a Mexican emigrant living in Chicago, invited Manríquez y Zárate to help him form the Unión Nacionalista Mexicana, an umbrella group for Cristero supporters in the United States.

As mentioned in Chapter 3, Fernández was a Mexican emigrant in Chicago who had founded the Beneficient Society Pro-Mexico, a Catholic organization with branches in Illinois, Indiana, Wisconsin, and Michigan.[23] In the spring of 1928, Fernández suggested to exiled members of the Liga in California and Texas that they form a single organization to channel funds and generate publicity for the Cristero cause. In doing so, he sought to overcome the divisions between Mexican political exiles such as René Capistrán Garza (who had fallen out with the rest of the Liga); Luis Bustos (who felt betrayed by the Mexican hierarchy, and particularly by Bishop Díaz); and other exiles such as the Chávez Hayhoe brothers in Los Angeles; Carlos P. Landero and J. Molinar y Rey in El Paso; Guillermo Ortíz Monasterio in New York City; and various other possible collaborators.[24]

To help consolidate support, Fernández wrote to Manríquez y Zárate—who had only recently arrived in Los Angeles—and invited him to become involved, with the hope that the bishop would use his considerable influence among Mexicans in Los Angeles and Texas to convince Mexican Catholic associations to help form the confederation. After receiving Fernández's proposal the bishop stated that the idea struck him as "wonderful, and very conducive to the end that is proposed: the true commingling of intellects and hearts of the Mexicans residing in exile." He suggested that Fernández reach out to the ACJM and other organizations, and that he arrange a meeting of Mexican Catholic leaders.[25] As Fernández embarked on the project, Manríquez y Zárate would repeatedly write with strong encouragement for his efforts.[26]

Over the next several months, Fernández worked tirelessly toward the goal of uniting the leaders of the most prominent Mexican Catholic organizations in the United States in Texas—which had fragmented after the split between the conciliatory Mexican hierarchy and the Liga in early 1928—in order to work out an agreement about the proposed confederation. These groups included smaller local organizations such as the Liga Pro Mexico, of Los Angeles and El Paso; and the Liga Católica, of Laredo and El Paso; as well as two of the transnational organizations with outposts in both Mexico and the United States, the Liga (LNDLR) and the ACJM.[27]

Fernández arranged for the UNM's founding conference to be held in El Paso between July 23 and 26, 1928. There, the participants drew up a charter and a constitution, complete with articles and statutes. These outlined that the organization would be classified as a federation of societies; that each regional branch of the Unión would send funds to the Central Committee every month; that the UNM would be open to any Mexican "of good faith"; that the organization would publish a weekly column in *La Voz de la Patria* (the Mexican Catholic newspaper published in Los Angeles by the ACJM); and that Bishop Manríquez y Zárate would serve as the organization's advisor.[28]

According to the UNM's constitution, the organization had four main goals. First, it aimed to relieve the "public necessities" of Mexico through fundraising. Second, it planned to use some of the funds to produce propaganda about the Church-state conflict. A third goal was to "instruct and prepare Mexicans in their civic and patriotic duties." Finally, it aimed to "procure the well-being of its members" by collecting a minimum of twenty-five cents per month. The UNM's constitution also recognized the supreme authority of the Liga in Mexico. All twelve attendees of the founding conference signed the document, including Carlos Fernández, as well as prominent lay political exiles such as Carlos de Silva, a leader of the ACJM, and Luis Chávez Hayhoe, a Liga member in Los Angeles.[29] Less than a month later, the Union Nacionalista's statutes and

FIGURE 5.3 Unión Nacionalista Mexicana letterhead, 1928
Source: Jorge Ferrer to Comite Directivo de la LNDLR, December 18, 1928, UNAM-MPV, Document 5112, Inv. No. 6611.

regulations received official approval from the Liga's Directive Committee in Mexico City.[30] Its official letterhead is shown in Figure 5.3.

By December of 1928, the Unión Nacionalista leadership decided to relocate its central headquarters to Los Angeles. There, the bishop attended an opening ceremony, and the organization set up offices on 124 West 36th Street.[31] In a letter to a friend in Mexico, the UNM's new president, Jorge Ferrer, reported that

> The Unión Nacionalista has become consolidated with great success. I lead it, along with Manríquez y Zárate. Other men of equal stature form a group that supports us. At last we have achieved accord with a respectable group of the episcopate. Certainly it has cost an enormous amount of work to silence so much discord—but [this has] stopped definitively.[32]

The vision of the UNM went beyond simply overcoming divisiveness between Mexican lay political exiles. In fact, the Mexican exiles who collaborated to create the organization stated that their goals also included

> maintaining in exile the integrity of our faith, the conservation of our religious and patriotic ideals, and the spiritual union with our prelates and brothers who, some in exile and others in Mexico,

work tirelessly to obtain, with divine help, the triumph of God's Holy Cause in our unfortunate country.[33]

It is evident that the Unión Nacionalista differed from other efforts by Cristero supporters within the Mexican diaspora, because its founders emphasized not only the need to respond to the religious crisis in Mexico, but also community-oriented goals and connections in the United States, as well as a strong Mexican nationalism that was integrally linked to religious identity. Specifically, they wished to promote religious identity and religious devotion ("by maintaining in exile the integrity of our faith"), as well as a version of national consciousness that was inseparable from their Catholic faith ("the conservation of our religious and patriotic ideals"). Furthermore, the organization's leaders explicitly emphasized the connections not only between Mexicans in different parts of the diaspora, but also between those US-based emigrants and their Cristero brethren at home in Mexico. These ideas seemed also to be popular with the emigrant members of the UNM, which by late 1928 claimed forty-six different branches in cities around the United States.[34] Its broad-based appeal would empower the UNM, under the leadership of Manríquez y Zárate, to transcend the persistent factionalism among lay Catholic exiles in the United States, and to continue to play a prominent role among Cristero supporters in the United States even after the signing of the arreglos, and into the early 1930s.

The Bishop of Huejutla and the Union Nacionalista Mexicana, 1929–1934

When the Church and state reached a settlement in 1929, Manríquez y Zárate was despondent. Indeed, the bishop, who was living in Los Angeles at the time, refused to support the agreements, on the grounds that they ignored the demands of the popular insurgency. In a letter to Miguel Palomar y Vizcarra, the head of the Liga in Mexico, he confessed: "rarely have I felt dispirited and shipwrecked in the middle of a battle, but now I find myself weighed down with a profound malaise and a mortal sadness."[35]

At the same time, however, the bishop held on to the hope that the armed conflict could be rekindled, even after the arreglos. Shortly after the accords were signed, Manríquez y Zárate called on members of the Liga to abandon Mexico and cross the border, where "thousands of Mexicans will receive you with open arms."[36] Eventually, he thought, Mexican Cristero supporters in the United States—with the help of their expansive new organization, the Unión Nacionalista Mexicana—might be able to launch "new crusades that would go later to fight in Mexico for the reconquest of liberty."[37]

Manríquez y Zárate was right to focus on the US community, for after the arreglos, the bishop of Huejutla was prohibited from returning to Mexico. The Mexican government had informally required his continued exile during the negotiations over the settlements in the summer of 1929. Excluded from the ranks of the conciliatory hierarchy, the bishop's power to influence matters south of the Rio Grande was more limited than ever. In addition, the beginning of the global economic depression after October 1929, as well as the repatriation of up to five hundred thousand Mexican emigrants between 1929 and the early 1930s, threatened to put an end to Cristero activism in the United States. After all, Mexican emigrant communities had suffered a double blow: a collapse of local economies (and subsequent joblessness), as well as the subsequent departure of many members of the community.[38]

Despite these challenges, Bishop Manríquez y Zárate and the UNM would continue to assume a central position in Cristero activism in the United States during the early 1930s. Under his direction, the organization would minister to and mobilize within Mexican emigrant communities, as well as galvanize them to support Catholic politics the Cristero cause. For several years after the 1929 arreglos, the Unión Nacionalista continued to produce propaganda aimed at Cristero supporters in the United States. A typical example was a pamphlet, published in Los Angeles in September 1930, containing updates relevant to the religious problem (for example, the news that Ambassador Dwight Morrow—reviled by Cristeros for his role in negotiating the arreglos—would be stepping down); editorials excoriating the Mexican government (one called Calles and his supporters "bandits and assassins, traitors to the Country and absolutely lacking in morals"); and critiques of regional leaders such as the aggressively anticlerical Tabasco governor Tomás Garrido Canabal—who, the writer argued "should be called Cannibal" and was "corrupting at all speed the Tabascan youth, teaching them to blaspheme God."[39]

During the early 1930s, the UNM also sponsored community meetings, including several in San Bernardino, a town about sixty miles to the east of Los Angeles whose Mexican population had grown impressively during the 1920s to about eight thousand people.[40] Many of the details about these meetings were transcribed, thanks to the efforts of several Mexican government employees who—concerned about the continued activities of Cristero dissidents in the United States—infiltrated several UNM events in southern California. Speaking at one of these gatherings in 1931, Manríquez y Zárate implored his listeners to unite in order to bring about the defeat of the current Mexican government. Reportedly, the audience included several hundred members of Catholic parishes and Catholic societies, as well as influential members of the Mexican emigrant community such as Juan Enciso, a rich landowner in Colton (a town close to San Bernardino) and a principal figure among Mexican Catholics, and Roberto Islas, director of the conservative San Bernardino newspaper *El Sol.*[41]

At a subsequent meeting in the neighboring town of Colton, hosted by the Colton branch of the Unión Nacionalista, consular informants reported that Jorge Prieto Laurens, the prominent anti-government exile and sometime Cristero supporter with connections to the Liga, gave a welcoming address to the Bishop, "making him seem like one of the martyrs of the Catholic cause" and praising the fact that "now he is in a free country in which he can speak without fear of being assassinated."[42] Next, Manríquez y Zárate addressed the Colton audience, asking them—just as he had in San Bernardino—to lend their moral and financial support to resisting the Mexican government. He then made several specific requests of his audience that ranged from the pragmatic to the militant: first, that the members join the registry of the Unión Nacionalista, so that "we can present the names of 100,000 or more"; second, that the Catholics prepare themselves "to defend hand-to-hand our legitimate rights, and if it is necessary, making use of arms"; third, that they donate their money to the cause, because "we need it in order to bring about our fight for the liberty of Mexico"; and finally, that those present dedicate themselves to "attacking the Revolution and its tyrants, investing their lives without fear and for the cause of God."[43] As his address demonstrates, despite the generally more pacific character of post-1929 emigrant Catholic activism, the bishop had still not given up completely on the possibility of organizing militant action. Furthermore, his efforts were not limited to California; according to one consular report, the bishop was planning a tour throughout the United States in order to further publicize the Church-state problems of Mexico.[44]

Despite the efforts of Mexican consular officials in San Bernardino to monitor and prevent Manríquez y Zárate's seditious activities, by the winter of 1932 the bishop and the members of the Union Nacionalista Mexicana were still avidly promoting a pro-Cristero, anti-government campaign within the emigrant community. A confidential report from a Mexican secret agent in Los Angeles stated that Manríquez y Zárate, together with Archbishop Orozco y Jiménez (who had also been denied reentry into Mexico after the 1929 arreglos) were organizing the "católico-rebeldes" of California in order to collect funds "by any way possible (raising bonds, evening events, collections for pious works, etc., etc.)."[45]

Notwithstanding Manríquez y Zárate's continued efforts, there are signs that the Depression was hampering his fundraising activities. Noting that the prelate was in a "most trying" financial situation, given that he had no steady income and was supporting several young men in their studies for the priesthood, an association calling itself "The General Committee for the Celebration of the Silver Anniversary of the Most Excellent and Most Reverend Bishop of Huejutla" sought to raise funds in order to pay for the festivities, as well as to "tender [Manríquez y Zárate] a pecuniary offering, however modest." Appealing to Cardinal Mundelein of Chicago, the writers stated that the "general situation of the Spanish speaking colonies of the United States [was] . . . extremely hard at present."[46]

Even in the wake of the Depression, however, the bishop and the broader community of Mexican emigrants continued their efforts on behalf of the Cristero cause. In fact, the bishop seems to have viewed the repatriations of Mexican emigrants after the Great Depression as an opportunity to spread the Cristero message even more widely: the same agent reported that Manríquez y Zárate was distributing "propaganda among all of those who are voluntarily and forcefully being repatriated so that, upon their arrival in the homeland, they are ready for the rebellion that the clergy will lead."[47] (Priests in other places apparently tried to keep Mexicans from repatriating for reasons related to the Cristero conflict; Dennis Nodín Valdés discussed the case of a priest in Detroit who encouraged Mexicans to resist deportation, lest they "be drafted as soldiers to fight against the Cristeros".[48]) The bishop also continued his active publication schedule: in 1932 the government of Mexico accused him in absentia of violating Article 130 of the Mexican constitution after he published his eleventh *Message to the Civilized World*.[49] And in 1933, another of the bishop's pastoral letters, published in Laredo, was distributed within Mexican border states by airplane.[50] Additionally, other Cristero activists within the Mexican emigrant community continued their anti-government activities during the worst years of the Depression. In southern California, there was unrest in Brawley, led by some Knights of Columbus who held a large meeting at the Church of Saint Margaret Mary in 1932,[51] while in Calexico, the consul noted that "the activities that the enemies of the Government are currently undertaking" are principally connected to "those who are affiliated with the Catholic party."[52]

Although it is possible that the UNM continued organizing among Mexican emigrants after 1934, archival records provide little evidence of its continued existence. Bishop Manríquez y Zárate—who, by 1934, had left Los Angeles for San Antonio—would continue to reach out to Mexican Cristero supporters in the United States, sometimes even traveling to visit distant Mexican emigrant communities. A Mexican emigrant newspaper in Chicago announced in February of 1937 that Manríquez y Zárate would officiate at a Mass in that city, at the Mexican Catholic church of Saint Francis.[53] Meanwhile, the bishop continued to publish his forceful opinions: in July of 1938, he released a pamphlet entitled "Reflections about the Current Situation in Mexico"; during that same year, he published a polemic against communism, vividly titled *Fighting with the Beast*.[54] He also began a spirited campaign for the canonization of Juan Diego, the indigenous man who is still revered by Mexican Catholics as the witness to the apparition of the Virgin of Guadalupe in 1531 (he was eventually canonized in 2002).[55] The bishop would not return to Mexico until 1944, when he was elderly and infirm. When he recalled his years in the United States—where he never learned English—he was less than enthusiastic: "During seventeen years," he wrote, "I ate the most bitter bread of exile. Oh, what sorrow for me to be so far from the [Fatherland] and to have no hope of returning!"[56]

Effectively, the bishop's years in exile were the last active years of his life: he died in 1951, afflicted with diabetes. Yet even if he regretted his time in the United States, it was nevertheless tremendously influential for those Mexican emigrants who supported the Cristero cause. Although if his attempts to channel financial and militant support to the Cristero battlefields would prove somewhat less fruitful after 1929, his efforts—and those of the UNM—to rally Mexican Catholics around an alternative nationalism that promoted religious identity and opposed the anticlerical policies of the Revolutionary government were certainly effective, drawing large crowds and provoking the ire and concern of Mexican government representatives in the United States. Yet Manríquez y Zárate was not the only voice to proclaim an explicitly religious Mexican nationalism within emigrant communities during the 1930s. In Los Angeles, several other emigrant Catholic leaders organized religious events and activities that provided Mexican emigrants with a forum to publically express and claim their religious identity.

Religious Nationalism on Display in Southern California

The annual procession to the Virgin of Guadalupe on Los Angeles' East Side had first begun in 1928 as a modest event sponsored by a Mexican Catholic women's organization, the Hijas de María and other Mexican Catholic individuals. By the early 1930s, however, it had become a more significant occasion, as the city's Mexican Catholic organizations continued to increase in number and strength.[57] For example, the Holy Name Society, founded in 1929 by José Orozco (a nephew of Jalisco's exiled archbishop, Francisco Orozco y Jiménez) had grown to about forty chapters in southern California. Additionally, the ACJM had 1,300 registered members, and its sister organization, the ACJF, had 1,400 members. Sponsored by these groups, the Guadalupe march had become a tradition that was advertised in regional Mexican newspapers. It had also attracted the approval and participation of Los Angeles bishop John Cantwell, who had been a powerful advocate of the exiled Mexican clergy during the 1926–29 period, as well as support (and possibly funding) from Catholic oil magnate Edward Doheny, who had been a central figure in the Teapot Dome scandal of the early 1920s.[58]

The 1934 march was particularly memorable because it was also an explicitly political protest against the new administration of Mexican president Lázaro Cárdenas. It attracted some forty thousand participants, the vast majority of Mexican origin, who gathered to express their opposition to Mexican anticlericalism, as well as to the government's promotion of socialist education programs, which many Catholics opposed bitterly.[59] In fact, 1934 was a particularly tumultuous year, with multiple clashes between Church and state over the issue of socialist education. Even the formerly conciliatory hierarchy—some of whom were once again in exile in the United States—was gravely concerned over the renewed violence, and the Mexican emigrant press provided continuous updates as events developed.[60] In response to these events in their homeland, the organizers of the Los Angeles procession of 1934 aimed to launch "a diocesan-wide campaign of prayer for the restoration of religious freedom in Mexico."[61]

On the afternoon of December 9, five processional divisions assembled near the Monte Carlo Chapel, on the corner of Hunter and Concord Streets. Traveling north on Concord to Eighth Street, west to Boyle Avenue, and north again, they marched to St. Elizabeth's Church in the heart of the Mexican East Side, where they assembled on the lawn in front of an altar. The first division was composed of the police escort, Boy Scouts, "Indians in tribal dress," the church hierarchy, and the diocesan executive committee. The second was comprised of the Knights of Columbus Band, Mexican Holy Name branches, and the Damas Católicas. The third contained the Loyola High School Band and the Mexican Holy Name branches from outside of Los Angeles. The fourth included the Paulist Cadets' Band, American representatives of the diocese, and—following the Mexican marchers—Italian, Japanese, and Polish Holy Name societies. Fifth and last were the women's organizations from Mexican parishes.[62]

The fact that the march drew participants from a variety of ethnic and emigrant groups, as well as from native-born US Catholics, was a striking indication that, by the mid-1930s, the approach of Mexico's Cristero supporters had expanded to include new participants—including Catholic members of other ethnic communities—and therefore to publicize the crisis in Mexico to a much wider audience. In addition, the parade also promoted a strong and vibrant Mexican nationalism, similar to that espoused by Bishop Manríquez y Zárate and the Unión Nacionalista Mexicana, which sent a clear message to participants about the centrality of the Mexican Catholic Church within the history of the nation.

The event incorporated numerous nationalistic and religious themes. As the *Los Angeles Times* reported, "the Mexican flag will be prominent in the parade and will be carried at the left of the Stars and Stripes."[63] According to the *Los Angeles Times*, the parade also attracted a contingent of Yaqui Indians, who wore their tribal costumes and performed a "Feather Dance," led by their chief, dressed as the "Devouring Eagle." (The participation of Yaquis in the event is particularly interesting, since members of this indigenous group had also supported the Gándara rebellion along the border, just a few years previously.) Other floats carried "beautiful Mexican maidens posed as the Holy Virgin of Guadalupe," with the floats themselves depicting "the five appearances of the Virgin to Juan Diego, an Indian . . . on Mont Tepeyac."[64]

This mixture of the religious and political was also evident in the prayers and speeches at the event. When the marchers arrived at their destination, Bishop Cantwell blessed the crowd and preached a sermon in front of the Los Angeles Orphanage. Cantwell "sternly rebuked the Mexican officials for 'persecuting the lowly and the unprotected' in their disfranchisement of the Catholic Church in that country," declaring that "Those who take the sword shall perish by the sword!" One of the speakers simultaneously brought up indigenous concerns, religion, and criticism of Mexico's revolutionary government: Father Isidore, a Passionist missionary exiled from Mexico, decried Mexican officials for "shooting down the poor Indian for protecting his faith." The audience "applauded these speeches with the ubiquitous cry of '¡Viva Cristo Rey!'"[65]

It is evident from the day's events, then, that the parade had multiple functions. First and foremost, it drew public attention and responses to the ongoing religious conflict in Mexico. The march was billed as "a memorial service for those who had suffered persecution in Mexico" and certainly attracted many who wished to protest the Mexican government. Second, by simultaneously displaying national and religious symbols such as the flag and the image of the Virgin of Guadalupe, it inspired the Mexican community to create and confirm a national identity that was explicitly religious.[66] Finally, the march also offered the chance for Mexicans in Los Angeles to make a statement to the broader, non-Mexican population of the city. As one scholar explains, the event provided "the opportunity to promote what [its organizer, Orozco] called 'Mexican consciousness.'" Concerned that Anglo discrimination and racism directed against Mexican emigrants would generate a sense of inferiority, Orozco viewed the march—and the organization—"as a way to resuscitate ... ethnic pride" as well as to assert "Mexicanness" in the increasingly multicultural setting of Los Angeles.[67]

Another function of the march was less overt, but certainly important: by mixing politics and religion so openly, Mexicans in Los Angeles were performing a political act that was no longer possible for Catholics in Mexico. By 1934, the Mexican Catholic hierarchy had successfully replaced the autonomous Liga in Mexico with Acción Católica, a group under the direct control of the Episcopate. The massive Liga-organized popular demonstrations of the Cristero War years had served as a way of showcasing the power of the laity to both the Mexican government and the conciliatory hierarchy—and it was this power that the Mexican Church needed to curtail in order to maintain the modus vivendi, or accommodative relationship, between Church and state. According to historian Matthew Butler, within Mexico such marches and demonstrations, particularly the festival of Cristo Rey, were "scaled down" after 1929; and popular participation was channeled into "emasculated, privatized" celebrations of the Virgin of Guadalupe.[68] Thus, the 1934 procession in Los Angeles signaled to Mexicans on both sides of the border that collective public action was still alive and well among Mexican Catholic communities in the diaspora, in stark contrast to Mexico.

Given that this form of religious patriotism stood in contrast to the secular nationalism promoted by the Mexican government, the 1934 march in Los Angeles alarmed local consular officials. The city's Mexican consul, Alejandro V. Martínez, sponsored conferences and went on the radio to argue that the organizers of the march were "enemies of Mexico's social, economic, and cultural progress" and to discourage Mexican citizens from participating in the processions.[69] In San Bernardino, whose Mexican community staged a similar procession only a week after the one in Los Angeles, Consul Hermolao Torres actively tried to stop the event. He was unsuccessful: some two to three thousand people participated. This was particularly impressive, since San Bernardino had a population of about eight thousand at the time.[70]

After the marches, Mexicans in both San Bernardino and Los Angeles rallied in protest of both consuls, declaring that they had attempted to quash their constitutional protections of religious freedom; their protests even prompted an investigation by State Department officials. Shortly afterward, both Torres and Martínez were eventually transferred to posts outside of the United States, leading historian Francisco Balderrama to conclude that "religious fervor among la raza was much stronger than the patriotic ties linking the colonia to the consulates." According to Balderrama, the march in 1934 is still remembered by members of the Los Angeles Mexican community as "the most popular ever held."[71]

By incorporating a broader lesson about Mexican nationalism, and by expanding their audience to include native-born Americans and other emigrant and ethnic groups, Cristero supporters in southern California had broadened their message, and set the stage for the survival of a specific Mexican Catholic identity within their communities. Yet this was not the only location where Mexican emigrant religious expression would revolve around the Church-state conflict. Along the border, as news of religious clashes between the Mexican government and Catholic activists continued to reach emigrant communities, Cristero supporters in the

United States remained deeply concerned with ongoing events in Mexico. Throughout the 1930s, there would be continuous Cristero activism within Mexican families, communities, and organizations, especially in southern California and the US Southwest. These activities are particularly well documented in the personal files of one emigrant family that lived in the borderlands during and after the Cristero War.

Cristero Activism in the Borderlands

The family of María and Ignacio de la Torre emigrated from Mexico to Nogales, Arizona, in late 1927. Before leaving their homeland, the de la Torre parents, both born in 1878, had lived across west-central Mexico: originally from Zacatecas and Guanajuato, they had also resided in Aguascalientes; by 1922, they had moved to San Luis Potosí. Eventually, they would relocate to Tampico, Tamaulipas, until they finally crossed into the United States with several of their eight adult children.

As devout and active Catholics, the de la Torre family had close friends among Mexico's Catholic clergy, as well as among the leadership of the Liga and the ACJM. It was only natural, then, that the couple and several of their children became directly involved in the Cristero cause during the 1920s and 1930s. Three of their sons became priests: Ignacio, who would found several religious organizations and eventually rise to the position of vicar general in the Archdiocese of Hermosillo, Sonora; and Francisco and Carlos, who were Jesuits in Nogales, Sonora. Their son Alfonso became a Cristero soldier, and was killed in a battle near the town of Suaqui de Batuc, Sonora, in 1935[72]; and their son Luis was also a participant in the Cristero movement. Their daughter María who would remain in the United States after emigrating in the late 1920s, did not directly participate in the armed movement, but her fiancé, Fidel Muro, was a Cristero who was killed by federal troops in 1928.[73]

Given their collective experiences during the Cristero War, and their close ties to Catholic figures in Mexico, it was only natural that the de la Torre family members in exile in the United States would remain deeply involved in the Cristero conflict from across the border. As a result, their personal archives are replete with communications between various family members and a wide network of Catholic activists at home in Mexico, as well as across the southwestern United States. Although the de la Torre family was certainly more connected with the Cristero movement than the majority of emigrant families, the documents that they collected nevertheless demonstrate that the Cristero diaspora—the widespread network of US-based Cristero supporters, sympathizers, and activists—was still present and active during the 1930s. In addition, it provides evidence that these affiliations extended geographically across a wide area, from the US-Mexico borderlands to southern California, and well into Mexico. Finally, the de la Torre family's papers showcase the post-arreglos tendency of the Cristero diaspora to move away from militancy, and toward broader expressions of religious nationalism.

Diasporic connections are evident in the the de la Torre family documents, which range in date from the early 1920s to the 1950s. These are especially apparent in the letters between de la Torre family members and the two exiled bishops most important to Cristero activism in the United States. The first was Bishop Juan Navarrete, who was an influential Cristero supporter for his diocese in Sonora during the 1920s—and who had provided the militant revolutionist José Gándara with his blessing, and perhaps also with tactical support. Navarrete had been a close confidante of the de la Torre family since at least 1919. In particular, the bishop had taken a strong interest in the education and religious formation of Ignacio, Jr., the family member who would go on to become a priest in the Diocese of Sonora. He also wrote to various other members of the family, including Francisco, Alfonso, and Luis, in order to consult with them about their activities in support of the Catholic movement in Mexico.[74] This correspondence would continue throughout the decade; in 1930, the Bishop wrote to Ignacio de la Torre, Jr. about initiatives that could be taken in Mexico after the passage of legal religious reforms.[75] The family also exchanged numerous letters with bishop Manríquez y Zárate about the Cristero movement and their work to support it from the United States during the early 1930s. Furthermore, they collected the bishop's published works, especially the various manifestos and tracts that he wrote during the 1930s.[76]

In addition to their communications with the exiled prelates, the de la Torre family also kept abreast of developments related to the Catholic struggle on both sides of the border, particularly in northern Mexico and the United States. They collected numerous documents related to the activities of religious individuals and societies in the northern Mexican states of Tamaulipas, as well as documents from activities in San Luis Potosí, Aguascalientes, and Sonora. In addition, they received and saved a variety of printed material produced by Mexican Catholics and their religious societies and organizations in the United States. One particularly interesting example was a Spanish-language flyer entitled "Intimate Proclamation to Christ the King," produced by the Liga of "Liberty of the Rights of Man," in El Paso, Texas, and printed in 1932. The flyer, whose authors are unknown, purportedly represented the "Colonia Católica Mexicana" (Mexican Catholic Colony) in that city, and a line underneath the text stated that more than a thousand people had signed it. The document offered both a direct address to Christ and a candid rebuke of the Mexican state. It declared that the Mexican government had, "after tricking the people; robbing temples; cruelly pursuing your Priests and disseminating corrupt doctrines; and betraying the will of your faithful—declared against you a war to the death and rejected your power, keeping you out of public places and overturning your monument."[77] The authors of the flyer then went on to proclaim their submission to Christ and to ask for his "blessing and protection."[78] While this flyer shared some similarities with the printed material distributed during the 1920s and discussed in previous chapters, it also seemed to tack away from the overt militancy of some of the earlier materials. It did not call upon readers to take action; rather, it simply listed the aggressions of the Mexican government, while appealing to Christ for help.

Just as they had during the 1920s, Mexican emigrants who supported the Cristero cause continued to publish periodicals for the Spanish-speaking audience in the years after the arreglos, and these were assiduously collected by the de la Torre family. These publications were extremely critical of the Mexican government. One of these was a newsletter published in Los Angeles by an organization called the Popular Committee for Mexican Defense (although not much is known about this organization, it did have an additional branch in Seguin, Texas).[79] The publication—like those of the 1920s—frequently criticized the Mexican government for its anticlerical actions. Making its position even clearer, its masthead declared that "the triumph of evil lies in the cowardice of Catholics."[80] It also articulated the views of the Mexican Catholic hierarchy: its March 1935 issue, for example, reprinted a speech from archbishop Leopoldo Ruíz, now the apostolic delegate of Mexico, which stated that "the [Mexican] government, far from achieving the betterment of the poorest classes, is ruining society and rapidly pushing the country into chaos."[81]

The contents of the Popular Committee's newsletter also indicated that emigrant Cristero supporters during the 1930s were increasingly concerned with the dissemination of information, rather than with direct action: many of the issues focused on informing readers that religious persecution was continuing in Mexico despite the arreglos. The newsletter frequently reprinted reports of persecutions ongoing in Mexico during 1935, including in Guadalajara, Mexico City, Toluca, and in the Yucatan, in order to dispel any perception that the religious problem had been solved. One issue, for example, included an article sarcastically entitled "In Mexico There Is No Religious Persecution," which went on to describe the various abuses of the Mexican government toward Mexican Catholics. To make this point even clearer, the newsletter's authors published a subsequent item entitled "The Mexican Flag Trampled. Wolves in Sheep's Clothing. Mexico, Wake up!"[82]

The Popular Committee for Mexican Defense was not the only publication informing its readership about the continued religious crisis in Mexico. One booklet, published in 1935 by Félix Navarrete, conveyed a similar message in a disquisition whose title asserted that "Yes, There Is Persecution in Mexico: Here Is the Proof."[83] Finally, another newsletter in the de la Torre family's collection, *Desde México*, ran from 1926 through 1937. Its coverage compiled religious and political news from many cities in Mexico by date, and reported on incidents of violence, the closing of Catholic schools, Mexican anticlerical decrees, and the activities of Mexican socialists, communists, and other anticlerical Mexican political parties and groups.[84] Taken together, these publications helped to generate sympathy for persecuted Catholics, while simultaneously providing a strong critique of the Revolutionary government of Calles's successors (before 1934) and President Lázaro Cárdenas (after 1934).

In another parallel with the 1926–29 period, there is evidence that Mexican Catholics in the United States during the 1930s continued to disseminate religious messages by radio, as well. Two of these addresses survive in the de la Torre family's documents. In 1937 Miguel Palomar y Vizcarra, who had served as president of the Liga in Mexico during the war years, gave a speech entitled "The Virgin of Guadalupe, Symbol and Bastion of Hispanicity," which was transmitted by a Los Angeles radio station on June 7, 1937.[85] Two years later, the parish priest of the Church of Our Lady of Guadalupe in Los Angeles, Manuel Angel Canseco, gave a talk on the KGER station about "the origin and development of the devotion to Our Lady of Guadalupe in the Archdiocese of Los Angeles since 1923."[86] The former address, in particular, emphasized the intertwined themes of religion and nationalism that had become so predominant within the Cristero diaspora during the 1930s.

The de la Torre papers—in addition to archival materials from other US collections—also demonstrate a connection between Mexican Catholics in the United States and a Catholic organization that was growing in importance in Mexico during the late 1930s. This was the Union Nacional Sinarquista (UNS), which was founded in May 1937 by Salvador Abascal of Morelia, Michoacán. Abascal came from a deeply Catholic family; he was the son of Adalberto Abascal, a prominent Catholic and member of the Knights of Columbus, and a co-founder of a secretive Catholic organization, known only as "La U," that was active during the Cristero War years.[87]

Given his upbringing, it is not surprising that Salvador Abascal was drawn to clandestine Catholic societies. In fact, two years before he founded the UNS, he had joined another secret organization, called "Las Legiones," which had been established by a Catholic activist in Jalisco. Shortly afterward, with Abascal's help, Las Legiones extended to Mexico City, Querétaro, and Morélia. Each of the Legion's separate-sex chapters (also called legions) consisted of up to a thousand men or women. The organization was not meant to foment an armed movement; rather, it produced verbal and written propaganda against the socialist schools or other aspects of the Mexican government that Catholics resisted during the 1930s. Importantly, Las Legiones would also become a transnational organization. In an interview decades later, Abascal recalled his travels in the United States, where he founded chapters of Las Legiones "from sea to sea across all of the South: from Brownsville to San Francisco, California, and northwards to San Antonio." It was from this cross-border network, Abascal recalled, that *sinarquismo* arose; the UNS was in fact meant to become the public wing of Las Legiones. In other words, it was to be an organization that openly expressed the clandestine goals and activities of its predecessor.[88]

As the historian Jason Dormady explains, the UNS, like Las Legiones, was not a militant organization. Rather, it was an explicitly Catholic political movement that aimed to restore Catholicism to its purportedly proper place "as a state-sponsored institution."[89] As a part of this goal, the UNS promoted conservative national heroes and symbols that had been rejected by the Revolutionary state, such as the pro-Catholic Mexican emperor Agustín de Iturbide and his tricolor flag. The UNS also advocated social programs that rejected revolutionary land distribution policies in favor of the workers circles described in the papal encyclical *Rerum novarum* (1891). At its peak in 1941, the organization attracted some five hundred thousand members across Mexico, including numerous former Cristero soldiers, and Abascal even launched an ambitious (albeit short-lived) colonization scheme in Baja, California, which attempted to bring the UNS's vision of society to life.[90]

The UNS drew enthusiastic participation from numerous Mexican emigrants in various parts of the United States, many of whom had already joined Las Legiones. By 1941, there were chapters in Los Angeles and Fresno, California, as well as Indiana Harbor, just outside of Chicago. These US outposts, according to Dormady, "would consistently contribute more than the chapters of the UNS in Mexico, most probably because they were earning wages far higher than their Mexican counterparts."[91] In 1944, an associate of the de la Torre family noted that "friends in the United States" had lent seven thousand pesos, and that this had been invested in "diverse necessities of the Movement"; another seven thousand was also sent by emigrants for use in the Sinarquista press.[92] The Los Angeles chapter, called the UNS's Comité Organizador Regional de California, was particularly active. Its members had access to a printing press, where they printed pamphlets and booklets with instructions on how to join the organization. The de la Torre family archives contain one such booklet, which called upon "true Mexican patriots" to unite in order to attain "the salvation of the fatherland."[93] Through such publications, the UNS promoted an alternative Catholic nationalism that appealed to many within the Mexican diaspora in the United States.[94] But the UNS was not the only channel for transnational religious patriotism. During the same time, a Mexican community near El Paso was constructing an even more tangible reminder of the connections between Catholic symbols and Mexican nationhood.

A Monument along the Border

In 1933, a group of Mexican Catholics outside of El Paso, Texas, began a campaign to construct a monumental statue of Christ the King along the US-Mexico border. The twenty-nine-foot-high limestone statue, portraying a cassocked Jesus standing atop a globe, stands to this day atop the Sierra de Cristo Rey, a mountain just nine miles west of downtown El Paso (see Figure 5.4). The drive to build the statue began in Smeltertown, a neighborhood that had formed around the American Smelting and Mining Company on the outskirts of El Paso. Its residents, the

FIGURE 5.4 Mount Cristo Rey at sunrise
Source: © 2014 Brian Wancho.

majority of whom were employed at the smelter, were almost all emigrants from Mexico.

The statue was the brainchild of Father Lourdes Costa, the local parish priest and an emigrant from Spain (Costa may have been among the
many foreign-born priests exiled from Mexico during the late 1920s, but
the records are unclear). After conceiving of the idea one day while looking at the mountain, then known as the Sierra de Muleros, Father Costa
and sixteen others hiked up to its summit on October 28, 1933. The next
day, he introduced the plan to his parishioners at the church of San José
del Río in Smeltertown. He received an enthusiastic response: soon afterward, Smeltertown residents launched a volunteer effort to construct the
statue on the mountaintop. Anthony Schuler, the bishop of El Paso, also
endorsed the plan, and contributed funds from the Diocese of El Paso.
Cleofás Calleros, head of the Immigration Bureau of the National Catholic
Welfare Conference—the organization that had been so instrumental in
helping refugee religious to enter the United States during the Cristero
War years—would supervise the construction and financing of the Christ
the King statue.[95]

The Smeltertown parishioners' efforts would take them five years,
countless hours of unpaid labor, and incredible physical effort. In the

process of building the monument, the men of the parish would carry close to fifty-two thousand pounds of material to the summit of Mount Cristo Rey.[96] After parishioners placed a rough wooden cross at the site, students at the Smelter Vocational School built an iron cross and installed it. Other parishioners worked on building a two-and-a-half mile road to the top of the mountain. In 1937 Father Costa solicited Urbici Soler, a Catalan sculptor who had created several other monumental works. Soler accepted the job, and the statue was completed on October 29, 1939.[97]

Since the residents of Smeltertown were people who already had difficult and taxing day jobs, their enthusiasm for this religious project seems remarkable. Yet the El Paso region had a notably ardent Mexican Catholic population, and one that had been profoundly affected by the Cristero War. After 1926, El Paso was the city where most of the religious refugees initially arrived, and dozens of them would stay there during the war years, thanks to the work of the Immigration Bureau's Cleofas Calleros. El Paso was also home to Cristero border revolutionist José Gándara, as well as a large community of Cristero supporters and Catholic organizations.[98] Certainly, El Paso was the most vocally Catholic city from the standpoint of the print media: it was home not only to the ardently pro-Cristero newspaper *El Diario de El Paso*, but also to *Revista Católica*, which was produced and edited by Jesuits.[99]

Thanks to the predominance of this staunchly pro-Cristero community, it stands to reason that the construction of the Christ the King statue, only a few short years after the signing of the arreglos, would have political and religious meaning for many Mexican emigrants residing in the El Paso area. In fact, the statue may have had a direct symbolic connection to another statue that any Mexican emigrants from the west-central region would have recognized: the monument to Christ the King on El Cubilete, a mountain outside of Guanajuato, in the geographic center of Mexico. The monument, which Mexican Catholics had begun in 1923, was later destroyed by the Mexican federal troops during the Cristero War. (It was rebuilt in 1940, and still stands today.) Furthermore, the construction of the statue of Christ the King to be facing south—into Mexico—would have been extremely politically significant to Mexicans in the area, clearly articulating the message that the Mexican Catholic community in the United States was watching Mexico, and monitoring the development of Church-state relations there.

By 1938, however, relations between Church and state in Mexico had finally begun to improve. The Cárdenas government, seeking conciliation

with the Catholic opposition, had backed away from the campaigns of
socialist education. Under Cárdenas's successor, Manuel Ávila Camacho,
the Church-state conflict seemed to have been resolved for good, as Ávila
Camacho famously declared "*Soy creyente*"—I am a believer—while preparing to take the presidency, thus offering an olive branch to Catholics
in Mexico. Furthermore, other political problems had also begun to
occupy the minds of Mexicans, and of many others throughout the world,
as Europe and Asia became embroiled in conflict and the United States
moved closer to entry into the Second World War.

Thus, the Mexicans who participated in the construction of the Christ
the King statue framed it not only as a response to religious restriction
and persecution in Mexico, but also as a symbol of transnational cooperation and hope in a time of global conflict. Father Costa expressed these
sentiments in a hymn of dedication to the statue, which celebrated "two
peoples embracing each other . . . they are more than neighbors, because
they are united in a bond of mutual defense and security. They are Old
Mexico and the United States." He emphasized the new possibilities of collaboration between the United States and Mexico, pointing out that "with
their powerful voice [they] can be the first to raise the 'Alarm' against athe-
ist irrational Communism." In the conclusion of his hymn, he hearkened
back to Church's mission to elevate the figure of Christ as the king of all
nations, and reiterated the battle cry of the Cristeros:

> *Happy are the people that obey Your Law!*
> *Happy are the souls that form your Flock!*
> *¡Viva Cristo Rey!*[100]

After the construction of the statue, the Diocese of El Paso sponsored
a pilgrimage to the Villa de Guadalupe in Mexico City, in December 1938.
Individual parishioners could sign up with their parish. At the pilgrimage, representatives from El Paso brought a tile mosaic with an image of
the Virgin of Guadalupe to her shrine, in the north of Mexico City. There,
the abbot of the shrine blessed the image. His words reflected the transnational nature of the endeavor: "this [blessing] represents the embrace that
the Mexicans of this side of the Río Bravo give to their compatriots that
live in North America."[101]

After the pilgrimage, the participants placed the mosaic at the statue
of Cristo Rey on December 18, the diocesan festival of Our Lady of
Guadalupe. Bishop Schuler urged parishioners to attend the ceremony to

show gratitude to the "undeniable [*sic*] Catholic, and always Guadalupan people south of the Río Grande." His letter was read aloud during all of the Masses of December 8 in the diocese. On the following year, a pilgrimage of dedication drew twelve thousand people to Smeltertown from the El Paso area and further afield. Its general intention—the goal for which all the pilgrims prayed—was "For the Kingdom of Christ: Pray that Christ conquers, reigns, and governs all of the Nations involved in the Second World War."[102] By now, Cristero supporters in the United States had expanded their message to incorporate prayers for global peace as well as opposition to the threat of communism.

Today, the statue of Christ the King still stands on Mount Cristo Rey, and continues to attract thousands of Catholics each year for its annual pilgrimage, held annually during the feast of Christ the King, on the last Sunday of October. The event typically begins with a procession led by the bishops of Las Cruces and El Paso; pilgrims follow, some walking on their knees, in the time-honored tradition of Mexican and other Catholic worshippers. When they arrive at the summit of the mountain, they can participate in a Mass that is held there. The cross is lit overnight on the night before the pilgrimage, shining out as a beacon of Mexican religious identity on the US-Mexico border.[103]

A Legacy of Cristero Activism

By the late 1930s and 1940s, the character of Mexican migration to the United States had changed. Despite the trauma of the Great Depression and the repatriation campaigns, a small but significant Mexican American middle class had arisen in many communities, with a growing number of skilled, semiskilled, and professional workers and increasing economic stability. It might be assumed, then, that these emigrants and their children became less involved with the politics of the homeland, and more concerned with events in the United States.[104] Certainly there were many such developments Mexican Americans enlisted in the Second World War and then returned home; became more involved in the widespread labor movements of the 1930s and 1940s; and fought for civil rights in an era of continued racism and segregation.

Yet the activities of Catholic activists within the Cristero diaspora—including the formation of Catholic activist organizations like the Union Nacionalista Mexicana; the great religious processions in southern California; the involvement of families like the de la Torres in varied forms of transnational Catholic activism, including sinarquismo; and the construction of a Christ the King monument along the border—indicate that there were continuous expressions of Catholic identity within Mexican emigrant communities during the 1930s and 1940s, as the diaspora responded to the events of the Second Cristiada. Although the activities of the Cristero diaspora would become notably less militant than they had been in the 1920s, they were more successful at instilling a sense of religious nationalism. In addition, these activities forged new connections among Mexican emigrant communities, other Catholic ethnic groups in the United States (such as the groups that participated in the Los Angeles march), and world events such as the Second World War and the perceived threat of communism.

In the decades to come, memories of the Cristero conflict would remain salient within Mexican emigrant communities, even as overtly Cristero political activism diminished.[105] In their parishes, in convents and monasteries, and within their homes, Mexican emigrants across the United States repeated stories to their children and grandchildren about what had happened during the 1920s and 1930s. These stories would continue to inform their religious beliefs, their political identities, and even their ongoing relationship to the Mexican government. They would also help to fuel the rise of new religious devotions to the saints and martyrs of the Cristero War.

6

Memories, Myths, and Martyrs

SOMETIME IN THE 1980s, a Mexican emigrant named Jesús Buendía Gaytán staggered through the northernmost reaches of the Sonoran desert. He was tantalizingly close to the US border, but hopelessly lost. Lacking water or shelter in the merciless terrain, he was well along the horrific descent into hyperthermia common to hundreds of border-crossers every year: profuse sweating; dehydration and muscle cramps; then vomiting, violent shaking, hallucinations, and an excruciating death.

In the harsh desert day, blinded by the sun, the broiling heat, and his own profound exhaustion, Buendía must have thought that the old pickup truck wending its way toward him was a figment of his imagination. Yet as he stumbled toward it, it grew steadily closer, and finally stopped just next to him. The metal door creaked open and a man got out: he was thin and pale, with dark hair and bright blue eyes.

¿Tiene sed, amigo? Like an angel of mercy, the man handed him a bottle of water and a bit of food, and Buendía knew he was saved. After a while, the man passed him a few crumpled dollar bills, and then told Buendía how to get out of the desert and across the border to California. As he said a grateful goodbye, the emigrant asked the blue-eyed man his name. "Toribio Romo," he replied, "from Santa Ana de Guadalupe, in Jalisco. After you're all settled, come and look for me."

Several years later, Buendía had saved up enough money from his work as a farm laborer in California to return home to Zacatecas. As soon as he could, he went to find the man who had rescued him in the desert. It wasn't easy: Santa Ana de Guadalupe was a tiny *ranchería*, really nothing more than a gravel-road hamlet nestled in the fertile highland region of Los Altos de Jalisco. But it wasn't too far from the southern edge of Zacatecas, Buendía's home state. When he got to the municipal seat of

Jalostitlán, locals directed him to follow the two-lane highway southward out of town. "When you get to Santa Ana," they said, "you'll find Toribio Romo in the parish church."

Upon arriving at the ranchería, Buendía trudged up a small hill and entered the little chapel, a solid, squat building made of dark gray volcanic stone and topped by a modest, three-bell *campanario*. As he settled into a wooden pew to get his bearings, he looked around. There, in the dim light above the altar, were two images: a picture of the Virgin of Guadalupe, and a gold-framed, black-and-white photo of a young man with dark hair and a pale face. Startled, Buendía stood up. It was unmistakable: the man in the photo was Toribio Romo, his desert savior.

As Buendía would shortly discover, Toribio Romo González had been dead for nearly half a century. The young priest was, in fact, a martyr of the Cristero War. Born in 1900 in Santa Ana de Guadalupe, he had entered the seminary at the precocious age of twelve, and by 1923 he had made his ordination vows. Only three years later, Father Toribio was on the run from the federal troops, disguising himself in peasants' overalls so that he could pass unheeded from town to town, saying clandestine masses and administering the sacraments to the determined faithful. After two years, the federales caught up with him in an abandoned factory in the town of Tequila, where he had been living in hiding with his sister María. On the morning of February 25, 1928, they burst into the room where he had been sleeping, and shot him to death.

For at least forty years after he was killed, Toribio Romo was largely forgotten outside of Jalisco. Within the state, he was remembered primarily by the townspeople of Santa Ana de Guadalupe, many of whom belonged to the expansive Romo family. By the early 2000s, however, his reputation had grown on both sides of the border, when an increasing number of emigrants began describing their miraculous encounters with the saint. (Jesús Buendía Gaytán was the first person to tell his story to the media, in 2002—some two decades after his experience in the desert.)[1]

The emigrants' stories differed in detail: sometimes the saint drove a truck; other times he was walking; and in one instance, he sat next to an emigrant on an airplane. Nevertheless, they were consistent in theme. Emigrants who saw him invariably noted his pale skin and blue eyes. Whenever he appeared, Father Toribio mentioned his own name. Finally, he usually invited them to visit him in the town of Santa Ana de Guadalupe, where, upon arriving, they were shocked to learn that he had died long before.[2]

In May of 2000, Pope John Paul II canonized Toribio Romo, along with twenty-five other Mexican priests who had died at the hands of Mexican federales during the Cristero War. Thanks to his new status as a saint, and his ever-growing reputation among emigrants, Toribio Romo has now become an economic patron of his hometown. By 2002 Santa Ana de Guadalupe had begun receiving thousands of visitors every weekend. Today, most of those who come to visit the shrine of Santo Toribio are emigrants or their relatives, either giving thanks for a safe journey, or praying for his protection for their next venture north. At the shrine, people visit the old church, which holds the saint's mortal remains, vials of his blood, and the clothing he was wearing when he was killed. There, they leave photos, *testimonios* describing their personal stories, and offerings.[3]

Today, Toribio Romo, who never left his home state while alive, has become the unofficial patron saint of Mexican emigrants, supplanting even Juan Soldado, the popular folk saint of Tijuana. He is often called *el santo pollero*, or the "coyote" saint, for his protection of undocumented emigrants.[4] Many Mexican emigrants, before making the journey across the desert, buy prayer cards emblazoned with his image in stores along the border.[5] They cultivate their devotion to him in the United States, as well: in Chicago (where there is a mural of his image in the Mexican neighborhood of Pilsen, shown in Figure 6.1), Los Angeles, and other US cities, there are now Santo Toribio shrines, Catholic churches, community centers, and even businesses.[6] In 2011 the church of Santa Ana de Guadalupe lent a statue of Santo Toribio Romo to the Diocese of Oakland, California; the statue attracted up to fifty thousand visitors—most of them Mexican emigrants—over the course of three weeks. The tour was repeated and expanded in July 2014.[7]

No one knows exactly why Toribio Romo, a Cristero martyr who lived and died in Jalisco, is now an object of such fervent transnational devotion—and of course, for those who have seen Santo Toribio in the desert, such a miraculous event needs no explanation. Yet the story of the santo pollero is certainly worthy of further historical investigation and contextualization, for it illustrates how a martyr of the Cristero War—which was, after all, a relatively brief conflict—has continued to hold deep meaning for many Mexican emigrants. Indeed, devotion to the memories, myths, and martyrs of the Cristero War has endured across both time (through multiple generations of Mexican families) and space (from the Mexican interior to cities and towns across the United States).

FIGURE 6.1 Mural of Santo Toribio Romo in Chicago's Pilsen neighborhood
Source: Photo courtesy of Les Kordylewski.

The persistence of Cristero devotion across space is explained relatively easily by the geography of twentieth-century Mexican migration. During the 1920s, the majority of Mexican emigrants came from the west-central region, where the Cristero War was fought most intensely. In the cities and towns of Jalisco, Michoacán, Guanajuato, and southern Zacatecas, the war has been continuously memorialized since the 1920s. Just as Santo Toribio's image hangs in the church of Santa Ana de Guadalupe, images of Cristero martyrs adorn Catholic churches, cathedrals, and chapels throughout the area.[8]

To this day, a majority of Mexican emigrants still come from the same region: the top three sending states continue to be Jalisco (Toribio Romo's home state), Michoacán, and Guanajuato.[9] Even though the generation that fought in the war—and fled to the United States during the 1920s—is now gone, the children and grandchildren of Cristeros and their opponents continue to migrate to the United States in large numbers. Thus, it is likely that many of the recent emigrants from this region have encountered the images and symbols of the Cristero War—including, possibly, the image of Santo Toribio—in their hometowns. These regional ties suggest one explanation for why the story of a Cristero martyr from Jalisco continues to resonate so profoundly among so many emigrants to the United States. In addition to these geographic linkages, multigenerational family networks have helped to ensure the relevance of the Cristero War in the decades since it ended. The experiences of these family members during the war years have been repeated not only between successive generations, but also among family members on both sides of the border.[10]

Family Memories of the Cristero War

To better understand how transnational family memories about the Cristero War endured across time and space, I interviewed six descendants of Cristero emigrants, all of whom had either grown up in the United States or spent a part of their lives there, and who ranged in age from their mid-sixties to their late eighties. Using a semi-structured, open-ended interview format, I invited each person to tell me their life stories, to share their memories of their families' involvement with the Cristero War, and to convey their opinions about religion, migration, and contemporary Mexico.[11] Their narratives—supplemented with archival accounts as well as historical data about Mexican religious institutions in the United States—demonstrate how the legacy of the Cristero War not only endured, but was actively cultivated within some Mexican families.

The interviews revealed several common themes. First, each of the interviewees came from a family that crossed the border as a direct or indirect result of the Cristero conflict. Second, these families then memorialized the Cristero conflict across generations: both through oral and written informational networks, such as stories told within the family, letters from home, and newspaper articles; and through contacts with religious refugees who had resettled within their communities. Then, with the help of these connections, these families developed devotional practices toward relatives who had participated in the Cristero conflict and whom they came to see as martyrs. Finally, they constructed narratives about Mexico—and Mexican politics—that would persist across generations. For this reason, the family memories of Cristero descendants comprise a set of oral histories that shed light on the ways that multiple generations of Mexicans and Mexican Americans perceived the Cristero War, and, based on these perceptions, formed beliefs about themselves, their families, and their homeland. As historian Mary Chamberlain explains, "memory as a source offers a clue not merely to past experiences, but to the interpretations of, and meanings given to, such experiences."[12] Thus, these family memories help explain why symbols of the Cristero War—such as Toribio Romo—continue to hold deep meaning for many Mexican emigrants.

Six Descendants of Cristero Emigrants

As we have seen in the previous chapters, the violence of the Cristero War prompted new waves of emigration in Mexico's west-central states. Within the families of each of the six descendants interviewed, the religious conflict was either a direct or indirect cause of their family's migration. Those who fled the conflict went to numerous different destinations in the United States, especially California, the US Southwest, and Midwestern cities such as Detroit, Milwaukee, and Chicago.

Severino López—a gregarious Claretian priest with a flat Midwestern twang—grew up in Illinois as a child of Mexican emigrants who were refugees of the religious conflict. His father, Don Severino López, who had been active in the ACJM, fled to California in 1915 during the Mexican Revolution, and then returned to Mexico in 1920. There, he began to promote the Catholic cause as a journalist, "condemning what he described as Marxist tactics of the government." In 1926, after warnings from friends, Don Severino emigrated to Joliet, Illinois, "where the paisanos—fellow Mexicans—had arranged a place for him to stay."[13] His wife and their four children (including Severino) joined him the following year.[14]

Like Severino López, Adelina Huerta grew up in Chicago. As she recalled solemnly, Adelina's paternal grandfather, Salvador Huerta Gutiérrez, and her great-uncle, Ezequiel Huerta Gutiérrez, were arrested, tortured, and then executed in April 1927 by federal troops in Guadalajara, where they had both been active members of the Catholic resistance and associates of Cristero leader Anacleto González Flores. The loss of Adelina's grandfather prompted a wave of emigration within the Huerta family; her grandfather and uncle had been the sole supporters of large families, and when they died, their older children were forced to seek employment. Adelina's father, the son of Salvador Huerta, moved to Chicago when he was eighteen years old; another uncle came to Chicago as well, and a few of his siblings went to Los Angeles.[15]

The city of Los Angeles was also the destination for the parents of María Teresa Venegas, who had lived in the Cristero stronghold of Zapotlanejo, Jalisco. When the war broke out, María's father and uncle, Miguel and Alfonso Venegas, became Cristero soldiers. After a few months in the army, Miguel decided to reunite with his family. But when he returned to Zapotlanejo, he found out that a local *cacique*, or political boss, was determined to kill him. He collected his wife, Dolores, and their children and left for the United States. In Los Angeles, Miguel and Dolores opened a Mexican grocery store, and eventually raised ten children. María Teresa, their only daughter, grew up to join a religious order, earn her PhD, and become the family's unofficial historian.[16]

María Teresa Amador Díaz—a cheerful, forceful, and sharp-witted grandmother who currently lives in the northern city of Monterrey, Mexico—is the niece of José de Jesús Manríquez y Zárate, the bishop of Huejutla. During the bishop's long exile to the United States (1927–51), numerous members of his large and devoted family followed him across the border—first to El Paso and then to California—to provide him assistance and support. To earn a living, María Teresa's parents worked in the fields in California, and eventually opened a small grocery store in Los Angeles. María Teresa was born while the family was still in El Paso; although she went back to Mexico as a child, she then returned to the United States as a teenager to serve as her uncle's housekeeper in San Antonio.[17]

Margarita Gándara, a vibrant and outspoken artist, also spent her life going back and forth across the border. Now in her eighties, Gándara is the daughter of the El Paso artist and Cristero revolutionary José Gándara. Throughout her life, she has maintained her family's deep ties to the El Paso-Ciudad Juárez region. Her grandfather, José María Gándara, had been the first family member to come to the United States: a prosperous lawyer from Chihuahua, he was reportedly threatened with death by Pancho Villa during the Mexican Revolution. Fluent in English, José María and his young family (including José Gándara, Margarita's father) pretended to be Americans in order to escape to El Paso. For many years after José became a Catholic revolutionary during the late 1920s, he remained on the US side of the border, since crossing into Mexico could mean imprisonment or death. When she grew up, Margarita became a painter and sculptor, living first in Ciudad Juárez and eventually moving to El Paso.[18]

José Luis de la Torre is a calm-spoken and analytical family man who lives in Tempe, Arizona, and works as a property manager. He came from a border-area family as well, but spent most of his early life in Mexico before migrating to the United States in 1973. During the Cristero War, his entire family—father, mother, grandparents, aunts and uncles—had sought exile in Nogales, Arizona. José's grandparents were close confidantes of Juan Navarrete, the bishop of Sonora; many of their eight children (including José's father, Luis) had played key roles in the Cristero uprising, and one of their sons (José's uncle, Alfonso) was killed in the conflict. After the war, some family members stayed in the United States; others, such as José's father, returned to various parts of Mexico.[19]

In describing the reasons for their families' migration to the United States, the six Cristero emigrant descendants clearly identified the religious conflict in Mexico as the primary cause. At the same time, they also acknowledged economic factors that influenced their families' decisions to cross the border. In the Venegas family, for example, Miguel Venegas left because the political spat with the cacique threatened not only his life, but also his family business in Jalisco. Once he settled in the United States, his family's grocery store in Los Angeles kept him tied to California, even after the war had ended. In the case of the Gándara family, the initial emigrant, grandfather José María, came to El Paso because he had been employed as a lawyer for the American Smelting and Refining Company, which had a smelting plant in that city. Likewise, Adelina Huerta's father came to Chicago primarily to provide financial support for his mother and siblings at home in Mexico, although he might not have migrated if his father had not been killed during the Cristero War.

This blending of political and economic "push factors" means that these Mexican emigrant families cannot be strictly categorized as either "political" or "labor" emigrants. The people I interviewed clearly indicated that religious persecution during the Cristero War was the primary cause of their migration. Yet economic reasons also played a role. This blurring of categories is helpful when considering the continued migration of Mexicans to the United States during the rest of the twentieth century. While economic causes for migration may have been more important for subsequent generations of Mexican emigrants, there is no reason to believe that they left their religious practices or beliefs behind when they crossed the border. In fact, the family narratives of Cristero emigrants indicate that the opposite was true.

Multigenerational Narratives of the Cristero Conflict

Within emigrant Mexican families affected by the Cristero War, news about the religious conflict circulated continuously and transnationally. As discussed in previous chapters, the families of these emigrants, including their young children, kept themselves informed about events in Mexico either through external sources (newspapers, community events, and social groups) or internal sources (family stories or letters from Mexico). Taken together, this information would fuel not only their continued awareness of the conflict, but also their devotion to Cristero symbols, memories, and martyrs.

The Venegas family constantly discussed the war during the 1920s and 1930s. María Teresa's father, Miguel Venegas, corresponded almost weekly with family members at home in Mexico, using code words in order to throw off the government censors who monitored the mail. When he received responses from his parents or siblings in Mexico, he would read them aloud to his children in Los Angeles. In addition to these updates, the family read *La Opinión*, the conservative Los Angeles Mexican newspaper, every day. Through the newspaper, according to María Teresa Venegas, "we kept tabs on what was happening in Mexico."

In some cases, family members not only read the news, but also produced it: in Chicago, Severino López's father, Don Severino López, began publishing a small newspaper called *La Avispa* (*The Hornet*). The newspaper's purpose, as Severino described it, was "to inform the large contingency of people in Chicago who were from Jalisco, Guanajuato, and Michoacán what was taking place in Mexico ... [it] acted also as a tool of support for the Cristero movement taking place back home." Don Severino's activities went beyond publishing the newspaper: he also gathered funds to send money back to the Cristero troops. As Severino López recalled, the family's friends and neighbors

> were all sympathetic and they all cooperated with my father in sending funds to help the movement. They would have various gatherings to raise funds: they would run a dance or plays, and my dad was gathering funds at the theater around the feasts of the 16th of September [Mexico's Independence Day]. People would gather in one of the halls; we would have a queen and things like that.

Within Severino's family, then, the religious war in Mexico was not only a frequent topic of conversation, but the object of community action. As a result, he grew up surrounded by news of the conflict. "I would pick up bits of information, and we would read letters from home and so forth," he stated.

José Luis de la Torre, who grew up in Mexico, also described how his family shared narratives about their experiences during the Cristero War. This was especially important to him, since, as a student in Mexican public schools, José was not taught about the religious conflict. His father frequently told him stories about his family's activities during the war, which included political intrigue, militancy, a dramatic escape across the border to Nogales, and the battlefield deaths of both an uncle and his aunt's fiancé. In addition, his father often read him letters from other family members who had been involved in the conflict. Later, when he went to college in Monterrey, he lived with his uncle Carlos, a Jesuit priest. "My uncle told me all the anecdotes," he recalled, "and I began reading more of the correspondence of my family, and the history of the war." Eventually, he would become the unofficial historian of his family, collecting their letters and accounts of the war and compiling them for a book that he plans to publish.

Encounters with Religious Refugees

For the children of the Cristero-era emigrants, their families were not the only source of knowledge about—and devotion to—the symbols, martyrs, and narratives of the religious conflict. Within many Mexican communities in the United States, emigrant family members attended the increasing numbers of Catholic schools and parishes that were staffed by Mexican priests and nuns. As discussed in Chapter 2, up to 2,500 refugee clergy—priests, nuns, seminarians, and bishops—came to the United States from Mexico during the war years. Most of them then resettled within new and existing parishes in Mexican emigrant neighborhoods. As a result, emigrants who wished to attend Catholic church services during the Cristero War years could often attend Mass given by a priest from Mexico—and even in some instances, a priest who came from their hometown. By the end of the decade, the number of Mexican national parishes had multiplied, and most of them were run and staffed by religious refugees.[20] Additionally, pious emigrant families who had supported the

Cristero cause were particularly interested in pursuing Catholic religious education for their children. During the Cristero War years, the refugee priests, seminarians, and nuns provided a way to meet that demand, as seminaries and boarding schools relocated wholesale from Mexico; and religious orders opened new schools for poor Mexican emigrants in the United States.

For the families of Cristero descendants, these Catholic parishes and schools would allow them to continue to practice their religion almost as they had done before leaving Mexico. In Chicago, Severino López's family attended the Mexican parish of Our Lady of Guadalupe, and they eventually enrolled their children in parish schools. The family expressed great pride, recalled Severino, because Our Lady of Guadalupe was "the first church that was built by Mexicans." Likewise, Adelina Huerta and her siblings grew up attending a Mexican parish; her family regularly attended Mass at St. Francis of Assisi, the other Mexican parish in Chicago. The family of María Teresa Venegas also attended a Mexican parish: Our Lady Queen of Angels Church, in the heart of the city's oldest Mexican neighborhood. There, they participated in Sunday Mass, as well as in other forms of worship, such as novenas and the adoration of the Blessed Sacrament.

Not only could Mexican emigrant families attend Mexican churches and send their children to Mexican parochial schools in the United States, but they could also join Mexican religious orders. During the war years, entire communities of nuns and monks relocated their convents and monasteries to the United States. These included the Sisters of Perpetual Adoration, whose superior, Mother Gertrudis, led a group of nuns from Guadalajara to southern California in July of 1926;[21] the Seminario Nacional Mexicano de San Felipe Neri-Castroville, Texas;[22] and the Carmelite Sisters of the Most Sacred Heart of Los Angeles, who came to the United States after their director, Mother Luisita, crossed the border in disguise.[23] This latter order would eventually grow into a multiethnic group of female religious, which has been credited by one scholar with becoming an "important presence in the conservative postconciliar American church" and reviving "the Tridentine lifestyle and devotions."[24] (Another well-known exile religious institution, the Montezuma Seminary of New Mexico, would operate from 1937 until 1972. As historian Anne Martínez argues, however, it generally trained priests who would return to Mexico, and did not have a significant impact within Catholic communities—either Mexican or non-Mexican—in the United States.[25])

Through education, church attendance, and community interactions, the families of Cristero emigrants regularly encountered the religious refugees in their daily lives. Adelina Huerta's father, for example, worked for the Claretian Order in Chicago, where he repaired their presses. Her awareness of the order would later influence her decision to join the Xavieran Missionary order when she grew up. Severino López had similar interactions: his own exposure to the Claretian community in Chicago, as well as his parents' involvement in religious devotional societies (his mother became a member of the Guadalupana Society and his father belonged to the Vincent de Paul Society), eventually prompted Severino to become a Claretian Missionary priest.

In some cases, religious refugees were also family members. María Teresa Venegas had relatives who belonged to religious orders. Two of her aunts had been cloistered nuns who had fled to San Francisco after the outbreak of the war with their order, the Sisters of Perpetual Adoration. "My aunts were always after me [to become more involved in the Catholic faith]" she remembered fondly. "I liked that kind of life; they were so joyful." At age eighteen, at the encouragement of her aunts, she took religious vows, joining the Sisters of the Immaculate Heart of Mary in 1970.[26]

Of course, not all of the children of Cristero emigrants went to Mexican Catholic schools or grew up to join religious orders. José Luis de la Torre, who grew up in Mexico and attended public schools, eventually married and had three children. María Teresa Amador Díaz, likewise, never took holy vows, although two of her children would eventually do so. And in some instances, the descendants of Cristero emigrants moved away from their religious upbringing altogether. Margarita Gándara, the daughter of the Cristero militant José Gándara, experienced religion as a pervasive influence during her early life. Her father's two sisters were deeply devout. As a result, she stated, "I harbored this horrific fear of hell—they said if you ate meat on Friday, even a sliver of chicken, you'd go to hell." After her father's failed revolt, his own faith was severely shaken, and for a while he felt so disillusioned by the Catholic Church that he developed a drinking problem. This experience—as well as the "fanaticism" of her two aunts—was traumatic to Margarita. She coped with her mixed feelings about religion after becoming a painter in Ciudad Juárez; during her long career, she frequently grappled with religious themes in her art.

Thus, for the descendants of Cristero emigrants, religious devotion and practice was common within their families, and was often formative—but it was not universally determinative of religious identity in later life. For

Margarita Gándara, and surely for many others, this intense religious practice would eventually influence her to move away from active participation in Catholic life.[27] Nevertheless, her family's dramatic involvement with the Cristero cause remained significant in her life narrative. For the other five people I interviewed, their families' ability to maintain their religious practices despite their physical separation from Mexico would prove instrumental in their continued sense of religious devotion, and in the centrality of the Cristero War to their narratives of migration and family life in the United States.

A Shared History of Martyrdom

Regardless of the levels of religiosity and varied career paths of the people I interviewed, they all shared a common practice: a deep veneration for deceased relatives, whom they viewed as having been persecuted by the Mexican government as a result of their Catholic faith. Irrespective of the circumstances of their death, all of these deceased relatives were seen as martyrs within their surviving families.

In the popular Catholic tradition, martyrdom is especially valued, since those who are killed because of their faith are believed to ascend straight to heaven and become saints, where they can intercede directly to God for those on earth, as well as grant the prayers of their faithful.[28] Within Mexico, most Cristeros and their families believed that the people who were killed by federal troops during the war were martyrs, regardless of whether they were officially declared to be so by the Catholic Church.[29] For most religious Mexicans, a martyr in the family was a great honor, and the culture of martyrdom was widely celebrated during the war years on both sides of the border. In December 1928, for example, the US-based Mexican Catholic newspaper *La Voz de la Patria* ran an ad announcing the sale of a hundred-page booklet, compiled by the exiled bishop José de Jesús Manríquez y Zárate, "illustrated with photographs of our martyrs."[30]

Among the families I interviewed, the martyrdom of relatives was perhaps most important within Adelina Huerta's family. Her maternal grandfather, Salvador Huerta Gutiérrez, and her great-uncle, Ezequiel Huerta Gutiérrez, had been pacifists who did not take up arms, and died after being tortured and shot in front of a firing squad. As a result of the circumstances of their death, the two men also received official recognition from the Catholic Church: they were beatified in 2005.

Even before their beatification, however, their families venerated them as martyrs. Adelina's father, who was thirteen when his own father was executed, remembered the event well, and discussed his vivid memories within the family. Indeed, Adelina and her siblings grew up with the knowledge that family members had been martyred for their religious beliefs. She later recounted how it had affected her family life:

> My father always talked about it—kept the story alive—we always knew that [my grandfather and uncle] were martyred . . . [We had] a history of the *revolución cristera* and my grandfather and my uncle's pictures were in there. Most of my father's side of the family, they always talked about it; [we knew that if] we needed anything we should pray to my grandfather because he was a martyr.

Salvador and Ezequiel Huerta Gutiérrez each had numerous children, and some of these stayed in Mexico. Adelina's cousin, who lived in Mexico, wrote about making relics from the bloodstained shirt that Salvador had been wearing during his execution. "Emotions as well as thoughts galloped through my head. I knew I had his blood in my veins . . . But this was . . . having his blood on my hand; he shed his blood in his martyrdom."[31] Thus, within the Mexican side of the family, the martyrs were venerated just as much as on the American side.

María Teresa Venegas, the daughter of the Los Angeles shop owner who fled Los Altos de Jalisco, also had a family member who was killed during the Cristero War. This was her father Miguel's brother, Alfonso, who had operated a small printing press that published pro-Cristero tracts. Federal troops found the press, near San José de Gracia, and fired into the building with machine guns; Alfonso and a companion were killed. In this case, the family did not receive confirmation of his death until around 1960, when a witness came forward. However, they assumed he had died after 1930, and regarded him as a martyr to the Cristero cause. According to María Teresa Venegas, for her and her many siblings, "these were very strong direct connections to someone we consider a martyr."

María Teresa Venegas's uncle was not the only person that her family venerated. Her great-aunt, María de Jesús Sacramentado Venegas (commonly known as Madre Nati) belonged to the Daughters of the Sacred Heart of Jesus, which operated a hospital in Guadalajara. During the war, she kept the hospital open and ministered to the sick, despite the threat of reprisal from federal troops. After her death in 1959, she was credited with a number of miracles; subsequently, she was canonized in 2000, and became Mexico's first female saint. María Teresa also remembered looking through a book by the Mexican Jesuit and historian Mariano Cuevas that her parents kept on a coffee table: "At the end of the book were page after page about martyrs. So for me as a child growing up I remember sitting there quietly [and] going through photos . . . That to me was a very deep influence—thinking of the martyrs and how cool it would be to become a martyr." For María Teresa as for many devout Catholics, martyrdom was something to be honored, and even wished for, as it was the purest and most noble expression of devotion to Christ.

Within José Luis de la Torre's family, there were numerous deaths of family members whom relatives later considered to be martyrs. His aunt María, who never married, had a boyfriend who was executed by soldiers in 1928; his uncle Alfonso was a Cristero soldier who was killed in 1935 near the town of Suaqui de Batuc, in Sonora; and another aunt was also considered a martyr, having been killed by soldiers while bringing food and supplies to the Cristeros. (The remains of his uncle, Alfonso de la Torre, are now interred in the border region, at the Sanctuary of Our Lady of Guadalupe in Nogales, Sonora.) Within the de la Torre family, these martyred ancestors were remembered and revered by their many descendants.

In some cases, the family martyrs had died before the Cristero War, albeit at the hands of the same anticlerical leaders who would eventually participate in the religious conflict. Severino López recounted the story of his aunt, Josefa Parra, who had been killed during the Mexican Revolution when General José García Inés Chávez raided the town:

> the soldiers were looking for young ladies to abuse. The soldiers grabbed her . . . [and] she ran into a burning building rather than being caught . . . she died defending her chastity.

After Josefa's death, the townspeople began to venerate "*las quemaditas*" (the little burned ones), as they called Josefa and another woman who had died with her. Soon, the local parish church began documenting "prayers answered and favors received."[32] Eventually, Catholic officials began the process of canonization for the two women, although the effort reportedly stalled in the late twentieth century. Despite her lack of institutional recognition, however, Josefa was venerated within the López family.

This sense of devotion was also present within the family of María Teresa Amador Díaz, the niece of José de Jesús Manríquez y Zárate. Although her uncle did not die in the war, and therefore is not considered a saint or a martyr, her family nevertheless considered him to have been a holy man who was a victim of persecution, and therefore martyr-like in character.[33] As María Teresa stated,

> My uncle was a saint; he was so brave. Calles was a demon. My uncle fought for all of his life. He was the beacon of the family, and he was exiled from Mexico. He only came back to die, when he was very sick. We all venerated him.

This devotion to martyrs and saints of the Cristero War, and particularly within the families of Cristero descendants, is widely established in Mexico, and is commonly expressed in the practice of establishing physical spaces in chapels, churches, and cathedrals where the martyrs can be honored.

In the United States, this practice is certainly not limited to the six families I interviewed. In fact, there is increasing evidence in the popular press that this practice of devotion to martyred ancestors, common within each of the families of the descendants I spoke with, is extensive within numerous other Mexican emigrant families with ties to the Cristero conflict. In 2012, after the US release of *For Greater Glory*, a film about the Cristero conflict, a variety of other family narratives surfaced in the Catholic popular press, as reporters became aware of the history of the Cristero War and sought to speak with descendants of Cristeros in the United States.[34] In Los Angeles, the Meza family described the life history of their patriarch, José Meza Gálvez, a Cristero soldier who was killed in Michoacán. His daughter, María, emigrated to the United States in the 1970s, and had fourteen children. Within her family, the story of her martyred father was a central narrative that was foundational to their continued religiosity.[35]

A Mexican emigrant from Jalisco, Salvador Gómez, cited the story of his two uncles, who were Cristero soldiers. Within his family, who emigrated to Detroit in the 1970s, the stories of his uncles' exploits were repeated and remembered. A member of Detroit's Holy Redeemer parish, Gómez described his uncles' involvement in the war as an exercise in devotion: "Sometimes they would eat once a day, sometimes nothing to eat for three days, or have no water. But they preferred to die to not believing in God." In addition, Gómez described how the memories of the conflict continue to reverberate within his community in Detroit: a grandson of a federal colonel (an enemy of the Cristeros) is a neighbor of his. Apparently, however, this grandson now identifies with the Cristero side of the conflict: "he says his grandfather is a bad man," according to Gómez.[36] Numerous other interviews in the media recount similar family narratives among emigrants in diverse locations across the United States.[37]

The interviews with the descendants of Cristero emigrants, in combination with recent accounts by other emigrant families, indicate that these family-oriented martyr devotions persist across generations, and are transnational in nature. By maintaining strong and enduring devotions to Cristero martyrs within their families, Mexican emigrants have also cultivated memories and narratives about the Cristero War. These can help explain why the Cristero saint Toribio Romo has generated such a large devotional following among Mexican emigrants. For many of them, Saint Toribio is part of a larger historical narrative that they are intimately familiar with, thanks to the stories of their parents and grandparents.

A Complex Relationship to the Homeland

For the people I interviewed, memories and experiences of the Cristero conflict affected not only devotional practices, but also their perceptions of Mexico and Mexican history. Their relationship to their homeland was a complex mixture of positive and negative: they expressed love and nostalgia for Mexico, but also wariness, and in some cases outright suspicion, toward the Mexican government. Furthermore, they developed historical narratives about Mexico that contradicted the official state narratives taught in Mexican schools and popularized by the Mexican state. (For most of the twentieth century, Mexican children did not learn about the Cristero War in school, since government-distributed public school textbooks largely excluded the history of religion and the Church-state conflict. This did not change until 1992, when official primary school textbooks began to include an examination of the Cristero War.)[38]

Given the centrality of religious devotion to the lives of Cristero emigrant descendants, this critical stance toward Mexican nationalism and Mexican history is not surprising. As we have seen in earlier chapters, for Mexican emigrants during the Cristero War, quotidian religious practice was infused with contemporary Mexican politics. During the 1920s and 1930s, the act of going to Mass or participating in parochial processions or communal prayers was often a political statement. After all, as discussed in Chapter 3, Mexican priests and bishops in exile in the United States frequently spoke out against the Mexican government, and urged their parishioners to support the Cristero cause. Thus, simply attending such events—such as the celebrations of Corpus Christi or the Feast of Christ the King in Los Angeles—subjected participants to strong critiques of Mexico's anticlerical government.

This mixture of sentiments—a combination of deep nostalgia and love for Mexico and criticism of its modern government—was expressed by Severino López, the Claretian priest who grew up Chicago. Although he never returned to Mexico during his childhood, he always felt a connection to his homeland. As he put it, "as a Mexican American, I have always followed and preserved my interest in Mexico." In his adult life he did return to Mexico for several short visits: during his career as a missionary, he completed a stint in Guerrero, and later in his life, he would make a visit to Guanajuato to attend a ceremony for the beatification of a martyred priest. These connections, however, did not preclude a critical stance toward the government. In his memoirs, he expressed nostalgia for the pre-Revolutionary period:

> There was a time when [Mexico] enjoyed a relative peace and prosperity during the reign of Porfirio Diaz . . . [his] administration was characterized by a period of stability and a strong economy . . . there was a marked interest in education . . . this gave rise to middle class intellectuals and professionals.[39]

This generous description of the *porfiriato* provides a counterpoint to the narratives promoted by Mexico's Revolutionary government within Mexican emigrant communities. These narratives invariably described Porfirio Díaz as a ruthless dictator, and lionized his enemies, the military heroes of the Mexican Revolution.[40] In Severino López's memory, by contrast, Revolutionary heroes were instigators of violence, and the Porfirian period was a kind of golden age that was disrupted by the violence and chaos of the Revolution.

Such historical counternarratives were certainly present among Mexican Cristero supporters in the United States during the 1920s. Supporters of the Cristero cause, when they recounted the history of Mexico, tended to emphasize Catholic heroes such as Miguel Hidalgo and José María Morelos, the priests who helped launch Mexico's independence movement; or Agustín de Iturbide, Mexico's first national leader during independence, who included support for the Church in his political platform. When Simón Tenorio launched his Catholic revolt along the border, for example, his group's manifesto claimed to "initiate an armed movement under the flag of the three guarantees and with the spirit to vindicate the death of the Father of our country, Don Agustín de Iturbide."[41] Thus, Severino López's portrayal of Porfirio Díaz as a national hero, written in 2004, echoes historical narratives expressed by Cristero supporters on both sides of the border during the 1920s and 1930s.

Like Severino López, María Teresa Venegas—the daughter of the Los Angeles shopkeeper who had fought for the Cristero army—expressed a somewhat ambivalent assessment of her relationship to her homeland. During her childhood, she recalled that her family felt a pervasive sense of wariness: her father "never, never" trusted the Mexican government, either at the local or national level. Within their Mexican neighborhood in Los Angeles, her father was careful to keep his opinions about Mexico to himself. Even to the members of his family, he minimized his own role in the religious conflict, only revealing that he had been a Cristero soldier after María Teresa began to interview him about the topic toward the end of his life. After the war ended, her family continued their oppositional activities, attending clandestine meetings of the Sinarquistas (the ultra-right Catholic political organization that formed in Mexico during the 1930s and had chapters on both sides of the border). "It was very hush-hush," she recalled. "We had to be very careful attending this particular event."

Despite this continued opposition toward the Mexican government—and the sense of wariness and caution that went along with that opposition—María Teresa Venegas's family retained lasting and positive connections to Mexico, and to their hometown in Jalisco, for most of her lifetime. They occasionally returned to Mexico—once for a period of two years—and she describes a feeling of great joy and a sense of belonging each time they went back:

The trips to Mexico were incredible for us, a wonderful feeling, because we could visit and meet our relatives and be with them. Once we crossed the border, we became something different. I no longer felt inferior. Then when we crossed [back into the United

States] you could feel this shutting down right away. So these were powerful reasons for loving Mexico.

Thus, for María Teresa Venegas and her family, support for the Cristero cause did not preclude a sense of deep fondness for their homeland, even if these feelings were tempered by their opposition to the policies of the Revolutionary state.

Like María Teresa Venegas, Margarita Gándara also expressed both love for Mexico and an abiding ambivalence for the politics of her homeland. As a child, her father took her on a trip to Mexico so that she could become familiar with the country. There, she was struck by the beauty of the scenery, and influenced by Mexican visual culture—particularly the compelling surrealist paintings of Mexican artist Rufino Tamayo. When she herself became an artist in the 1960s, the El Paso native relocated to Ciudad Juárez, where she maintained a thriving studio and gained local recognition.[42]

When the city's drug-related violence became endemic, however, Margarita refused to pay the *quota*, or bribes, to the local gangs. Soon, she began to receive threats of kidnapping and violence. As a result, she returned to El Paso, where she became a vocal critic of the Mexican government. "There's no police—the soldiers, the government, it's just all corrupt," she stated. She described her recurrent sense of relief upon returning to the United States: "I always breathe—*phew*—because I feel [a sense of] that protection that the US citizen has." Her own experience was just another event in a city with a long history of exile, and she likened her own exile to her father's and grandfather's flight from Mexico in the 1910s and 1920s. "El Paso is now full of escaped Mexicans," she said, "including me."

For at least one family, that of María Teresa Amador Díaz, this critical stance toward the Mexican government was especially focused on the PRI (the *Partido Revolucionario Institutional*), which was founded by President Calles and dominated Mexican politics for much of the twentieth century. As such, Mexican Cristero families viewed the PRI as the party responsible for the Cristero War. Throughout the twentieth century, the family of María Teresa Amador Díaz would back the conservative PAN (*Partido Acción Nacional*), which was founded by prominent Catholics after the Cristero War.[43] Thus, for the families of Cristero emigrants to the United States, the memories of the Cristero War had the potential to influence not only their feelings about the homeland and their narratives about the history of Mexico, but also their lasting alliance to specific political parties in Mexico.

Enduring Resonance

The experiences and family narratives of the Cristero emigrant descendants interviewed here—Severino López, Adelina Huerta, María Teresa Amador Díaz, María Teresa Venegas, José Luis de la Torre, and Margarita Gándara—indicate that the Cristero War had a multigenerational, transnational impact on Mexican emigrant families. For the families of the interviewees, the experience of migration was linked to the religious conflict in Mexico: they framed their migration in terms of exodus, escape, or exile. Upon migrating, they remained aware of that religious conflict through informational networks that included letters from home, newspaper articles, and family stories. They continued to participate in daily Catholic life through education in Catholic schools, attendance at parish churches, and contact with the members of exiled religious orders. The families also cultivated a sense of strong devotion to family members whom they considered martyrs. Finally, all of these themes—exile, Catholic devotion, and martyrdom— fueled a complex, and at times ambivalent, relationship to Mexico as a nation, and to Mexican historical narratives and political realities. For the descendants of Cristero emigrants that I interviewed, their abiding love for Mexico was accompanied by a critical stance toward the Mexican government and a belief that the history of the Cristero War, long left out of state-sponsored narratives during the twentieth century, was centrally important to their own identity as Mexicans or Mexican Americans.[44]

These devotional practices and counter narratives offer a historical contextualization that can help explain the surging popularity of Santo Toribio Romo, the Cristero martyr from Jalostitlán, among Mexican emigrants during the last several decades. The family memories of the descendants of Cristero emigrants demonstrate the ways in which the events of the Cristero War continued to hold deep historical meaning for at least some Mexicans—not only in the years and decades immediately after the war, but throughout the twentieth century and up to the present day. The cult of Santo Toribio Romo, the Cristero martyr who shepherds emigrants across the border, is but one example of the long and complex legacy of the Cristero diaspora.

Epilogue

CRISTEROS RESURGENT

IN 2008, THE Mexican historian and priest Manuel Olimón Nolasco recounted a road trip that he had taken a few years earlier, along California's famous and dramatic coastal highway, Route 1. As he drove, he turned on the radio and happened upon a station that

> began to play, one after another, a Rosary of Cristero *corridos*. Many, many *corridos*, with lyrics that sang of the deeds of marginalized personalities from a history that, despite so many interpretations, silences, and oversights, has had a concrete and true achievement ... Surely, I thought then and I remember today, the Cristero memory has stayed alive in more than just a corner of California, fueled by the presence—and later the loving memory—of exiles: natives of Jalisco, Colima, and Nayarit.[1]

It is certainly true that the memory of the Cristero War has remained alive in California, as well as in many other parts of the United States and Mexico. In 2006, *The New York Times Magazine* published an article entitled "Nuevo Catholics," which argued that Hispanic immigrants have revitalized the Catholic Church in the United States. In a discussion about Mexicans in Los Angeles, the author stated that

> one key to the history of the city (mostly forgotten by non-Latinos) is the fact that the great migration of Mexican nationals northward in the past 30 years has a precedent in the 1920s, when waves of emigrants flowed into California after the failure of the Cristero

rebellion ... On one level, this is all ancient history, yet for many new immigrants from Mexico, the echoes linger on.[2]

This statement, as well as Olimón Nolasco's experience on the highway, underscores a key argument of this book: that the Cristero War has continued to resonate in the collective memory of many contemporary Mexican emigrants in the United States. And in fact, it is now apparent that, during the first two decades of the twenty-first century, the Cristero War has reemerged as a polarizing issue in Catholic popular culture on both sides of the border. Almost ninety years after the war began, Mexico's Cristeros—who once seemed destined to fade into obscurity, their history left out of Mexican textbooks and largely forgotten by US Catholics—are resurgent.

This renewed popularity comes about partly as the result of concerted efforts by Mexican and US Catholic organizations, especially members of the Knights of Columbus. The organization campaigned for the canonization of twenty-five priests and laymen killed during the Cristero War (they were canonized by Pope John Paul II in 2000; a smaller group was canonized by Pope Benedict XVI in 2006). Over the past decade, these Cristero saints—who include Toribio Romo, as well as beatified Mexican Cristero figures such as Father Miguel Pro—have generated an increasing following among Catholics in both countries.

This growing devotion to the saints of the Cristero War was on full display in 2006, when the US Knights of Columbus sponsored a multi-city tour of the holy relics of six Mexican saints (all of whom had been Knights during their lifetimes) to Catholic parishes across the United States and Mexico. The martyrs' relics consisted of bone fragments embedded inside a large golden cross, which the Catholic faithful could kneel before, touch, or kiss, as they made their prayers to the saints. In each of the US cities where the relics arrived—in Houston, Tucson, Los Angeles, San Antonio, Chicago, and New York—Catholic parishes, most of them with a large population of Mexican-origin parishioners, sponsored special masses to mark the occasion. At these events, parishioners lined up to venerate the Cristero martyrs, while several solemn Knights of Columbus, dressed in their signature black, white, and red regalia, stood guard beside the golden cross.[3] In 2012, the tour of the relics was repeated on the US side of the border.[4]

The latter tour coincided with two other major public events involving both the Knights and the Cristeros. The first of these was the June 2012 release of *For Greater Glory*, the first big-budget Hollywood film about the Cristero War. The movie, which starred well-known actors such as Peter O'Toole, Eva Longoria, and Andy Garcia, was produced by Pablo José Barroso, a Mexican businessman, and filmed entirely in English. During the months leading up to the movie's release, the US Knights of Columbus helped to generate publicity for the film, featuring a film still of actor Andy Garcia in character as General Enrique Gorostieta, the leader of the Cristero army, on the cover of the May issue of *Columbia*, the Knights' national magazine.

During the same month that *For Greater Glory* was released, the US Council of Catholic Bishops announced the first annual "Fortnight for Freedom," a "special period of prayer, study, catechesis, and public action" meant to highlight the cause of religious liberty in the United States. During the Fortnight, which took place from June 21 through July 4, 2012, and was repeated in 2013, some Catholic commentators, including members of the Knights of Columbus, framed the history of the Cristero War as directly relevant to contemporary US politics, arguing that the restriction of religious liberties in Mexico during the 1920s and 1930s was analogous to the contemporary struggle between the Catholic hierarchy and the administration of President Barack Obama, which had recently announced a mandate requiring religious institutions to provide birth control to their employees under the Affordable Care Act (something that the US Catholic hierarchy strongly opposed).[5]

Within the Mexican emigrant community, some Cristero descendants expressed agreement with that comparison. In an interview with *The Catholic Sun*, a publication of the Phoenix Catholic Diocese, a Mexican parishioner of the church of St. Francis Xavier named Rosie Villegas-Smith recounted her family's experiences during the Cristero War. After viewing the film *For Greater Glory*, she said, she felt proud of her family's resistance to the Mexican government. In the United States, she added, the government "is trying to take away our religious rights. We won't allow it. Our ancestors didn't permit it, and neither will we."[6] To Villegas-Smith and other American Catholics, the history of the Cristero War as depicted in the film provided a vivid allegory of religious opposition to a tyrannical government—one that was equivalent to their opposition to the Obama government's health-care mandate.

For a number of Catholics on the US side of the border, including many Mexican Americans, the Cristero War and the Cristero martyrs had emerged not only as objects of religious devotion, but also as a heroic emblem for conservative Catholics opposed to the social reforms of some US politicians. This deployment of the Cristero War as part of a particular political agenda is also a reminder that, just as there were during the 1920s and 1930s, there are deep political divisions within emigrant communities, and Mexican Americans—like many other emigrant groups—cannot necessarily be expected to vote in a bloc at the beginning of the twenty-first century.

In contemporary Mexico as well, the topic of Church-state relations and the Cristero War has likewise resurfaced in both political debates and the public imagination during the 2000s and 2010s. Numerous recent events contributed to this resurgence, most importantly the rise of the PAN to national power between 2000 and 2012. The 2000 election of presidential candidate Vicente Fox—who had openly genuflected before the image of the Virgin of Guadalupe—led many to wonder whether the Church would begin to assume a more prominent role in Mexican politics. And indeed, the moralizing campaigns of the PAN; the debate over abortion in Mexico City and the rise of the Pro-Vida lay organization; the political interventions of Cardinal Norberto Rivera Carrera; and the new prominence of ultraconservative lay organizations such as the Legionarios de Cristo seemed to indicate that the Catholic Church was increasingly willing to take a public stance in Mexican politics. Although the PAN lost the presidency in 2012, during the years of the PAN administration the meaning and legacy of the Cristero conflict became a topic of much more open discussion within the political landscape in Mexico. (Sometimes this discussion became quite controversial, as in 2007, when Mexico's Miss Universe candidate wore a hoop skirt emblazoned with printed images related to the war, including priests in front of the firing squad and executed Cristeros hanging from telegraph poles.)[7]

All of these events—the binational tour of Cristero relics, the debate over the movie *For Greater Glory* in the United States, and the renewed salience of the Cristero War as a topic of discussion, investigation, and debate in Mexico—have seemingly put an end to decades of public silence about the Cristero War on both sides of the border. Yet this recent surge of popular interest in the religious conflict of the 1920s and 1930s did not arise in a vacuum. This book has demonstrated that, thanks to the Great Migration of the 1920s, the Cristero War became a transnational conflict that had a profound impact on tens of thousands of Mexican emigrants during the war years. These emigrants, religious refugees, and political exiles—who were wealthy and poor, men and women, Indian, mestizo, and white—collaborated and competed in order to respond to the crisis and resist the anticlerical Mexican government from abroad. Together, they forged diasporic connections across regions and cities, as well as back to their homeland, in order to advance their political goals. Although their efforts to organize militant revolts from the United States were thwarted by internal divisions and external repression, they nevertheless developed a strong sense of religious nationalism, which would continue to inform the memories and identities of their descendants. In the end, it is apparent that the Cristero War comprises an integral, deeply felt part of Mexican American popular religiosity. As historians and other scholars continue to assess the impact of the war, the actions, interactions, and ideologies of the Cristero diaspora must be taken into consideration. Newer religious devotions, such as that of Santo Toribio, indicate that the legacy of the Cristero War—particularly its history of martyrdom and militancy—will continue to retain symbolic significance, and to shape religious and political identities, for Mexican Catholics on both sides of the border.

Notes

INTRODUCTION

1. Informe Número 394 [no author], Del Rio, Texas, August 14, 1927, in SRE, LE 822-8.

2. According to Acuña, "from the late nineteenth century on, Chihuahuan workers migrating into the United States named their barrios Chihuahuitas (Little Chihuahua) . . . a Chihuahuita was a place of refuge, where they could preserve their identity." Rodlofo F. Acuña, *Corridors of Migration: the Odyssey of Mexican Laborers, 1600–1933* (Tucson, AZ: University of Arizona Press, 2007), 1–2.

3. Clipping from the newspaper *La Razon*, February 27, 1927, in the AGN, IPS Vol. 33, Expediente 5.

4. Tenorio named several other men involved in the plot, including a Ramón Muzquiz of Eagle Pass, Texas; Coronel Fernando Ortegón, of Del Rio, Texas, and his nephew in Paint Rock, Texas; J. H. Avitud, a journalist from Paint Rock, Texas; Colonel Donaciano Maldonado of San Antonio, Texas; and a "north-American of the last name Smith" who supplied the horses. Tenorio also indicated that Félix Díaz was involved in funding or directing the movement. Díaz, a nephew of Mexico's former president Porfirio Díaz, lived in the United States during the 1910s and 1920s, and was among the many disaffected exiles opposed to the successive Mexican governments after the Revolution of 1910–20. Report from A. Granguillheme, Delegado de Migración in Piedras Negras, to the Secretaría de Gobernación, August 13, 1927, in AGN, Vol. 231, Expediente 30.

5. Informe Número 394 [no author], Del Rio, Texas, August 14, 1927, in SRE, LE 822-8; "Simon Tenorio et al," report by Agent J. J. Lawrence, August 18, 1927, in NACP, State RG 59, Decimal File 812.00/28745.

6. "Simon Tenorio et al," report by Agent J. J. Lawrence, August 18, 1927, in NACP, State RG 59, Decimal File 812.00/28745.

7. Report from A. Granguillheme, Delegado de Migración in Piedras Negras, to the Secretaría de Gobernación, August 13, 1927, in AGN, IPS, Vol. 231, Expediente 30; clipping from the newspaper *La Razon*, July 31, 1927, in AGN, IPS, Vol. 231, Expediente 30.

8. Informe Número 394 [no author], Del Rio, Texas, August 14, 1927, in SRE, LE 822-8.

9. Pascual Robles in San Antonio to Genaro S. Valadez in Del Rio, Texas, July 26, 1927, in SRE, LE 852-4.

10. María L. Carrasco in San Angelo, Texas to Pascual Robles, May 25, 1927, in SRE, LE 852-4.

11. San Antonio Consul General to Mr. Gus Johns, Department of Justice Agent in San Antonio, August 11, 1927, in SRE, LE 852-4; Simón Muñoz in Detroit to Genaro S. Valadez in Del Rio, Texas, July 29, 1927, in SRE, LE 852-4.

12. Report from A. Granguillheme, Delegado de Migración in Piedras Negras, to the Secretaría de Gobernación, August 13, 1927, in AGN, IPS, Vol. 231, Expediente 30.

13. Report from Agent 47 in San Antonio to the Jefe del Departamento Confidencial, December 28, 1927, in AGN, IPS, Vol. 54, Expediente 10.

14. A. Granguillhome, Delegado de Migracion in Piedras Negras, to the Secretaría de Gobernación, August 20, 1927, in AGN, IPS, Vol. 231, Expediente 30.

15. Jean Meyer, *The Cristero Rebellion: The Mexican People Between Church and State, 1926–1929* (Cambridge: Cambridge University Press, 1976), 178.

16. The history of Mexican migration to the United States began with the annexation of more than half of Mexico's territory by the United States in 1848. For more on the history of late-nineteenth-century population movements in the borderlands, see José Ángel Hernández, *Mexican American Colonization during the Nineteenth Century: A History of the U.S.-Mexico Borderlands* (New York: Cambridge University Press, 2012).

17. US immigration statistics provide only a rough indication of emigrant population growth and decline, since a significant number of Mexican emigrants during the period went uncounted by border officials and census-takers. In 1926, using money orders and US and Mexican census and immigration data, Manuel Gamio pointed out that Mexican emigration was still highly cyclical, and that government sources were unreliable on both sides of the border. In Manuel Gamio, "Number of Mexican Immigrants in the United States," in *Mexican Immigration to the United States: A Study of Human Migration and Adjustment* (Chicago: University of Chicago Press, 1930), 1–12. The US Bureau of the Census, Censuses of Population, 1910–1940 estimated 1.5 million, as cited in Oscar J. Martínez, *Mexican-Origin People in the United States: A Topical History* (Tucson, AZ: University of Arizona Press, 2001), 14.

18. The extensive literature on Mexican exiles during the Revolution includes W. Dirk Raat, *Revoltosos: Mexican Rebels in the United States, 1903–23* (College Station, TX: Texas A&M University Press, 1981); Peter Henderson, *Mexican Exiles in the Borderlands, 1910–1913* (El Paso, TX: Texas Western Press, 1979); Michael M. Smith, "The Mexican Secret Service in the United States, 1910–1920," *The Americas* Vol. 59, No. 1 (2002), 65–85; Victoria Lerner Sigal, "Espionaje y Revolución Mexicana," *Historia Mexicana* Vol. 44, No. 4 (1995), 617–42, and "Los exiliados de la Revolución Mexicana en Estados Unidos, 1910–1940," in *La comunidad mexicana en Estados Unidos. Aspectos de su historia*, ed. Fernando Saúl Alanis Enciso (Mexico City: CONACULTA, 2004), 71–126; David Dorado Romo, *Ringside Seat to a Revolution: An Underground Cultural History of El Paso and Juárez, 1893–1923* (El Paso, TX: Cinco Puntos Press, 2005); Charles H. Harris II and Louis R. Salder, *The Secret War in El Paso: Mexican Revolutionary Intrigue, 1906–1920* (Albequerque, NM: University of New Mexico Press, 2009); Nancy Aguirre, "Porfirismo during the Mexican Revolution: Exile and the Politics of Representation, 1910–1920" (PhD diss., University of Texas, El Paso, 2012); Ward Albro, *Always a Rebel: Ricardo Flores Magon and the Mexican Revolution* (Fort Worth, TX: Texas Christian University Press, 1992); Thomas C. Langham, *Border Trials: Ricardo Flores Magón and the Mexican Liberals* (El Paso, TX: Texas Western Press, 1981); Linda B. Hall, *Revolution on the Border: The United States and Mexico 1910–1920* (Albuquerque, NM: University of New Mexico Press, 1988); and Elliott Young, *Catarino Garza's Revolution on the Texas-Mexico Border* (Durham, NC: Duke University Press, 2004).

19. For a deeper discussion of how the term "diaspora" has been applied to Mexican emigrants, see Alexandra Délano, *Mexico and Its Diaspora in the United States: Policies of Emigration since 1848* (New York: Cambridge University Press, 2011), 4. Specifically, she states that "a number of authors have established certain criteria to establish whether a group can be designated as a diaspora, mostly coinciding with the premise that a dispersed population's identification with a real or imagined homeland and maintenance of emotional or social ties with it is a key feature of a diaspora." Délano, 2, n 2.

20. Dufoix also cites William Safran's six criteria for diasporas: (1) "their or their ancestors' dispersion from a center to at least two peripheral foreign regions"; (2) "the persistence of a collective memory concerning their homeland"; (3) "the certainty that their acceptance by the host society is important"; (4) "the main-tenance of an often idealized homeland as a goal of return"; (5) "the belief in a collective duty to engage in the perpetuation, restoration, or security of the country of origin"; and (6) "the maintenance of individual or collective rela-tions with the country of origin." As we shall see in this chapter and those fol-lowing, the Cristero diaspora meets most, if not all, of these criteria, with the

possible exception of the third. See Stéphane Dufoix, *Diasporas*, trans. William
Rodamor (Berkeley, CA: University of California Press, 2006), 60.

21. Francisco Balderrama is among the scholars who have studied Mexicans who
supported the Revolutionary government during the 1920s and 1930s. See
his essay, "Revolutionary Mexican Nationalism and the Mexican Immigrant
Community in Los Angeles during the Great Depression: Memory, Identity,
and Survival," in *The Mexican Revolution: Conflict and Consolidation,
1910–1940*, ed. Douglas W. Richmond and Sam W. Haynes (College Station,
TX: Texas A&M University Press, 2013), 117–34. See also Dennis Nodín Valdéz,
"Mexican Revolutionary Nationalism and Repatriation during the Great
Depression," *Mexican Studies/Estudios Mexicanos* Vol. 4, No. 1 (Winter 1988),
1–23. For a more recent study, and one that is unique in tracing the divisions
between "liberals" and "traditionalists" within a Mexican community, see
John Henry Flores, "On the Wings of the Revolution: Transnational Politics
and the Making of Mexican American Identities" (PhD diss., University of
Illinois at Chicago, 2009).

22. For a discussion of the role of class within several generations of the Mexican
emigrant population during the 1920s and 1930s, see Richard A. Garcia, *Rise
of the Mexican American Middle Class: San Antonio, 1929–1941* (College Station,
TX: Texas A&M University Press, 1991).

23. Letter from a group of Mexican residents of Perris, California, to President
Plutarco Elias Calles, April 23, 1926, AGN, D-Gob., Vol. 39, Expediente
2-347 (2-2).

24. These collections included the Archivo General de la Nación; the Archivo
Histórico Genaro Estrada, Secretaría de Relaciones Exteriores; the Archivo
Histórico de la Universidad Nacional Autónoma de México; the Archivo Histórico
del Arzobispado de México; and the Archivo Cristero at the Centro de Estudios
de Historia de México CARSO (formerly CONDUMEX). I also consulted the
Archivos de la Secretaría de Educación Pública and the Hemeroteca Nacional
de México. Finally, I visited several regional archives, including the Archivo
Historico de Jalisco in Guadalajara and the Archivo General de Guanajuato in the
city of Guanajuato. Thanks to the kindness of Professor Fernando Saúl Alanís
Enciso, I was able to consult copies of records from local archives in San Luis
Potosí as well. These local records, however, provided fewer relevant sources than
the national collections, and most of this narrative relies on documents from the
national collections in Mexico City.

25. In the Washington, DC, region, I consulted the National Archives and Records
Administration holdings in College Park and Washington, DC; the American
Catholic History Research Center at the Catholic University of America; the
Library of Congress; and the records of the Special Collections department
at Georgetown University Library. In New Haven, Connecticut, I visited the
Knights of Columbus Supreme Council Archives. To research what happened

on the borderlands, I went to El Paso, where I examined documents in the C. L. Sonnichsen Special Collections Department at the University of Texas at El Paso; thanks to research assistance by Timothy R. Homan and Robin Zenger, I was able to view materials from the University of Arizona Libraries Special Collections. In California, I made use of various manuscripts and documents at the Bancroft Library at the University of California, Berkeley; thanks to research assistance from James Adams, I was able to view documents from the Department of Archives and Special Collections at Loyola Marymount University, Los Angeles. I also visited numerous collections in Chicago, including the Special Collections Research Center at the University of Chicago; the Archives and Special Collections at Loyola University—Chicago; the Archives of the Claretian Missionaries; and the Archives and Records Center of the Archdiocese of Chicago. Finally, I consulted the microform collections of the Chicago Public Library and the East Chicago Public Library in East Chicago, Indiana.

26. Since the 1960s, the historical literature on the Cristero War has focused predominantly on its popular roots, thanks to the influence of scholars such as Alicia Olivera de Bonfil and Jean Meyer, who began compiling oral histories and archival records in order to explain popular participation and popular religiosity. See Alicia Olivera de Bonfil (who later published under the name Alicia Olivera Sedano), *Aspectos del conflicto religioso de 1926 a 1929, sus antecedentes y consecuencias* (Mexico City: Instituto Nacional de Antropología e Historia, 1966); Jean Meyer, *La Cristiada*, 4 Vols. (Mexico City: Siglo Veintiuno Editores, 1976) and *The Cristero Rebellion: The Mexican People Between Church and State, 1926–1929*. Until the early 2000s, much of this scholarship generally focused on the west-central region, particularly Jalisco and Michoacán. See Jim Tuck, *The Holy War in Los Altos: A Regional Analysis of Mexico's Cristero Rebellion* (Tucson, AZ: University of Arizona Press, 1982); Jennie Purnell, *Popular Movements and State Formation in Revolutionary Mexico: The Agraristas and Cristeros of Michoacán* (Durham, NC: Duke University Press, 1999); Marjorie Becker, *Setting the Virgin on Fire: Lázaro Cárdenas, Michoacán Peasants, and the Redemption of the Mexican Revolution* (Berkeley, CA: University of California Press, 1995); Christopher Boyer, *Becoming Campesinos: Politics, Identity, and Agrarian Struggle in Postrevolutionary Michoacán, 1920–1935* (Stanford, CA: Stanford University Press, 2003); Matthew Butler, *Popular Piety and Political Identity in Mexico's Cristero Rebellion: Michoacán, 1927–1929* (New York: Oxford University Press, 2004).

Historian Adrian Bantjes, in an incisive historiographical essay, argued that while the turn toward straightforward, respectful examinations of popular religiosities and local belief systems has been a positive one, Cristero scholarship is nonetheless hobbled by "temporal limitations and generalizations based on the rather exceptional case of the Bajío." See "Religion and the Mexican

Revolution: Toward a New Historiography," in *Religious Culture in Modern Mexico*, ed. Martin Austin Nesvig (Lanham, MD: Rowman & Littlefield, 2007), 242. In a subsequent essay, Bantjes called for a national overview of "the variables that may have triggered cycles of local and regional religious violence," arguing against the parochialism of scholarship that equates the religious conflict with west-central Mexico. Furthermore, he asserts that "popular resistance" can itself be interpreted in new ways, encompassing not only the decision to take up arms, but also peaceful events such as demonstrations, boycotts, and petitions. "The Regional Dynamics of Anticlericalism and Defanaticization in Revolutionary Mexico," in *Faith and Impiety in Revolutionary Mexico*, ed. Matthew Butler (New York: Palgrave Macmillan, 2007), 111 and 122. Several of the other essays in *Faith and Impiety* go far in overturning such monolithic conceptions, including Alan Knight, "The Mentality and Modus Operandi of Revolutionary Anticlericalism," 21–56; Matthew Butler, "Trouble Afoot? Pilgrimage in *Cristero* Mexico City," 149–66; Massimo De Giuseppe, "'El Indio Gabriel': New Religious Perspectives among the Indigenous in Garrido Canabal's Tabasco (1927–1930)," 225–43; and Edward Wright-Rios, "A Revolution in Local Catholicism? Oaxaca, 1928–34," 243–59.

Even more recently, scholars on both sides of the border have begun to produce new examinations of the Cristero conflict that move beyond the religious heartland states of Jalisco and Michoacán. These studies include Edward Wright-Rios's *Revolutions in Mexican Catholicism: Reform and Revelation in Oaxaca, 1887–1934* (Durham, NC: Duke University Press, 2009); Benjamin Smith's, *The Roots of Conservatism in Mexico: Catholicism, Society, and Politics in the Mixteca Baja, 1750–1962* (Albuquerque, NM: University of New Mexico Press, 2012); and Ben Fallaw's *Religion and State Formation in Postrevolutionary Mexico* (Durham, NC: Duke University Press, 2013), which examines Catholic popular movements in Guanajuato, as well as the understudied states of Campeche, Guerrero, and Hidalgo. Recent publications in Mexico include Félix Brito R., "*Una óptica del movimiento social Cristero desde la periferia: caso Sinaloa. 1926–1929*," in *Movimientos sociales, Estado y religion en América Latina Siglos XIX y XX*, ed. Franco Savarino and Alejandro Pinet (Mexico: Escuela Nacional de Antropología e Historia, 2008); Enrique Bautista González, *La Guerra Olvidada: La cristera en Nayarit: 1.926–1.929* (Guadalajara: Taller editorial La Casa del Mago, 2008); and Julia Preciado Zamora, *Por las faldas del Volcán de Colima: Cristeros, agraristas y pacíficos* (Colima: Publicaciones de la Casa Chata, Centro de Investigaciones y Estudios Superiores en Antropología Social, Archivo Histórico del Municipio de Colima, 2007). Preciado's book, in addition to expanding the regional study of the Cristero conflict, also takes a new approach by not only investigating those who fought, but also people who stayed out of the conflict (whom she labels *pacíficos*). All of these studies not only expand historical conceptions of the geography of the religious conflict, but also provide excellent evidence to advance the argument that religion was far more central to Mexican political and social identity throughout the nineteenth and twentieth centuries than many scholars had previously assumed.

27. In contrast to the popular histories, which have focused on the regional and national dimensions of the Cristero conflict, there is an extensive historiography that explores the international aspects of the conflict. Here, historians have generally focused on how the relevant actors in Mexico interacted with various individuals, organizations, institutions, and national governments outside of Mexico, including the Vatican as well as the United States and other countries, during the war years. See, for example, David Bailey, *¡Viva Cristo Rey! The Cristero Rebellion and the Church-State Conflict in Mexico* (Austin: University of Texas Press, 1974), which focuses on the relationship between Church and state in Mexico during the war and pays close attention to the roles of various diplomatic actors in the United States and Rome. Similarly, Servando Ortoll's "Catholic organizations in Mexico's national politics and international diplomacy (1926–1942)" (PhD diss., Columbia University, 1987) contributes a compelling analysis of the roles of the Knights of Columbus, the US Catholic hierarchy, and Mexican Catholic organizations in the conflict. Robert Quirk, in *The Mexican Revolution and the Catholic Church, 1910–1929* (Bloomington: Indiana University Press, 1973), also focused on institutional actors, dismissing the popular revolt as a scattered and badly organized uprising. On the international reaction to the Cristero conflict, see J. Antonio López Ortega, *Las naciones extranjeras y la persecucion religiosa* (Mexico City: Edición privada, 1944); more recently, Jean Meyer published an edited volume that examines the international response to Mexico's religious crisis, *Las naciones frente al conflicto religioso en México* (Mexico City: CIDE/Tusquets Editores México, 2010). A fascinating new study by Maurice Demiers examines the impact of the Cristero conflict on Catholics in Quebec. Demiers, *Connected Struggles: Catholics, Nationalist, and Transnational Relations between Mexico and Québec, 1917–1945* (Montréal: McGill Queens University Press, 2014). For more on diplomacy, see also María del Carmen Collado Herrera, *Dwight W. Morrow: reencuentro y revolución en las relaciones entre México y Estados Unidos, 1927–1930* (Mexico City: Instituto Mora, 2005) and Manuel Olimón Nolasco, *Diplomacia insólita: el conflicto religioso en México y las negociaciones cupulares (1926–1929)* (Mexico City: Instituto Mexicano de Doctrina Social Cristiana, 2006). Stephen Andes has examined the relationship between the Vatican and Mexican Catholic organizations, taking advantage of newly available sources in the Vatican Secret Archives (ASV), in *The Vatican and Catholic Activism in Mexico and Chile: The Politics of Transnational Catholicism, 1920–1940* (Oxford: Oxford University Press, 2014).

28. Various scholars have specifically focused on the actions of American Catholics who supported Mexican exiles, notably Jean Meyer, *La cruzada por*

México: Los católicos de Estados Unidos y la cuestión religiosa en México (Mexico
City: Tusquets Editores México, 2008) and Matthew Redinger, *American
Catholics and the Mexican Revolution, 1924–1936* (Notre Dame: University of
Notre Dame Press, 2005). In particular, Redinger offers a thorough and very
interesting analysis of the ways in which various American Catholic organiza-
tions, particularly the Knights of Columbus, the NCWC, and the Extension
Society, responded to the Church-state conflict in Mexico, including the "problem" of religious refugees. However, the activities of Mexican exiles and emigrants are largely left out of his narrative, and indeed, out of the majority of the
international studies of the Cristero War. Two exceptions are Yolanda Padilla's
Los desterrados: exiliados católicos de la Revolución Mexicana en Texas, 1914–1919
(Aguascalientes, Ags., Mexico: Universidad Autónoma de Aguascalientes,
2009), although this monograph considers the role of Mexican bishops in
the United States in the pre-*Cristero* years of 1914–19; and David Bailey's *¡Viva
Cristo Rey!*, which devotes some attention to the activities of Mexican political
exiles (particularly members of the Liga Nacional Defensora de la Libertad
Religiosa) in the United States.

29. While numerous recent histories of Mexican emigration have focused on
    the pre-1940 period, many of these have chosen to examine the labor move-
    ment, race and ethnicity, and community formation. In general, the effects
    of the Cristero War on Mexican emigrants are mentioned in passing, if at all.
    Studies of labor include Rodlofo F. Acuña, *Corridors of Migration: The Odyssey
    of Mexican Laborers, 1600–1933* (Tucson, AZ: The University of Arizona Press,
    2007); Matt García, *A World of Its Own: Race, Labor, and Citrus in the Making
    of Greater Los Angeles, 1900–1970, Studies in Rural Culture* (Chapel Hill, NC:
    University of North Carolina Press, 2001); Gilbert González, *Mexican Consuls
    and Labor Organizing: Imperial Politics in the American Southwest* (Austin, TX:
    University of Texas Press, 1999); Camille Guerin-Gonzales, *Mexican Workers
    and American Dreams: Immigration, Repatriation, and California Farm Labor,
    1900–1939* (New Brunswick, NJ: Rutgers University Press, 1994); Zaragosa
    Vargas, *Proletarians of the North: A History of Mexican Industrial Workers in the
    Midwest, 1917–1933* (Berkeley, CA: University of California Press, 1993). Vicki
    Ruíz, *Cannery Women, Cannery Lives: Mexican Women, Unionization, and
    the California Food Processing Industry, 1930–1950*, 1st ed. (Albuquerque, NM:
    University of New Mexico Press, 1987).

    Other scholars of the period have focused on race, ethnicity, and the pro-
    cess of creating a "Mexican American" identity; the landmark study is George
    Sánchez, *Becoming Mexican American: Ethnicity, Culture and Identity in
    Chicano Los Angeles, 1900–1945* (New York: Oxford University Press, 1993);
    other valuable works include David Montejano, *Anglos and Mexicans in the
    Making of Texas, 1836–1986* (Austin, TX: University of Texas Press, 1987);
    Douglas Monroy, *Thrown Among Strangers: The Making of Mexican Culture*

in Frontier California (Berkeley, CA: University of California Press, 1990) and *Rebirth: Mexican Los Angeles from the Great Migration to the Great Depression* (Berkeley, CA: University of California Press, 1999); Stephen Pitti, *The Devil in Silicon Valley: Northern California, Race, and Mexican Americans* (Princeton, NJ: Princeton University Press, 2003); and Neil Foley, *The White Scourge: Mexicans, Blacks, and Poor Whites in Texas Cotton Culture* (Berkeley, CA: University of California Press, 1999).

Although they are fewer in number, Mexican historians writing on the topic of emigration to the United States include Fernando Saúl Alanís Enciso, whose publications on the period include *Que se queden allá: el gobierno de México y la repatriación de mexicanos en Estados Unidos (1934–1940)* (Tijuana: El Colegio de la Frontera Norte; San Luis Potosí: El Colegio de San Luis, 2007); and the sociologist Jorge Durand, whose publications on the topic include the edited volume *Migración México-Estados Unidos: Años Veinte* (Mexico City: Consejo Nacional para la Cultura y las Artes, 1991); Jorge Durand and Patricia Arias, *La Experiencia Migrante: Iconografía de la Migración México-Estados Unidos* (Mexico City: Alianza del Texto Universitario, 2000); Jorge Durand and Michael M. Smith, "*El Cosmopolita* de Kansas City (1914–1919): Un periódico para mexicanos," *Frontera Norte* Vol. 13, No. 24 (July–December 2001), 7–30. See also Moisés González Navarro, *Los Extranjeros en México y Los Mexicanos en el Extranjero, 1821–1970, Volúmenes I–III* (Mexico City: El Colegio de México, 1994).

Until recently, however, relatively few studies focused deeply on the intersections between religion and politics in Mexican emigrant communities. Instead, the general trend in Mexican migration history has been to continue the regional approach of earlier scholars, with an expanding focus on less-studied Mexican communities in the United States, specifically those outside of California and the borderlands. Notable recent examples include Michael Innis-Jiménez's *Steel Barrio: The Great Mexican Migration to South Chicago, 1915–1940* (New York: New York University Press, 2013); Gabriela Arredondo, *Mexican Chicago: Race, Identity, and Nation, 1916–39* (Chicago: University of Illinois Press, 2008); Julie Weise, "Mexican Nationalisms, Southern Racisms: Mexicans and Mexican Americans in the U.S. South, 1908–1939," *American Quarterly* Vol. 60, No. 3 (September 2008), 749–77; see also Monica Perales, *Smeltertown: Making and Remembering a Southwest Border Community* (Chapel Hill, NC: University of North Carolina Press, 2010). Many of these works aim to define and discuss the ways that Mexican communities forged their identities within the context of US racial relations and the pressure of ethnic assimilation.

30. Several earlier historical studies point out that migration during the 1920s was partially caused by the conflict; still, however, these tend to focus more on economic factors as a cause of migration. See, for example, Lawrence

Cardoso, "Mexican Emigration to the United States, 1900–1930: An Analysis of Socio-Economic Causes" (PhD diss., University of Connecticut, 1974); Francisco A. Rosales, "Mexican Immigration to the Urban Midwest During the 1920s" (PhD diss., Indiana University, 1978); John R. Martínez, *Mexican Emigration to the United States, 1910–1930* (San Francisco: R and E Research Associates, 1971). Other studies that mention Cristero emigrant activities briefly include Vicki Ruíz, *Cannery Women, Cannery Lives*; Zaragosa Vargas, "Life and Community in the 'Wonderful City of the Magic Motor': Mexican Immigrants in 1920s Detroit," *Michigan Historical Review* Vol. 15 (Spring 1989), 45–68; and Mike Davis, *City of Quartz: Excavating the Future in Los Angeles* (London, New York: Verso, 1990).

Almost as soon as the great emigration of the early 1920s began, the phenomenon drew the scrutiny of scholars from a variety of disciplines, especially sociology and history. Studies of Mexican migration to the United States during this period are immensely valuable for compiling a statistical portrait of the demographic distribution, regions of origin, and regions of settlements of emigrants, especially since government recordkeeping on both sides of the border left much to be desired. Nevertheless, although these scholars did investigate religion, many of them assumed that Mexican migrants would become more secularized after enough time in the supposedly "modern" United States. See Manuel Gamio, *The Life Story of the Mexican Immigrant: Autobiographic Documents Collected by Manuel Gamio* (Chicago: University of Chicago Press, 1930. Reprint, Toronto: Dover Publications, 1971); Manuel Gamio, *Mexican Immigration to the United States: A Study of Human Migration and Adjustment*; Paul S. Taylor, "A Spanish-Mexican Peasant Community: Arandas in Jalisco, Mexico," *Ibero-Americana* Vol. 4 (1933): 1–94; Paul S. Taylor, *An American-Mexican Frontier: Nueces County, Texas* (Chapel Hill, NC: The University of North Carolina Press, 1934); Paul S. Taylor, *Mexican Labor in the United States: Chicago and the Calumet Region*, University of California Publications in Economics, Vol. 7, No. 2 (Berkeley, CA: University of California, 1932); The Robert Redfield Papers, (1925–1958), Department of Special Collections, Joseph Regenstein Library, University of Chicago; Emory Stephen Bogardus, *The Mexican in the United States*, Social Science Series No. 8 (Los Angeles: University of Southern California Press, 1934). For Spanish-language studies, see Alfonso Fabila, *El problema de la emigración de obreros y campesinos mexicanos* (Mexico City: Talleres Gráficos de la Nación, 1929) and Enrique Santibáñez, *Ensayo acerca de la inmigración mexicana en los Estados Unidos* (San Antonio, TX: Clegg, 1930); Gustavo Doron González, *Problemas migratorios de México: Apuntamientos para su resolución* (Mexico City: Talleres de la Cámara de Diputados, 1925); Andres Landa y Piña, *El Servicio de Migración en México* (Mexico City: Talleres Gráficos de la Nación, 1930); Secretaría de Relaciones Exteriores, *La Migración y protección de mexicanos en el extranjero: Labor de la*

Secretaría de Relactiones Exteriores en Estados Unidos de América y Guatemala (Mexico City: Imprenta de la Secretaría de Relaciones Exteriores, 1928). For a comprehensive discussion of both the Spanish- and English-language historiography of Mexican emigration to the United States, see Fernando Alanís Enciso, *Historiografía de la emigración de trabajadores mexicanos a Los Estados Unidos (1900–1932)* (Tijuana: El Colegio de la Frontera Norte, 1994).

31. Until recently, it was relatively rare to find historical studies that make equal use of archival collections on both sides of the US-Mexico border. Today, a growing number of historians are producing fascinating work on Mexican migration by conducting transnational archival research. Notable examples include José Angel Hernández, *Mexican American Colonization*; Kelly Lyttle Hernández's *Migra! A History of the U.S. Border Patrol* (Berkeley, CA: University of California Press, 2010); Benjamin Heber Johnson, *Revolution in Texas: How a Forgotten Rebellion and Its Bloody Suppression Turned Mexicans into Americans* (New Haven, CT: Yale University Press, 2003). Notable earlier examples include González, *Mexican Consuls and Labor Organizing* and Elliot Young, *Catarino Garza's Revolution*.

Outside of the discipline of history, some seminal works on transnational approaches to the study of migration include Nina Glick Schiller, Linda G. Basch, and Cristina Szanton Blanc, *Towards a Transnational Perspective on Migration: Race, Class, Ethnicity, and Nationalism Reconsidered*, Vol. 645, *Annals of the New York Academy of Sciences* (New York: New York Academy of Sciences, 1992); Roger Rouse, "Mexican Migration and the Social Space of Post-Modernism," *Diaspora* Vol. 1 (1991), 8–23; and Michael P. Smith and Luis Guarnizo, *Transnationalism from Below*, Vol. 6, *Comparative Urban and Community Research* (New Brunswick, NJ: Transaction Publishers, 1998). More recent work by sociologist David Fitzgerald, including "A Nation of Emigrants? Statecraft, Church-Building, and Nationalism in Mexican Migrant Source Communities" (PhD diss., University of California, Los Angeles, 2005), and *A Nation of Emigrants: How Mexico Manages Its Migration* (Berkeley, CA: University of California Press, 2009) takes a transnational approach in discussing the role of the Catholic Church, the Mexican state, and immigration policy.

32. Historians have examined diasporic connections between a variety of emigrant groups and political causes in their homelands. See, for example, Terry Golway, *Irish Rebel: John Devoy and America's Fight for Ireland's Freedom* (New York: St. Martin's Press, 1998); Joséph Rappaport, *Hands Across the Sea: Jewish Immigrants and World War I* (Lanham, MD: Hamilton Books, 2005); Daniel Soyer, *Jewish Immigrant Associations and American Identity in New York, 1880–1939* (Detroit: Wayne State University Press, 2002); Robert Mirak, *Torn Between Two Lands, Armenians in America 1890 to World War I* (Cambridge, MA: Harvard University Press, 1983), 20; Isabel Kaprielian-Churchill, *Like*

Our Mountains: A History of Armenians in Canada (Montreal: McGill-Queen's University Press, 2005); Eiichiro Azuma, *Between Two Empires: Race, History, and Transnationalism in Japanese America* (New York: Oxford University Press, 2005). Although her subject is religion and contemporary Mexican migration, Leah Sarat, in *Fire in the Canyon: Religion, Migration, and the American Dream* (New York: New York University Press, 2013), compares contemporary Mexican emigrants to other emigrant groups such as the Irish and Italians, noting that they, like many others, rely on religious beliefs to comfort and strengthen them as they prepare to cross the US-Mexico border (126) and asserting that "crossing the border is also a deeply religious matter. The journey confronts people with hard-hitting questions about life, death, and the limits of human power" (3).

33. Scholars of working-class Mexican emigrants have often portrayed them primarily as labor emigrants subject to broader economic forces, at the risk of ignoring the political or religious causes of their migration. For a recent example, see Gilbert González, *Guest Workers or Colonized Labor?: Mexican Labor Migration to the United States* (Boulder, CO: Paradigm Publishers, 2007). According to Stéphane Dufoix, there is a tendency within migration studies to categorize migration as either voluntary/involuntary or political/economic, and subsequently to classify "voluntary" emigrants as "economic" and "involuntary" emigrants as "political." Such categories, he explains, create artificial divisions that encourage studies of "voluntary/economic" emigrants to leave out the political dimension of those emigrants' experiences. Instead, Dufoix acknowledges—and I agree—that there is slippage between these categories (Dufoix, *Diasporas*, 60). In the case of Mexican emigrants, while economic causes might have been the main force driving migration for much of the twentieth century, the volatile politics of the homeland both compounded these economic "push factors" (on the Mexican side, at least) and provoked separate waves of emigration that would not have occurred otherwise.

34. For a very useful essay on the history of the study of Mexican American religion, see the introduction to Gastón Espinosa and Mario T. García (eds.), *Mexican American Religions: Spirituality, Activism, and Culture* (Durham, NC: Duke University Press, 2008), 1–16. In it, the authors trace the "geneology" of Mexican American religious studies, describing how the field has developed from the early twentieth-century "church-sponsored" institutional histories and matter-of-fact reports on the religious practices of Mexican communities in the Southwest to, more recently, a new and much more varied interest in popular devotions.

35. Lourdes Celina Vázquez investigates collective memory and "the persistence of Cristero thought [*pensamiento*] in the Catholic vision of the world in western Mexico" in *Guerra cristera: narrativa, testimonios y propaganda* (Guadalajara: Editorial Universitaria, Universidad de Guadalajara, 2012),

246. For a fascinating discussion about religion and collective memory, see Elizabeth Castelli, *Martyrdom and Memory: Early Christian Culture Making* (New York: Columbia University Press, 2004), 11–19.

36. Numerous scholars of Mexican emigration who investigate the role of Catholicism and the Catholic Church during the 1920s and 1930s discuss the impact of the Cristero War, although they generally do not use sources from Mexico, and only rarely do they consider whether and how the Cristero War might have had a long-term impact on religious identity and community formation. Nevertheless, these studies provide invaluable information about the ways that different US-based Mexican communities experienced the Cristero conflict. See Jay P. Dolan and Gilberto Miguel Hinojosa, *Mexican Americans and the Catholic Church, 1900–1965*, Notre Dame History of Hispanic Catholics in the U.S., Vol. 1 (Notre Dame, IN: University of Notre Dame Press, 1994); and Roberto R. Treviño, *The Church in the Barrio: Mexican American Ethno-Catholicism in Houston* (Chapel Hill, NC: University of North Carolina Press, 2006); Malachy McCarthy, "Which Christ Came to Chicago: Catholic and Protestant Programs to Evangelize, Socialize, and Americanize the Mexican Emigrant, 1900–1940" (PhD diss., Loyola University of Chicago, 2002); and Timothy M. Matovina, *Guadalupe and Her Faithful: Latino Catholics in San Antonio from Colonial Origins to the Present* (Baltimore, MD: Johns Hopkins University Press, 2005). Monica Perales's *Smeltertown* has a very good account describing how the Cristero war affected the Mexican community outside of El Paso, but its focus is limited to this specific community, and it does not investigate how the conflict may have continued to impact the community after the 1920s.

Works that cover more recent history include Mario T. García's *Católicos: Resistance and Affirmation in Chicano Catholic History* (Austin, TX: University of Texas Press, 2008) and David Badillo, *Latinos and the New Immigrant Church* (Baltimore, MD: Johns Hopkins University Press, 2006). These studies are extremely helpful for an understanding of Mexican American Catholicism, but do not use sources from Mexico; rather, they rely on archival material from the United States. Several recent books by scholars outside the field of history provide compelling case studies that narrate and explain transnational religious practice among contemporary Mexican emigrants. See Leah M. Sarat, *Fire in the Canyon*; Elaine A. Peña, *Performing Piety: Making Space Sacred with the Virgin of Guadalupe* (Berkeley, CA: University of California Press, 2011); R. Andrew Chesnut's *Devoted to Death: Santa Muerte, the Skeleton Saint* (New York: Oxford University Press, 2012); and Alfredo Mirandé, *Jalos, USA: Transnational Community and Identity* (South Bend, IN: Notre Dame University Press, 2014).

Historians, as well, have produced recent studies that investigate the transnational aspects of Mexican religious devotions, including Jennifer Scheper

Hughes, *Biography of a Mexican Crucifix: Lived Religion and Local Faith from the Conquest to the Present* (New York: Oxford University Press, 2010) and Christina Heisser, "Thanks to God and the Virgin of San Juan: Migration and Transnational Devotion during the 'Mexican Miracle,' 1940–1970" (PhD diss., Indiana University, 2012).

37. See, for example, Socorro Castaneda-Liles, "Our Lady of Guadalupe and the Politics of Cultural Interpretation," and Kay Turner, "*Voces de Fe:* Mexican American *Altaristas* in Texas," both in Gastón Espinosa and Mario T. García (eds.), *Mexican American Religions*, 153–79 and 180–205. Roberto R. Treviño, in his valuable study of Mexican ethno-Catholicism in Houston, likewise focuses on popular traditions such as *guadalupanismo, altarcitos,* and *quinceañeras,* with only a very brief discussion of the impact of the Cristero War on the Houston community. Treviño, *The Church in the Barrio,* 67, 74–75.

38. Here I agree with Matthew Jacobson, who explains that "recasting the immigrant experience as largely an emigrant experience" can more effectively demonstrate how the homeland remains central to "migrants' ideological geographies." Matthew Frye Jacobson, *Special Sorrows: The Diasporic Imagination of Irish, Polish, and Jewish Immigrants in the United States* (Berkeley, CA: University of California Press, 2002), 2.

CHAPTER 1

1. James W. Wilkie, "Statistical Indicators of the Impact of National Revolution on the Catholic Church in Mexico, 1920–1967," *Journal of Church and State* Vol. 12, No. 1 (1970), 92. See also Linda A. Curcio-Nagy, "Faith and Morals in Colonial Mexico," in *The Oxford History of Mexico*, ed. Michael C. Meyer and William H. Beezley (New York: Oxford University Press, 2000), 143–74. The essays in *Religious Culture in Modern Mexico*, edited by Martin Austin Nesvig, provide a comprehensive exploration of the intersections between Catholicism, national identity, and popular culture in Mexico (New York: Rowman & Littlefield Publishers, 2007). For two excellent studies of Mexican popular religious practices that have persisted from the colonial period to the present, see Richard C. Trexler, *Reliving Golgotha: The Passion Play of Ixtapalapa* (Cambridge: Harvard University Press, 2003) and Jennifer Scheper Hughes, *Biography of a Mexican Crucifix.*

2. For more on Protestant evangelization during the early twentieth century, see Jean-Pierre Bastian, *Los disidentes: sociedades protestantes y revolución en México, 1872–1911* (Mexico D.F.: Fondo de Cultura Económica and El Colegio de México, 1989) and Deborah Baldwin, *Protestants and the Mexican Revolution: Missionaries, Ministers, and Social Change* (Chicago: University of Illinois Press, 1990).

3. Matthew Butler, *Popular Piety and Political Identity in Mexico's Cristero Rebellion*, 9–10, 143; for a more detailed discussion of the varieties of religiosity and devotion across Mexican regions, see Butler, ed., "A Revolution in Spirit? Mexico, 1910–1940," in *Faith and Impiety in Revolutionary Mexico*, 12–16.

4. For a seminal work on the intricate and layered relationships between priests and townspeople in central Mexico, see William B. Taylor, *Magistrates of the Sacred: Priests and Parishioners in Eighteenth-Century Mexico* (Palo Alto, CA: Stanford University Press, 1996).

5. Luis González y González, *San José de Gracia: Mexican Village in Transition* (Austin, TX: University of Texas Press, 1982), 50.

6. Richard C. Trexler discusses the tensions between Catholic clergy and Mexican popular religious culture, describing how church authorities disapproved of the Ixtapalapa Passion parade on the grounds that it was "full of folklore." *Reliving Golgotha*, 78.

7. Benjamin Smith, *The Roots of Conservatism in Mexico*, 10.

8. On parish priests, see Taylor, *Magistrates of the Sacred*, 77–238. For a fascinating exploration of women's spiritual and political life inside a Mexican convent, see Margaret Chowning, *Rebellious Nuns: The Troubled History of a Mexican Convent, 1752–1863* (New York: Oxford University Press, 2006).

9. Father Pedro M. Bustos to Sr. Diego Gutierrez, Cacalotenango, Guerrero, September 20, 1928, in AGN, IPS, Vol. 233, Expediente 62.

10. Manuel Gamio, *The Life Story of the Mexican Immigrant*, 4.

11. Gamio, *The Life Story of the Mexican Immigrant*, 60.

12. See Pamela Voekel, "Liberal Religion: The Schism of 1861," in *Religious Culture in Modern Mexico*, ed. Martin Austin Nesvig, 78–105.

13. On liberalism and peasant culture, see Florencia E. Mallon, *Peasant and Nation: The Making of Postcolonial Mexico and Peru* (Berkeley and Los Angeles: The University of California Press, 1995).

14. For an excellent exploration of the enduring effects of popular conservatism in Mexico, see Smith, *Roots of Conservatism*. See also K. Aaron von Oosterhout, "Confraternities and Popular Conservatism on the Frontier: Mexico's Sierra del Nayarit in the Nineteenth Century," *The Americas* Vol. 71, No. 1 (July 2014), 101–30. For a discussion of the particular nationalist vision put forth by the Catholic hierarchy during the late eighteenth and early nineteenth centuries, see Brian F. Connaughton, *Clerical Ideology in a Revolutionary Age: The Guadalajara Church and the Idea of the Mexican Nation, 1788–1853* (Trans. Mark Alan Healy; Calgary, Alberta and Boulder: University of Calgary Press and University Press of Colorado, 2003).

15. Legislation in 1874 "forbade the performance of a "religious act of public worship" anywhere other than inside places of public worship," Trexler, *Reliving Golgotha*, 67. Brian Stauffer's forthcoming diss., "Victory on Earth or in

Heaven: Religion, Reform, and Rebellion in Michoacán, Mexico, 1869–1877," will provide a valuable investigation of the *religioneros*.

16. Alicia Olivera de Bonfil, *Aspectos del conflicto religioso*, 44. For more on the rise of popular devotions, see Margaret Chowning, "The Catholic Church and the Ladies of the Vela Perpetua: Gender and Devotional Change in Nineteenth-Century Mexico," *Past & Present* Vol. 221, No. 1 (November 2013), 197–237.

17. Stephen Andes, *The Vatican and Catholic Activism*, 25.

18. For the seminal study on the Tomochic rebellion, see Paul Vanderwood, *The Power of God Against the Guns of the Government: Religious Upheaval in Mexico at the Turn of the Nineteenth Century* (Stanford, CA: Stanford University Press, 1998).

19. Andes, *The Vatican and Catholic Activism*, 26. For more on the rise of social Catholicism during the late nineteenth century, see Manuel Ceballos Ramírez, *El catolicismo social: un tercero en discordia, Rerum Novarum, la "cuestión social" y la movilización de los católicos mexicanos* (1891–1911) (Mexico City: El Colegio de Mexico, 1991).

20. According to Yolanda Padilla, Archbishop José Mora y del Río lent money to Huerta after he had ordered the assassination of Madero. She argues that this loan "is considered the 'original sin' of the hierarchy or, in other words, the drop that knocked over the glass of *carrancista* anticlericalism, which before had not been expressed in such open or dominant form." Yolanda Padilla, *Los desterrados: exiliados católicos de la Revolución Mexicana en Texas*, 30.

21. Ben Fallaw, "Varieties of Mexican Revolutionary Anticlericalism: Radicalism, Iconoclasm, and Otherwise, 1914–1935," *The Americas* Vol. 65, No. 4 (April 2009), 481–509; Alan Knight, "The Mentality and Modus Operandi of Mexican Anticlericalism," in *Faith and Impiety*, ed. Matthew Butler, 21–56.

22. Andes, *The Vatican and Catholic Activism*, 48–50.

23. Padilla, *Los desterrados*, 239; James Talmadge Moore, *Acts of Faith: The Catholic Church in Texas, 1900–1950* (College Station, TX: Texas A&M University Press, 2002), 81–82; Joséph J. Thompson, *The Diamond Jubilee of the Archdiocese of Chicago* (Des Plaines, IL: St. Mary's Training School Press, 1920).

24. Padilla, *Los desterrados*, 67, 241.

25. Padilla, *Los desterrados*, 86; "The Knights of Columbus in Mexico," brochure dated August 7–9, 1923, in ACUA-NCWC, Mexican Files, Box 148, Folder 28.

26. On the "U," see Andes, *The Vatican and Catholic Activism*, 51–54; see also Yves Solis, "Asociación espiritual o masonería católica: la U," *ISTOR* Vol. 9, No. 33 (Summer 2008), 121–37.

27. Olivera de Bonfil, *Aspectos del conflicto religioso*, 92.

28. Following the release of the papal encyclical *Quas Primas* in 1925, which advocated a more overtly public and political role for the church, Mexican Catholic leaders also promoted popular devotion to the cult of Christ the King. Indre

Cuplinskas argues that the devotion to Christ the King was linked to a vision of militant Catholicism that viewed Christ as the supreme leader and the members of Catholic organizations such as Catholic action as "soldiers of Christ." Indre Cuplinskas, "Guns and Rosaries: The Use of Military Imagery in the French-Canadian Catholic Student Newspaper *JEC*," *CCHA Historical Studies* Vol. 71 (2005): 7–28. See also Anscar Chupungo, *Liturgies of the Future: The Process and Methods of Inculturation* (New York: Paulist Press, 1989), 208.

29. State governments were implementing the anticlerical constitutional articles, particularly Tomás Garrido Canabal, as well as in Hidalgo, Chiapas, and Tabasco. In Jalisco and Colima, state governments had closed a number of seminaries and parochial schools. See Robert Quirk, *The Mexican Revolution and the Catholic Church*, 150.

30. David Bailey, *¡Viva Cristo Rey!*, 55–56. Olivera de Bonfil, *Aspectos del conflicto religioso*, 117.

31. Quirk, *The Mexican Revolution and the Catholic Church*, 151.

32. Quirk, *The Mexican Revolution and the Catholic Church*, 161–69.

33. Olivera de Bonfil, *Aspectos del conflict religioso*, 153.

34. Olivera de Bonfil, *Aspectos del conflicto religioso*, 136, 156.

35. Olivera de Bonfil, *Aspectos del conflicto religioso*, 179, map 2.

36. Situación militar de la Defensa Armada en el año de 1927, Boletín del 29 de diciembre de 1927, cited in Olivera de Bonfil, *Aspectos del conflicto religioso*, 185.

37. Olivera de Bonfil, ed. *La literatura cristera* (Mexico City: Instituto Nacional de Antropologia e Historia, 1994), 159–60.

38. Fernando M. González, *Matar y morir por Cristo Rey: aspectos de la Cristiada* (Mexico City: Instituto de Investigaciones Sociales, Universidad Nacional Autónoma de México/Plaza y Valdés, 2001), 18.

39. Quirk, *The Mexican Revolution and the Catholic Church*, 191; "Mexican Survivors Tell Train Horrors," *The New York Times*, April 22, 1927, 1.

40. "Por qué combatí a los Cristeros" in Lourdes Celina Vázquez Parada, *Testimonios Sobre la Revolución Cristera: Hacia una Hermenéutica de la Conciencia Histórica* (Guadalajara: Universidad de Guadalajara, 2001), 149–53.

41. Jean Meyer estimates that one hundred thousand combatants were killed. *The Cristero Rebellion*, 178.

42. Enrique Gorostieta, "Manifesto a la Nacion," October 28, 1928. Cited in Olivera de Bonfil, *Aspectos del conflicto religioso*, 205.

43. Meyer, *The Cristero Rebellion*, 53.

44. Detailed accounts of the settlements can be found in Olimón Nolasco, *La Diplomacia insólita: el conflicto religioso en México y las negociaciones cupulares (1926–1929)*; Matthew Redinger, *American Catholics and the Mexican Revolution, 1924–1936* (Notre Dame, IN: University of Notre Dame Press, 2005); and Andes, *The Vatican and Catholic Activism*.

45. Meyer, *The Cristero Rebellion*, 57.

46. The border region has long been a sphere of transnational economic, political, and cultural exchange. For a longer discussion, see John Tutino, "Capitalist Foundations: Spanish North America, Mexico, and the United States," in *Mexico and Mexicans in the Making of the United States*, ed. John Tutino (Austin, TX: University of Texas Press, 2012), 36–84.

47. Lawrence Cardoso, *Mexican Emigration to the United States*, 9.

48. For a detailed description of the hacienda system during the Porfiriato, see Friedrich Katz, "Labor Conditions on Haciendas in Porfirian Mexico: Some Trends and Tendencies," *The Hispanic American Historical Review* Vol. 54, No. 1 (February 1974): 1–47.

49. For a more localized and detailed history on the social ramifications of the transition from subsistence agriculture to a market economy in rural Mexico, see Paul Friedrich, *Agrarian Revolt in a Mexican Village* (Chicago: University of Chicago Press, 1977).

50. Jorge Durand and Patricia Arias, *La experiencia migrante: iconografía de la migración México-Estados Unidos*, 23; Cardoso, *Mexican Emigration to the United States*, 13–14.

51. Cardoso, *Mexican Emigration to the United States*, 41–44.

52. Francisco A. Rosales, "Mexican Immigration to the Urban Midwest," 45.

53. Rosales, "Mexican Immigration to the Urban Midwest," 52.

54. Cardoso, *Mexican Emigration to the United States*, 14; and Paul S. Taylor, "A Spanish-Mexican Peasant Community: Arandas in Jalisco, Mexico," 35.

55. Rosales, "Mexican Immigration to the Urban Midwest," 70; Cardoso, *Mexican Emigration to the United States*, 18–20; Carey McWilliams, *North From Mexico: The Spanish-Speaking People of the United States* (Philadelphia: J. B. Lippincott Company, 1949), 179.

56. The solicitations were often quite specific: "From one thousand to fifteen hundred Mexican laborers will be needed on these clearings, who, besides being employed for quite a while, will be able to maintain themselves until the coming cotton season." Translated clipping from *Excelsior*, December 16, 1925, in State RG 59, Decimal File 812.5611/3.

57. Rosales, "Mexican Immigration to the Urban Midwest," 82.

58. Report by J. E. Trout, Immigration Inspector at Laredo, Texas, October 14, 1923, in NA, INS RG 85, "Subject Correspondence Files; Part 2: Mexican Immigration, 1906–1930," Case file No. 55639/550.

59. Paul S. Taylor, "A Spanish-Mexican Peasant Community," 35, 41.

60. Marilyn Bowman, "Labor Migration on Mexico's Southern Border, 1880–1941: The Quest for Regulation and Its Aftermath" (PhD diss., University of Minnesota, 1987), 138.

61. Rosales, "Mexican Immigration to the Urban Midwest," 54.

62. Meyer, *La Cristiada*, Vol. 1, 176.

63. Luis González y González, *San José de Gracia: Mexican Village in Transition*, Texas Pan American Series, trans. John Upton (Austin, TX: University of Texas Press, 1982), 158.

64. Meyer, *The Cristero Rebellion*, 180.

65. Marylin P. Davis, *Mexican Voices, American Dreams: An Oral History of Mexican Immigration to the United States* (New York: Henry Holt & Co, 1991), 11.

66. Anonymous letter "From one woman to her friend," November 18, 1927, in ACUA-NCWC, Mexican Files, Box 146, Folder 19.

67. *El Excelsior* clipping from May 21, 1928, translated from Spanish to English (no title given), in ACUA-NCWC, Mexican Files, Box 146, Folder 20; Report from the Aguascalientes Consulate, September 30, 1927, in NACP, Foreign Service RG 84, Consular Correspondence from Aguascalientes, Subject Group 811.11; Report from the Guadalajara Consulate, February 1, 1927, in NACP, Foreign Service RG 84, Consular Correspondence from Guadalajara, Subject Group 800.

68. Report from the Guadalajara Consulate, May 7, 1927, in NACP, Foreign Service RG 84, Consular Correspondence from Guadalajara, Subject Group 800.

69. Confidential Report from Consul John W. Dye, Ciudad Juárez Consulate, October 4, 1926, in NACP, Foreign Service RG 84, Consular Correspondence from Ciudad Juárez, Subject Group 800.

70. Report from the Guadalajara Consulate, June 3, 1927, in NACP, Foreign Service RG 84, Consular Correspondence from Guadalajara, Subject Group 800.

71. "El éxodo de braceros ha continuado interminable," *El Universal*, May 28, 1927, clipping in UNAM-Traslosheros, Caja 99, Expediente 717, Foja 6339.

72. José Orozco, "¡*Esos Altos de Jalisco!* Emigration and the Idea of Alteño Exceptionalism, 1926–1952" (PhD diss., Harvard University, 1997), 145.

73. Rosales, "Mexican Immigration to the Urban Midwest," 211.

74. Zaragosa Vargas, "Life and Community in the 'Wonderful City of the Magic Motor'," 60.

75. Dolan and Hinojosa, *Mexican Americans and the Catholic Church*, 185.

76. Meyer, *The Cristero Rebellion*, 179.

77. Rosales, "Mexican Immigration to the Urban Midwest," 104.

78. Rosales, "Mexican Immigration to the Urban Midwest," 102.

79. Camille Guerin-Gonzales, *Mexican Workers and American Dreams*, 143.

80. George Sanchez, *Becoming Mexican American*, 46.

81. Paul S. Taylor, *Mexican Labor in the United States: Chicago and the Calumet Region*, 49. Rosales found that of 1,016 immigrants to the Chicago area from 1920 to 1925, 214 came from Guanajuato, 201 came from Jalisco, and 260 from Michoacán, while 68 came from Mexico City. Rosales, "Mexican Immigration to the Urban Midwest," 107.

82. Vargas, "Life and Community in the 'Wonderful City of the Magic Motor'," 48.

83. Report by J. E. Trout, Immigration Inspector at Laredo, Texas, October 14, 1923, in INS RG 85, "Subject Correspondence Files; Part 2: Mexican Immigration, 1906–1930," Case file No. 55639/550.

84. Taylor, "A Spanish-Mexican Peasant Community," 42.

85. There were 555,850 men and 334,986 women, according to José M. Davila, "The Mexican Migration Problem." Address delivered at the Friends of Mexican [*sic*] Conference at Claremont, January 1929, in NACP, State RG 59, Decimal File 812.5611/18.

86. Douglas Monroy, *Rebirth*, 65.

87. For a discussion of both the labor movement and the patriotic societies, see Gilbert González, *Mexican Consuls and Labor Organizing*, especially Chapter 2, "Organizing *México de afuera* in Southern California," 37–81.

88. Manuel Gamio, *Mexican Immigration to the United States*, 115–16.

89. Emory Bogardus, in his 1934 study of Mexicans in the United States, argued that exposure to US culture liberalized emigrants. Bogardus is quoted in Richard A. García, *Rise of the Mexican American Middle Class: San Antonio, 1929–1941* (College Station, TX: Texas A&M University Press, 1991), 50. Paul Taylor, in a study of Mexicans in Chicago, claimed that "institutions of family and religion weaken" among emigrants to the United States because of differing work habits, *Mexican Labor in the United States: Chicago and the Calumet Region*, 280. Likewise, Francisco Rosales noted in a 1978 dissertation that religiosity declined among Mexicans in 1920s East Chicago because "the familiar time structure based on night and day, Sundays and feast days, became irrelevant." Rosales, *Mexican Immigration to the Urban Midwest During the 1920s*, 180. More recently, Richard García agreed with Bogardus, and claimed that Catholicism "was not a magnet for daily participatory activism" among Mexican working-class emigrants in San Antonio. García, *Rise of the Mexican American Middle Class*, 153. Finally, in his study of Mexicans in Los Angeles, George Sánchez asserts that due to Protestant evangelization, exposure to secular culture, and the Americanization of the US Church, "Catholic religious practice . . . increasingly narrowed to the province of women, and became less a community function and more a set of rituals performed at home." Sánchez, *Becoming Mexican American*, 11.

CHAPTER 2

1. With the permission of *The Catholic Historical Review*, parts of chapters 2 and 3 are reproduced and adapted from Julia G. Young, "Cristero Diaspora: Mexican Immigrants, the U.S. Catholic Church, and Mexico's Cristero War, 1926–1929," *The Catholic Historical Review* Vol. 98, No. 2 (April 2012), 271–300.

2. "El Mayor Tobin no tomará parte en los festejos que organiza la Junta Patriótica de San Antonio" and "Renuncia a su candidatura de reina," *La Prensa*, August

1, 1926, 1; "El Sr. Obispo Drossaerts pide a sus diocesanos mexicanos de San Antonio que se abstengan de participar en las fiestas de Independencia," *Mexico*, July 30, 1926, 1.

3. "Border Mexicans Excoriate Calles: They Hand Protest to Consul at San Antonio, Charging Murder, Torture, and Tyranny," *The New York Times*, December 5, 1927, 25.

4. James Talmadge Moore, *Acts of Faith: The Catholic Church in Texas, 1900–1950* (College Station, TX: Texas A&M University Press, 2002), 102–03.

5. "Mas de Diez Mil Mexicanos Formaron en el Gran Desfile: Monseñor Manríque y Zárate pronunció el sermón final," clipping from *El Diario de El Paso*, June 14, 1928, UNAM-Traslosheros, Caja 100, Expediente 724, Foja 6897. "Corpus Christi Fete Gay Event: Ten Thousand of City's Latin Presidents [sic] Participate," *Los Angeles Times*, June 11, 1928, A2.

6. Malachy McCarthy, "Which Christ Came to Chicago," 214.

7. *Announcements*, April 1, 1928, OLG Parish.

8. "Truce for Return of Bishops Denied by Archbishop Ruiz," National Catholic Welfare Conference press release, June 3, 1929, in ACUA-NCWC, Mexican Files, Folder 7, Box 148. According to an article in the *New York Herald Tribune*, the National Catholic Welfare Conference estimated that about nine out of ten Mexican exiles came to the United States. "Rev. J. J. Burke's Part in Mexico Peace Revealed," *New York Herald Tribune*, July 2, 1929. On the flight of religious refugees to countries other than the United States, see J. Antonio Lopez Ortega, *Las naciones extranjeras y la persecucion religiosa*, 107.

9. Moore, *Acts of Faith*, 81–82; Yolanda Padilla, *Los desterrados*, 23, 184.

10. Henry Krause, American Vice Consul of San Luis Potosí, to Alexander W. Weddel, American Consul General of Mexico City, July 21, 1926, in NACP, Foreign Service RG 84, Consular Correspondence from San Luis Potosí, Subject Group 811.11. See also "Churches Looted in Mexican Drive, Refugees Charge," *The Washington Post*, March 5, 1926, 3.

11. "Mayor is Lynched by Mob in Mexico; Fired at a Priest: Catholics Now Fearful of Church Seizures if Clergy Retire," *The Washington Post*, July 28, 1926, 1.

12. Sr. Barbara Miller, "The Role of Women in the Mexican Cristero Rebellion: *Las Señoras y Las Religiosas*," *The Americas* Vol. 40, No. 3 (January 1984), 303–23, 314.

13. "Los sacerdotes rebeldes van a ser deportados: Una circular de la Secretaría de Guerra a los Jefes de las Operaciones Militares," clipping from *Excelsior*, February 14, 1927, AGN-IPS, Vol. 209, Expediente 6.

14. Unnamed consular official in Guadalajara to Secretary of State Frank Billings Kellogg in Washington, February 3, 1927, NACP, State Department Central File, State RG 59, Decimal File 812.404/754.

15. Unnamed employee of the consulate of Piedras Negras, Coahuila, to the Ministry of the Interior, June 1, 1927, AGN-IPS, Vol. 230, Expediente 21.

16. Marjorie Sánchez-Walker, "Migration Quicksand: Immigration Law and Immigration Advocates at the El Paso-Ciudad Juárez Border Crossing, 1933–1941" (PhD diss., Washington State University, 1999), 278.

17. Booklet entitled "Bishop Anthony Schuler, S. J.," in the archives of the Catholic diocese of El Paso, Texas.

18. Office memorandum and news clippings, February 23, 1928, ACUA-NCWC, Mexican Files, Box 146, Folder 20. Other accounts of expulsions of priests and nuns can be found scattered throughout the Confidential Department archives. See "Expulsión de sacerdote sinaloense," in AGN-IPS, Vol. 229, Expediente 16; and "Aprehensión de sacerdotes, algunos son expulsados del país," in AGN-IPS, Vol. 58, Expediente 15.

19. Letter on behalf of Bishop Schuler from Bishop Kelly, fall 1929, in ACUA-NCWC, Mexican Files, Box 150, Folder 25.

20. "Mexican Survivors Tell Train Horrors," *The New York Times*, April 22, 1927, 1.

21. G-2 report from the military attaché of the US embassy in Mexico City, April 24, 1927, in NACP, MID RG 165, 2657-G-616, Doc. 7. See also "Testimony to the Apostolic Delegate in Washington, D.C., from six bishops regarding deportation to San Antonio Texas," April 26, 1927, in ACUA-NCWC, Mexican Files, Box 147, Folder 14, and Quirk, *The Mexican Revolution and the Catholic Church*, 190.

22. "Bishop Diaz Arrives Hopeful of Victory: Church Will Win in Mexico as It Has Elsewhere, Expelled Prelate Declares," *The New York Times*, February 2, 1927, 4.

23. David Bailey, *¡Viva Cristo Rey!*, 143.

24. See, for example, Pedro Vera y Zuria, *Diario de mi Destierro* (El Paso: Editorial Revista Catolica, 1927).

25. "Report on exiled clergy in the United States," 1927, in Archives of the Catholic Archdiocese of Chicago, Document No. 1927-G-1 (3).

26. Dolan and Hinojosa, *Mexican Americans and the Catholic Church*, 163; Mike Davis, *City of Quartz*, 330–31.

27. Rev. Msgr. Harry C. Koenig, ed., *Caritas Christi Urget Nos: A History of the Archdiocese of Chicago* (Chicago, IL: The New World Publishing Company, 1981), 1006.

28. "Report on exiled clergy in the United States," 1927, in Archives of the Catholic Archdiocese of Chicago, Document No. 1927-G-1 (3).

29. Dolan and Hinojosa, *Mexican Americans and the Catholic Church*, 21, 135.

30. Dolan and Hinojosa, *Mexican Americans and the Catholic Church*, 65, 161, 256.

31. Bishop Francis Kelley, "Memorandum on Mexico," May 30, 1934, in ACUA-NCWC, Mexican Files, Box 150, Folder 25. For a more detailed history of the activities of Francis Kelley, see Anne M. Martínez, *Catholic Borderlands: Mapping Catholicism onto American Empire, 1905–1935* (Lincoln: University of Nebraska Press, 2014).

32. Dolan and Hinojosa, *Mexican Americans and the Catholic Church*, 167–68.

33. Bresette, "Mexicans in the United States: A Report of a Brief Survey," in ACUA-NCWC, Mexican Files, Box 148, Folder 36.

34. Dolan and Hinojosa, *Mexican Americans and the Catholic Church*, 167–68.

35. See McCarthy, "Which Christ Came to Chicago," 183–298. For a fascinating recent study on the history of the Latino Pentecostal movement in the United States that includes a valuable discussion of Mexican and Mexican American involvement in the movement, see Gaston Espinosa, *Latino Pentecostals in America: Faith and Politics in Action* (Cambridge: Harvard University Press, 2014).

36. Dolan and Hinojosa, *Mexican Americans and the Catholic Church*, 180–82.

37. Bresette, "Mexicans in the United States: A Report of a Brief Survey," in ACUA-NCWC, Mexican Files, Box 148, Folder 36.

38. Moore, *Acts of Faith*, 81–82.

39. Douglas Slawson, "The National Catholic Welfare Conference and the Church-State Conflict in Mexico, 1925–1929," *The Americas* Vol. 47, No. 1 (July, 1990), 66–67.

40. "Immigration: A Statement Regarding Immigration to the United States ... Prepared for the Official Catholic Yearbook," 1928, UTEP-Calleros, MS 231, Series II.

41. Immigration case files, in UTEP-Calleros, MS 231, Series II, Box 11.

42. Immigration case files, UTEP-Calleros, MS 231, Series II, Box 11; Father Theo. Laboure in San Antonio to Rev. Jesus Prieto in Laredo, June 13, 1929, NACP, RG 84, Consular Correspondence from Nuevo Laredo, Subject Group 811.11. Calleros and his office also took responsibility for communicating US immigration laws to the Mexican immigrant community; one pamphlet, produced in 1925, explained the US laws and offered words of counsel and warning, and gave the address of the NCWC's Office of Immigration in Juárez. "Algunas Reglas de importancia para los inmigrantes que pasan por la frontera mexicana a los estados unidos," in UTEP-Calleros, MS 231, Series II, Box 7.

43. "Cleofas Calleros," Oral History Interview No. 157, The Institute of Oral History, The University of Texas at El Paso.

44. Chicago, Archives of the Catholic Archdiocese of Chicago, "Report on Exiled Clergy in the United States," 1927, Document No. 1927-G-1 (3); Richard A. García, *Rise of the Mexican American Middle Class*, 28, 35–36; Report from Agent 47 in San Antonio to the Jefe del Departamento Confidencial, April 25–26, 1927, AGN-IPS, Vol. 54, Expediente 10.

45. Bresette, *Mexicans in the United States: A Report of a Brief Survey*, in ACUA-NCWC, Mexican Files, Box 148, Folder 36.

46. Sister Lilliana Owens, S. L. *Most Reverend Anthony J. Schuler, SJ, DD, First Bishop of El Paso, and Some Catholic Activities in the Diocese Between 1915–1942*, Jesuit Studies—Southwest, Number Three (El Paso: Revista Catolica Press, 1953), 320–21.

47. Letter on behalf of Schuler from Bishop Francis Kelley, Diocese of Oklahoma, fall 1929, in ACUA-NCWC, Mexican Files, Box 150, Folder 25. "News Items," May 10, 1929, in ACUA-NCWC, Mexican Files, Box 148, Folder 6. Report from C. T. Valdivia, Presbitero at the Centro Propagandista de la Fe in Colton, CA, to the Ministro de Gobernación, August 12, 1927, in AGN-IPS, Vol. 225, Expediente 15; Report from Cónsul General in El Paso to Secretario de Gobernación, August 30, 1934, in AGN, Fondo Dirección de Gobierno, Vol. 126, Expediente 2.340 (73) 66; Report from Delegado de Migración, Piedras Negras, Coahuila, to the Secretaria de Gobernación, February 26, 1927, in AGN-IPS, Vol. 227, Expediente 34.

48. George Sánchez, *Becoming Mexican American*, 46.

49. Dolan and Hinojosa, *Mexican Americans and the Catholic Church*, 163.

50. Samuel Ortegon, "The Religious Status of the Mexican Population of Los Angeles" (Master's thesis, University of Southern California, 1932), 45–47. Other accounts place the number at fifty; see Davis, *City of Quartz*, 330–31. "Los Angeles Now Second Largest Mexican City—Mission Problem Acute," *The Tidings*, May 18, 1927, in UNAM-Traslosheros, Caja 100, Expediente 724, Foja 6858.

51. Juan R. García, *Mexicans in the Midwest, 1900–1932* (Tucson: University of Arizona Press, 1996), 27, 46, 43, 239; Francisco A. Rosales, "Mexican Immigration to the Urban Midwest During the 1920s," 165.

52. "Crónica de la Cuasi-Residencia de los Misioneros Hijos del Corazón de María en Chicago, Illinois, U.S.A., Octubre 1924–Agosto 1946," OLG Parish. Badillo, in Dolan and Hinojosa, *Mexican Americans and the Catholic Church*, 256. Anne M. Martínez, "Bordering on the Sacred: Religion, Nation, and U.S.-Mexican Relations, 1910–1929" (PhD diss., University of Minnesota, 2003), 148; Rosales, "Mexican Immigration to the Urban Midwest," 165; McCarthy, "Which Christ Came to Chicago," 212.

53. Bishop Emmanuel Ledvina to the Rev. Eugene J. McGuinness, August 13, 1926, in Loyola-Chicago-CCES, Box 23, Folder 2. Ledvina was particularly sympathetic to the Cristero refugees: he had been named an honorary canon of the Basilica of Our Lady of Guadalupe in 1919 due to his work with exiles and refugees during the Revolution. Moore, *Acts of Faith*, 161.

54. Bishop John Cantwell to the Extension Society, May 16, 1927, in Loyola Chicago-CCES, Box 66, Folder 2.

55. McCarthy, "Which Christ Came to Chicago," 198, 202.

56. Owens, *Most Reverend Anthony J. Schuler*, 320–31.

57. Sánchez-Walker, "Migration Quicksand," 25.

58. Owens, *Most Reverend Anthony J. Schuler*, 334.

59. Letter of appeal sent from the Supreme Council of the Knights of Columbus to all United States Grand Knights, August 26, 1926, NCWC Box 149, Folder 3.

60. Report of the Knights of Columbus Mexican Program, February 11, 1931, in KOC, Document 11-2-069-01.

61. Sanchez-Walker, "Migration Quicksand," 280.

62. "Los Colegios Catolicos de Sonora se van al Extranjero," *La Prensa*, July 30, 1926, 9; "Las monjas de León pasan al Estado de Arizona," *La Prensa*, August 10, 1926, 4; "200,000 Mexico Students Go to Schools in U.S.: War on Catholics Results in Big Exodus," *The Chicago Tribune*, August 19, 1928, 14.

63. The Congregation of the Perpetual Adorers to Mr. & Mrs. Cleofas Calleros, December 14, 1928, in UTEP-Calleros, MS231, Series II.

64. Dolan and Hinojosa, *Mexican Americans and the Catholic Church*, 58.

65. García, *Rise of the Mexican American Middle Class*, 35.

66. Nancy Aguirre, "Porfirismo during the Mexican Revolution," 112–51.

67. Quirk, *The Mexican Revolution and the Catholic Church*, 190. "Informes Confidenciales Emitidos por 10-B," October 15, 1926, in Fideicomiso Archivos Plutarco Elias Calles, Mexico City, Collección FEC, Serie 0906, Expediente 7, Document 1554.

68. Jorge Prieto Laurens, *Anécdotas históricas de Jorge Prieto Laurens* (Mexico City: B. Costa-Amic Press, 1977), esp. 159–69.

69. Jurgen Buchenau, *Plutarco Elias Calles and the Mexican Revolution* [Latin American Silhouettes Series] (New York: Rowman and Littlefield, 2006), 101.

70. See, for example, the case of Manuel Valle, y V., who was deported to the United States "solamente por ser miembro Liga Defensa Religiosa [*sic*]" in April 1927. Delegate of the Migration Office in Ciudad Juárez to the Ministry of the Interior, April 19, 1927, AGN-IPS, Vol. 228, Expediente 3. See also Victoria Lerner, "Los exiliados de la Revolución Mexicana," 83.

71. Lerner, "Los exiliados de la Revolución Mexicana," 92.

72. "Mexico News Item," February 27, 1928, in NCWC Collection 10, Box 149, Folder 8.

73. Phil J. Divver, *Knights of Columbus Historical Review* (Knights of Columbus California State Council, [n.p.] 1967), 176–77.

74. Report of the Knights of Columbus Mexican Program, February 11, 1931, in KOC, Document 11-2-069-01.

75. "Report concerning Mrs. Carlota Landero de Algara," Nuevo Laredo, August 1, 1927, in AGN-IPS, Vol. 49, Expediente 3.

76. Lerner, "Los exiliados," 89–91. See also Prieto Laurens, *Anécdotas históricas*, 168–69.

77. Report from Agent 47 in San Antonio to the Jefe del Departamento Confidencial, February 28, 1927, in AGN, IPS, Vol. 54, Expediente 10.

78. Report by Department of Justice agent J. J. Lawrence, San Antonio, August 11, 1927, in NACP, State RG 59, Decimal File 812.00/28639.

79. René Capistrán Garza to John J. Burke, December 5, 1926, in ACUA-NCWC, Mexican Files, Box 149, Folder 7; Report from Agent 47 in San Antonio to

the Jefe del Departamento Confidencial, January 24, 1927, in AGN, IPS, Vol. 2053-A, Expediente 5.

80. Jorge Prieto Laurens relocated there by 1929; as did Guillermo Prieto-Yeme; Vasconcelos passed through the city, as well. See Prieto Laurens, *Anécdotas históricas*, 156, 163.

81. Guillermo Prieto-Yeme to Judge Alfred B. Tally, October 13, 1925, in GU-America, Box 18, Folder 27.

CHAPTER 3

1. "Mexico News Items," August 23, 1927, in ACUA-NCWC, Mexican Files, Box 146, Folder 19. Anselmo Padilla's death is also briefly described in Jean Meyer, *La Cristiada* Vol. 3, No. 301 (Mexico City: Siglo Veintiuno Editores, 1976), fn79.

2. "Estadísticas Históricas de México 2009," INEGI, 2010, cuadro 3.7, 2a parte. (Retrieved: http://www.inegi.org.mx/prod_serv/contenidos/espanol/bvinegi/productos/integracion/pais/historicas10/EHM2009.pdf.)

3. Raúl Coronado, *A World Not to Come: A History of Latino Writing and Print Culture* (Cambridge: Harvard University Press, 2013), 281.

4. See Michael M. Smith, "Carrancista Propaganda and the Print Media in the United States: An Overview of Institutions," *The Americas* Vol. 52, No. 2 (October 1995), 155–74; Nicolás Kanellos, "Recovering and Re-Constructing Early Twentieth-Century Hispanic Immigrant Print Culture in the US," *American Literary History* Vol. 19, No. 2 (Summer 2007), 438–55; Jorge Durand and Michael M. Smith, "*El Cosmopolita* de Kansas City." See also Rudolph Vecoli, "The Italian Immigrant Press and the Construction of Social Reality, 1850–1920," in *Print Culture in a Diverse America*, ed. James Philip Dankey and Wayne A. Wiegand (Champaign, IL: University of Illinois Press, 1998), 17–33.

5. Nancy Aguirre, "Porfirismo during the Mexican Revolution," 243.

6. Richard A. García, *Rise of the Mexican American Middle Class*, 225.

7. Aguirre, "Porfirismo during the Mexican Revolution," 226–27, 244, 262.

8. Sister Lilliana S. L. Owens, *Most Reverend Anthony J. Schuler*, 190.

9. Report from C. T. Valdivia, Presbitero at the Centro Propagandista de la Fe in Colton, California, to the Ministro de Gobernación, August 12, 1927, in AGN, IPS, Vol. 225, Expediente 15; Report from Cónsul General in El Paso to Secretario de Gobernación, August 30, 1934, in AGN, D-Gob., Vol. 126, Expediente 2.340 (73) 66; Report from El Delegado de Migracion, Piedras Negras, Coahuila, to the Secretaría de Gobernación, February 26, 1927, in AGN, IPS, Vol. 227, Expediente 34.

10. "News Items," May 10, 1929, in ACUA-NCWC, Mexican Files, Box 148, Folder 6.

11. Pamphlet entitled "LA RAZON," July 31, 1927, in AGN, IPS, Vol. 231, Expediente 30.

12. Report by Department of Justice Agent H. J. Kheen in Los Angeles, September 20, 1927, in NA State RG 59, Decimal File 812.404/837.

13. Interview by author with Severino López, C.M.F., October 18, 2006.

14. Dolan and Hinojosa, *Mexican Americans and the Catholic Church*, 195; see also Spencer Leitman, "Exile and Union in Indiana Harbor: Los obreros católicos 'San José' and El Amigo del Hogar, 1925–1930," *Revista chicano-riquena* Vol. 2 (1974), 50–57, 52.

15. "Un Día en mi Patria," *El Amigo del Hogar*, May 8, 1927, 3.

16. "Dios y el Pueblo" and "Mayo mes de María," *El Amigo del Hogar*, May 15, 1927, 3.

17. "Mártires de Zamora, Mex.," *El Amigo del Hogar*, August 7, 1927, 2; "Exitativa a los Católicos de la colonia Mexicana" and "Los Mártires de Leon Guanajuato: ¡Cristianos a las Fieras!," *El Amigo del Hogar*, July 24, 1927, 1–2.

18. "Los Mártires" and "Notas Breves relativas a Mexico," *El Amigo del Hogar*, July 7, 1927, 2–3.

19. "Revisando la Prensa" *El Amigo del Hogar*, August 13, 1927, 1.

20. "La idea de la Biblioteca se abre paso" and "Recuerdos de los beneficios que debe Mexico a la Religion Catolica," *El Amigo del Hogar*, June 5, 1927, 1, 4.

21. Pamphlet with the heading: "*¡Alerta Católicos! Al pueblo mexicano y en particular a la clase trabajadora*," 1926, in UNAM-MPV-LNDLR, Caja 47, Expediente 346, Folio 7689.

22. A letter to the president of the Knights of Columbus from a Mexican consular representative in Los Angeles in September of 1926 warned of revolutionary activities in El Paso fomented by exiled members of the ACJM. These included Jorge Prieto Laurens, a member of Adolfo de la Huerta's revolutionary cadre; Pedro Vazquez Cisneros, an editor of a Mexican newspaper in El Paso; and Rene Capistran Garza. The letter further warned that the men were plotting to start a newspaper (to be called *El Continental*) and to distribute pamphlets around town. E. Traslosheros to James A. Flaherty, September 23, 1926, in GU-America, Box 38, Folder 5.

23. Report from Enrique Santibañez, Consul General of Mexico in San Antonio, to the Mexican Ambassador in Washington, April 9, 1929, in SRE, LE 817. See also Ransom Patrick Cross, "Hands Across the Border: The Role of the U.S. Catholic Church in Assisting Mexican Catholics during the Religious Crisis in Mexico, 1926–1929" (MA thesis, University of Texas at El Paso, 1994).

24. Report from Cónsul C. Palacios Roji, Nogales, Arizona to the Cónsul of Mexico in Calexico, California. February 28, 1928, in SRE, LE 863–12.

25. *¡Viva Cristo Rey! Mensaje al Mundo Civilizado por el obispo de Huejutla*, San Antonio, Texas, July 12, 1927, in SRE, LE 852, Legajo 4, Document 213.

26. Report from the Department of Justice to the Department of State (no agent name) containing translated version of pamphlet, May 8, 1928, in NACP, State RG 59, Decimal File 812.00/29168.

27. Report by Department of Justice Agent H. J. Kheen in Los Angeles, September 20, 1927, in NA State RG 59, Decimal File 812.404/837.

28. Parts of the speech are reproduced in Pedro Vera y Zuria, *Diario de mi destierro*, 44.

29. Archbishop Ruiz y Flores stated to *La Opinión* that the Mexican Church looked "with sympathy, especially at a time like this, on any candidate or party who sincerely promises the religious liberties to which all citizens have a right." Clipping from *La Opinión*, December 7, 1928, translated to English, in ACUA-NCWC, Mexican Files, Box 148, Folder 5.

30. Report from Consul John W. Dye in Ciudad Juárez to Department of State, November 5, 1929, in NACP, Foreign Service RG 84, Consular Correspondence from Ciudad Juárez, Subject Group 800; see also Adolfo Tamayo in Fresno, California, to President Emilio Portes Gil, August 31, 1929, in AGN, EPG, Vol. 18, Expediente 672/217, Legajo 15.

31. Report from Edmundo L. Aragon, Consul of Calexico, to Secretary of Foreign Relations, March 3, 1930, in SRE, LE 863-14. Memorandum concerning political campaigns in the United States by Agent 24 in San Antonio, January 22, 1929, in AGN, IPS, Vol. 54, Expediente 11. For more on Vasconcelos's work within Mexican emigrant communities, see John Skirius, "Vasconcelos and México de Afuera (1928)," *Aztlán—International Journal of Chicano Studies Research* Vol. 7, No. 3 (Fall 1976), 479–97.

32. See "Hispanic Radio: U.S. Spanish-Language Broadcasting," in Christopher H. Sterling and Cary O'Dell, eds., *The Concise Encyclopedia of American Radio* (New York: Routledge, 2010), 351.

33. Report from Juan Achondo, Consul of Mexico in Tucson, to SRE, November 30, 1926, in AGN, IPS, Vol. 2053-A, Expediente 4.

34. Melissa Johnson, "Pre-Television Stereotypes: Mexicans in U.S. Newsreels, 1919–1932," *Critical Studies in Mass Communication* Vol. 16, No. 4 (1999), 424.

35. Dolan and Hinojosa, *Mexican Americans and the Catholic Church*, 185.

36. Jean Meyer and Ulises Íñiguez Mendoza, *La Cristiada en imagines: del cine mudo al video* (Guadalajara: University of Guadalajara Press, 2006), 17–18.

37. Report from Miguel M. Dominguez in Kansas City to J. L. Deister, September 15, 1928, in AGN, IPS, Vol. 234, Expediente 29.

38. "Mexico News Item," translated clipping from *La Voz de la Patria*, December 16, 1928, NCWC. Mexican Files, Box 146, Folder 20.

39. Report from Agent 47 in San Antonio to the Jefe del Departamento Confidencial, March 3, 1926, in AGN, IPS, Vol. 54, Expediente 9.

40. Report from Agents 19 & 21 to Jefe del Departamento Confidencial, January 10, 1927, in AGN, IPS, Vol. 227, Expediente 20.

41. Report from Enrique Santibañez, Consul General of Mexico in San Antonio, to the Mexican Ambassador in Washington, April 9, 1929, in SRE, LE 817.

42. "Announcements," January 20, 1927, OLG Parish.

43. Jesus Fuentes Davila, Jefe de la Guarnición, to the President of Mexico, April 26, 1927, in AGN, IPS, Vol. 228, Expediente 15.

44. Jefe del Departamento at the SRE to Jefe del Departamento Confidencial, March 25, 1927, in AGN, IPS, Vol. 228, Expediente 15.

45. News clipping from the *San Antonio Express*, October 1, 1927, in ACUA-NCWC, Mexican Files, Box 146, Folder 19.

46. Confidential Agent Number 47 to the Confidential Department, March 3, 1926, in AGN, IPS, Vol. 54, Expediente 9.

47. "Crónica," August 1, 1926, OLG Parish.

48. "Announcements," January 20, 1927, OLG Parish.

49. "Mexicans of South to Erect Shrine to Our Lady of Guadalupe," *Los Angeles Tidings*, June 9, 1928, quoted in Dolan and Hinojosa, *Mexican Americans and the Catholic Church*, 185.

50. Matthew Butler, "Trouble Afoot? Pilgrimage in *Cristero* Mexico City," 156.

51. In 1927—just as the Cristero War was gaining strength in the Mexican heartland—Mexican consulates in the United States received a directive from the SRE "to develop special plans for Mexican Independence Day celebrations and other national holidays." Organization of the *fiestas patrias* was often delegated to the *comisiones honoríficas*, groups of emigrants that worked under the direct supervision of the consulates. The fiestas patrias typically featured displays of the Mexican flag, the national anthem, nostalgic songs, poems, skits, plays, music, and dancing. See González, *Mexican Consuls and Labor Organizing*, 56–57.

52. "Mas de Diez Mil Mexicanos Formaron en el Gran Desfile: Monseñor Manríque y Zárate pronunció el sermón final," *El Diario de El Paso*, June 14, 1928, clipping in UNAM-Traslosheros, Caja 100, Expediente 724, Foja 6897. The event was large enough to garner a mention in the *Los Angeles Times* as well. "Corpus Christi Fete Gay Event: Ten Thousand of City's Latin Presidents Participate," *Los Angeles Times*, June 11, 1928, A2.

53. For a broader discussion on hometown associations, see José C. Moya, "Immigrants and Associations: A Global and Historical Perspective," *Journal of Ethnic and Migration Studies* Vol. 31, No. 5 (2005), 833–64.

54. "The Knights of Columbus in Mexico," Brochure dated August 7, 8, and 9, 1923, NCWC Box 148, Folder 28.

55. "Tepeyac Council No. 2635," in Peter T. Conmy, *Seventy Years of Service: History of the Knights of Columbus in California, 1902–1972* (New Haven, CT: Knights of Columbus Press, 1972), 176–77.

56. Timothy M. Matovina, *Guadalupe and Her Faithful*, 111.

57. Report from Agent No. 21 to Jefe del Departamento Confidencial, Ciudad Juárez, February 16, 1927, in AGN, IPS, Vol. 2053-A, Expediente 5.

58. Malachy McCarthy, "Which Christ Came to Chicago," 220.

59. Dolan and Hinojosa, *Mexican Americans and the Catholic Church*, 195.

60. Carlos Férnandez to the National Catholic Welfare Conference, May 7, 1928, in UNAM-LNDLR, Document 4050, Inv. No. 5050; Carlos Fernández to Salvador Chavez Hayhoe, May 7, 1928, in UNAM-LNDLR, Document 4071, Inv. No. 5051; Carlos Fernández and associates to Rev. D. Zaldívar, Chicago, May 11, 1928, in UNAM-LNDLR Document 4089, Inv. No. 5089.

61. Mexico City, Archivo Histórico, UNAM, Carlos Fernández to the National Catholic Welfare Conference, May 7, 1928, Fondo Manuel Palomar y Vizcarra, UNAM-LNDLR, Document 4050, Inv. No. 5050; Carlos Fernández to Salvador Chavez Hayhoe, May 7, 1928, UNAM-LNDLR, Document 4071, Inv. No. 5051; Carlos Fernández and associates to Rev. D. Zaldívar, Chicago, May 11, 1928, UNAM-LNDLR Document 4089, Inv. No. 5089; Carlos Fernández to Guillermo Prieto-Yeme in San Antonio, March 13, 1928, UNAM-LNDLR 3954, Document, Inv. No. 4855.

62. See González, *Mexican Consuls and Labor Organizing*, 56–57.

63. "Renuncia a su candidatura de reina," *La Prensa*, August 1, 1926, 1.

64. *Mexico*, "Los Mexicanos de Tucson, Arizona no Haran Festejos En Septiembre," August 21, 1926; Letter from the Club Latino de Tucson to the *Tucson Citizen*, August 7, 1926, in SRE, LE 710, Document 485.

65. "Rara Conducta de los Mexicanos en Los Angeles, Cal.: Por los recientes conflictos entre el gobierno y el clero, se abstendran de participar en las fiestas patrias," *México*, August 21, 1926, 1.

66. Report from Agent No. 9 in Hermosillo, Sonora, to Jefe del Departamento de Gobernación, September 27, 1926, in AGN, IPS, Vol. 246, Expediente 15.

67. Report from Agent (no number given) in San Antonio to Jefe del Departamento Confidencial, April 21, 1926, in AGN, IPS, Vol. 2053-A, Expediente 4.

68. "Border Mexicans Excoriate Calles: They Hand Protest to Consul at San Antonio, Charging Murder, Torture, and Tyranny," *The New York Times*, December 5, 1927, 25.

69. Letter from a group of Mexican residents of Perris, California, to President Plutarco Elias Calles, April 23, 1926, in AGN, D-Gob., Vol. 39, Expediente 2-347 (2-2).

70. "Border Mexicans Excoriate Calles: They Hand Protest to Consul at San Antonio, Charging Murder, Torture, and Tyranny," *The New York Times*, December 5, 1927, 25.

71. David Bailey, *!Viva Cristo Rey!*, 143.

72. Francisco A. Rosales, "Mexican Immigration to the Urban Midwest," 165.

73. González, *Mexican Consuls and Labor Organizing*, 42.

74. Guillermo Prieto-Yeme to Wilfred Parsons, October 13, 1926, in GU-Americas, Box 18, Folder 27.

75. "La voz de los emigrados," *Diario de El Paso*, December 6, 1927, clipping in UNAM-Traslosheros, Caja 100, Expediente 721, Foja 6604.

76. Carlos Fernández to Salvador Chavez Hayhoe, 5/7/1928, in UNAM-LNDLR, Document 4071, Inv. No. 5051.

77. "Fue instalada aqui la Unión Nacionalista," *La Opinión*, December 11, 1928, clipping in UNAM-Traslosheros, Caja 103, Expediente 735, Foja 7653.

78. José de Jesús Manríquez y Zárate to Miguel Palomar y Vizcarra, April 29, 1929, in INAH-MPV.

79. Manuel Gamio, *The Life Story of the Mexican Immigrant*, 170.

80. Gamio, *The Life Story of the Mexican Immigrant*, 211.

81. Gamio, *The Life Story of the Mexican Immigrant*, 173–74.

82. Gamio, *The Life Story of the Mexican Immigrant*, 179–80.

83. Gamio, *The Life Story of the Mexican Immigrant*, 43.

84. See the collection of letters from residents of the United States in support of Calles's anticlerical reforms, in AGN, O-C, Vol. 104-L-23, Expediente 3, Anexo 2.

85. Unsigned letter from a Mexican emigrant in Los Angeles to President Calles, July 1926, in AGN, O-C, Vol. 104-L-23, Expediente 4, Anexo 1.

86. "Nota [que] Se Dirigen al Presidente de Mexico Los Obreros Mexicanos de Chicago," *México*, August 7, 1926, 2.

87. C. T. Valdivia of the Centro Propagandista de la Fe, Colton, California, to the Secretario de Gobernación, September 8, 1926, in AGN, D-Gob., Vol. 125, Expediente 2.340 (73) 3.

88. "En Gary Se Condenó a los Católicos de Todas las Épocas" *México*, April 2, 1927, 1. For more on the conflicts between "liberal" and "traditionalist" (i.e., Catholic) Mexicans in Chicago and the Midwest, see John Henry Flores, "On the Wings of the Revolution," Chapter II, 59–88.

89. J. M. Chávez in Saginaw, Michigan, to the President of Mexico, August 19, 1926, in AGN, O-C, Vol. 104-L-23, Expediente 4, Anexo 1.

90. Antonio Rodríguez in Chicago to the President of Mexico, October 16, 1927, in AGN, IPS, Vol. 2053-A, Expediente 6.

91. "Situación Militar de la Defensa Armada en el año de 1927," Bulletin of the LNDLR, December 29, 1927, cited in Alicia Olivera de Bonfil, *Aspectos del conflicto religioso de 1926 a 1929, sus antecedentes y consecuencias* (Mexico City: Instituto Nacional de Antropología e Historia, 1966), 185.

92. Olivera de Bonfil, *Aspectos del conflicto religioso*, 209.

93. Charles H. Harris III and Louis R. Sadler, *The Secret War in El Paso*, 32.

94. Harris and Sadler, *The Secret War in El Paso*, 37, 87–88, 149.

95. See W. Dirk Raat, *Revoltosos: Mexican Rebels in the United States*, 229–56. See also the *Presidential Proclamation* of January 7, 1924, in NACP, State RG 59, Decimal File 812.24/596. To gain this approval, those who wished to ship weapons were required to fill Department of State Form Mex., "Application for License to Export Arms or Munitions of War to Mexico," in NACP, State RG 59, Decimal File 811.24/677.

96. Report from Department of Justice Agent Manuel Sorola in San Antonio, February 7, 1928, in NACP State RG 59, Decimal File 812.00/211122.

97. G-2 Report from Informant S-1 to Commanding General, 8th Corps Area, Fort Sam Houston, Texas, March 20, 1928, in NACP, MID RG 165, 2657-G-605, Document 68.

98. G-2 Report from A. S. Balsam, Major, 25th Infantry, in Nogales, Arizona, to Assistant Chief of Staff, Fort Sam Houston, Texas, March 31, 1928, in NACP, MID RG 165, 2657-G-605, Document 127-3.

99. Informe Número 390 [no author], Del Rio, Texas, August 11, 1927, in SRE, LE 822-8; Report from Department of Justice Agent J. J. Lawrence, November 7, 1927, in NACP, State RG 59, Decimal File 812.00/28963.

100. Report from Consul C. Palacios Rojí, Nogales, Arizona, to the Cónsul of Mexico in Calexico, California, February 28, 1928, in SRE, LE 863-12.

101. Report from the Consul of Calexico to C. Palacios Rojí, the Consul of Nogales, March 15, 1928, in SRE, LE 863-12.

102. Report from the Subsecretarío of Relaciones Exteriores to the Secretarío de Gobernación, March 7, 1928, in AGN, IPS, Vol. 232, Expediente 48.

103. Report from Luis Pérez Abreu, Consul of Rio Grande City, to Secretary of Foreign Relations, June 27, 1927, in SRE, LE 852-5.

104. Telegram from Consul Lubbert in San Francisco to SRE, June 20, 1927, in SRE, LE 852-3.

105. Report by Department of Justice Agent John K. Wren, El Paso, August 24, 1927, in NACP State RG 59, Decimal File 812.24/449.

106. Report by Department of Justice Agent John K. Wren, El Paso, July 15, 1927, in NACP Justice RG 60, Classified Subject File 71-1-6, Box 12339; Report by Department of Justice Agent J.J. Lawrence, San Antonio, August 11, 1927, in NACP State RG 59, Decimal File 812.00/28639.

107. Report from Consul Lubbert in San Francisco to SRE, October 11, 1927, in SRE, LE 852-3.

108. Department of Justice Agent John K. Wren to the Department of State, October 14, 1927, in NACP, State RG 59, Decimal File 812.00/28898.

109. Report of Special Agent John L. Haas in the case entitled "Pacific Arms Company, Guillermo Rosas, Jr., M. Garcia Herrera, et al., Mexican Matters, in DOJ RG 60, Classified Subject File No. 71-1-2.

110. Manríquez y Zárate to Miguel Palomar y Vizcarra, November 3, 1928, in INAH-MPV.

111. Manríquez y Zárate to Miguel Palomar y Vizcarra, December 24, 1928, in UNAM-MPV-LNDLR, Caja 50, Expediente 372, Folio 10630.

112. Manríquez y Zárate to Miguel Palomar y Vizcarra, September 15, 1928, in INAH-MPV.

113. Manríquez y Zárate to Miguel Palomar y Vizcarra, July 15, 1928, in INAH-MPV.

114. Manríquez y Zárate to Miguel Palomar y Vizcarra, November 3, 1928, in INAH-MPV.

115. Report from Agent 47 in San Antonio to the Jefe del Departamento Confidencial, February 9, 1927, in AGN, IPS, Vol. 228, Expediente 23.

116. Report from Agent 47 in San Antonio to Jefe del Departamento Confidencial, February 28, 1927, in AGN, IPS, Vol. 54, Expediente 10.

117. Report from the *Official mayor* of the SRE, Mexico City, September 20, 1926, in SRE, LE 858-2.

118. Report from A. F. Carrillo, Consul, San Antonio, May 4, 1927, in SRE, LE 852-4.

119. G-2 Report from Robert J. Halpin, Major, General Staff, in Fort Sam Houston, Texas to Assistant Chief of Staff, War Department General Staff, April 7, 1928, in NACP, MID RG 165, 2657-G-605, Document 128-1.

120. Report from Viceconsul L. H. Obregón in Los Angeles to SRE, May 23, 1927, in SRE, LE 846-3.

121. Translated clipping from *La Opinión*, February 7, 1928, in ACUA-NCWC, Mexican Files, Box 146, Folder 20.

122. Félix Brito R., "Una óptica del moviemiento social Cristero desde la periferia," 119.

123. Report from Department of Justice Agent Gus T. Jones in San Antonio, August 11, 1928, in NACP State RG 59, Decimal File 812.00/29287.

124. A. P. Carrillo to the Secretaría de Relaciones Exteriores, July 21, 1927, SRE LE 852-4.

125. Department of Justice report filed in San Antonio, Texas, Jesus Martínez Galvan, Francisco Castillano [*sic*] and Bernadi Orizaga [*sic*], October 24, 1928, in NACP, Justice RG 60, Classified Subject File 71-1-0.

126. Report from Agent 29 in San Antonio to Jefe del Departamento Confidencial, November 8, 1928, in AGN, IPS, Vol. 234, Expediente 15; Report from Secret Agent 29 in San Antonio to the Jefe del Departamento Confidencial, November 1928 [no exact date], in AGN, IPS, Vol. 54, Expediente 10.

127. Report from E. Medina, Procurador General de la Republica, to the Subsecretario de Gobernación, June 13, 1929, in AGN, IPS, Vol. 234, Expediente 15.

128. Report from Agent 2 to the Jefe del Departamento Confidencial, June 16, 1927, in AGN, IPS, Vol. 230, Expediente 39.

129. Carlos Fernández to unnamed correspondent, April 22, 1927, in UNAM-MPV-LNDLR, Caja 48, Expediente 353, Folio 8498; Alert to border officials, January 21, 1927, in AGN, IPS, Vol. 226, Expediente 7.

130. Report from Confidential Agent (no number given) in San Antonio to Jefe del Departamento Confidencial, April 21, 1926, in AGN, IPS, Vol. 2053-A, Expediente 4.

131. Manríquez y Zárate to Miguel Palomar y Vizcarra, October 24, 1928, in INAH-MPV.

132. Bailey, ¡*Viva Cristo Rey!*, 107.

133. Memorandum, January 7, 1927, in ACUA-NCWC, Mexican Files, Box 149, Folder 8; Consul General A. P. Carillo in San Antonio to SRE, January 22, 1927, in SRE, LE 853; Report from Laredo, Texas to the SRE, February 7, 1927, in SRE, LE 846 (3); Report from Agent J. J. Lawrence, San Antonio, October 13, 1927, in NACP State RG 59, Decimal File 812.00/28903; Report from A. P. Carillo, Consul General in San Antonio, to the SRE, May 23, 1927, in SRE, LE 852-4; Assistant Attorney General Geo R. Farnull to Frank B. Kellogg, Secretary of State, December 1, 1927, in NACP, Justice RG 60, Classified Subject File 71-1-47, Box 12340.

134. See, for example, a flyer entitled "Libertad Religiosa" and signed by J. G. Escobar, March 1929, in SRE, LE 817.

135. José Gándara to Frank B. Kellogg, December 17, 1926, in NACP, State RG 59, Decimal File 812.00/28132.

136. Report of the US War Department concerning José Gándara, February 25, 1938, in NACP, MID RG 165, 2657-G-657, Document 260, Box 1665; "Another Revolution in Mexico Believed Nipped by Arrests Near Tucson ... New Uprising Called Purely Religious," *Tucson Citizen*, clipping in NA, INS RG 85, Subject Correspondence Files, Part 2, Mexican Immigration, 1906–1930, Case File 55598/459-A.

137. John O. Risoeher S. J. to Wilfred Parsons, January 16, 1927, in GU-America, Box 18, Folder 28.

138. E. Traslosheros to James A. Flaherty, September 23, 1926, in GU-America, Box 38, Folder 5.

139. Report from Agent 2 to the Jefe del Departamento, June 16, 1927, in AGN, IPS, Vol. 230, Expediente 39.

140. Confidential Memorandum from William F. Montavon to John J. Burke regarding José F. Gándara, February 4, 1930, in ACUA-NCWC, Mexican Files, Box 150, Folder 17.

141. Confidential Memorandum from William F. Montavon to John J. Burke regarding José F. Gándara, February 4, 1930, in ACUA-NCWC, Mexican Files, Box 150, Folder 17.

142. Report from Agent 9 in Hermosillo, Sonora, to Jefe del Departamento de Gobernación, October 30, 1926, in AGN, IPS, Vol. 246, Expediente 15.

143. The conflicts between the Mexican government and the Yaqui Indians had a long history that predated the 1920s. For further reference, see Evelyn Hu-DeHart, *Yaqui Resistance and Survival: The Struggle for Land and Autonomy, 1821–1910* (Madison: University of Wisconsin Press, 1984). See also a clipping from a newspaper article in the *Nogales Herald* about bands of Yaquis seeking refuge in the United States [Full title obscured from microfilm], *Nogales*

Herald, May 9, 1927, in NA, INS RG 85, Subject Correspondence Files, Part 2: Mexican Immigration, 1906–1930, Case File 55598/459-A.

144. Confidential Memorandum from William F. Montavon to John J. Burke regarding José F. Gándara, February 4, 1930, in ACUA-NCWC, Mexican Files, Box 150, Folder 17.

145. Official at Embassy of Mexico in Washington to Franklin Mott Gunther, US Department of State, June 21, 1927, in SRE, LE 822-4.

146. Report from Agent 2 in Ciudad Juárez to the Jefe del Departamento Confidencial, July 6, 1927, in AGN, IPS, Vol. 230, Expediente 64.

147. Report from Agent 2 in Chihuahua to Jefe del Departamento Confidencial, 7/12/1927, in AGN, IPS, Vol. 230, Expediente 64.

148. "Shipment of Rifles Recalled in Trial of Esteban Borgaro," *Tucson Citizen,* June 18, 1927, clipping in NA, INS RG 85, Subject Correspondence Files, Part 2: Mexican Immigration, 1906–1930, Case File 55598/459-A.

149. Report from Consul of Tucson to Consul General in El Paso, June 26, 1927, in AGN, IPS, Vol. 230, Expediente 39.

150. Report from Agent 2 in Chihuahua to the Jefe del Departamento Confidencial, October 7, 1927, in AGN, IPS, Vol. 230, Expediente 64.

151. "Second Group of Yaquis Is Arrested Here," *Arizona Daily Star,* June 25, 1927, clipping in NA, INS RG 85, Subject Correspondence Files, Part 2: Mexican Immigration, 1906–1920, Case File 55598/459-A; Telegram from employee of SRE in Mexico City to Secretaria de Gobernación, June 27, 1927, in AGN, IPS, Vol. 230, Expediente 39.

152. Confidential Memorandum from William F. Montavon to John J. Burke regarding José F. Gándara, February 4, 1930, in ACUA-NCWC, Mexican Files, Box 150, Folder 17.

153. "Two Years in Prison and $1000 Fine, Fate of Border Disturber," *Tucson Citizen,* December 2, 1927, 2. It appears from the archival documents that the case was never retried.

154. "Gandara Charged with Violating Nation's Neutrality Law," *Tucson Citizen,* September 9, 1927, 3.

155. These included Frank Curley, Judge Samuel L. Patee, James D. Barry, Tom K. Richey, W. H. Fryer, and Lynn D. Smith. "Navarrete at Bar: Catholic Bishop of Sonora on Trial in Federal Court Here," *Tucson Citizen,* November 22, 1927, 1; "Directed Verdict of Not Guilty Is Asked in Conspiracy Case," *Tucson Citizen,* November 26, 1927, 2.

156. "Navarrete at Bar: Catholic Bishop of Sonora on Trial in Federal Court Here," *Tucson Citizen,* November 22, 1927, 1.

157. "Yaqui Troops Link Bishop's Name with Revolt," *Tucson Citizen,* November 23, 1927, 2.

158. "Bishop Navarrete Freed: Instructed Verdict for Cleric Ordered by Presiding Judge," *Tucson Citizen,* November 29, 1927, 3.

159. "Another Revolution in Mexico Believed Nipped by Arrests Near Tucson . . . New Uprising Called Purely Religious," *Tucson Citizen*, June 26, 1927, clipping in INS Case File 55598/459-A.

160. Report from Enrique Liekens, Consul General in El Paso, to Secretary of Foreign Relations, June 28, 1927, in SRE, LE 822-6.

161. "Argument Made in Conspiracy Hearing Today: Case of Gándara and Borgaro Submitted This Afternoon," *Tucson Citizen*, November 30, 1927, 3.

162. Private memorandum by John J. Burke ("Some Thoughts on the Bp. Navarrete Case"), November 7, 1927, in ACUA-NCWC, Mexican Files, Box 145, Book 1; "Archbishop Defends Accused Mexican," The *Washington Post*, September 17, 1927, clipping in ACUA-NCWC, Mexican Files, Box 147, Folder 14; Documents concerning Navarrete case, in ACUA-NCWC, Mexican Files, Box 147, Folder 14; John I. Reilly to the Honorable Ralph H. Cameron, National Republican Club. November 14, 1927, in NACP, Justice RG 60, Classified Subject File 71-1-2 Nos. 1-49, Box 12338; John J. Burke to Archbishop Hanna, October 31, 1927, in ACUA-NCWC, Mexican Files, Box 150, Folder 38.

163. "Two Years in Prison and $1000 Fine, Fate of Border Disturber," *Tucson Citizen*, December 2, 1927, 2.

164. E. J. Geehan to Director, Bureau of Investigation, December 5, 1927, in NACP, State RG 59, Decimal File 812.00/28935; "Gándara Found Guilty of Fomenting Rebellion," *Tucson Citizen*, December 1, 1927, 2; Report from Confidential Agent in Ciudad Juárez, Chihuahua, to Jefe del Departamento Confidencial, July 11, 1927, in AGN, IPS, Vol. 230, Expediente 39; "Higher Court Will Pass on Gándara Case: Appeal and Stay of Execution Is Granted," *Tucson Citizen*, December 4, 1927, 2.

165. Wilfred Parsons to Archbishop Drossaerts, April 1930, in GU-America, Box 38, Folder 24.

166. Confidential Memo on the 1929 Revolution by John J. Burke, March 5, 1929, in ACUA-NCWC, Mexican Files, Box 145, Book 3.

167. John J. Burke to John T. McNicholas, Archbishop of Cincinnati, January 2, 1931, in ACUA-NCWC, Mexican Files, Box 148, Folder 12.

168. Copy of presidential pardon by Herbert Hoover to José Gándara, March 31, 1930, in NACP, Justice RG 60, Classified Subject File 71-1-2, Box 12338.

169. Jefe del Departamento de Gobernación to the Delegado de Migración, September 6, 1929, in AGN, IPS, Vol. 230, Expediente 39; Statement by José Gándara to the Consul General of Mexico in El Paso, July 27, 1929, in AGN, IPS, Vol. 230, Expediente 39.

170. Manuel C. Tellez, Ambassador of Mexico, to William D. Mitchell, US Attorney General, March 27, 1930, in NACP, Justice RG 60, Classified Subject File 71-1-2, Box 12338.

171. Author interview with Margarita (Mago) Gándara, June 25, 2013.

172. Letter from M. T. Gándara to Robert F. Kennedy, September 5, 1964, in NACP, Justice RG 60, Classified Subject File 71-1-2, Box 12338.

173. For more on indigenous participation in religious revolts, see Adrian Bantjes, *As If Jesus Walked on Earth: Cardeniso, Sonora, and the Mexican Revolution* (Oxford: SR Books, 1998); Antonio Avitia Hernández, *El Caudillo Sagrado: Historia de las rebeliones cristeras en el estado de Durango* (Mexico City: Impresos Castellanos, 2000); Ben Fallaw, " 'The Devil Is Now Loose in Huejutla': The Bishop, the SEP, and the Emancipation of the Indian in Hidalgo," in *Religion and State Formation in Revolutionary Mexico*, 63–100.

CHAPTER 4

1. For a more detailed history of the ecobarista uprising, see René Valenzuela, "Chihuahua, Calles and the Escobar Revolt of 1929" (PhD diss., University of Texas at El Paso, 1975).

2. Escobar's supporters also included Fausto Topete, the former governor of Sonora; Francisco Manzo, a former military general; Gilberto Valenzuela, former candidate for the Mexican presidency; Jorge Prieto Laurens, a dela-huertista and Catholic supporter; and Enrique Estrada, who had led a Catholic-supported border revolt of his own in the summer of 1926. "Escobar Declared Canadian Refugee: Score of Mexican Generals, Sick or Destitute, Are in Los Angeles," *The Washington Post*, May 10, 1929, clipping in ACUA-NCWC, Mexican Files, Box 148, Folder 6; Consul Vázquez in Nogales to SRE, March 18, 1929, in SRE, LE 693-2.

3. Report from Department of Justice Agent Manuel Sorola, March 3–13, 1929, in NACP, Justice RG 60, Classified Subject File 71-1-0, Box 12338.

4. Report from Department of Justice Agent C. B. Winstead in Los Angeles regarding Dionisio Alvarez, Jorge Padilla, and Ramon Hernandez Chavez, March 9, 1929, in NACP, Justice RG 60, Classified Subject File 71-1-71, Box 12340.

5. Telegram from Consul Liekens in El Paso to the President of Mexico, March 10, 1929, in SRE, LE 695; Consul Vázquez in Nogales to SRE, March 10, 1929, in SRE, LE 693-2.

6. Enrique Santibanez, Consul in San Antonio, to Subsecretario de Relaciones Exteriores, March 13, 1929, April 4, 1929, and April 9, 1929, in SRE, LE 814-2.

7. Flyer entitled "Libertad Religiosa" and signed by J. G. Escobar, March 1929, in SRE, LE 817.

8. Statement made by Raúl Madera in the office of the district director of Immigration, El Paso, April 13, 1929, in NACP, Foreign Service RG 84, Consular Correspondence from Ciudad Juárez, Subject Group 800.

9. News clippings related to the 1929 revolt, March 9, 1929, in NACP, Foreign Service RG 84, Consular Correspondence from Ciudad Juárez, Subject Group 800.

10. Translated clipping from *La Prensa*, March 15, 1929, in ACUA-NCWC, Mexican Files, Box 148, Folder 6.

11. "Escobar Declared Canadian Refugee: Score of Mexican Generals, Sick or Destitute, Are in Los Angeles," *The Washington Post*, May 10, 1929, clipping in ACUA-NCWC, Mexican Files, Box 148, Folder 6.

12. See Douglas Slawson, "The National Catholic Welfare Conference and the Church-State Conflict in Mexico," 55–93.

13. Matthew Redinger, *American Catholics and the Mexican Revolution*, 117.

14. Petition from the Liga to John Burke, March 13, 1926, in ACUA-NCWC, Mexican Files, Box 149, Folder 7.

15. José Mora y del Río, Archbishop of Mexico, to John J. Burke, May 2, 1926, in ACUA-NCWC, Mexican Files, Box 149, Folder 7. He added: "It is humiliating for us, Mexicans, to be reduced to asking for money from those who are foreigners, but when we see in danger of shipwreck everything—our religious, civic, and social institutions—we can [do nothing] but solicit aid from those whom we know to have generous souls and noble hearts."

16. Liga committee to John J. Burke and NCWC, May 13, 1926, and Burke's response, May 14, 1926, in ACUA-NCWC, Mexican Files, Box 149, Folder 7.

17. Robert Quirk, *The Mexican Revolution and the Catholic Church*, 167. A list of attendees can be found in a report from agent F. de la Garza in San Antonio to the Confidential Department, June 28, 1926, in AGN, IPS, Vol. 54, Expediente 9.

18. David Bailey, *¡Viva Cristo Rey!*, 103. The failed tour is well known by historians and has been recounted in Quirk, *The Mexican Revolution and the Catholic Church*, 194, and Alicia Olivera de Bonfil, *Aspectos del conflicto religioso*, 142–44.

19. René Capistrán Garza to Wilfred Parsons, n.d., in GU-America, Box 38, Folder 21.

20. Bailey, *¡Viva Cristo Rey!*, 105.

21. *Presidential Proclamation* of January 7, 1924, in NACP, State RG 59, Decimal File 812.24/596.

22. Memorandum from the Secretaria Particular of the Jefe del Departamento Confidencial to the Secretaria de Gobernación, October 7, 1926, in AGN, IPS, Vol. 238, Expediente 11.

23. Bailey, *¡Viva Cristo Rey!*, 104.

24. Redinger, *American Catholics*, 119–23; Letter from the Knights of Columbus Supreme Council, September 14, 1927, in GU-America, Box 18, Folder 28.

25. Report from consul or agent [name obscured] at Tucson, Arizona, to Consul General of Mexico, El Paso, Texas, June 16, 1927, in AGN, IPS, Vol. 230, Expediente 56; "New Rebellion Against Calles Discovered Here," *Tucson Citizen*, June 26, 1927, clipping in NA, INS RG 85, Subject Correspondence Files, Part 2, Mexican Immigration, 1906–1930, Case File 55598/459-A.

26. Clipping from *El Excelsior*, February 5, 1927, in ACUA-NCWC, Mexican Files, Box 146, Folder 32.

27. Report from the SRE to Consuls in the United States and to the Oficina de Migración, 1926, in SRE, LE 852 (5).

28. Memorandum of the LNDLR, September 15, 1927, in CARSO, Fondo CLXXXVI, Carpeta 5, Legajo 380–466, Document 422.

29. National Catholic Welfare Conference press release, December 13, 1926, in ACUA-NCWC, Mexican Files, Box 149, Folder 7.

30. See general correspondence between Wilfred Parsons and Mexican exiles, in GU-America, Box 39.

31. Stephen Andes, *The Vatican and Catholic Activism*, 98.

32. See Bailey, *¡Viva Cristo Rey!*, 122–29; Andes, *The Vatican and Catholic Activism*, 95–99.

33. News clipping from *La Prensa*, translated into English, July 24, 1927, in ACUA-NCWC, Mexican Files, Box 149, Folder 8.

34. Report from Agent 47, in San Antonio to the Jefe del Departamento Confidencial, February 12, 1927, in AGN, IPS, Vol. 54, Expediente 10.

35. Bailey, *¡Viva Cristo Rey!*, 152; Memorandum by John J. Burke, March 27, 1926, in ACUA-NCWC, Mexican Files, Box 149, Folder 10. Carlos Blanco and Tercero came to the NCWC on March 27, 1926.

36. Bailey, *¡Viva Cristo Rey!*, 211.

37. Olivera de Bonfil, *Aspectos del conflicto religioso*, 150.

38. Bailey, *¡Viva Cristo Rey!*, 186.

39. While Díaz claimed that these instructions came from the Vatican, there is some doubt about this within the secondary literature; Bailey states that Rome did not condemn the rebellion or prohibit Catholics from participating, but Díaz's goal was to take control over the Cristero movement, which was by that point out of episcopal power. Bailey, *¡Viva Cristo Rey!*, 170.

40. Pascual Díaz to Luis Bustos, January 7, 1928, in ACUA-NCWC, Mexican Files, Box 147, Folder 23.

41. Memorandum of the LNDLR, December 11, 1927, in CARSO, Fondo CLXXXVI, Carpeta 5, Legajo 380–466, Document 458.

42. See Mae M. Ngai, "Braceros, 'Wetbacks,' and the National Boundaries of Class," in *Impossible Subjects: Illegal Aliens and the Making of Modern America* (Princeton, NJ: Princeton University Press, 2005), 127–66. For a contemporary account of the formation of the Migration Service, see Andrés Landa y Piña, *El Servicio de Migración en México*.

43. See Dirk W. Raat, *Revoltosos*, 229–56. *Presidential Proclamation* of January 7, 1924, in NACP, State RG 59, Decimal File 812.24/596.

44. Report from consul or agent [name obscured] at Tucson, Ariz. to Consul General of Mexico, El Paso, Texas, June 16, 1927, in AGN, IPS, Vol. 230, Expediente 56; Report from Rafael Aveleyra, Consul Particular of El Paso, to Consul of Mexico, Denver, January 13, 1927, in SRE, LE 822-6; Telegram from Enrique Liekens, Consul General in El Paso, to SRE, May 19, 1927, in SRE, LE 822-6.

45. Summary of the border situation by Department of Justice Agent Gus. T. Jones, May 7, 1927, in NACP, State RG 59, Decimal File 812.00/28415.

46. Eugene Cunningham, "The Border Patrol," published in FRONTIER STORIES (Garden City, NY), August 1928, copy available in NA, INS RG 85, Subject Correspondence Files, Part 2: Mexican Immigration, 1906–1930, Case File 55598/459-C.

47. "Border Patrol Travels Far to Catch Suspects: Thirty-Four Men, Working on de la Huerta and Other Cases, Go 4854 Miles," *Arizona Daily Star*, May 24, 1927, clipping in NA, INS RG 85, Subject Correspondence Files, Part 2: Mexican Immigration, 1906–1930, Case File 55598/459-A; "Weekly Report of Border Patrol Shows Activity in Mex. Gun Capture," *Tucson Daily Citizen*, May 23, 1927, clipping in NA, INS RG 85, Subject Correspondence Files, Part 2: Mexican Immigration, 1906–1930, Case File 55598/459-A. For an excellent recent history of the transnational development of the Border patrol, see Kelly Lyttle Hernández's *Migra! A History of the U.S. Border Patrol*.

48. Raat, *Revoltosos*, 236.

49. Report from Department of Justice Agent Gus T. Jones in San Antonio, August 24, 1927, in NACP, State RG 59, Decimal File 812.00/28703.

50. Report from DOJ Agent A. A. Hopkins concerning Enrique Estrada, July 13, 1927, in NACP, Justice RG 60, Classified Subject File 71-1-3, Box 12338. Of great interest to government agents was where Estrada had gotten the money he used to purchase supplies, although it was rumored that the money came from Estrada's wife's family, "extremely wealthy residents of Jalisco," or that it was furnished by the Catholic hierarchy of Mexico or the oil interests of the United States.

51. Report from DOJ Agent A. A. Hopkins in Los Angeles, October 15, 1926, in NACP, Justice RG 60, Classified Subject File 71-1-3, Box 12338. Summary Report of Trial with History of Case. Defendants: Personnel and History. Notes on Estrada recruits by Department of Justice Agent A. A. Hopkins in Los Angeles, December 1, 1926, in NACP, Justice RG 60, Classified Subject File 71-1-3, Box 12338.

52. Report from Department of Justice Agent A. A. Hopkins in Los Angeles, October 15, 1926, in NACP, Justice RG 60, Classified Subject File 71-1-3, Box 12338.

53. See FBI article, "A Byte out of FBI History: Homeland Security "Between the Wars"." (Retrieved: https://www2.fbi.gov/page2/aug03/estrada081503.htm.)

54. Report from Department of Justice Agent Gus T. Jones on border situation, May 7, 1927, in NACP, State RG 59, Decimal File 812.00/28415.

55. Report from Emiliano Tamez, Consul of Eagle Pass, Texas, to Secretary of Foreign Relations, May 11, 1927, in SRE, LE 822-5.

56. With the permission of *The Americas*, parts of this section are reproduced and adapted from Julia G. Young, "The Calles Government and Catholic Dissidents: Mexico's Transnational Projects of Repression, 1926–1929," *The Americas* Vol. 70, No. 1 (July 2013), 271–300.

57. *Guía del Fondo de la Secretaria de Gobernación*, Introduction. (Retrieved: http://www.estudioshistoricos.inah.gob.mx/guia/INTRODGIPSCOMP.pdf.)

58. Memorandum from Francisco Delgado to the Secretaría de Gobernación, December 14, 1925, AGN-IPS, Vol. 43, Expediente 30.

59. Circular from Francisco Delgado, January 22, 1926, AGN-IPS, Vol. 43, Expediente 30.

60. "Guía del Fondo de la Secretaría de Gobernación"; Aaron W. Navarro, *Political Intelligence and the Creation of Modern Mexico* (Philadelphia: The Pennsylvania State University Press, 2010), 153, 159.

61. Joseph A. Stout Jr., "El poder y la autoridad en México: el Departamento Confidencial, 1922–1945" (paper presented at the XIII Reunión de Historiadores de México, Estados Unidos y Canadá, Querétaro, Mexico, October 29, 2010), 5.

62. Report from Fernando de la Garza to the head of the Departamento Confidencial, November 8, 1927, in AGN-IPS, Vol. 266, Expediente 39.

63. Report by Manuel Tello and Ignacio González G. to the head of the Departamento Confidencial, April 3, 1925, in AGN-IPS, Vol. 15, Expediente 30.

64. Report by Agent C. I. Flores to the head of the Departamento Confidencial, March 27, 1925, in AGN-IPS, Vol. 50, Expediente 1.

65. See blacklists in AGN-IPS, Vol. 208, Expediente 18.

66. Wilfred Parsons, *Mexican Martyrdom: Firsthand Accounts of the Religious Persecution in Mexico (1926–1935)* (Charlotte, NC: TAN Books, 1936), 60.

67. Report from F. de la Garza to Francisco Delgado, June 17, 1926, in AGN-IPS, Vol. 54, Expediente 9.

68. Report from F. de la Garza to the Confidential Department, June 28, 1926, in AGN-IPS, Vol. 54, Expediente 9.

69. Confidential letter from an informant in Los Angeles to Genaro Estrada, Secretary of Foreign Relations, March 8, 1928, in AGN-IPS, Vol. 232, Expediente 48.

70. Harry Walsh, US Consul in Nuevo Laredo, to John W. Dye, US Consul in Ciudad Juárez, August 26, 1926, in NACP, Foreign Service RG 84, Consular Correspondence from Ciudad Juárez, Subject Group 800.

71. List of banned publications, November 1, 1935, in GU-Americas, Box 19, Folder 18.

72. There are few if any published studies about Mexican citizens being blacklisted from returning to Mexico. American citizens living in Mexico helped to create blacklists of German sympathizers in Mexico during World War I, according to Yolanda de la Parra, "La Primera Guerra Mundial y la prensa mexicana," in *Estudios de Historia Moderna y Contemporánea de México*, ed. Álvaro Matute (Mexico: Universidad Nacional Autónoma de México, Instituto de Investigaciones Históricas), Vol. 10 (1986), 155–76.

73. Blacklists were created during the delahuertista rebellion and again between 1926 and 1930. See AGN-IPS, Vol. 206, Expediente 09; and AGN-IPS, Vol. 207, Expedientes 2-4.

74. Report from Agent 47 to the head of the Departamento Confidencial, February 12, 1927, in AGN-IPS, Vol. 54, Expediente 10.

75. The list of clerical names can be found in AGN-IPS, Vol. 33, Expediente 21, and Vol. 208, Expediente 17.

76. Telegram from Gonzalo Vázquez, senior officer in the Departamento de Gobernación, to the Servicio de Migración, August 20, 1926, in AGN-IPS, Vol. 2053-A, Expediente 4.

77. Memorandum from the head of the Departamento Confidencial to the head of the Servicio de Migración, December 11, 1928, in AGN-IPS, Vol. 295, Expediente 28.

78. The archives of the Confidential Department contain a full box of blacklists filed between October 1928 and December 1928. See AGN-IPS, Vol. 295, Expedientes 11 and 20.

79. E. Portes Gil, Secretaría de Gobernación, to the head of the Departamento Confidencial, February 20, 1930, in AGN-IPS, Vol. 295, Expediente 42.

80. Confidential Agent in Ciudad Reynosa, Tamaulipas, to the Secretaría de Gobernación, November 28, 1928, in AGN-IPS, Vol. 295, Expediente 33.

81. Santiago A. Martínez, Migration Delegate in Nogales, to the Mexican Consulate in Tucson, August 13, 1926, in SRE, LE 710, Doc. 537.

82. List of the members of the Club Latino de Tucson, n.d. [prob. September 1926], in SRE, LE 710, Doc. 483.

83. See blacklists in AGN-IPS, Vol. 236, Expedientes 1–4.

CHAPTER 5

1. See Robert Quirk, *The Mexican Revolution and the Catholic Church, 1910–1929* (Bloomington, IN: Indiana University Press, 1973), 215–47.

2. Portes Gil's statement also clarified the interpretation of some of the anticlerical laws, particularly those concerning the registration of priests, religious education, and the right to petition the government. "Declaraciones públicas del Presidente Provisional Emilio Portes Gil y de Mons. Ruiz y Flores, 21 de junio 1929, published in *El Universal*, 22 de junio de 1929, reproduced in Olimón Nolasco, *Diplomacia insolita*, 111–12.

3. Statement of Archbishop Ruiz y Florez, June 21, 1929, reproduced in Manuel Olimón Nolasco, *Diplomacia insólita: el conflicto religioso en México y las negociaciones cupulares (1926–1929)* (Mexico City: Instituto Mexicano de Doctrina Social Cristiana, 2006), 113.

4. David Bailey, *¡Viva Cristo Rey! The Cristero Rebellion and the Church-State Conflict in Mexico* (Austin, TX: University of Texas Press, 1974), 285.

5. Rodolfo Acuña, *Corridors of Migration: The Odyssey of Mexican Laborers, 1600–1933* (Tucson, AZ: University of Arizona Press, 2007), 188.

6. "El Regreso de los Prelados que se hallan en S. Antonio," *La Opinion*, June 28, 1929, clipping in UNAM-Traslosheros, Caja 105, Expediente 743, Foja 8285.

7. Olimon Nolasco, *Diplomacia insólita*, 88; J. Antonio Lopez Ortega, *Las naciones extranjeras y la persecucion religiosa* (Mexico City: Edición privada, 1944), 361.

8. Miguel Venegas to Juan Venegas, July 17, 1929, translated by María Teresa Venegas in *Letters Home: Mexican Exile Correspondence from Los Angeles, 1927–1932* (self-published, 2012), 64.

9. See Mary Kay Vaughan, *Cultural Politics in Revolution: Teachers, Peasants, and Schools in Mexico, 1930–1940* (Tucson, AZ: University of Arizona Press, 1997).

10. The historiography of the second Cristero War is far more limited than that of the 1926–29 period. A brief review of this literature can be found in Enrique Guerra Manzo, "El fuego sagrado. La segunda cristiada y el caso de Michoacán (1931–1938)," *Historia Mexicana* Vol. 55, No. 2 (2005), 513–75. Ben Fallaw contributes an excellent study of two regional outbreaks of *La Segunda* in Guerrero and Guanajuato in *Religion and State Formation in Postrevolutionary Mexico* (Durham, NC: Duke University Press, 2013), Chapters 4 and 5.

11. Stephen Andes, *The Vatican and Catholic Activism in Mexico and Chile: The Politics of Transnational Catholicism, 1920–1940* (Oxford: Oxford University Press, 2014), 147.

12. For more on Manríquez y Zárate's life and long exile in the United States, see Julia G. Young, "Un obispo cristero en Estados Unidos: el exilio de José de Jesús Manríquez y Zárate, 1927–1932," in *Los guachos y los mochos: once ensayos cristeros*, ed. Julia Preciado Zamora and Servando Ortoll (Morelia, Mexico: Jitanjáfora Press, 2009), 61–80; Pbro. Lauro Lopez Beltran, *Manríquez y Zárate, Primer Obispo de Huejutla, Sublimador de Juan Diego, heroic defensor de la Fe: Obra conmemorativa del Quinto Centenario del Natalicio de Juan Diego: 1474–1974* (Mexico City: Editorial Tradición, 1974); Andrés Galván Amador, "Llegada del Obispo," in *El Tordo: Memorias y Anécdotas de un Huasteco* (Tampico, Mexico: Servicios Gráficos, 2006), 21–32; Ben Fallaw describes how the bishop, while in exile in the United States, remained deeply involved in the affairs of his diocese, communicating regularly with family members and priests who had remained in the area. Fallaw, "The Devil Is Now Loose in Huejutla: The Bishop, the SEP, and the Emancipation of the Indian in Hidalgo," in *Religion and State Formation in Revolutionary Mexico*, 63–100.

13. Cónsul Liekens in El Paso, Texas, to the Consulate of New York, October 5, 1927, SRE, LE 822, Legajo 6, Document 38.

14. *¡Viva Cristo Rey! Mensaje al Mundo Civilizado por el obispo de Huejutla*, San Antonio, Texas, July 12, 1927, in SRE, LE 852, Legajo 4, Document 213.

15. "Monseñor Zárate relata sus penalidades," *La Prensa*, April 26, 1927, clipping in AGN, IPS, Vol. 225, Expediente 15, Document 110.

16. *¡Viva Cristo Rey! Mensaje al Mundo Civilizado por el obispo de Huejutla*, San Antonio, Texas, July 12, 1927, in SRE, LE 852, Legajo 4, Document 213.

17. LNDLR Memorandum, July 23, 1927, in CARSO, Fondo CLXXXVI, Carpeta. 5, Legajo 380–466, Documento 404.

18. Department of Justice Agent John K. Wren to the Department of State, October 14, 1927, in NACP, State RG 59, Decimal File 812.00/28898.

19. "Mas de Diez Mil Mexicanos Formaron en el Gran Desfile: Monseñor Manríque y Zárate pronunció el sermón final," *El Diario de El Paso*, June 14, 1928, clipping in UNAM-Traslosheros, Caja 100, Expediente 724, Foja 6897.

20. Manríquez y Zárate to Miguel Palomar y Vizcarra, November 3, 1928, in INAH-MPV.

21. For a series of insightful essays on Mexican revolutionary nationalism, see Mary Kay Vaughan and Stephen E. Lewis, *The Eagle and the Virgin: Nation and Cultural Revolution in Mexico, 1920–1940* (Durham, NC: Duke University Press, 2006).

22. Manríquez y Zárate to Miguel Palomar y Vizcarra, November 3, 1928, in INAH-MPV. For a brief discussion on religious nationalism as it relates to emigration, see Peter van der Veer, *Religious Nationalism: Hindus and Muslims in India* (Berkeley, CA: University of California Press, 1994), 108. Douglass Sullivan-González presents a fascinating analysis of the interlinkages between religion and nationalism in Rafael Carrera's Guatemala, describing how religious discourse was deployed in support of a conservative nation-building project. Douglass Sullivan-González, *Piety, Power, and Politics: Religion and Nation Formation in Guatemala, 1821–1871* (Pittsburgh, PA: University of Pittsburgh Press, 1998), 81–119.

23. Carlos Fernández to the National Catholic Welfare Conference, May 7, 1928, in UNAM-LNDLR, Document 4050, Inv. No. 5050; Carlos Fernández to Salvador Chávez Hayhoe, May 7, 1928, in UNAM-LNDLR, Document 4071, Inv. No. 5051; Carlos Fernández and associates to Rev. D. Zaldívar, Chicago, May 11, 1928, in UNAM-LNDLR Document 4089, Inv. No. 5089.

24. Carlos Fernández to Luis Ruiz y Rueda in San Antonio, May 7, 1928, in UNAM-LNDLR, Document 4072, Inv. No. 5052; F. Urdanivia in El Paso to Agustín Sanchez in Chicago, March 14, 1928, in UNAM-LNDLR, Document 3955, Inv. No. 4856; Memorandum concerning the ACJM in the United States, April 18, 1928, UNAM-MPV-LNDLR, Caja 49, Expediente 363, Folio 9574-9577.

25. José de Jesús Manríquez y Zárate in Los Angeles to CF, May 17, 1928, in UNAM-MPV-LNDLR, Caja 49, Expediente 364, Folio 9672.

26. Miguel Palomar y Vizcarra to José de Jesús Manríquez y Zárate, August 22, 1928, in UNAM-MPV-LNDLR, Caja 50, Expediente 368, Folio 10160.

27. Carlos Fernández to Rev. D. Zaldívar, May 11, 1928, in UNAM-LNDLR, Document 4086, Inv. No. 5080.

28. Liga Comite Directivo in Mexico City to Jorge Bernardi in San Francisco, August 18, 1928, in UNAM-LNDLR, Document 4510, Inv. No. 5836.

29. Minutes of the Unión Nacionalista Mexicana in meeting in El Paso, July 23–26, 1928, in UNAM-LNDLR, Documents 4444-4451, Inv. No. 5712-5725.

30. Liga Comite Directivo in Mexico City to Jorge Bernardi in San Francisco, August 18, 1928, in UNAM-LNDLR, Document 4510, Inv. No. 5836.

31. Jorge Ferrer, President of the UNM, to Comite Directivo de la LNDLR, Mexico City, December 18, 1928, in UNAM-LNDLR, Document 5112, Inv. No. 6611.

32. Jorge Ferrer to "Querido amigo," December 25, 1928, in UNAM-LNDLR, Document 5148, Inv. No. 6731.

33. "Memorial de la UNM al Santo Padre," December 18, 1928, in UNAM-MPV-LNDLR, Caja 50, Expediente 372, Folio 10610.

34. "Fue instalada aqui la Unión Nacionalista," *La Opinión*, December 11, 1928, clipping in UNAM-Traslosheros, Caja 103, Expediente 735, Foja 7653.

35. Manríquez y Zárate to Miguel Palomar y Vizcarra, June 25, 1929, in INAH-MPV.

36. Manríquez y Zárate to Miguel Palomar y Vizcarra, June 25, 1929, in INAH-MPV.

37. Manríquez y Zárate to Miguel Palomar y Vizcarra, June 25, 1929, in INAH-MPV.

38. The Depression disproportionately impacted Mexican workers in Los Angeles, who generally held the lowest-paying, least desirable, and least secure jobs. Furthermore, repatriation drives and the voluntary exodus of poverty-stricken emigrants resulted in a loss of about a third of the population: In 1930 there were about 167,000 Mexicans living in Los Angeles County; by 1940, between eighty and a hundred thousand of these had left. Nevertheless, "most of the Mexicans sent back to Mexico eventually returned to Los Angeles." Antonio Rios-Bustamante and Pedro Castillo, *An Illustrated History of Mexicans in Los Angeles, 1781–1985* (Los Angeles: Chicano Studies Research Center, University of California, 1986), 135–54. For more on the repatriation period, see Francisco E. Balderrama and R. Raymond Rodríguez, *Decade of Betrayal: Mexican Repatriation in the 1930s* (Albuquerque, NM: University of New Mexico Press, 2006); Mae M. Ngai, *Impossible Subjects: Illegal Aliens and the Making of Modern America*, 127–66; and Fernando Alanís Enciso, "No cuenten conmigo: La pólitica de repatriación del gobierno mexicano y sus nacionales en Estados Unidos, 1910–1928," *Mexican Studies*/Estudios Mexicanos Vol. 19, No. 2 (Summer 2003), 401–31.

39. Pamphlet and letter sent from Carlos M. Gama in Whittier, California, to Secretarío de Gobernación, November 5, 1930, in AGN, D-Gob., Vol. 126, Expediente 2.340 (73) 37.

40. Albert Camarillo, *Chicanos in a Changing Society: From Mexican Pueblos to American Barrios in Santa Barbara and Southern California, 1848–1930*, (Cambridge: Harvard University Press, 1979), 207.

41. Report from the Mexican consulate in San Francisco to the Consul in Los Ángeles, August 28, 1931, in AGN, POR, Vol. 74, Expediente 24/6253/1931; Unsigned letter to C. Agente del Ministerio Público, Mexico City, n.d. [1931], in

AGN, POR, Vol. 74, Expediente 24/5898/1931. Report from the Mexican consulate in San Bernardino, California, to the Secretarío de Relaciones Exteriores, August 27, 1931, in AGN, POR, Vol. 74, Expediente 24/6409/1931.

42. Report from the Mexican consulate in San Bernardino, California, to the Secretarío de Relaciones Exteriores, August 27, 1931, in AGN, POR, Vol. 74, Expediente 24/6409/1931.

43. Report from the Mexican consulate in San Bernardino, California, to the Secretarío de Relaciones Exteriores, August 27, 1931, in AGN, POR, Vol. 74, Expediente 24/6409/1931.

44. Report from the Mexican consulate in San Bernardino, California, to the Secretarío de Relaciones Exteriores, August 27, 1931, in AGN, POR, Vol. 74, Expediente 24/6409/1931.

45. Report from Agent 1 in Los Angeles to the Jefe del Departamento Confidencial, February 22, 1932, in AGN, IPS, Vol. 226, Expediente 16, Document 60.

46. "Comite General Pro Celebración Bodas de Plata Del Excmo. y Rmo. Sr. Obispo de Huejutla" in Los Angeles to George Cardinal Mundelein in Chicago, September 12, 1932, in Loyola Chicago-CCES, Box 21, Folder 1.

47. "Comite General pro Celebración," in Loyola Chicago-CCES, Box 21, Folder 1.

48. Dennis Nodín Valdés, "Mexican Revolutionary Nationalism and Repatriation during the Great Depression," 1–23, 15.

49. "The Bishop of Huejutla Cited for Trial," article translated to English from the Mexican newspaper *El Nacional*, May 4, 1932, in NACP, MID RG 165, 2657-G-616, Document 68.

50. Cleofas Calleros to José de Jesús Manríquez y Zárate, December 6, 1933, in UTEP-Calleros, MS 173, Box 21.

51. Report from Consul of Calexico to SRE, prob. July 30, 1932 [date unclear], in SRE, LE 863-15.

52. Report from Consul of Calexico to SRE, February 18, 1932, in SRE, LE 863-15.

53. Clipping from *El Ideal Mexicano*, February 14, 1937, in the Chicago Public Library, Chicago Foreign Language Press Survey, Vol. IV, No. 17.

54. "Reflections about the current Situation in Mexico;" DLT, Box 5, Folder 2; José de Jesús Manríquez y Zárate [Exmo. Y Rvmo. Sr. Obispo de Huejutla], *Luchando con la bestia* [self-published, 1938].

55. Beltran, *Manríquez y Zárate, Primer Obispo de Huejutla*, 262.

56. Manríquez y Zárate in *Revista Juan Diego*, Septiembre 1948, 15, cited in Beltran, *Manríquez y Zárate, Primer Obispo de Huejutla*, 258.

57. For more on Mexican religious organizations in Los Angeles, see Samuel Ortegón, "The Religious Status of the Mexican Population of Los Angeles" (MA Thesis, University of Southern California, 1932).

58. Francisco E. Balderrama, *In Defense of La Raza: The Los Angeles Mexican Consulate and the Mexican Community, 1929 to 1936* (Tucson, AZ: University of Arizona Press, 1982), 77.

59. Dolan and Hinojosa, *Mexican Americans and the Catholic Church, 1900–1965*, 185–86.

60. Olimón Nolasco writes that Leopoldo Ruiz y Flores, in exile once again, delivered a long manifesto from San Antonio at the College of the Incarnate Word, which was republished in *La Prensa*. Manuel Olimon Nolasco, *Asalto a las conciencias. Educación, política y opinión pública. 1934–1935* (Mexico City: Instituto Mexicano de Doctrina Social Cristiana, 2008), 120.

61. "Catholics to Parade: Forty Thousand March Today," *Los Angeles Times*, December 9, 1934, 4.

62. "Catholics to Parade," *Los Angeles Times*, December 9, 1934, 4.

63. "Catholics to Parade," *Los Angeles Times*, December 9, 1934, 4.

64. "Yaquis of Mexico Join in Guadalupe Ceremony," *Los Angeles Times*, December 10, 1934, A1.

65. "Yaquis of Mexico Join in Guadalupe Ceremony," *Los Angeles Times*, December 10, 1934, A1; Balderrama, *In Defense of La Raza*, 80.

66. The image of the Virgin of Guadalupe has long been connected to Mexican nationalism; see Eric R. Wolf, "The Virgin of Guadalupe: A Mexican National Symbol," *The Journal of American Folklore*, Vol. 71, No. 279 (January–March, 1958), 34–39; see also David Brading, *Mexican Phoenix: Our Lady of Guadalupe: Image and Tradition Across Five Centuries* (New York: Cambridge University Press, 2003).

67. Douglas Monroy, *Rebirth: Mexican Los Angeles from the Great Migration to the Great Depression*, 52.

68. According to Butler, "pilgrimage was thus part of a wider, if temporary pattern of decentralization by which a persecuted Church leased a significant degree of power to the laity . . . The dangers of laicization became apparent in 1928." Matthew Butler, "Trouble Afoot?," 162–63.

69. Balderrama, *In Defense of La Raza*, 78.

70. Camarillo, *Chicanos in a Changing Society*, 207.

71. Balderrama, *In Defense of La Raza*, 78–87.

72. "Murió un General Cristero," *El Imparcial* de Hermosillo, Sonora, February 28, 1968, in DLT Box 1, Folder 20.

73. "Biographical Note," Online finding aid for the de la Torre Family papers. (Retrieved: http://www.azarchivesonline.org/xtf/view?docId=ead/uoa/UAMS420.xml.)

74. Juan Navarrete to Ignacio de la Torre, July 26, 1920, in DLT, Box 2, Folder 15.

75. Juan Navarrete to Ignacio de la Torre, Sr., December 23, 1930, in DLT, Box 2, Folder 15.

76. Correspondence between Manríquez y Zárate and members of the de la Torre family, in DLT, Box 2, Folder 13; José de Jesús Manríquez y Zárate, "Exposicion y Protesta," May 30, 1934, in San Antonio, in DLT, Box 3, Folder 2; José de Jesús Manríquez y Zárate, "Reflexiones sobre la actual Situación de México," July 16,

1938, DLT, Box 5, Folder 2; José de Jesús Manríquez y Zárate, "Fourth Message to the Civilized World," 1935, in DLT, Box 5, Folder 1.

77. This refers to the monument of Christ the King at Cubilete, Guanajuato, which was destroyed by federal troops during the Cristero War (it was later rebuilt, and still stands today).

78. "Intimate Proclamation to Christ the King," October 12, 1932, in DLT, Box 3, Folder 2.

79. Newsletter of the *Comité Popular de la Defensa Mexicana*, April 1935, in DLT, Box 4, Folder 26. The same issue announced that a subcommittee of the Popular Committee for Mexican Defense had been founded in Seguin, Texas.

80. Newsletters of the *Comité Popular de la Defensa Mexicana*, Issues No. 3 (February 15, 1935) to No. 9 (March 29, 1935), in DLT, Box 4, Folder 2.

81. March 1935 newsletter of the *Comité Popular de la Defensa Mexicana*, in DLT, Box 4, Folder 2.

82. "*Organo Oficial del Comité Popular de la Defensa Mexicana*," in DLT, Box 4, Folder 26.

83. "Pamphlets, 1935," in DLT, Box 5, Folder 1.

84. "*Desde México*" (1934–1937), in DLT, Box 4, Folder 8.

85. "Pamphlets, 1936–1939," in DLT, Box 5, Folder 2.

86. "Once Pláticas acerca del origen y desarrollo de la devoción a Nuestra Senora de Guadalupe en la Arquidiócesis de Los Angeles, desde el año de 1923," July 19, 1939, in DLT, Box 5, Folder 22.

87. See Yves Solis, "Asociación espiritual o masonería católica: la U," 121–37.

88. Interview by James W. Wilkie with Salvador Abascal, August 17, 1964, from "Oral history interviews with Mexican political leaders and other personalities: Mexico, 1964–1965," University of California, Bancroft Library, 59–61. According to scholars, the UNS also arose from an organization called La Base, founded in 1934, whose objective was to "install the Christian social order in Mexico, fight against Communism, Masonry and against the application of the anticlerical laws." For more on Sinarquismo and the UNS, see Tania Hernández Vicenio, "El Partido Acción Nacional en la Oposición, 1939–1999," in *Los Matices de la Rebeldía: Las oposiciones Políticas y sociales*, ed. Alicia Olivera Sedano (Mexico City: Instituto Nacional de Antropología e historia, 2010), 85; see also Jean Meyer, *El sinarquismo. Un fascismo mexicano? 1937–1947* (Mexico City: Editorial Joaquin Mortiz, 1975); V. Rubén Aguilar and P. Guillermo Zermeño, *Religión, Política y Sociedad: El Sinarquismo y la iglesia en México (Nueve Ensayos)* (Mexico City: Universidad Iberoamericana, Departamento de Historia, 1992); and Jason Dormady, *Primitive Revolution: Restorationist Religion and the Idea of the Mexican Revolution, 1940–1968* (Albuquerque, NM: University of New Mexico Press, 2011).

89. Dormady, *Primitive Revolution*, 135.

90. Dormady, *Primitive Revolution*, 107, 126.

91. Dormady, *Primitive Revolution*, 116.

92. Gustavo Arizmendi, secretary of Colonization of the María Auxiliadora Colony to R. B. Alvarez, November 30, 1944, in DLT, Box 2, Folder 17.

93. Booklet entitled "Comité Organizador Regional de California, Unión Nacional Sinarquista," 1937, in DLT, Box 2, Folder 17.

94. There is evidence that other Mexican Catholic organizations were recruiting and working within the United States during the 1930s as well. According to Father Miguel Darío Miranda, head of the Mexican Social Secretariat, a Spanish priest named Manuel Mendez planned to return to Los Angeles, where he had been in exile previously, in order to try to organize Catholic Action groups in Mexican parishes. Memorandum, April 4, 1933, in ACUA, NCWC Box 148, Folder 11.

95. "History," published on the home page of Mount Cristo Rey Restoration Committee. (Retrieved: http://mtcristorey.com.) See also "Correspondence related to Mt. Cristo Rey," in UTEP-Calleros, Box 20, Folder 12.

96. Monica Perales, *Smeltertown*, 89.

97. "History," home page of Mount Cristo Rey. (Retrieved: http://mtcristorey. com.)

98. Report from IPS Agent 6 in Chihuahua City, Chihuahua, to Jefe del Departamento Confidencial, November 25, 1927, in AGN, IPS, Vol. 231, Expediente 24; Report from Agent No. 21 to Jefe del Departamento Confidencial, Ciudad Juárez, February 16, 1927, in AGN, IPS, Vol. 2053-A, Expediente 5.

99. S. L. Sister Lilliana Owens, *Most Reverend Anthony J. Schuler*, 190.

100. Monseñor Lourdes F. Costa, from his unpublished book "El Rosario del Poeta" o "Poemas de la Sierra de Cristo Rey," Misterios Gloriosos. UTEP-Calleros, Document 5.5.

101. "Mount Cristo Rey," in UTEP-Calleros, Box 20, Folder 12, Document 5.5.

102. "Mount Cristo Rey," in UTEP-Calleros, Box 20, Folder 12, Document 5.5.

103. "Upcoming events," home page of Mount Cristo Rey (Retrieved: http:// mtcristorey.com.); Rudy Gutierrez, "Thousands Attend 74th Annual Mt. Cristo Rey Pilgrimage," *El Paso Times*, October 28, 2013. (Retrieved: http:// www.elpasotimes.com/ci_24398758/thousands-attend-74th-annual-mt-cristo-rey-pilgrimage.)

104. See David Montejano, *Anglos and Mexicans in the Making of Texas*, 298–99. See also José E. Limón, "Transnational Triangulation: Mexico, the United States, and the Emergence of a Mexican American Middle Class," in John Tutino, *Mexico and Mexicans in the Making of the United States* (Austin, TX: University of Texas Press, 2012), 236–56, 239.

105. There is evidence, however, that the Cristero War continued to impact public religious devotion during the 1950s: Roberto R. Treviño describes how, at one of the popular annual Christ the King celebrations in Houston, three elderly

survivors of the Cristero War "held up a small tattered banner on which was a picture of Christ the King" and then "in unison exclaimed, 'Viva Cristo rey!'" These celebrations, says Treviño, demonstrated how "in Houston's barrios people held fast to the memory of religious and historical events that entwined to define their Mexicanness." Treviño, *The Church in the Barrio*, 67.

CHAPTER 6

1. Marco A. García Gutiérrez, "Toribio Romo González, Protector de los mojados: Es un espejismo del desierto que hace milagros de carne y hueso," *Contenido*, June 1, 2002. (Retrieved: http://www.zermeno.com/Toribio_Romo.html.)

2. There are numerous accounts of the apparitions of Toribio Romo in the contemporary news media, many of which appear online. See Alfredo Corchado, "The Migrant's Saint: Toribio Romo Is a Favorite of Mexicans Crossing the Border," *The Dallas Morning News*, July 22, 2006 (Retrieved: http://www. banderasnews.com/0607/nr-migrantssaint.htm.); Mario Muñoz, "*Santo que no es conocido, no es venerado*," *El Informador*, July 15, 2012 (Retrieved: http://www.informador.com.mx/suplementos/2012/389975/6/santo-que-no-es-conocido-no-es-venerado.htm.); Laura Sánchez, "*Santo Toribio: pollero divino*," *El Universal*, October 6, 2013. (Retrieved: http://www.eluniversal. com.mx/estados/2013/santo-toribio-pollero-divino-956206.html.) The scholarly literature on Toribio Romo is also growing. See Alfredo Mirandé, *Jalos, USA*; Alfredo Mirandé, "Toribio Romo, el Padre Pollero," *Aztlán: A Journal of Chicano Studies* Vol. 38, No. 2 (Fall 2013), 95–122; Fernando Guzmán Mundo, "*Santo Toribio. De mártir de los altos a santo de los emigrantes*," *Revista estudios del hombre* Vol. 25 (2012), 107–27.

3. David Agren, "Cristero Martyr Now Popular Patron of Migrants Heads to U.S.," *Catholic News Service*, May 31, 2012 (Retrieved: http://www.catholic-news.com/data/stories/cns/1202255.htm.); Ginger Thompson, "Santa Ana de Guadalupe Journal: A Saint Who Guides Migrants to a Promised Land," *The New York Times*, August 14, 2002, A4.

4. A *coyote* is a smuggler who assists Mexican emigrants in crossing the border. This is particularly interesting, since Toribio Romo was actually opposed to migration: according to his nephew, he wrote a play entitled "Let's Go North!" that lampooned returned emigrants and discouraged Mexicans from leaving home. David Romo, "My *Tío*, the Saint," *Texas Monthly*, November 2010. See also Cathy Sze, "A Q&A With David Dorado Romo," *Texas Monthly*, November 2010. (Retrieved: http://www.texasmonthly.com/story/qa-david-dorado-romo ?fullpage=1.)

5. Laura Sánchez and Daniel Aguilar, "Immigrants in Tijuana Have a New Saint: 'Toribio,'" *SanDiegoRed.com*, n.d. (Retrieved: http://www.sandiegored. com/noticias/41649/Immigrants-in-Tijuana-have-a-new-Saint-Toribio/.)

6. Such places include the mission church to Saint Toribio Romo in Chatsworth, Georgia; the Botánica Santo Toribio Romo in Los Angeles; the Saint Toribio Romo Society in Chicago, Illinois; the Centro De Capacitación Toribio Romo in San Diego, California; the Shrine to Saint Toribio Romo in Holy Redeemer Catholic Church, Detroit, Michigan; and others.

7. Grace Rubenstein, "Tour Draws Immigrants to Honor Their Saint," *The New York Times*, July 1, 2011. (Retrieved: http://www.nytimes.com/2011/07/01/us/01bctoribio.html?_r=0.) Esmerelda Bermudez, "Faithful Flock to See Statue of Santo Toribio, the Immigrants' Saint," *The Los Angeles Times*, July 12, 2014. (Retrieved: http://www.latimes.com/local/la-me-immigrants-saint-20140713-story.html.)

8. Throughout Jalisco, for example, the Cristero War and its dead are commemorated with statues in public spaces, museum displays, parish churches, chapels, and shrines. The blog *"Santos, Martires y Cristeros"* (Accessible: http://rutacristerajalisco.blogspot.com) documents many such places.

9. See "Regional and State Origins of Mexicans Who Registered in Mexico's Matrícula Consular Program, 2006," in Douglas Massey, Jacob S. Rugh, and Karen A. Pren, "The Geography of Undocumented Mexican Migration," *Mexican Studies*/Estudios Mexicanos Vol. 26, No. 1 (Winter 2010), 129–52.

10. Families have always transferred knowledge, practices, and ideologies from one generation to the next, and Mexican emigrants, refugees, and exiles of the Cristero War were no exception. For a more detailed discussion on family, society, and memory, see Alisse Waterston and Barbara Rylko-Bauer, "Out of the Shadows of History and Memory: Personal Family Narratives in Ethnographies of Rediscovery," *American Ethnologist* Vol. 33, No. 3 (2006), 397–412; Paul Connerton, *How Societies Remember* (Cambridge: Cambridge University Press, 1989); "Introduction," in Jacob J. Climo and Maria G. Catell, eds., *Social Memory and History: Anthropological Perspectives* (Lanham, MD: AltaMira Press, 2002), 1–39; Daniel M. Wegner, "Transactive Memory: A Contemporary Analysis of the Group Mind," in *Theories of Group Behavior*, ed. B. Mullen and G. R. Goethals (New York: Springer-Verlag, 1989), 185–208. For perspectives on transnational family narratives, see Mary Chamberlain and Selma Leydesdorff, "Transnational Families: Memories and Narratives," *Global Networks* Vol. 4, No. 3 (2004), 227–41.

11. I am very grateful both to the people whom I interviewed, and to the archivists who helped connect me to them. Malachy McCarthy, Archivist for the Claretian Missionaries, introduced me to Severino López and Adelina Huerta; Clay Stalls, Manuscripts Coordinator at the William H. Hannon Library at Loyola Marymount University, California, introduced me to María Teresa Venegas; and Verónica Reyes-Escudero, Borderlands Curator and Associate Librarian of the University of Arizona Libraries Special Collections, introduced me to José Luis de la Torre. I contacted Margarita Gándara after reading

an article about her life (Ramón Rentería, "From 'Art Queen' to Exile: Juárez Muralist Mago Gándara Seeks Her 'Revenge' in New Show," *El Paso Times*, August 21, 2011. (Retrieved: http://www.elpasotimes.com/ci_18724347.) Isabel Garza, the daughter of María Teresa Amador Díaz, contacted me by e-mail in 2012 and subsequently facilitated my interview with her mother.

12. Mary Chamberlain, "Family Narratives and Migration Dynamics: Barbadians to Britain," *New West Indian Guide/Nieuwe West-Indische Gids* Vol. 69, No. 3/4 (1995), 253–75.

13. Father Severino López, C.M.F., *El Poche: Memoirs of a Mexican American Padre* (Chicago: Claretian Publications, 2004).

14. Author interview with Severino López, October 18, 2006.

15. Author interview with Adelina Huerta, August 1, 2006.

16. Author interview with María Teresa Venegas, August 27, 2013.

17. Author interview with María Teresa Amador Díaz, July 17, 2012.

18. Author interview with Margarita Gándara, June 25, 2013.

19. Author interview with José Luis de la Torre, November 9, 2013.

20. Davis, *City of Quartz*, 330–31; Rosales, "Mexican Immigration to the Urban Midwest," 165; Malachy McCarthy, "Which Christ Came to Chicago," 212.

21. "Early History of the San Francisco Monastery," excerpted from the *Crónica del Monasterio de San Francisco, CA 1928–1938* by Sister María del Cristo Rey; translated and edited by Bali K. Nelson, 2010. (Retrieved: http://adorejesus. org/About_Early_History_San_Francisco_Community.aspx.)

22. Ann Lozano, "Seminary of St. Philip for Mexican Students," *Handbook of Texas Online*, Published by the Texas State Historical Association. (Retrieved: http:// www.tshaonline.org/handbook/online/articles/iwso1.)

23. "Our Beginnings," Carmelite Sisters of the Most Sacred Heart of Los Angeles. (Retrieved: http://www.carmelitesistersocd.com/timeline/.)

24. Darryl V. Caterine, *Conservative Catholicism and the Carmelites: Identity, Ethnicity, and Tradition in the Modern Church* (Bloomington and Indianapolis, IN: Indiana University Press, 2001), 18, 38.

25. Anne Martínez, *Catholic Borderlands*, 215–22. For more on the Montezuma Seminary, see L. Medina, *Historia del Seminario de Montezuma. Sus precedentes, fundación y consolidación, 1910–1953* (Mexico City: Editorial Jus, 1962). Among the Seminary's graduates is Mexican historian Manuel Olimón Nolasco.

26. María Teresa Venegas's relationship to the Church was not without problems, however. "I had a struggle with authority in terms of women in the Catholic Church," she recalled. During the 1960s, her religious community had a confrontation with James Cardinal McIntyre and the Sisters gave up on their vows and became a lay community. For more on this community, see Richard Lee Colvin, "Idealistic Lay Group Is Legacy of Nuns' Split with Church in 1970," *Los Angeles Times*, April 3, 1993. (Retrieved: http://articles.latimes. com/1993-04-03/local/me-18589_1_immaculate-heart-community.)

27. Interestingly, the nephew of Saint Toribio Romo falls into this camp: he writes that his father, an emigrant from Mexico, was not interested in the family saint. "An avid Dallas Cowboys fan, he'd rather be related to Tony Romo … Santo Toribio was never a subject of conversation in our immediate family. He was almost a taboo, a vestige of the past we had collectively left behind." David Romo, "My *Tío*, the Saint," *Texas Monthly*, November 2010. (Retrieved: http://www.texasmonthly.com/story/qa-david-dorado-romo?fullpage=1.)

28. *Catechism of the Catholic Church*, 2473–74. (Retrieved: http://www.vatican.va/archive/ENG0015/_INDEX.HTM.) For a deeper history of martyrdom, see Elizabeth Castelli, *Martyrdom and Memory: Early Christian Culture Making*, and Joseph M. Bryant, "The Sect-Church Dynamic and Christian Expansion in the Roman Empire: Persecution, Penitential Discipline, and Schism in Sociological Perspective," *The British Journal of Sociology* Vol. 44, No. 2 (June 1993), 303–39. For a compelling study of the increasing importance of Mexican martyrdom and transnational Catholicism, see Marisol López-Menendez, "The Holy Jester: Martyrdom, Social Cohesion and Meaning in Mexico: The Story of Miguel Agustin Pro SJ, 1927–1988" (PhD diss., New School University, 2012).

29. Importantly for the history of the Cristero conflict, people who took up arms in defense of their faith could not be declared martyrs, as martyrs cannot have participated in violent acts.

30. "Mexico News Item," translated clipping from *La Voz de la Patria*, December 16, 1928, NCWC. Mexican Files, Box 146, Folder 20.

31. María Guadalupe Alatorre Huerta, *Salvador Huerta Gutiérrez: Family Memories*, trans. Adelina Huerta González (Tlaquepaque, Jalisco: Ediciones Católicas de Guadalajara, n.d.), 83.

32. Severino López, *El Poche: Memoirs of a Mexican American Padre*, 25.

33. Technically, people who suffer but do not die for their faith are termed "confessors."

34. For more on the ways that Mexican Americans have received artistic interpretations of the Revolution, see the essays in Jaime Marroquín Arredondo, Adela Piñeda Franco, and Magdalena Mieri, eds., *Open Borders to a Revolution: Culture, Politics, and Migration* (Washington, DC: Smithsonian Institution Scholarly Press, 2013).

35. Doris Benavides, "Cristero War Took Her Father But Strengthened Her Faith, Says Woman," *Catholic News Service*, May 22, 2012. (Retrieved: http://www.catholicsun.org/2012/05/22/cristero-war-took-her-father-but-strengthened-her-faith-says-woman/.)

36. Robert Delaney, "Cristero War Still Echoes in Local Man's Memories," *The Michigan Catholic: A Publication of the Archdiocese of Detroit*, May 17, 2012. (Retrieved: http://themichigancatholic.com/2012/05/cristero-war-still-echoes-in-local-mans-memories/.)

37. See J. D. Long-García, "¡Viva Cristo Rey!: Mexican Religious Liberty War Inspires Catholics Today," *The Catholic Sun*, June 21, 2012. (Retrieved: http://www.catholicsun.org/2012/06/21/viva-cristo-rey-mexican-religious-liberty-war-inspires-catholics-today/.); Julio Morales, "Vista Latina: Cristero War Film 'For Greater Glory' Touches Local Family," *Imperial Valley Press*, June 4, 2012. (Retrieved: http://articles.ivpressonline.com/2012-06-04/mexican-history_32037695.); Kathryn Jean Lopez, "Son of *Cristero* Talks *For Greater Glory*, Religious Freedom," www.patheos.com, September 11, 2012. (Retrieved: http://www.patheos.com/blogs/kathrynLópez/2012/09/son-of-cristero-talks-for-greater-glory-religious-freedom/.)

38. Richard Blaine McCornack, "Attitudes toward Religious Matters in Mexican School History Textbooks," *The Americas* Vol. 15, No. 3 (January 1959), 235–47; Dennis Gilbert, "Rewriting History: Salinas, Zedillo, and the 1992 Textbook Controversy," *Mexican Studies/Estudios Mexicanos* Vol. 13, No. 2 (Summer 1997), 271–97, 282–83.

39. Severino López, *El Poche*, 17–18.

40. See Gabriela Arredondo, *Mexican Chicago: Race, Identity, and Nation, 1916–39* (Chicago: University of Illinois Press, 2008), 163.

41. "Simón Tenorio et al.," report by Agent J. J. Lawrence, August 18, 1927, NACP, State RG 59, Decimal File 812.00/28745.

42. Ramon Rentería, "From 'Art Queen' to Exile: Juárez Muralist Mago Gándara Seeks Her 'Revenge' in New Show," *El Paso Times*, August 21, 2011. (Retrieved: http://www.elpasotimes.com/ci_18724347.)

43. According to Tania Hernández Vicenio, many PAN members had previously participated in Acción Católica, la Unión Nacional de Estudiantes Católicos, el Movimiento Familiar Cristiano, los Cursillos de Cristiandad, and the Unión Nacional de Padres de Familia. "El Partido Acción Nacional en la Oposición, 1939–1999," in *Los Matices de la Rebeldía: Las oposiciones Políticas y sociales* (Mexico City: Instituto Nacional de Antropología e Historia, 2010), 90. For deeper investigations of the PAN and its historical connections to earlier Catholic groups such as the ACJM, see Yemile Mizrahi, *From Martyrdom to Power: The Partido Acción Nacional in Mexico* (South Bend, IN: Notre Dame University Press, 2003); Donald J. Mabry, *Mexico's Acción Nacional: A Catholic Alternative to the Revolution* (Syracuse, NY: Syracuse University Press, 1973).

44. In the United States as well, the history of the Cristero War receded from public awareness until very recently. Despite the fact that, during the 1920s, millions of American Catholics had mobilized in vocal support of Mexico's Cristeros, by the 1940s the violence was largely over, and US Catholics had moved on to other pressing issues, such as the Church's response to the Second World War and the intensifying tensions between Catholics and Protestants. See

Patrick W. Carey, "American Catholic Ecumenism on the Eve of Vatican II, 1940–1962," *U.S. Catholic Historian* Vol. 28, No. 2 (Spring 2010), 1–17.

EPILOGUE

1. Manuel Olimón Nolasco, "Prólogo," in Enrique Bautista González, *La Guerra Olvidada: La cristera en Nayarit: 1.926–1.929* (Guadalajara: Taller editorial La Casa del Mago, Guadalajara, 2008), 13.

2. "Nuevo Catholics: Home on the Altar," *The New York Times Magazine*, December 24, 2006, E40.

3. Lourdes Medrano, "Six Mexican Saints' Relics to Visit City on U.S. Tour," *Arizona Daily Star*, July 17, 2006. (Retrieved: http://tucson.com/ lifestyles/faith-and-values/six-mexican-saints-relics-to-visit-city-on-u-s/ article_bd9ca6b0-4d9d-5282-a3e0-7955e5a51ef7.html.)

4. "Relics of 6 Martyred Priests Tour U.S.," www.zenit.org, May 3, 2012. (Retrieved: http://www.zenit.org/en/articles/relics-of-6-martyred-priests-tour-us.)

5. Hillary Senour, "HHS Mandate 'Ominous' Threat to Religious Liberty, Priest Says," *Catholic News Agency*, June 2, 21012. (Retrieved: http:// www.catholicnewsagency.com/news/hhs-mandate-ominous-threat-to-religious-liberty-priest-says/.)

6. J. D. Long-Garcia, "¡Viva Cristo Rey!: Mexican Religious Liberty War Inspires Catholics Today," *The Catholic Sun*, June 21, 2012. (Retrieved: http://www.catholicsun.org/2012/06/21/viva-cristo-rey-mexican-religious-liberty-war-inspires-catholics-today/.)

7. For a discussion of the recent resurgence of the Cristero War as a topic of discussion and debate in Mexico's visual culture, see Daniel Chávez, "From *Miss Cristera to The Desert Within*: Towards a Contemporary War of Images in Mexico," *Studies in Hispanic Cinemas* Vol. 9, No. 1 (2012): 63–79.

Bibliography

ARCHIVAL SOURCES

ACUA-NCWC: The American Catholic History Research Center at the Catholic University of America, National Catholic Welfare Conference Collection

AGN: Archivo General de la Nacion, Mexico City

    D-Gob.: Fondo Dirección General de Gobierno

    EPG: Fondo Emilio Portes Gil

    IPS: Dirección General de Investigaciones Políticas y Sociales

    O-C: Fondo Obregón-Calles

    POR: Fondo Pascual Ortíz Rubio

CARSO: CARSO Centro de Estudios de Historia de Mexico, Mexico City, Archivo Cristero

DLT: De la Torre Family Papers, University of Arizona Library Special Collections, Tucson, Arizona

GU-America: Booth Family Center for Special Collections, Georgetown University Library, *America* magazine archives

INAH-MPV: Instituto Nacional de Antropología e Historia, Archivo Miguel Palomar y Vizcarra, Serie Conflicto Religioso, rollo de microfilm sin numero

KOC: Knights of Columbus Supreme Council Archives, New Haven, Connecticut

Loyola Chicago-CCES: Loyola University Chicago Archives, Catholic Church Extension Society Records, Diocesan Correspondence

NA: National Archives Building, Washington, DC

    INS RG 85: Records of the Immigration and Naturalization Service

NACP National Archives at College Park

    Foreign Service RG 84: State Department Foreign Service Post Files

    Justice RG 60: General Records of the Department of Justice

    MID RG 165: Military Intelligence Division

    State RG 59: State Department Central File, Record Group 59

OLG Parish: Records of the parish of Our Lady of Guadalupe, Claretian Missionary Archives, Chicago

SRE, LE: Secretaría de Relaciones Exteriores, Archivo Histórico Genaro Estrada, Legajos Encuadernados

UNAM: Archivo Histórico de la Universidad Nacional Autónoma de México

  LNDLR: Fondo Liga Nacional Defensora de la Libertad Religiosa

  MPV-LNDLR: Fondo Manuel Palomar y Vizcarra, Serie Liga Nacional Defensora de la Libertad Religiosa

  Traslosheros: Fondo Manuel Palomar y Vizcarra, Serie Colección Traslosheros

UTEP-Calleros: C. L. Sonnichsen Special Collections Department of the University of Texas at El Paso Library, Cleofas Calleros Papers

PERIODICALS

El Amigo del Hogar
Catholic News Agency
Catholic News Service
The Catholic Sun
The Chicago Tribune
The Dallas Morning News
The El Paso Times
El Informador
The Los Angeles Times
México
New York Herald Tribune
The New York Times
La Prensa
Texas Monthly
Tucson Citizen
El Universal
Washington Post

BOOKS, ARTICLES, AND ONLINE SOURCES

Acuña, Rodolfo F. *Corridors of Migration: The Odyssey of Mexican Laborers, 1600–1933*. Tucson, AZ: University of Arizona Press, 2007.

Aguirre, Nancy. "Porfirismo during the Mexican Revolution: Exile and the Politics of Representation, 1910–1920." PhD diss., University of Texas, El Paso, 2012.

Albro, Ward. *Always a Rebel: Ricardo Flores Magon and the Mexican Revolution*. Fort Worth, TX: Texas Christian University Press, 1992.

Amador, Andrés Galván. "Llegada del Obispo." In *El Tordo: Memorias y Anécdotas de un Huasteco*, 21–32. Tampico: Servicios Gráficos, 2006.

Andes, Stephen. *The Vatican and Catholic Activism in Mexico and Chile: The Politics of Transnational Catholicism, 1920–1940*. Oxford: Oxford University Press, 2014.

Arredondo, Gabriela. *Mexican Chicago: Race, Identity, and Nation, 1916–39*. Chicago: University of Illinois Press, 2008.

Arredondo, Jaime Marroquín, Adela Piñeda Franco, and Magdalena Mieri, eds. *Open Borders to a Revolution: Culture, Politics, and Migration*. Washington, DC: Smithsonian Institution Scholarly Press, 2013.

Azuma, Eiichiro. *Between Two Empires: Race, History, and Transnationalism in Japanese America*. New York: Oxford University Press, 2005.

Badillo, David. *Latinos and the New Immigrant Church*. Baltimore, MD: Johns Hopkins University Press, 2006.

Bailey, David. *¡Viva Cristo Rey! The Cristero Rebellion and the Church-State Conflict in Mexico*. Austin, TX: University of Texas Press, 1974.

Balderrama, Francisco. *In Defense of La Raza: The Los Angeles Mexican Consulate and the Mexican Community, 1929 to 1936*. Tucson, AZ: University of Arizona Press, 1982.

Balderrama, Francisco. "Revolutionary Mexican Nationalism and the Mexican Immigrant Community in Los Angeles during the Great Depression: Memory, Identity, and Survival." In *The Mexican Revolution: Conflict and Consolidation, 1910–1940*, edited by Douglas W. Richmond and Sam W. Haynes, 117–34. College Station, TX: Texas A&M University Press, 2013.

Balderrama, Francisco E., and Raymond R. Rodríguez. *Decade of Betrayal: Mexican Repatriation in the 1930s*. Albuquerque, NM: University of New Mexico Press, 2006.

Baldwin, Deborah. *Protestants and the Mexican Revolution: Missionaries, Ministers, and Social Change*. Chicago: University of Illinois Press, 1990.

Bantjes, Adrian. *As If Jesus Walked on Earth: Cardeniso, Sonora, and the Mexican Revolution*. Oxford: Scholarly Resources Books, 1998.

Bantjes, Adrian. "The Regional Dynamics of Anticlericalism and Defanaticization in Revolutionary Mexico." In *Faith and Impiety in Revolutionary Mexico*, edited by Matthew Butler, 111–30. New York: Palgrave Macmillan, 2007.

Bantjes, Adrian. "Religion and the Mexican Revolution: Toward a New Historiography." In *Religious Culture in Modern Mexico*, edited by Martin Austin Nesvig, 223–54. Lanham, MD: Rowman and Littlefield, 2007.

Bastian, Jean-Pierre. *Los disidentes: sociedades protestantes y revolución en México, 1872–1911*. Mexico D. F.: Fondo de Cultura Económica and El Colegio de México, 1989.

Becker, Marjorie. *Setting the Virgin on Fire: Lázaro Cárdenas, Michoacán Peasants, and the Redemption of the Mexican Revolution*. Berkeley, CA: University of California Press, 1995.

Beltran, Pbro. Lauro Lopez. *Manríquez y Zárate, Primer Obispo de Huejutla, Sublimador de Juan Diego, heroic defensor de la Fe: Obra conmemorativa del*

Quinto Centenario del Natalicio de Juan Diego: 1474–1974. Mexico City: Editorial Tradición, 1974.

Bogardus, Emory Stephen. *The Mexican in the United States.* Social Science Series No. 8. Los Angeles: University of Southern California Press, 1934.

Bowman, Marilyn. "Labor Migration on Mexico's Southern Border, 1880–1941: The Quest for Regulation and Its Aftermath." PhD diss., University of Minnesota, 1987.

Boyer, Christopher. *Becoming Campesinos: Politics, Identity, and Agrarian Struggle in Postrevolutionary Michoacán, 1920–1935.* Stanford, CA: Stanford University Press, 2003.

Brading, David. *Mexican Phoenix: Our Lady of Guadalupe: Image and Tradition Across Five Centuries.* New York: Cambridge University Press, 2003.

Bryant, Joseph M. "The Sect-Church Dynamic and Christian Expansion in the Roman Empire Persecution, Penitential Discipline, and Schism in Sociological Perspective." *The British Journal of Sociology* Vol. 44, No. 2 (June 1993): 303–39.

Buchenau, Jurgen. *Plutarco Elias Calles and the Mexican Revolution.* Latin American Sillouettes Series. New York: Rowman and Littlefield, 2006.

Butler, Matthew. *Popular Piety and Political Identity in Mexico's Cristero Rebellion: Michoacán, 1927–1929.* New York: Oxford University Press, 2004.

Butler, Matthew. "Trouble Afoot? Pilgrimage in *Cristero* Mexico City." In *Faith and Impiety in Revolutionary Mexico,* edited by Matthew Butler, 149–66. New York: Palgrave Macmillan, 2007.

Camarillo, Albert. *Chicanos in a Changing Society: From Mexican Pueblos to American Barrios in Santa Barbara and Southern California, 1848–1930.* Cambridge: Harvard University Press, 1979.

Cardoso, Lawrence. "Mexican Emigration to the United States, 1900–1930: An Analysis of Socio-Economic Causes." PhD diss., University of Connecticut, 1974.

Cardoso, Lawrence. *Mexican Emigration to the United States, 1897–1931.* Tucson, AZ: University of Arizona Press, 1980.

Carey, Patrick W. "American Catholic Ecumenism on the Eve of Vatican II, 1940–1962." *U.S. Catholic Historian* Vol. 28, No. 2 (Spring 2010): 1–17.

Castaneda-Liles, Socorro. "Our Lady of Guadalupe and the Politics of Cultural Interpretation." In *Mexican American Religions: Spirituality, Activism, and Culture,* edited by Gastón Espinosa and Mario T. García, 153–79. Durham, NC: Duke University Press, 2008.

Castelli, Elizabeth. *Martyrdom and Memory: Early Christian Culture Making.* New York: Columbia University Press, 2004.

Caterine, Darryl V. *Conservative Catholicism and the Carmelites: Identity, Ethnicity, and Tradition in the Modern Church.* Bloomington and Indianapolis, IN: Indiana University Press, 2001.

Chamberlain, Mary. "Family Narratives and Migration Dynamics: Barbadians to Britain." *New West Indian Guide/Nieuwe West-Indische Gids* Vol. 69, No. 3/4 (1995): 253–75.

Chamberlain, Mary, and Selma Leydesdorff. "Transnational Families: Memories and Narratives." *Global Networks* Vol. 4, No. 3 (2004): 227–41.

Chesnut, R. Andrew. *Devoted to Death: Santa Muerte, the Skeleton Saint.* New York: Oxford University Press, 2012.

Daniel Chávez, "From *Miss Cristera* to *The Desert Within*: Towards a Contemporary War of Images in Mexico." *Studies in Hispanic Cinemas* Vol. 9, No. 1 (2012): 63–79.

Chowning, Margaret. "The Catholic Church and the Ladies of the Vela Perpetua: Gender and Devotional Change in Nineteenth-Century Mexico." *Past & Present* Vol. 221, No. 1 (November 2013): 197–237.

Chowning, Margaret. *Rebellious Nuns: The Troubled History of a Mexican Convent, 1752–1863.* New York: Oxford University Press, 2006.

Chupungo, Anscar. *Liturgies of the Future: The Process and Methods of Inculturation.* New York: Paulist Press, 1989.

Climo, Jacob J., and Maria G. Catell, eds. *Social Memory and History: Anthropological Perspectives.* Lanham, MD: AltaMira Press, 2002.

Collado Herrera, María del Carmen. *Dwight W. Morrow: reencuentro y revolución en las relaciones entre México y Estados Unidos, 1927–1930.* Mexico City: Instituto Mora, 2005.

Connaughton, Brian F. *Clerical Ideology in a Revolutionary Age: The Guadalajara Church and the Idea of the Mexican Nation, 1788–1853.* Trans. Mark Alan Healy. Calgary, Alberta, and Boulder, CO: University of Calgary Press and University Press of Colorado, 2003.

Connerton, Paul. *How Societies Remember.* Cambridge: Cambridge University Press, 1989.

Conmy, Peter T. *Seventy Years of Service: History of the Knights of Columbus in California, 1902–1972.* New Haven, CT: Knights of Columbus Press, 1972.

Coronado, Raúl. *A World Not to Come: A History of Latino Writing and Print Culture.* Cambridge, MA: Harvard University Press, 2013.

Cross, Ransom Patrick. "Hands Across the Border: The Role of the U.S. Catholic Church in Assisting Mexican Catholics during the Religious Crisis in Mexico, 1926–1929." MA Thesis, University of Texas at El Paso, 1994.

Cuplinskas, Indre. "Guns and Rosaries: The Use of Military Imagery in the French-Canadian Catholic Student Newspaper *JEC*." *CCHA Historical Studies* Vol. 71 (2005): 7–28.

Curcio-Nagy, Linda A. "Faith and Morals in Colonial Mexico." In *The Oxford History of Mexico*, edited by Michael C. Meyer and William H. Beezley, 143–74. New York: Oxford University Press, 2000.

Davis, Marilyn P. *Mexican Voices, American Dreams: An Oral History of Mexican Immigration to the United States*. New York: Henry Holt, 1991.

Davis, Mike. *City of Quartz: Excavating the Future in Los Angeles*. London, New York: Verso, 1990.

De Giuseppe, Massimo. " 'El Indio Gabriel': New Religious Perspectives among the Indigenous in Garrido Canabal's Tabasco (1927–1930)." In *Faith and Impiety in Revolutionary Mexico*, edited by Matthew Butler, 225–43. New York: Palgrave Macmillan, 2007.

Délano, Alexandra. *Mexico and Its Diaspora in the United States: Policies of Emigration since 1848*. New York: Cambridge University Press, 2011.

de la Parra, Yolanda. "La Primera Guerra Mundial y la prensa mexicana." In *Estudios de Historia Moderna y Contemporánea de México*, edited by Álvaro Matute. Mexico: Universidad Nacional Autónoma de México, Instituto de Investigaciones Históricas, Vol. 10 (1986): 155–76.

Demiers, Maurice. *Connected Struggles: Catholics, Nationalist, and Transnational Relations between Mexico and Québec, 1917–1945*. Montréal: McGill Queens University Press, 2014.

Divver, Phil J.; Knights of Columbus California State Council. *Knights of Columbus Historical Review*. [n.p.], 1967.

Dolan, Jay P., and Gilberto M. Hinojosa, eds. *Mexican Americans and the Catholic Church, 1900–1965*. The Notre Dame History of Hispanic Catholics in the United States Vol. 1. Notre Dame, IN: University of Notre Dame Press, 1994.

Dormady, Jason. *Primitive Revolution: Restorationist Religion and the Idea of the Mexican Revolution, 1940–1968*. Albuquerque, NM: University of New Mexico Press, 2011.

Dufoix, Stéphane. *Diasporas*. Translated by William Rodamor. Berkeley, CA: University of California Press, 2006.

Durand, Jorge. *Migración México-Estados Unidos: Años Veinte*. Mexico City: Consejo Nacional para la Cultura y las Artes, 1991.

Durand, Jorge, and Patricia Arias. *La Experiencia Migrante: Iconografía de la Migración México-Estados Unidos*. Mexico City: Alianza del Texto Universitario, 2000.

Durand, Jorge, and Michael M. Smith. "*El Cosmopolita* de Kansas City (1914–1919): Un periódico para mexicanos." *Frontera Norte* Vol. 13, No. 24 (July–December 2001): 7–30.

Enciso, Fernando Alanís Saul. *Historiografía de la emigración de trabajadores mexicanos a Los Estados Unidos (1900–1932)*. Tijuana: El Colegio de la Frontera Norte, 1994.

Enciso, Fernando Alanís Saul. "No cuenten conmigo: La política de repatriación del gobierno mexicano y sus nacionales en Estados Unidos, 1910–1928." *Mexican Studies*/Estudios Mexicanos Vol. 19, No. 2 (Summer 2003): 401–31.

Enciso, Fernando Alanís Saul. *Que se queden allá: el gobierno de México y la repatriación de mexicanos en Estados Unidos (1934–1940)*. Tijuana: El Colegio de la Frontera Norte; San Luis Potosí: El Colegio de San Luis, 2007.

Espinosa, Gaston. *Latino Pentecostals in America: Faith and Politics in Action.* Cambridge: Harvard University Press, 2014.

Espinosa, Gastón, and Mario T. García, eds. *Mexican American Religions: Spirituality, Activism, and Culture.* Durham, NC: Duke University Press, 2008.

Fabila, Alfonso. *El problema de la emigración de obreros y campesinos mexicanos.* Mexico City: Talleres Gráficos de la Nación, 1929.

Fallaw, Ben. *Religion and State Formation in Postrevolutionary Mexico.* Durham, NC: Duke University Press, 2013.

Fallaw, Ben. "Varieties of Mexican Revolutionary Anticlericalism: Radicalism, Iconoclasm, and Otherwise, 1914–1935." *The Americas* Vol. 65, No. 4 (April 2009): 481–509.

Fitzgerald, David. "A Nation of Emigrants? Statecraft, Church-Building, and Nationalism in Mexican Migrant Source Communities." PhD diss., University of California, Los Angeles, 2005.

Fitzgerald, David. *A Nation of Emigrants: How Mexico Manages Its Migration.* Berkeley, CA: University of California Press, 2009.

Flores, John Henry. "On the Wings of the Revolution: Transnational Politics and the Making of Mexican American Identities." PhD diss., University of Illinois at Chicago, 2009.

Foley, Neil. *The White Scourge: Mexicans, Blacks, and Poor Whites in Texas Cotton Culture.* Berkeley, CA: University of California Press, 1999.

Friedrich, Paul. *Agrarian Revolt in a Mexican Village.* Chicago: University of Chicago Press, 1977.

Gamio, Manuel. *The Life Story of the Mexican Immigrant: Autobiographic Documents Collected by Manuel Gamio.* Chicago: University of Chicago Press, 1930. Reprint, Toronto: Dover Publications, 1971.

Gamio, Manuel. *Mexican Immigration to the United States: A Study of Human Migration and Adjustment.* Chicago: University of Chicago Press, 1930.

García, Juan R. *Mexicans in the Midwest, 1900–1932.* Tucson, AZ: University of Arizona Press, 1996.

García, Mario T. *Católicos: Resistance and Affirmation in Chicano Catholic History.* Austin, TX: University of Texas Press, 2008.

García, Matt. *A World of Its Own: Race, Labor, and Citrus in the Making of Greater Los Angeles, 1900–1970.* Studies in Rural Culture. Chapel Hill, NC: University of North Carolina Press, 2001.

Garcia, Richard A. *Rise of the Mexican American Middle Class: San Antonio, 1929–1941.* College Station, TX: Texas A&M University Press, 1991.

Gilbert, Dennis. "Rewriting History: Salinas, Zedillo, and the 1992 Textbook Controversy" *Mexican Studies/Estudios Mexicanos* Vol. 13, No. 2 (Summer 1997): 271–97.

Golway, Terry. *Irish Rebel: John Devoy and America's Fight for Ireland's Freedom.* New York: St. Martin's Press, 1998.

González, Enrique Bautista. *La Guerra Olvidada: La cristera en Nayarit: 1.926–1.929.* Guadalajara: Taller editorial La Casa del Mago, Guadalajara, 2008.

González, Fernando M. *Matar y morir por Cristo Rey: aspectos de la Cristiada.* Mexico City: Instituto de Investigaciones Sociales, Universidad Nacional Autónoma de México/Plaza y Valdés, 2001.

González, Gilbert. *Guest Workers or Colonized Labor?: Mexican Labor Migration to the United States.* Boulder, CO: Paradigm Publishers, 2007.

González, Gilbert. *Mexican Consuls and Labor Organizing: Imperial Politics in the American Southwest.* Austin, TX: University of Texas Press, 1999.

González, Gustavo Doron. *Problemas migratorios de México: Apuntamientos para su resolución.* Mexico City: Talleres de la Cámara de Diputados, 1925.

González y González, Luis (Trans. John Upton). *San José de Gracia: Mexican Village in Transition* (Texas Pan American Series). Austin, TX: University of Texas Press, 1982.

Guerin-Gonzales, Camille. *Mexican Workers and American Dreams: Immigration, Repatriation, and California Farm Labor, 1900–1939.* New Brunswick, NJ: Rutgers University Press, 1994.

Guzmán Mundo, Fernando. "*Santo Toribio. De mártir de los altos a santo de los emigrantes.*" *Revista estudios del hombre* Vol. 25 (2012): 107–27.

Hall, Linda B. *Revolution on the Border: The United States and Mexico 1910–1920.* Albuquerque, NM: University of New Mexico Press, 1988.

Harris, Charles H. II, and Louis R. Salder. *The Secret War in El Paso: Mexican Revolutionary Intrigue, 1906–1920.* Albuquerque: University of New Mexico Press, 2009.

Heisser, Christina. "Thanks to God and the Virgin of San Juan: Migration and Transnational Devotion during the 'Mexican Miracle,' 1940–1970." PhD diss., Indiana University, 2012.

Henderson, Peter. *Mexican Exiles in the Borderlands, 1910–1913.* El Paso, TX: Texas Western Press, 1979.

Hernández, Antonio Avitia. *El Caudillo Sagrado: Historia de las rebeliones cristeras en el estado de Durango.* Mexico City: Impresos Castellanos, 2000.

Hernández, José Ángel. *Mexican American Colonization during the Nineteenth Century: A History of the U.S.-Mexico Borderlands.* New York: Cambridge University Press, 2012.

Hernández, Kelly Lyttle. *Migra! A History of the U.S. Border Patrol.* Berkeley, CA: University of California Press, 2010.

Hu-DeHart, Evelyn. *Yaqui Resistance and Survival: The Struggle for Land and Autonomy, 1821–1910.* Madison, WI: University of Wisconsin Press, 1984.

Huerta, María Guadalupe Alatorre. *Salvador Huerta Gutiérrez: Family Memories.* Translated by Adelina Huerta González. Tlaquepaque, Jalisco: Ediciones Católicas de Guadalajara, n.d.

Hughes, Jennifer Scheper. *Biography of a Mexican Crucifix: Lived Religion and Local Faith from the Conquest to the Present*. New York: Oxford University Press, 2010.

Innis-Jiménez, Michael. *Steel Barrio: The Great Mexican Migration to South Chicago, 1915–1940*. New York: New York University Press, 2013.

Jacobson, Matthew Frye. *Special Sorrows: The Diasporic Imagination of Irish, Polish, and Jewish Immigrants in the United States*. Berkeley, CA: University of California Press, 2002.

Johnson, Benjamin Heber. *Revolution in Texas: How a Forgotten Rebellion and Its Bloody Suppression Turned Mexicans into Americans*. New Haven, CT: Yale University Press, 2003.

Johnson, Melissa. "Pre-Television Stereotypes: Mexicans in U.S. Newsreels, 1919–1932." *Critical Studies in Mass Communication* Vol. 16, No. 4 (1999): 417–35.

Kanellos, Nicolás. "Recovering and Re-Constructing Early Twentieth-Century Hispanic Immigrant Print Culture in the US." *American Literary History* Vol. 19, No. 2 (Summer 2007): 438–55.

Kaprielian-Churchill, Isabel. *Like Our Mountains: A History of Armenians in Canada*. Montreal; Ithaca: McGill-Queen's University Press, 2005.

Katz, Frederick. "Labor Conditions on Haciendas in Porfirian Mexico: Some Trends and Tendencies." *The Hispanic American Historical Review* Vol. 54, No. 1 (February 1974): 1–47.

Knight, Alan. "The Mentality and Modus Operandi of Mexican Anticlericalism." In *Faith and Impiety in Revolutionary Mexico*, edited by Matthew Butler, 21–56. New York: Palgrave Macmillan, 2007.

Koenig, Rev. Msgr. Harry C., ed. *Caritas Christi Urget Nos: A History of the Archdiocese of Chicago*. Chicago: New World Publishing, 1981.

Landa y Piña, Andres. *El Servicio de Migración en México*. Mexico City: Talleres Gráficos de la Nación, 1930.

Langham, Thomas C. *Border Trials: Ricardo Flores Magón and the Mexican Liberals*. El Paso, TX: Texas Western Press, 1981.

Laurens, Jorge Prieto. *Anécdotas históricas de Jorge Prieto Laurens*. Mexico City: B. Costa-Amic Press, 1977.

Leitman, Spencer. "Exile and Union in Indiana Harbor: Los obreros católicos 'San José' and El Amigo del Hogar, 1925–1930." *Revista chicano-riquena* Vol. 2 (Winter, 1974): 50–57.

Limón, José E. "Transnational Triangulation: Mexico, the United States, and the Emergence of a Mexican American Middle Class." In *Mexico and Mexicans in the Making of the United States*, edited by John Tutino, 236–56. Austin, TX: University of Texas Press, 2012.

López, Severino, C. M. F. *El Poche: Memoirs of a Mexican American Padre*. Chicago: Claretian Publications, 2004.

López Menéndez, Marisol. "The Holy Jester: Martyrdom, Social Cohesion and Meaning in Mexico: The Story of Miguel Agustin Pro SJ, 1927–1988." PhD diss., New School University, 2012.

Mabry, Donald J. *Mexico's Acción Nacional: A Catholic Alternative to the Revolution.* Syracuse, NY: Syracuse University Press, 1973.

Mallon, Florencia E. *Peasant and Nation: The Making of Postcolonial Mexico and Peru.* Berkeley and Los Angeles: University of California Press, 1995.

Manzo, Enrique Guerra. "El fuego sagrado. La segunda cristiada y el caso de Michoacán (1931–1938)." *Historia Mexicana* Vol. 55, No. 2 (2005): 513–75.

Martínez, Anne M. "Bordering on the Sacred: Religion, Nation, and U.S.-Mexican Relations, 1910–1929." PhD diss., University of Minnesota, 2003.

Martínez, Anne M. *Catholic Borderlands: Mapping Catholicism onto American Empire, 1905–1935.* Lincoln, NE: University of Nebraska Press, 2014.

Martínez, John R. *Mexican Emigration to the United States, 1910–1930.* San Francisco: R and E Research Associates, 1971.

Martínez, Oscar J. *Mexican-Origin People in the United States: A Topical History.* Tucson, AZ: University of Arizona Press, 2001.

Massey, Douglas, Jacob S. Rugh, and Karen A. Pren. "The Geography of Undocumented Mexican Migration," *Mexican Studies/Estudios Mexicanos* Vol. 26, No. 1 (Winter 2010): 129–52.

Matovina, Timothy M. *Guadalupe and Her Faithful: Latino Catholics in San Antonio from Colonial Origins to the Present.* Baltimore, MD: Johns Hopkins University Press, 2005.

McCarthy, Malachy. "Which Christ Came to Chicago: Catholic and Protestant Programs to Evangelize, Socialize, and Americanize the Mexican Emigrant, 1900–1940." PhD diss., Loyola University of Chicago, 2002.

McCornack, Richard Blaine. "Attitudes toward Religious Matters in Mexican School History Textbooks." *The Americas* Vol. 15, No. 3 (January 1959): 235–47.

McWilliams, Carey. *North from Mexico: The Spanish-Speaking People of the United States.* Philadelphia, PA: J. B. Lippincott, 1949.

Medina, Luis. *Historia del Seminario de Montezuma. Sus precedentes, fundación y consolidación, 1910–1953.* Mexico City: Editorial Jus, 1962.

Meyer, Jean. *La Cristiada.* 4 Vols. Mexico City: Siglo Veintiuno Editores, 1976.

Meyer, Jean. *La cruzada por México: Los católicos de Estados Unidos y la cuestión religiosa en México.* Mexico City: Tusquets Editores México, 2008.

Meyer, Jean. *The Cristero Rebellion: The Mexican People Between Church and State, 1926–1929.* Cambridge: Cambridge University Press, 1976.

Meyer, Jean. *Las naciones frente al conflicto religioso en México.* Mexico City: CIDE/Tusquets Editores México, 2010.

Meyer, Jean. *El sinarquismo. Un fascismo mexicano? 1937–1947.* Mexico City: Editorial Joaquin Mortiz, 1975.

Meyer, Jean, and Ulises Íñiguez Mendoza. *La Cristiada en imagines: del cine mudo al video*. Guadalajara: University of Guadalajara Press, 2006.

Miller, Sr. Barbara. "The Role of Women in the Mexican Cristero Rebellion: *Las Señoras y Las Religiosas*." *The Americas* Vol. 40, No. 3 (January 1984): 303–23.

Mirak, Robert. *Torn Between Two Lands, Armenians in America 1890 to World War I*. Cambridge, MA: Harvard University Press, 1983.

Mirandé, Alfredo. *Jalos, USA: Transnational Community and Identity*. South Bend, IN: Notre Dame University Press, 2014.

Mirandé, Alfredo. "Toribio Romo, el Padre Pollero." *Aztlán: A Journal of Chicano Studies* Vol. 38, No. 2 (Fall 2013): 95–122.

Mizrahi, Yemile. *From Martyrdom to Power: The Partido Acción Nacional in Mexico*. South Bend, IN: Notre Dame University Press, 2003.

Monroy, Douglas. *Rebirth: Mexican Los Angeles from the Great Migration to the Great Depression*. Berkeley, CA: University of California Press, 1999.

Monroy, Douglas. *Thrown Among Strangers: The Making of Mexican Culture in Frontier California*. Berkeley, CA: University of California Press, 1990.

Moore, James Talmadge. *Acts of Faith: The Catholic Church in Texas, 1900–1950*. College Station, TX: Texas A&M University Press, 2002.

Montejano, David. *Anglos and Mexicans in the Making of Texas, 1836–1986*. Austin, TX: University of Texas Press, 1987.

Moya, Jose C. "Immigrants and Associations: A Global and Historical Perspective." *Journal of Ethnic and Migration Studies* Vol. 31, No. 5 (2005): 833–64.

Navarro, Aaron W. *Political Intelligence and the Creation of Modern Mexico*. Philadelphia, PA: Pennsylvania State University Press, 2010.

Navarro, Moisés González. *Los extranjeros en México y los Mexicanos en el extranjero, 1821–1970, Volúmenes I–III*. Mexico City: El Colegio de México, 1994.

Nesvig, Martin Austin, ed. *Religious Culture in Modern Mexico*. New York: Rowman and Littlefield Publishers, 2007.

Ngai, Mae M. *Impossible Subjects: Illegal Aliens and the Making of Modern America*. Princeton, NJ: Princeton University Press, 2005.

Olimon Nolasco, Manuel. *Asalto a las conciencias. Educación, política y opinión pública. 1934–1935*. Mexico City: Instituto Mexicano de Doctrina Social Cristiana, 2008.

Olimon Nolasco, Manuel. *Diplomacia insólita: el conflicto religioso en México y las negociaciones cupulares (1926–1929)*. Mexico City: Instituto Mexicano de Doctrina Social Cristiana, 2006.

Olivera de Bonfil, Alicia. *Aspectos del conflicto religioso de 1926 a 1929, sus antecedentes y consecuencias*. Mexico City: Instituto Nacional de Antropología e Historia, 1966.

Olivera Sedano, Alicia, ed. *Los Matices de la Rebeldía: Las oposiciones políticas y sociales*. Mexico City: Instituto Nacional de Antropología e Historia, 2010.

Orozco, José. "*¡Esos Altos de Jalisco!* Emigration and the Idea of Alteño Exceptionalism, 1926–1952." PhD diss., Harvard University, 1997.

Ortega, J. Antonio López. *Las naciones extranjeras y la persecucion religiosa.* Mexico City: Edición privada, 1944.

Ortegon, Samuel. "The Religious Status of the Mexican Population of Los Angeles." Master's thesis, University of Southern California, 1932.

Ortoll, Servando. "Catholic Organizations in Mexico's National Politics and International Diplomacy (1926–1942)." PhD diss., Columbia University, 1987.

Owens, Sister Lilliana S. L. *Most Reverend Anthony J. Schuler, SJ, DD, First Bishop of El Paso, and Some Catholic Activities in the Diocese Between 1915–1942.* El Paso, TX: Revista Catolica Press, 1953.

Padilla, Yolanda. *Los desterrados: exiliados católicos de la Revolución Mexicana en Texas, 1914–1919.* Aguascalientes: Universidad Autónoma de Aguascalientes, 2009.

Parsons, Wilfred. *Mexican Martyrdom: Firsthand Accounts of the Religious Persecution in Mexico (1926–1935).* Charlotte, NC: Tan Books, 1936.

Perales, Monica. *Smeltertown: Making and Remembering a Southwest Border Community.* Chapel Hill, NC: University of North Carolina Press, 2010.

Peña, Elaine A. *Performing Piety: Making Space Sacred with the Virgin of Guadalupe.* Berkeley, CA: University of California Press, 2011.

Pitti, Stephen. *The Devil in Silicon Valley: Northern California, Race, and Mexican Americans.* Princeton, NJ: Princeton University Press, 2003.

Preciado Zamora, Julia. *Por las faldas del Volcán de Colima: Cristeros, agraristas y pacíficos.* Colima: Publicaciones de la Casa Chata, Centro de Investigaciones y Estudios Superiores en Antropología Social, Archivo Histórico del Municipio de Colima, 2007.

Preciado Zamora, Julia, and Servando Ortoll, eds. *Los guachos y los mochos: once ensayos Cristeros.* Morelia: Editorial Jitanjáfora Press, 2009.

Prieto Laurens, Jorge. *Anecdotas Historicas de Jorge Prieto Laurens.* Mexico City: B. Costa-Amic Editor, 1977.

Purnell, Jennie. *Popular Movements and State Formation in Revolutionary Mexico: The Agraristas and Cristeros of Michoacán.* Durham, NC: Duke University Press, 1999.

Quirk, Robert. *The Mexican Revolution and the Catholic Church, 1910–1929.* Bloomington, IN: Indiana University Press, 1973.

Raat, W. Dirk. *Revoltosos: Mexican Rebels in the United States, 1903–23.* College Station, TX: Texas A&M University Press, 1981.

Ramírez, Manuel Ceballos. *El catolicismo social: un tercero en discordia, Rerum Novarum, la "cuestión social" y la movilización de los católicos mexicanos (1891–1911).* Mexico City: El Colegio de Mexico, 1991.

Rappaport, Joséph. *Hands Across the Sea: Jewish Immigrants and World War I.* Lanham, MD: Hamilton Books, 2005.

Redinger, Matthew. *American Catholics and the Mexican Revolution, 1924–1936*. Notre Dame, IN: University of Notre Dame Press, 2005.

Rios-Bustamante, Antonio, and Pedro Castillo. *An Illustrated History of Mexicans in Los Angeles, 1781–1985*. Los Angeles: Chicano Studies Research Center, University of California, 1986.

Romo, David Dorado. *Ringside Seat to a Revolution: An Underground Cultural History of El Paso and Juárez, 1893–1923*. El Paso, TX: Cinco Puntos Press, 2005.

Rosales, Francisco A. "Mexican Immigration to the Urban Midwest During the 1920s." PhD diss., Indiana University, 1978.

Rouse, Roger. "Mexican Migration and the Social Space of Post-Modernism." *Diaspora* Vol. 1 (1991): 8–23.

Rubén, Aguilar V., and Guillermo Zermeño Padilla. *Religión, Política y Sociedad: El Sinarquismo y la iglesia en México (Nueve Ensayos)*. Mexico City: Universidad Iberoamericana, Departamento de Historia, 1992.

Ruíz, Vicki. *Cannery Women, Cannery Lives: Mexican Women, Unionization, and the California Food Processing Industry, 1930–1950*. 1st ed. Albuquerque, NM: University of New Mexico Press, 1987.

Sánchez, George. *Becoming Mexican American: Ethnicity, Culture and Identity in Chicano Los Angeles, 1900–1945*. New York: Oxford University Press, 1993.

Sánchez-Walker, Marjorie. "Migration Quicksand: Immigration Law and Immigration Advocates at the El Paso-Ciudad Juárez Border Crossing, 1933–1941." PhD diss., Washington State University, 1999.

Santibáñez, Enrique. *Ensayo acerca de la inmigración mexicana en los Estados Unidos*. San Antonio, TX: Clegg, 1930.

Sarat, Leah M. *Fire in the Canyon: Religion, Migration, and the Mexican Dream*. New York: New York University Press, 2013.

Savarino, Franco, and Alejandro Pinet, eds. *Movimientos sociales, Estado y religion en América Latina Siglos XIX y XX*. Mexico: Escuela Nacional de Antropología e Historia, 2008.

Schiller, Nina Glick, Linda G. Basch, and Cristina Szanton Blanc. *Towards a Transnational Perspective on Migration: Race, Class, Ethnicity, and Nationalism Reconsidered*. Vol. 645. *Annals of the New York Academy of Sciences*. New York: New York Academy of Sciences, 1992.

Sigal, Victoria Lerner. "Espionaje y Revolución Mexicana." *Historia Mexicana* Vol. 44, No. 4 (1995): 617–42.

Sigal, Victoria Lerner. "Los exiliados de la Revolución Mexicana en Estados Unidos, 1910–1940." In *La comunidad mexicana en Estados Unidos. Aspectos de su historia*, edited by Fernando Saúl Alanis Enciso, 71–126. Mexico City: Conaculta, 2004.

Skirius, John. "Vasconcelos and México de Afuera (1928)." *Aztlán: International Journal of Chicano Studies Research* Vol. 7, No. 3 (Fall 1976): 479–97.

Slawson, Douglas. "The National Catholic Welfare Conference and the Church-State Conflict in Mexico, 1925–1929." *The Americas* Vol. 47, No. 1 (July 1990): 55–93.

Smith, Benjamin. *The Roots of Conservatism in Mexico: Catholicism, Society, and Politics in the Mixteca Baja, 1750–1962*. Albuquerque, NM: University of New Mexico Press, 2012.

Smith, Michael M. "Carrancista Propaganda and the Print Media in the United States: An Overview of Institutions." *The Americas* Vol. 52, No. 2 (October 1995): 155–74.

Smith, Michael M. "The Mexican Secret Service in the United States, 1910–1920." *The Americas* Vol. 59, No. 1 (2002): 65–85.

Smith, Michael P., and Luis Guarnizo. *Transnationalism from Below* Vol. 6, *Comparative Urban and Community Research*. New Brunswick, NJ: Transaction Publishers, 1998.

Solis, Yves. "Asociación espiritual o masonería católica: la U," *ISTOR* Vol. 9, No. 33 (Summer 2008): 121–37.

Soyer, Daniel. *Jewish Immigrant Associations and American Identity in New York, 1880–1939*. Detroit, MI: Wayne State University Press, 2002.

Stauffer, Brian. "Victory on Earth or in Heaven: Religion, Reform, and Rebellion in Michoacán, Mexico, 1869–1877." PhD diss., University of Texas, forthcoming.

Sterling, Christopher H., and Cary O'Dell, eds. "Hispanic Radio: U.S. Spanish-Language Broadcasting." In *The Concise Encyclopedia of American Radio*. New York: Routledge, 2010.

Stout, Joseph A. Jr. "El poder y la autoridad en México: el Departamento Confidencial, 1922–1945." Paper presented at the XIII Reunión de Historiadores de México. Estados Unidos y Canadá, Querétaro, Mexico, October 29, 2010.

Sullivan-González, Douglass. *Piety, Power, and Politics: Religion and Nation Formation in Guatemala, 1821–1871*. Pittsburgh, PA: University of Pittsburgh Press, 1998.

Taylor, Paul S. *An American-Mexican Frontier: Nueces County, Texas*. Chapel Hill, NC: University of North Carolina Press, 1934.

Taylor, Paul S. *Mexican Labor in the United States: Chicago and the Calumet Region*. University of California Publications in Economics Vol. 7, No. 2. Berkeley, CA: University of California, 1932.

Taylor, Paul S. "A Spanish-Mexican Peasant Community: Arandas in Jalisco, Mexico." *Ibero-Americana* Vol. 4 (1933): 1–94.

Taylor, William B. *Magistrates of the Sacred: Priests and Parishioners in Eighteenth-Century Mexico*. Palo Alto, CA: Stanford University Press, 1996.

Thompson, Joséph J. *The Diamond Jubilee of the Archdiocese of Chicago*. Des Plaines, IL: St. Mary's Training School Press, 1920.

Treviño, Roberto R. *The Church in the Barrio: Mexican American Ethno-Catholicism in Houston*. Chapel Hill, NC: University of North Carolina Press, 2006.

Trexler, Richard C. *Reliving Golgotha: The Passion Play of Ixtapalapa*. Cambridge, MA: Harvard University Press, 2003.

Tuck, Jim. *The Holy War in Los Altos: A Regional Analysis of Mexico's Cristero Rebellion*. Tucson, AZ: University of Arizona Press, 1982.

Turner, Kay. "*Voces de Fe:* Mexican American *Altaristas* in Texas." In *Mexican American Religions: Spirituality, Activism, and Culture*, edited by Gastón Espinosa and Mario T. García, 180–205. Durham, NC: Duke University Press, 2008.

Tutino, John. *Mexico and Mexicans in the Making of the United States*. Austin, TX: University of Texas Press, 2012.

Valdéz, Dennis Nodín. "Mexican Revolutionary Nationalism and Repatriation during the Great Depression." *Mexican Studies/Estudios Mexicanos* Vol. 4, No. 1 (Winter 1988): 1–23.

Valenzuela, René. "Chihuahua, Calles and the Escobar Revolt of 1929." PhD diss., University of Texas at El Paso, 1975.

van der Veer, Peter. *Religious Nationalism: Hindus and Muslims in India*. Berkeley, CA: University of California Press, 1994.

Vanderwood, Paul. *The Power of God Against the Guns of the Government: Religious Upheaval in Mexico at the Turn of the Nineteenth Century*. Stanford, CA: Stanford University Press, 1998.

Vargas, Zaragosa. "Life and Community in the `Wonderful City of the Magic Motor': Mexican Immigrants in 1920s Detroit." *Michigan Historical Review* Vol. 15, No. 1 (Spring 1989): 45–68.

Vargas, Zaragosa. *Proletarians of the North: A History of Mexican Industrial Workers in the Midwest, 1917–1933*. Berkeley, CA: University of California Press, 1993.

Vaughan, Mary Kay. *Cultural Politics in Revolution: Teachers, Peasants, and Schools in Mexico, 1930–1940*. Tucson, AZ: University of Arizona Press, 1997.

Vaughan, Mary Kay, and Stephen E. Lewis. *The Eagle and the Virgin: Nation and Cultural Revolution in Mexico, 1920–1940*. Durham, NC: Duke University Press, 2006.

Vázquez, Lourdes Celina. *Guerra cristera: narrativa, testimonios y propaganda*. Guadalajara: Editorial Universitaria, Universidad de Guadalajara, 2012.

Vázquez Parada, Lourdes Celina. *Testimonios Sobre la Revolución Cristera: Hacia una hermenútica de la conciencia histórica*. Guadalajara: Universidad de Guadalajara, 2001.

Vecoli, Rudolph. "The Italian Immigrant Press and the Construction of Social Reality, 1850–1920." In *Print Culture in a Diverse America*, edited by James Philip Dankey and Wayne A. Wiegand, 17–33. Champaign, IL: University of Illinois Press, 1998.

Venegas, Miguel. *Letters Home: Mexican Exile Correspondence from Los Angeles, 1927–1932*. Translated by María Teresa Venegas. Self-published, 2012.

Vera y Zuria, Pedro. *Diario de mi Destierro*. El Paso: Editorial Revista Catolica, 1927.

Voekel, Pamela. "Liberal Religion: The Schism of 1861." In *Religious Culture in Modern Mexico* [Jaguar Books on Latin America], edited by Martin Austin Nesvig, 78–105. Lanham, MD: Rowman and Littlefield, 2007.

von Oosterhout, K. Aaron. "Confraternities and Popular Conservatism on the Frontier: Mexico's Sierra del Nayarit in the Nineteenth Century." *The Americas* Vol. 71, No. 1 (July 2014): 101–30.

Waterston, Alisse, and Barbara Rylko-Bauer. "Out of the Shadows of History and Memory: Personal Family Narratives in Ethnographies of Rediscovery." *American Ethnologist* Vol. 33, No. 3 (2006): 397–412.

Wegner, Daniel M. "Transactive Memory: A Contemporary Analysis of the Group Mind." In *Theories of Group Behavior,* edited by Brian Mullen and George R. Goethals, 185–208. New York: Springer-Verlag, 1989.

Weise, Julie. "Mexican Nationalisms, Southern Racisms: Mexicans and Mexican Americans in the U.S. South, 1908–1939."*American Quarterly* Vol. 60, No. 3 (September 2008): 749–77.

Wilkie, James W. "Statistical Indicators of the Impact of National Revolution on the Catholic Church in Mexico, 1920–1967." *Journal of Church and State* Vol. 12, No. 1 (1970): 89–106.

Wolf, Eric R. "The Virgin of Guadalupe: A Mexican National Symbol." *The Journal of American Folklore* Vol. 71, No. 279 (January–March 1958): 34–39.

Wright-Rios, Edward. "A Revolution in Local Catholicism? Oaxaca, 1928–34." In *Faith and Impiety in Revolutionary Mexico,* edited by Matthew Butler, 421–51. New York: Palgrave Macmillan, 2007.

Wright-Rios, Edward. *Revolutions in Mexican Catholicism: Reform and Revelation in Oaxaca, 1887–1934.* Durham, NC: Duke University Press, 2009.

Young, Elliott. *Catarino Garza's Revolution on the Texas-Mexico Border.* Durham, NC: Duke University Press, 2004.

Young, Julia G. "The Calles Government and Catholic Dissidents: Mexico's Transnational Projects of Repression, 1926–1929." *The Americas* Vol. 70, No. 1 (July 2013): 63–91.

Young, Julia G. "Cristero Diaspora: Mexican Immigrants, the U.S. Catholic Church, and Mexico's Cristero War, 1926–1929." *The Catholic Historical Review* Vol. 98, No. 2 (April 2012): 271–300.

Index

Abascal, Adalberto, 148
Abascal, Salvador, 148–149
Acción Católica, 142
Affordable Care Act, 178
agraristas (rural supporters of the
    Calles government), 6, 27, 29
Aguascalientes (Mexico), 27
Aguirre, Nancy, 54, 64
Alcocer, Mariano, 55–56
Amador Díaz, María Teresa
    biographical background of, 161
    children and family of, 166
    Cristero War historical memory and,
        161, 175
    as niece of Manríquez y Zárate, 161, 170
    Partido Revolucionario Institutional
        and, 174
Amador Manríquez, José, 68
America (Jesuit magazine), 109
American Smelting and Mining
    Company, 149
Armenian diaspora, 9, 15
Asociación Católica de la Juventud
    Mexicana (ACJM). *See* Mexican
    Catholic Youth Association
Aurora (Illinois), 77
Ávila, Aurelia, 39, 78
Ávila Camacho, Manuel, 152
Avitud, J. H., 181n4

Baja California, 121, 149
Bajío region (Mexico), 27, 30, 34, 90

Balderrama, Francisco, 143
Bantjes, Adrian, 13, 185–186n26
Barragan, Heliodoro, 34
Barroso, Pablo José, 178
Bartres, Angelino, 81
Benedict XVI (pope), 177
Beneficent Society Pro-Mexico, 77, 80, 132
Big Wells (Texas), 78, 90
Blanchard, Father, 73
Blanco, Carlos, 56, 106, 111
The Book of Red and Yellow (Kelly), 48
Border Patrol. *See* United States
    Border Patrol
Borgaro, Esteban, 94–97
Bourbon Dynasty, 21
bracero program migrations
    (1942–1964), 6
Brady, Nicholas, 109
Brawley (California), 67, 71, 85, 139
Briones, Manuel, 56
Brownsville (Texas), 46, 74
Buckley Sr. William F., 109
Buendía Gaytán, Jesús, 155–156
Burke, John Joseph
    Cristero War and, 29, 48–49,
        106, 125
    Gándara and, 98
    the Liga and, 106–107
    National Catholic Welfare
        Conference leadership of, 29,
        48–49, 97–98, 106–107, 125
    Navarrete y Guerrero case and, 97

Bustos, Luis
  Díaz y Barreto and, 113, 132
  Knights of Columbus leadership of,
    25, 55, 110
  the Liga and, 2, 25, 55, 76, 110–111, 113
  Mexican Catholic Youth Association
    and, 76
  Mexico's exile of, 55, 76, 127
  Pacific Arms Company case and, 86
  Partido de Unión Nacional and, 110–111
  public lectures by, 69
  in San Antonio (Texas), 76
Butler, Matthew, 18–19, 74, 143

Caballeros de Colón. *See* Knights of
    Columbus (KOC)
Calexico (California), 139
Calleros, Cleofás, 49–50,
    150–151, 203n42
Calles, Plutarco Elías
  anticlerical policies of, 5–6, 10–11, 13,
    24–26, 41–43, 45, 59, 62, 69, 78,
    104, 127
  archival record of correspondence
    with, 10–11, 81, 83
  "blacklists" of Cristero diaspora
    members and, 121–123
  Catholic Church's opposition to, 2–3,
    5–6, 10–11, 13–14, 25–28, 107
  Cristero diaspora's opposition to, 3,
    9, 14, 39–41, 54–55, 60, 62, 64–65,
    69, 71, 73–74, 78–80, 97, 106, 109,
    117, 136, 142, 146, 160
  Cristero War and, 12, 45, 49, 61,
    118–122
  Cristero War negotiations and, 125
  emigrant publications' coverage of,
    65, 67
  escobarista revolt and, 101
  intelligence services and, 118–122
  Mexican American supporters of,
    81–83, 120–121
  Mexican Revolution and, 25
  as minister of war, 101
  non-Cristero opponents of, 91
  Partido Revolucionario Institutional
    and, 174
Canseco, Manuel Angel, 147
Cantwell, John J., 51–52, 140, 142
Capistrán Garza, René
  Cristero diaspora publications
    and, 65
  Díaz y Barreto and, 113
  Gándara and, 93
  the Liga and, 25, 27, 55, 57–58, 76,
    87, 90, 107–108, 110, 113, 132
  Mexican Catholic Youth Association
    and, 25, 76, 207n22
  Mexico's exiling of, 55–56, 76, 126–127
  military leadership of, 27, 55, 57
  Partido de Unión Nacional and, 111
  photo of, 57
  recruitment and fundraising efforts
    of, 57–58, 90, 107–110, 113
  in San Antonio (Texas), 58, 76, 90
  weapons smuggling and, 87
Cárdenas, Lázaro, 127, 140, 147, 151–152
Carmelite Sisters of the Most Sacred
    Heart, 165
Carranza, Venustiano
  anticlerical policies of, 24, 42
  Constitutionalist faction in Mexican
    Revolution and, 23
  emigrant press' coverage of,
    64–65
  Huerta overthrown by, 23
Caruana, George J., 26
Casanova, Juan, 20
Castellanos, Francisco, 88–89
Catholic Church. *See also specific*
    members and organizations
  Americanization policy in, 47
  Calles government opposed by, 2–3,
    5–6, 10–11, 13–14, 25–28, 107

colonial period in Mexico and, 20–21
Cristero War and, 2–3, 5–6, 15–16,
    27–28, 30, 41–46, 48–49, 60, 62,
    72–73, 93, 100, 104–108
escobarista revolt and, 104
Gándara uprising and, 98
Great Migration and, 59
the Inquisition in Spain and, 20–21
institutional *versus* popular, 19
Mexican American community's
    relations with U.S. branch of, 46–53
Mexican culture permeated by,
    18–20, 22, 132, 141
Mexican government restrictions on,
    5–6, 8, 10–11, 13, 21–26, 41–43, 55,
    59, 62–63, 69, 71, 73, 104, 127–128,
    140–142, 146–147, 151–152
Mexican regional variations in, 18–20
Mexican religious refugees' support
    from, 38, 41–42, 46, 49–53, 59
Mexican Revolution (1910-1920) and,
    22–24, 48
nineteenth-century Mexican politics
    and, 21–22
Partido Acción Nacional (PAN) and, 179
religious syncretism and, 19
role of clergy in, 19–20, 22, 26–27, 30
Vasconcelos presidential campaign
    and, 69, 71
War of the Reform (1858-1861) and, 21
Catholic Extension Society,
    47–48, 50–52
The Catholic Sun (Phoenix Diocese
    newspaper), 178
Catholic Union of San José (El Paso,
    Texas), 77
Centurioni, Pedro, 73
Cervantes, Manuel, 87
Chamberlain, Mary, 159–160
Chávez, J. M., 82–83
Chávez, José Luis, 34
Chávez, Miguel, 81

Chávez Hayhoe, Luis, 55, 111, 132–133
Chavinda (Mexico), 35
Chiapas (Mexico), 27
Chicago (Illinois)
    Calles supporters in, 81–82
    Church of Our Lady of Guadalupe in,
        40–41, 51, 73–74, 165
    collective associations in, 77, 80
    Cristero diaspora in, 13–14, 35, 40–41,
        46, 51–52, 59, 62, 73, 132, 162
    Cristero War relic tour and, 177
    descendants of Cristero diaspora in,
        160, 162–163, 165–166
    emigrant publications in, 66–67, 77
    Eucharistic Conference (1926) in, 107
    Great Migration and, 32, 35–36, 51
    Manríquez y Zárate in, 139
    Mexico's Confidential Department
        agents in, 120
    Saint Toribio Romo mural in, 157–158
    St. Francis Parish in, 51, 83, 139, 165
Chihuahua (Mexico), 30, 37, 104
Christ the King. *See* Cristo Rey
Church of Our Lady of Guadalupe
    (Chicago), 40–41, 51, 73–74, 165
Church of Our Lady of Guadalupe (Los
    Angeles), 147
Ciudad Juárez (Mexico)
    drug-related violence in, 174
    escobarista revolt and, 104
    Gándara uprising and, 94
    Margarita Gándara in, 161, 166, 174
    migration to the United States and,
        34, 43, 56
    weapons smuggling and, 121
Claretian priests, 47, 51, 73–74, 166
Club Latino de Tucson, 78, 123
Coahuila (Mexico), 27, 30
Colegio Pío Latino Americano (Rome), 22
Colima (Mexico), 13, 27, 176
College of the Incarnate Word (San
    Antonio, Texas), 45, 58

Colton (California), 137
Confidential Department (Mexico's
   Ministry of the Interior)
   blacklists of Mexican migrants
     barred from re-entry and, 121–123
   Cristero diaspora monitored by, 11,
     43, 119–124
   expansion of, 118–119
   interdiction of publications by, 121
   Mexican-American Calles supporters
     and, 120–121
   Mexican consulates in the United
     States and, 119–120
   secretive techniques of, 119–120
Corbella, Carmelo, 79
Cordi-Marian nuns, 51
Coronado, Raúl, 64
Corpus Christi (Texas)
   Cristero diaspora in, 51
   fundraising efforts in, 107
   Great Migration and, 35
Corpus Christi, feast of, 40, 74, 131, 172
corrido ballads, 27, 176
Costa, Lourdes, 150–152
Cristero diaspora. *See also under specific*
   locations
   anti-Communism among, 152–154
   blacklists of Mexican migrants
     barred from re-entry and, 121–123
   boycott of Mexican-sponsored
     patriotic festivals (1926) by,
     39, 77–78
   clergy members among, 2–3, 6, 17,
     39–46, 48–53, 59, 62, 68, 72–74,
     78, 81–86, 90, 93–94, 126–139,
     164–166, 172, 175 (*See also specific*
     individuals)
   collective associations among, 76–80
     (*See also specific organizations*)
   Cristero War's end and, 125–127
   definition of, 7–9
   descendants of, 154, 158–174
   diversity within, 10

emigrant print media and,
   63–69, 163
escobarista revolt (1929) and, 101–104
"exile" *versus* "refugee" terminology
   regarding, 16–17
films and newsreels among, 71–72
fundraising efforts and, 15, 53,
   56–59, 68, 73, 77, 83–87, 90, 98,
   100–103, 105–109, 218n15
Great Depression and, 136,
   138–139, 153
La Segunda (Second Cristada) and,
   127–128, 137–139, 145, 154
lay political exiles among, 54–59,
   68, 91, 105 (*See also specific*
   individuals)
martyrdom accounts among, 61–62,
   66, 72, 74, 102, 164, 167–171
Mexican American political
   opponents of, 63, 80–83
Mexican consulates in the United
   States and, 77–79, 109, 118–119,
   123, 139, 143, 209n51
Mexican government's monitoring
   of, 11, 43, 72–73, 79, 105, 117–124,
   137–139
Mexican Revolution and, 64, 137,
   146, 172
military fighting by members of,
   1–6, 13, 62, 65, 82, 91–95, 98–105,
   114, 117, 122–124, 141, 144, 161,
   181n4, 222n50
military recruiting efforts among,
   2–3, 6–7, 58, 68, 89–91, 90, 93,
   100, 111
Padilla murder and, 61–62
political infighting among, 110–114
political mobilization by, 39–40, 59,
   62–63, 68, 71, 74–75, 77–80, 124,
   128–129, 131, 139–144, 146–149,
   153–154
public lectures among, 69–71
radio broadcasts and, 71

religious life among, 7–8, 10, 16, 38,
40–41, 53, 59–60, 66, 72–75, 77,
100, 129, 135, 140–143, 149–153,
164–167, 171–172, 175
size of, 9–10
U.S. Catholic Church hierarchy and,
46, 49–53, 106–108
U.S. government's monitoring
of, 94–95, 105, 115–118, 120,
123–124, 131
weapons smuggling and, 62, 83–89,
94–95, 100, 114–118, 121
Cristero War. *See also* La Segunda
academic scholarship on, 13
Catholic Church and, 2–3, 5–6, 15–16,
27–28, 30, 41–46, 48–49, 60, 62,
72–73, 93, 100, 104–108
corrido ballads from, 27, 176
Cristero diaspora members' fighting
in, 1–6, 13, 62, 65, 82, 91–95,
98–105, 114, 117, 122–124, 141, 144,
161, 181n4, 222n50
Cristeros' public processions during, 74
emigrant publications' coverage of,
65–68
escobarista revolt (1929) and, 101–104
fundraising in United States for, 15,
53, 56–59, 68, 73, 77, 83–87, 98,
100–103, 105–110, 218n15
government forces' reconcentration
campaigns in, 33
government troops' use of torture in,
61–62, 160, 167
historical memory and, 16, 154,
158–160, 163–180
martyrdom accounts from, 156–157,
167–171, 177, 180
Mexican government intelligence
operations in the United States
and, 119–124
Mexican indigenous populations
and, 99–100
Mexican textbooks and, 171, 177

migration to the United States and,
7, 11–12, 14, 33–35, 37, 42–46, 51–53,
59, 151, 159–162, 175, 179–180
negotiations and formal end (1929)
of, 6, 12, 29, 106, 125
newsreel footage of, 71
rebels as aggressors in, 28–29, 33–34
rebels' military setbacks in, 4–5,
12–13, 26–27, 29
relic tour (2006) and, 177–178
religious motivation in, 27–28
spontaneous beginning of, 26
still photography from, 72
weapons smuggling in, 62, 83–89,
114–118, 121
Cristo Rey
feast day celebrations for, 24, 74–75,
131, 143, 153, 172
as inspiration for Cristero War
fighters, 3, 5, 26–27, 40, 61,
102–103, 131
monument at El Cubilete (Mexico)
for, 24, 77, 151, 228n77
monument at Sierra de Cristo Rey
(Texas) for, 129, 149–154
¡Viva Cristo Rey! battle cry and, 5, 131,
142, 152
Cruz Azul Mexicana, 78
Cuevas, Mariano, 169
Curley, Frank, 96

Damas Católicas, 141
Daughters of the Sacred Heart of Jesus,
168
de la Garza, Fernando, 122
de la Garza, Francisco, 120
de la Huerta, Adolfo
delahuertistas [followers of de la
Huerta] in the United States and,
55, 57, 82, 89, 101, 117
exile of, 91
uprising (1923) by, 33, 54–55, 105, 196n20
weapons smuggling and, 89

de la Huerta, Alfonso, 55
de la Mora, Miguel, 93
Délano, Alexandra, 9, 183n19
de la Peza, Manuel, 55
de la Torre, Alfonso, 144, 169
de la Torre, Carlos, 144, 164
de la Torre, Francisco, 144
de la Torre, Ignacio Jr., 144–145
de la Torre, Ignacio Sr., 144
de la Torre, José Luis
  biographical background of, 162
  children and family of, 166
  Cristero War historical memory and,
    164, 169, 175
  Cristero War martyrs in the family
    of, 169
  Mexico upbringing of, 164
  migration to United States of, 162
de la Torre, Luis, 144, 162
de la Torre, Maria (daughter), 144
de la Torre, Maria (mother), 144
Delgado, Francisco M., 119, 122
Del Rio (Texas), 2–3, 67, 73, 76
Department of Justice (United States)
  Bureau of Investigation and,
    115, 117
  Confidential Department (Mexico)
    and, 120
  Cristero diaspora monitored by,
    94–95, 105, 115–117, 120, 124, 131
  escobarista revolt and, 102
  Estrada uprising and, 102, 117, 122
  Gándara uprising and, 94–95, 115
  Manríquez y Zárate monitored by, 131
  Pacific Arms case and, 84–86, 89
  Tenorio uprising and, 1
Department of State (United States),
  34–35, 42, 49–50, 143
Desde México (newsletter), 147
de Silva, Carlos, 68, 133
Detroit (Michigan)
  Beneficient Society Pro-Mexico in, 77

Cristero diaspora in, 35, 51, 62,
  138, 160
Great Migration and, 32, 35–36
Holy Redeemer Parish in, 170–171
diaspora, definition of, 8–10, 183 nn19–20
Díaz, Félix, 54, 86, 91, 105, 181n4
Díaz, Porfirio
  church-state relations under, 22
  economic gains under, 31, 172
  exiled opponents of, 54, 172
  national railway system and, 31
  in the United States, 8, 54
Díaz y Barreto, Pascual
  Bustos and, 113, 132
  Church of Our Lady of Guadalupe
    (Chicago) and, 40
  Cristero War negotiations and, 86,
    112–113, 125, 219n39
  exile of, 45
  Gándara and, 93
  García Herrera and, 86
  the Liga and, 86, 111–113
  Manríquez y Zárate and, 130
  Mexico City bishopric of, 127
  photo of, 112
  Second Cristada and, 127
  weapons smuggling and, 85–86, 111
Diego, Juan, 18, 139, 141
Doheny, Edward, 140
Dolan, Jay P., 35
Dormady, Jason, 148–149
Dougherty, Dennis Cardinal, 97
Drossaerts, Arthur, 39, 50, 107
Dufoix, Stéphane, 9, 183n20, 192n33
Dunnegan, Momsen & Ryan
  (Tucson-based arms smuggling
  company), 108
Durango (Mexico), 104

Eagle Pass (Texas), 73, 88, 118
El Amigo del Hogar (Chicago
  newspaper), 66–67, 77

El Circulo de Obreros Católicos "San José" (Indiana Harbor), 66, 77
El Cubilete (Mexico), Monument of Christ the King at, 24, 77, 151, 228n77
El Diario de El Paso (newspaper), 52, 57, 61, 65, 74, 79, 151
El Eco de México, 57
Elgin (Illinois), 77
Elizondo, Jesús, 3
"El Mártir de Leon" (Torrente), 74
El Paso (Texas)
    Catholic Union of San José in, 77
    Corpus Christi march (1927) in, 40
    Cristero diaspora in, 2, 13–14, 39–40, 43, 46, 49–52, 54, 57–59, 61–62, 69, 93, 102, 106, 132, 151
    descendants of Cristero diaspora in, 161–162, 174
    El Diario de El Paso (newspaper) and, 52, 57, 61, 65, 74, 79, 151
    emigrant print media in, 52, 57, 61, 65, 74, 79
    escobarista revolt and, 102
    Gándara in, 92–93, 95, 151
    Gándara uprising and, 94
    Great Migration and, 50, 56
    Jesuits in, 82
    Knights of Columbus in, 76
    Liga Católica in, 133
    Liga Pro Mexico in, 133
    Mexican rail links to, 31
    Mexican Revolution refugees in, 54
    Mount Cristo Rey monument near, 129, 149–154
    National Catholic Welfare Conference and, 49
    Revista Católica newspaper in, 65
    San José del Río Church in, 150
    Smeltertown neighborhood in, 149–151, 153
    Villa de Guadalupe pilgrimage from, 152
    weapons smuggling and, 86–87

El Sagrado Corazón, 48
El Salvador (town in Mexico), 87
El Santo Nombre, 48
El Universal (Mexico City newspaper), 25, 34
Enciso, Juan, 137
Escobar, José Gonzálo, 101–104, 217n2
escobarista revolt (1929), 101–104, 114, 117, 123–124
Estrada, Enrique
    Department of Justice monitoring of, 102, 117, 122
    escobarista revolt and, 101–102, 217n2
    exile of, 55, 91
    failed uprising of, 82, 101, 105, 117, 122, 222n50
    imprisonment of, 117
Eucharistic Congress (Chicago, 1926), 107, 120
Eucharistic National Congress (Mexico City, 1924), 24
Extension (magazine of Catholic Extension Society), 48

Félix, Francisco, 96
Ferdinand Maximilian (archduke of Austria), 21–22
Fernández, Carlos, 77, 80, 132–133
Fernández, Nicolás, 94
Ferrer, Jorge, 134
Ferrocarril Central Mexicano, 31
Ferrocarril Nacional Mexicano, 31
Fighting with the Beast (Manríquez y Zárate), 139
First World War, 32, 48
Flores, Carlos I., 120
Flores Magón, Enrique and Ricardo, 8, 54
For Greater Glory (film), 170, 178–179
"Fortnight for Freedom" (U.S. Council of Catholic Bishops event), 178
Fox, Vicente, 179

Fresno (California), 149
Friedrich, Paul, 31
Fryer, William H., 96–97, 108
Fumasoni Biondi, Pietro, 97, 113

Galería de Mártires Mexicanos, 72, 167
Galindo, Juan, 94
Galveston (Texas), 46, 107
Gamio, Manuel, 20, 36–38, 81
Gándara, Carlos, 92, 94–95
Gándara, José
    biographical background of, 92
    Capistrán Garza and, 93
    Department of Justice monitoring of,
        94–95, 115
    in El Paso (Texas), 92–93, 95, 151
    imprisonment of, 97
    Knights of Columbus and,
        98–99, 108
    the Liga and, 93
    National Catholic Welfare
        Conference and, 98–99
    Navarrete y Guerrero and, 93–94, 145
    pardoning of, 99
    photo of, 92
    religiosity of, 93, 95
    trial (1927) of, 95–98, 108, 115
    uprising (1927) led by, 91–95,
        98–100, 104, 114, 117, 141, 161
    Yaqui Indians and, 96, 141
Gándara, José María, 161–162
Gándara, Margarita
    biographical background of, 161
    Cristero War historical memory and, 175
    as a painter, 166, 174
    religious experiences of, 166–167
    on traveling to Mexico, 174
Garcia, Andy, 178
García Herrera, Manuel, 86
García Inés Chávez, José, 169
García Naranjo, Nemesio, 54,
    65, 69–70

Garde, Cruz M., 65
Garrido Canabal, Thomás, 24, 136
Gary (Indiana), 77, 82
Garza, Catarino, 8
Gaxiola, José, 107–108
Gertrudis, Mother (superior in Sisters
    of Perpetual Adoration), 165
Godinez, Merced, 2
Gómez, Salvador, 170–171
González, Fernando, 88
González, Fernando M., 28
González, Pedro, 85
González Flores, Anacleto, 160
González y González, Luis, 33
González y Valencia, José María, 126
Gorostieta y Velarde, Enrique, 29, 178
Great Depression, 136, 138–139,
    153, 225n38
Great Migration (1920-1929)
    academic scholarship on, 14–15
    Cristero War and, 7, 11–12, 14, 33–35,
        37, 42–46, 51–53, 59, 151, 159–162,
        175, 179–180
    economic and demographic factors
        in, 30–32, 36, 162, 192n33
    geographic breakdown of, 7,
        32–33, 46
    labor unions and, 37
    Mexican Revolution refugees and,
        6, 13, 23, 30–31, 42, 48, 54, 92,
        160–161, 172
    mutual benefit associations and, 37
    numbers of immigrants in,
        6–7, 182n17
    Protestant ministries and, 37–38
    secularization and, 37–38, 200n89
    socioeconomic diversity of emigrants
        in, 33, 180
Guadalajara (Mexico), 30, 34, 66,
    147, 160
Guadalupana Society. *See* Sociedad
    Guadalupana

Guanajuato (Mexico)
  Cristero War in, 1, 6–7, 13, 27, 29–30,
    35, 66, 158
  the Liga in, 25, 27
  migration from, 7, 30, 33, 35–36, 66,
    158, 163
  Monument of Christ the King at El
    Cubilete in, 24, 77, 151, 228n77
  religious life in, 27
Guérin-Gonzales, Camille, 35
Guerra, Agustín L., 3
Guerra, José, 2
Guzmán, Vicente, 78

Hannah, Edward Joseph, 97
Hayes, Patrick Cardinal, 97
Heredia, Carlos María, 108
Hernández Vázquez, Soledad, 122
Hidalgo, Miguel, 173
Hinojosa, Gilberto Miguel, 35
Hispanic American Alliance, 78
*History of Religious Persecution in
  Mexico* (film), 71
Holy Name Society, 51, 80, 140–141
Hoover, Herbert, 99
Houston (Texas), 46, 107, 177
Huerta, Adelina
  biographical background of, 160
  Cristero War historical memory and,
    167–168, 175
  Cristero War martyrs in family of,
    167–168
  St. Francis Parish (Chicago) and, 165
  as Xavieran Missionary, 166
Huerta, Victoriano, 23, 54
Huerta Gutiérrez, Ezequiel, 160, 167–168
Huerta Gutiérrez, Salvador, 160,
    167–168

Iglesias, Wenceslao, 81
Immigration Acts of 1921 and 1924
  (United States), 32

Immigration Bureau. *See under*
  National Catholic Welfare
  Conference
Imperial Valley (California), 35, 117
Indiana Harbor (Indiana), 66–67,
    77, 149
the Inquisition, 20–21
"Intimate Proclamation to Christ
  the King" (1932 pro-Cristero
  flyer), 146
Irapuato (Mexico), 67
Irish American Catholic diaspora, 15
Isidore, Father, 142
Islas, Roberto, 137
Iturbide, Agustín, 21, 148, 173

Jacobson, Matthew Frye, 194n38
Jalisco (Mexico)
  Cristero War in, 1, 6–7, 13, 27, 29–30,
    34, 61, 87–88, 109, 158–159, 168
  Las Legiones in, 148
  the Liga in, 25, 27
  Los Altos region of, 27, 29–30, 34–35,
    61, 168
  migration from, 7, 30, 33–36, 66, 158,
    161–163, 168, 176
  religious life in, 27
  Venegas's travel to, 173–174
  weapons smuggling and, 87–88
the Jesuits, 21, 82
Jewish diaspora, 9, 15
John Paul II (Roman Catholic pope),
    157, 177
Joliet (Illinois), 77
Jones, Gus T., 115, 118
Juárez, Benito
  anticlerical policies of, 21, 24, 29
  Religionero Revolts and, 22
  in the United States, 8

Kansas City (Missouri), 46
Kelley, Francis Clement, 47–48, 106

Knights of Columbus (KOC)
  Columbia magazine and, 178
  Cristero War and, 6, 56, 58, 105,
    108–109
  Cristero War canonization
    campaigns of, 177
  Cristero War refugees and, 50, 52
  Cristero War relics tour (2006)
    and, 177
  escobarista revolt and, 102
  Gándara and, 98–99, 108
  For Greater Glory (film) and, 178
  growth during 1920s of, 24
  La Segunda and, 139
  the Liga and, 109
  in Mexico, 6, 24–25, 54–56, 76
  Mexico's Confidential Department
    monitoring of, 121, 123
  Mexico's exiled leaders of,
    54–55, 76
  Million Dollar Fund of, 52, 108
  Radio KNX and, 71
  Supreme Council of, 108
  Tepeyac Council and, 56, 76
  Virgin of Guadalupe procession (Los
    Angeles, 1934) and, 141
  weapons smuggling and, 87

La Avispa (Mexican Catholic newspaper
    in Chicago), 66, 163
La Base, 228n88
Lainé, Juan, 2, 55, 127
Landero, Carlos P., 132
Landero de Algara, Carlota, 56
La Opinión (Los Angeles newspaper),
    54, 65, 80, 163
La Prensa
  coverage of Manríquez y Zárate by,
    130
  escobarista revolt coverage of, 104
  as major Cristero diaspora
    publication, 54, 64–65, 67

Mexican American identity
    formation and, 64–65
  Prieto-Yeme and, 56, 79
La Razón, 2–3, 65
Laredo (Texas)
  Cristero diaspora in, 2, 46, 49, 54
  Liga Católica in, 133
  Mexican rail links to, 31
  weapons smuggling and, 87
La Reforma (Mexico, 1855–1876), 21
Lascuraín de Silva, Elena, 56
La Segunda ("The Second Cristada,"
    1930s rebellions)
  Catholic Church and, 127
  Cristero diaspora and, 6, 30, 127–128,
    137–139, 145, 154
  de la Torre family and, 145
  Knights of Columbus and, 139
  Manríquez y Zárate and, 137–139
Las Hijas de María, 48, 51, 77, 140
Las Legiones (secret Catholic society),
    148–149
La Vela Perpétua, 48
La Voz de la Patria (Mexican Catholic
    Youth Association newspaper),
    65–66, 68, 72, 133, 167
Ledvina, Emmanuel, 51
Legionarios de Cristo, 179
León (Mexico), 66, 74
Lerdo, Santiago, 81
Lerdo de Tejada, Sebastián, 22
Lerma River Basin (Mexico), 30
Lerner, Victoria, 57
"Let's Go North!" (Romo González),
    230n4
Ley Calles, 26, 41–42, 59
the Liga (National League for the
    Defense of Religious Liberty)
  Bustos and, 2, 25, 55, 76, 110–111, 113
  Capistrán Garza and, 25, 27, 55,
    57–58, 76, 87, 90, 107–108, 110,
    113, 132

Central Committee of, 133
conciliatory clergy's withdrawal of
support from, 111
Cristero War and, 2, 4, 6, 27, 29, 83,
87, 90–91, 106–114, 142
Cristero War's end and, 125–126
de la Torre family and, 144
Directive Committee and, 134
divisions among, 110–114
escobarista revolt and, 117
Estrada uprising and, 117
Executive Committee of, 25, 107, 113
founding of, 25
fundraising efforts and, 107–110
Knights of Columbus and, 109
Ley Calles and, 26
Manríquez y Zárate and, 131–132,
135–136
membership estimates from, 25
Mexico's exiling leaders of,
54–56, 76, 93
military consolidation efforts of, 29
Pacific Arms Company case and, 86
Partido de Unión Nacional and,
110–111
Unión Nacionalista Mexicana and,
80, 132–134
U.S. Catholic Church leaders and, 106
War Committee, 27
weapons smuggling and, 83, 87
Liga Católica, 133
Liga Nacional Defensora de la Libertad
Religiosa. *See* the Liga
Liga Pro Mexico, 133
Little Rock (Arkansas), 107
Longoria, Eva, 178
Longworth, Nicholas, 99
López, Don Severino, 160, 163
López, Severino
biographical background of, 160
Church of Our Lady of Guadalupe
(Chicago) and, 165

as Claretian priest, 166, 172
Cristero War historical memory and,
163–164, 169, 175
Cristero War martyrs in the family
of, 169
on Díaz's presidency, 172–173
Los Altos region (Jalisco, Mexico)
Cristero War and, 27, 29, 34, 61
economy of, 30
government establishment of
control in, 29
migration from, 35, 168
Los Angeles (California)
Carmelite Sisters of the Most Sacred
Heart in, 165
Church of Our Lady of Guadalupe
in, 147
Corpus Christi march (1928) in, 40,
74, 131, 172
Cristero diaspora in, 13–14, 35, 40,
45–46, 51–55, 58–59, 62, 68–69,
74, 86–87, 90, 102–103, 106, 131,
162, 172, 176–177
Cristero War relic tour and, 177
Cristo Rey celebration (1928) in, 131
descendants of Cristero diaspora in,
160–163, 173
emigrant print media in, 65, 67
escobarista revolt and, 102–104
Estrada's uprising and, 117
Fiesta de Cristo Rey (1928) in, 75, 172
Great Depression in, 225n38
Great Migration and, 35, 51
Knights of Columbus Tepeyac
Council in, 56, 76
La Opinión newspaper in, 54, 65,
80, 163
Liga Pro Mexico in, 133
Manríquez y Zárate in, 87, 114,
131–132, 135, 138
Mexican Catholic Youth Association
in, 55, 68

Los Angeles (California) (*cont.*)
  Mexican Independence Day festival
    boycott (1926) in, 78
  Mexico's secret agents in, 138
  political protests in, 78–79
  Popular Committee for Mexican
    Defense in, 146
  Radio KNX in, 71
  religious schools in, 54
  return migration to Mexico from,
    126
  Saint Toribio devotion in, 157
  Unión Nacionalista Mexicana in, 134
  Union Nacional Sinarquista in, 149
  Virgin of Guadalupe festival
    processions in, 140–143, 147
  weapons smuggling and, 88, 131
Los Caballeros de Guadalupe (Chicago),
    77
Loyola High School (Los Angeles), 141
Lozano, Ignacio, 54, 64–65
Lozano Saldana, Mrs. Rafael, 52
Luisita, Mother (director of Carmelite
    Sisters of the Most Sacred Heart of
    Los Angeles), 165

Madera, Raúl, 104
Madero, Francisco, 8, 23, 54
Maldonado, Donaciano, 181n4
Manríquez y Zárate, José de Jesus
  Corpus Christi march in Los
    Angeles (1928) and, 40, 131
  Cristero War and, 124, 135–136
  Cristo Rey celebration in Los Angeles
    (1928) and, 131
  death of, 139
  de la Torre family and, 145
  Department of Justice monitoring
    of, 131
  escobarista revolt and, 114
  exile of, 2, 40, 45, 114, 126, 136,
    139, 161

fundraising efforts of, 114, 129,
    137–138
  Galería de Mártires Mexicanos and,
    72, 167
  García Herrera and, 86
  Huejutla (Mexico) bishopric of, 129
  Juan Diego canonization campaign
    and, 139
  La Segunda (Second Cristada) and,
    137–139
  in Los Angeles, 87, 114, 131–132, 135, 138
  "Messages to the Civilized World"
    series of, 67, 129–131, 138
  Mexican government's monitoring
    of, 138
  photo of, 130
  recruitment of Cristero fighters and,
    90, 111
  in San Antonio, 139
  silver anniversary of, 138
  Unión Nacionalista Mexicana and,
    80, 128–129, 132–139, 141
  weapons smuggling and, 86–87,
    114, 131
Manzo, Francisco, 217n2
Mares, Pablo, 20
Martínez, Alejandro V., 143
Martínez, Anne, 165
martyrdom
  Cristeros' accounts of, 28, 61–62, 66,
    72, 74, 102, 164, 167–171
  historical memory and, 12, 15–16, 154,
    157, 167–171, 175, 179–180
  popular Catholic tradition and, 167
  Romo González and, 156–157, 175,
    177, 180
Matovina, Timothy, 77
Mazatlán (Mexico), 88
Melrose Park (Illinois), 77
"Messages to the Civilized World"
    series (Manríquez y Zárate), 67,
    129–131, 138

Mexican Catholic Youth Association
  (Asociación Católica de la Juventud
  Mexicana, or ACJM)
  Central Committee of, 25
  Cristero War and, 6
  de la Torre family and, 144
  La Voz de la Patria newspaper and,
    65–66, 68, 72, 133, 167
  the Liga and, 25
  Mexican Revolution and, 23–24
  Mexico's exiling leaders of, 54–56,
    76, 111, 207n22
  political pamphlets of, 67
  Southern California membership
    numbers and, 140
  Unión Nacionalista Mexicana and,
    133
Mexican Constitution
  Constitution of 1857 and, 29, 110–111
  Constitution of 1917 and, 23–26, 138
  restrictions against the Catholic
    Church in, 21–22, 25–26, 110, 138
Mexican consulates in the United
  States. *See under* Cristero diaspora
Mexican emigration
  bracero program migrations
    (1942–1964) and, 6
  Cristero War and, 7, 11–12, 14, 33–35,
    37, 42–46, 51–53, 59, 151, 159–162,
    175, 179–180
  economic and demographic
    reasons for, 6, 10, 15, 30–32, 36,
    162, 192n33
  Great Migration (1920–1929) and,
    6–7, 11–15, 23, 30–38, 42–46,
    48, 51–54, 59, 151, 159–162, 175,
    179–180, 182n17, 192n33, 200n8
  Mexican Revolution refugees and,
    6, 13, 23, 30–31, 42, 48, 54, 92,
    160–161, 172
  nineteenth century and, 8, 30
  regional networks in, 34–36

Saint Toribio Romo as unofficial
    patron saint of, 157–160, 171,
    175, 180
  secularization and, 37–38, 200n89
  transition toward permanent
    settlements in, 36–37
Mexican Episcopal Committee, 45, 113
Mexican Martyrs (film), 71
Mexican Revolution (1910-1920)
  anticlericalism and, 23–24, 42
  Catholic Church and, 22–24, 48
  Constitutionalist faction in, 23
  Cristero diaspora's views of, 64, 137,
    146, 172
  refugees from, 6, 13, 23, 30–31, 42,
    48, 54, 92, 160–161, 172
  weapons smuggling in, 84
Mexican Social Secretariat, 24
Mexico City
  Las Legiones in, 148
  religious persecutions of 1930s in,
    147
  religious violence in, 25
  Virgin of Guadalupe shrine in,
    71, 152
Meyer, Jean, 29, 35
Meza Gálvez, José, 170
Meza Gálvez, Maria, 170
Michoacán (Mexico)
  Cristero War in, 1, 6–7, 13, 27, 29–30,
    33, 66, 90, 109, 158, 170
  the Liga in, 25, 27
  migration from, 30, 33–36, 66,
    158, 163
  religious life in, 18–19, 27
  weapons smuggling and, 87
Migration Office (United States),
    120, 122
Migration Service (Mexico), 121–122
Milwaukee (Wisconsin), 32, 51, 77, 160
Ministry of Foreign Relations (Mexico),
    11, 77–78

Missionary Sisters of Our Lady of
Victory, 47
Mobile (Alabama), 46
Molinar y Rey, J., 132
Monclova (Mexico), 2
Monroy, Douglas, 36
Montezuma Seminary of New
Mexico, 165
Mora y del Río, José, 25, 45, 93,
196n20, 218n15
Morélia (Mexico), 148
Morelos, José María, 173
Morrow, Dwight, 29, 49, 125, 136
Mount Cristo Rey (Texas), 129, 149–154
Mundelein, George, 51
Muñoz, Simón, 3–4
Muro, Fidel, 144
Muzquiz, Ramón, 181n4

Naco (Arizona), 78
National Catholic War Council.
See National Catholic Welfare
Conference
National Catholic Welfare
Conference (NCWC)
Burke's leadership of, 29, 48–49,
97–98, 106–107, 125
Cristero War and, 97–99, 109
First World War and, 48
Gándara uprising and, 98–99
Immigration Bureau of, 46, 49–50,
52, 150–151
the Liga and, 107
National Cooperativist Party, 55
National League for the Defense of
Religious Liberty. *See* the Liga
Nava, María, 122
Navarrete, Félix, 147
Navarrete y Guerrero, Juan
arrest and trial (1927) of, 95–98
de la Torre family and, 145, 162
exile of, 45

Gándara uprising and, 93–94, 145
Yaqui Indians and, 93–94
Navarro, Father, 43
Nayarit (Mexico), 176
New York City, 43, 46, 177
Nodín Valdés, Dennis, 138
Nogales (Mexico), 121
"Nuevo Catholics" (*New York Times*
magazine article), 176–177
Nuevo Laredo (Mexico), 58, 122

Oakland (California), 157
Obama, Barack, 178
Oblate Fathers, 47
Obregón, Alvaro, 24, 54–55
Ojinaga (Mexico), 121
Olimón Nolasco, Manuel, 176–177
Olivera Sedano, Alicia, 27
Orizoga, Bernardo, 88–89
Orozco, José, 35, 140, 142
Orozco y Jiménez, Francisco, 126, 138
Ortegón, Fernando, 181n4
Ortiz Monasterio, Guillermo, 132
Ortiz Monasterio, José, 54, 113
Ortiz Rubio, Pascual, 127
Osorio, Isidro, 81
O'Toole, Peter, 178
Our Lady Queen of Angels Church
(Chicago), 165

Pacific Arms Company case (1927),
85–87
Padilla, Anselmo, 61–62, 65
Palomar y Vizcarra, Miguel, 25, 90, 147
Parra, Josefa, 169
Parsons, Wilfred, 97–98, 109
Partido Acción Nacional (PAN), 174, 179
Partido Católico Nacional (PCN), 23, 25
Partido de Unión Nacional (National
Union Party), 110
Partido Revolucionario Institucional
(PRI), 174

Perrin, Clarence V., 96
Philadelphia (Pennsylvania), 46
Phoenix (Arizona), 178
Pius IX (Roman Catholic pope), 22
Pius XI (Roman Catholic pope), 24
Plan de Iguala (Iturbide), 21
Ponce, Apolinar, 67, 85
Popular Committee for Mexican
　Defense, 146–147
Portes Gil, Emilio, 101, 125, 127, 222n2
Prieto Laurens, Jorge
　de la Huerta revolt and, 55
　escobarista revolt and, 101, 105, 217n2
　Manríquez y Zárate and, 137
　Mexican Catholic Youth Association
　　and, 55, 207n22
　National Cooperativist Party and, 55
　newspaper work of, 57
　public lectures by, 69
Prieto-Yeme, Guillermo, 56, 59, 65, 79
Pro, Miguel, 43, 177
Prohibition legislation in the United
　States (1920-1933), 114
Protestantism
　among Mexican Americans, 47,
　　82, 200n89
　in Mexico, 19, 21, 37–38
Pro-Vida (Catholic lay organization), 179

Querétaro (Mexico), 27, 30, 148
Quintanar, Moisés, 43

Radio KNX (Los Angeles), 71
Reform Laws of 1857, 22, 24, 29
Regalado, Francisca, 122
Religionero Revolts (Mexico, 1873-1877), 22
"The Religious Problem of Mexico"
　(García Naranjo), 69
religious syncretism, 19
Rerum novarum (1891 papal encyclical),
　22, 148
Revista Católica, 65, 151

Revista Mexicana, 65
Rio Grande City (Texas), 85, 87
Rivera Carrera, Norberto, 179
Riverside County (California), 35
Robert E. Lee Hotel (San Antonio), 2, 5, 58
Robles, Pascual
　Cristero War and, 2–3, 6, 84
　in Del Rio (Texas), 2
　La Razon and, 65
　the Liga and, 2
　Tenorio and, 2, 58, 65, 84–85
　weapons smuggling and, 84–85
Rodríguez, Abelardo, 127
Rodríguez, Antonio, 83
Rojos, J. C., 68
Romo González, Maria, 156
Romo González, Toribio (Santo Toribio)
　Buendía Gaytán and, 155–156
　canonization of, 157, 177
　Chicago mural of, 157–158
　churches named for, 231n6
　as Cristero War martyr, 156–157, 175,
　　177, 180
　Mexican migrants' devotion to,
　　157–160, 171, 175, 180
　migration-related ministry of,
　　155–157, 175
　opposition to migration by, 230n4
　relics of, 157
Rosales, Francisco, 35
Rosas, Guillermo, 86
Ruiz y Flores, Leopoldo
　Cristero War negotiations and, 29, 125
　exile of, 45
　Gándara and, 93
　on the Mexican government and
　　society, 146
Ruiz y Rueda, Luis and Ramón, 55–56,
　　107, 111

Sacred Heart Sisters, 49
Sáenz, Aaron, 67

Safran, William, 183n20
Sagrada Familia church (Mexico City),
  1926 violence at, 25
San Antonio (Texas)
  College of the Incarnate Word in,
    45, 58
  Confidential Department spies in,
    120
  Cristero diaspora in, 2, 13–14, 35, 39,
    45–46, 50–52, 54–55, 58–59, 62,
    67, 73–74, 76–77, 87–88, 93, 106
  Cristero War relic tour and, 177
  emigrant print media in, 64, 67, 72
  escobarista revolt and, 102
  the Liga in, 55, 67, 76, 86, 90, 113
  Manríquez y Zárate in, 129, 131
  Mexican Catholic Youth Association
    and, 67, 76
  Mexican Independence Day festival
    boycott (1926) in, 39, 78
  Mexican Revolution refugees in, 54
  political protests in, 78–79
  return migration to Mexico from,
    126
  Robert E. Lee Hotel in, 2, 5, 58
  San Fernando Cathedral in, 77, 102
  Sisters of Charity in, 85
  Vasallos and Vasallas de Cristo
    Rey in, 77
  weapons smuggling and, 88
  Young Catholics Club of San
    Fernando in, 39, 78
San Bernardino (California), 35,
  136–138, 143
Sánchez, George, 35–36
Sánchez, Plácido, 3, 5
Sánchez, Ramiro, 90
Sanctuary of Our Lady of Guadalupe
  (Nogales, Mexico), 169
San Diego (California), 121–122
San Diego (Texas), 46
San Elizario (Texas), 95

San Fernando Cathedral (San Antonio),
  77, 102
San Francisco (California), 88–89
San Francisco del Rincón (Mexico), 35
San José de Gracia (Mexico), 19, 33
San José del Río Church (El Paso), 150
San Julian (Mexico), 61
San Luis Potosí (Mexico), 27, 42
Santa Ana de Guadalupe (Mexico),
  155–158
Santo Toribio. *See* Romo González,
  Toribio
Schuler, Anthony, 50–51, 107, 150, 152–153
Scott, José, 71
Second World War, 152–154
Secret Service (Mexico), 94–95, 105,
  118, 138
Seminario Nacional Mexicano de San
  Felipe Neri (Castroville, Texas),
  48, 165
Sierra de Cristo Rey (Texas). *See* Mount
  Cristo Rey (Texas)
Sisters of Charity at the Good Shepherd
  Home (San Antonio, Texas), 85
Sisters of the Perpetual Adoration of the
  Blessed Sacrament, 52, 165–166
Smeltertown (El Paso, Texas
  neighborhood), 149–151, 153
Smith, Benjamin, 19
Sociedad Guadalupana, 48, 166
Soldado, Juan, 157
Soler, Urbici, 151
Sonora (Mexico)
  Cristero War in, 144, 169
  escobarista revolt and, 101–102, 104
  emigration from, 30, 37, 155
  Gándara uprising and, 93–94
Spain, 18, 20–21
St. Francis Parish (Chicago), 51, 83,
  139, 165
St. Philip Neri Seminary (Castroville,
  Texas), 48, 165

Tabasco (Mexico), 27, 127
Tamaulipas (Mexico), 27, 30, 122
Tamayo, Rufino, 174
Tamez, Emiliano, 118
Taylor, Paul, 33, 35–36
Tejeda, Adalberto, 45
Tenorio, Simón
  Iturbide and, 173
  recruiting by, 2–3, 6–7
  religious motivations of, 3, 95, 173
  Robles and, 2, 58, 65, 84–85
  in San Antonio, 2, 58
  surrender and imprisonment
    of, 5
  uprising led by, 1–6, 13, 62,
    65, 91–92, 99–100, 104, 114,
    117, 181n4
Tepeyac Council (Los Angeles). *See*
  under Knights of Columbus
Tercero, José, 106
Terrazas family, 52
Tobin, John Wallace, 39
Toluca (Mexico), 147
Topete, Fausto, 217n2
Torrente, Camilo, 73–74, 102
Torres, Hermolao, 143
Tort, James, 40
Traslosheros, Edelmiro, 56, 87
Traslosheros, Julio, 56
Traslosheros Gutiérrez, Francisco, 56
Tucson (Arizona)
  Club Latino in, 78, 123
  Cristero diaspora in, 45, 62
  Cristero War relic tour and, 177
  Gándara trial in, 95–96
  Gándara uprising and, 94–95, 115
  Hispanic American Alliance in, 78
  Mexican American radio in, 79
  Mexican Independence Day festival
    boycott (1926) in, 78
  weapons smuggling and, 87,
    89, 108

Unión de Católicos Mexicanos (La "U"),
  24
Unión Nacionalista Mexicana (UNM)
  broad coalition approach of, 128–129
  constitution and goals of, 133–135
  founding of, 80, 132–133, 153
  growth of, 80
  the Liga and, 80, 132–134
  Los Angeles headquarters of, 134
  Manríquez y Zárate and, 80,
    128–129, 132–139, 141
  Mexican government's monitoring
    of, 137
  pro-Cristero activism of, 136–139
  religious identity and, 135, 141
  in San Bernardino County, 136–137
Union Nacional Sinarquista (UNS),
  148–149, 173, 228n88
Union of Mexican Catholic Ladies
  (Unión de Damas Católicas
  Mexicanas), 6
United States. *See also specific cities and*
  government agencies
  agriculture in, 32, 36
  arms trafficking legislation in, 114
  demand for Mexican labor in, 32
  First World War and, 32, 36
  Immigration Acts of 1921 and 1924
    and, 32
  Prohibition legislation (1920-1933)
    in, 114
  railroad development in, 32
United States Border Patrol, 88, 94,
  115–116, 120
United States Council of Catholic
  Bishops, 178
United States Customs Office, 84, 116
Uranga y Sáenz, Francisco, 45
Urrea, Teresa de, 22

Valadez, Genaro, 2–3, 5
Valdespino y Díaz, Ignacio, 45

Valdiva, C. T., 82
Valenzuela, Gilberto, 101, 217n2
Valle, Miguel, 104
Vallela, Jose, 56
Vallvé, Antonio, 74
Vargas, Zaragosa, 35
Vasallos and Vasallas de Cristo
   Rey, 77
Vasconcelos, José, 69, 71
The Vatican
   Burke and, 49
   Calles government and, 26, 49
   Capistrán Garza and, 58
   Cristero War and, 13, 49, 109, 112–113
   Cristero War negotiations and, 125
   nineteenth century Mexican politics
      and, 22
   Second Cristada and, 127–128
Vázquez, Lourdes Celina, 15
Vazquez Cisneros, Pedro, 207n22
Vega, Padre, 88
Vélez, Graciano, 3
Venegas, Alfonso, 161, 168
Venegas, Dolores, 161
Venegas, María de Jesús Sacramentado
   ("Madre Nati"), 168
Venegas, María Teresa
   biographical background
      of, 161
   canonized great-aunt of,
      168–169
   conflicts with Catholic Church and,
      232n25
   Cristero War historical memory and,
      163, 168, 173, 175
   Cristero War martyrs in the family
      of, 168
   Our Lady Queen of Angels Church
      (Chicago) and, 165

   as Sisters of Perpetual Adoration
      nun, 166
   on traveling to Mexico, 173–174
Venegas, Miguel, 127, 161–163, 173
Vera y Zuria, Pedro, 45
Vertiz, Ricardo, 56
Villa, Pancho, 8, 23, 161
Villagómez, María, 122
Villareal, Antonio I., 55
Villegas-Smith, Rosie, 178
Virgin of Guadalupe
   academic scholarship on, 16
   apparition to Juan Diego (1531) of,
      139, 141
   celebrations of the feast day of, 18, 74,
      140–143, 152–153
   as inspiration for Cristero War
      fighters, 3–4, 27, 51, 95
   as Mexico's national emblem, 18
   pilgrimages to Mexico City shrine
      to, 71
   President Fox's genuflection
      before, 179
   "The Virgin of Guadalupe, Symbol
      and Bastion of Hispanicity"
      (Palomar y Vizcarra), 147

Walsh, Edmund, 29, 125
Walsh, Harry, 58
War of the Reform (Mexico,
   1858-1861), 21
Waukegan (Illinois), 77

Yaqui Indians
   Gándara trial and, 96
   Gándara uprising and,
      93–94, 99–100
   Navarrete y Guerrero and,
      93–94

Virgin of Guadalupe march (Los Angeles, 1934) and, 141

"Yes, There Is Persecution in Mexico: Here Is the Proof" (pamphlet), 147

Young Catholics Club of San Fernando (San Antonio, Texas), 39, 78

Ysleta (Texas), 73

Yucatán (Mexico), 147

Zacatecas (Mexico), 27, 29, 34–35, 158

Zamora (Mexico), 66

Zamora (weapons smuggling ship), 88

Zapata, Emiliano, 23

Zapotlanejo (Mexico), 161